Venezuela's Chavismo and Populism in Comparative Perspective

Populism is best understood as a Manichaean worldview linked to a characteristic language or discourse. Chavismo, the movement that sustains Hugo Chávez in Venezuela, is a paradigmatic instance of populism. Using a novel cross-country dataset on populist discourse, combined with extensive data from within Venezuela and across other countries, this book demonstrates that populist movements can be understood as responses to widespread corruption and economic crisis. The book analyzes the Bolivarian Circles and government missions in Venezuela, revealing how populist ideas influence political organization and policy. The analysis provides important insight into the nature of populism, including its causes and consequences, and addresses broader questions about the role of ideas in politics.

Kirk A. Hawkins is Assistant Professor of Political Science at Brigham Young University. He is a coauthor of *Latin American Party Systems* (Cambridge University Press). His work on political parties and populist movements has been published as several book chapters and in journals, including *Comparative Political Studies, Latin American Research Review,* and *Third World Quarterly.*

Venezuela's Chavismo and Populism in Comparative Perspective

KIRK A. HAWKINS
Brigham Young University

CAMBRIDGE
UNIVERSITY PRESS

Shaftesbury Road, Cambridge CB2 8EA, United Kingdom

One Liberty Plaza, 20th Floor, New York, NY 10006, USA

477 Williamstown Road, Port Melbourne, VIC 3207, Australia

314–321, 3rd Floor, Plot 3, Splendor Forum, Jasola District Centre, New Delhi – 110025, India

103 Penang Road, #05–06/07, Visioncrest Commercial, Singapore 238467

Cambridge University Press is part of Cambridge University Press & Assessment, a department of the University of Cambridge.

We share the University's mission to contribute to society through the pursuit of education, learning and research at the highest international levels of excellence.

www.cambridge.org
Information on this title: www.cambridge.org/9780521765039

© Kirk A. Hawkins 2010

This publication is in copyright. Subject to statutory exception and to the provisions of relevant collective licensing agreements, no reproduction of any part may take place without the written permission of Cambridge University Press & Assessment.

First published 2010
First paperback edition 2013

A catalogue record for this publication is available from the British Library

Library of Congress Cataloging-in-Publication data
Hawkins, Kirk Andrew, 1969–
Venezuela's Chavismo and populism in comparative perspective / Kirk A. Hawkins.
p. cm.
Includes bibliographical references and index.
ISBN 978-0-521-76503-9 (hardback)
1. Venezuela – Politics and government – 1999– 2. Populism – Venezuela.
3. Chávez Frías, Hugo. I. Title.
JL3831.H39 2010
320.987–dc22   2009029820

ISBN   978-0-521-76503-9   Hardback
ISBN   978-1-107-61783-4   Paperback

Cambridge University Press & Assessment has no responsibility for the persistence or accuracy of URLs for external or third-party internet websites referred to in this publication and does not guarantee that any content on such websites is, or will remain, accurate or appropriate.

Contents

List of Tables	*page* vii
Preface	ix
Acknowledgments	xi
1 Introduction	1
2 Chavismo, Populism, and Democracy	15
3 Measuring the Populist Discourse of Chavismo	50
4 Party System Breakdown and the Rise of Chavismo	86
5 The Causes of Populism in Comparative Perspective	131
6 Populist Organization: The Bolivarian Circles in Venezuela	166
7 Populist Policy: The Missions of the Chávez Government	195
8 Conclusion	231
Appendix A: The Populist Speech Rubric	251
Appendix B: Test of the Sampling Technique	255
Appendix C: Test of Interaction Effects	259
References	263
Index	287

List of Tables

3.1	Average populism scores for Latin American chief executives	page 76
3.2	Average populism scores for non–Latin American chief executives	77
4.1	Union density in Latin America	101
4.2	Responses to "country's most important problem"	106
4.3	Multinomial logit of vote choice (issues)	115
4.4	Multinomial logit of vote choice (candidate attributes)	120
4.5	Multinomial logit of vote choice (full model)	121
4.6	Estimated probabilities of voting for Chávez	127
5.1	Multivariate regressions on populism	155
5.2	Predicted level of populism, given corruption and economic growth	158
6.1	Attitudes toward regime types	185
6.2	Democratic methods	187
6.3	Content analysis of definitions of democracy	188
6.4	Attitudes toward social change	189
6.5	Membership in organizations and activities	191
7.1	Missions by origin and area of emphasis	203
7.2	Expected attributes of the Missions	215
7.3	Data sources on the Missions	216
7.4	Model results for Missions	219
B.1	Analysis of random samples of Lula and Cárdenas speeches	256
C.1	Multinomial logit of vote choice (with interaction)	260

Preface

This book was born out of the last stages of my dissertation research nearly 10 years ago. I first traveled to Venezuela in 1999 to study why the traditional system of political parties had broken down. For several months I interviewed former party leaders and scholars of traditional Venezuelan politics, a process that gradually educated me in the history and workings of the old Punto Fijo system. However, as I worked, it became clear that something new and important was taking shape in Venezuela, something that very few academics were studying yet. This was the movement led by Hugo Chávez, or "Chavismo," which was taking the place of the old party system.

Seeing Chavismo as the real story was my first step in a process of discovery; the second step came when I began to understand the distinct qualities of Chavismo as a populist movement. My academic training is in the "new institutionalism," meaning that I study the causes and consequences of formal rules and political organization, particularly political parties, using rational-choice theory. Hence, when my first interviews of Chavista leaders took place in December 1999, I focused on the leadership of what was then the movement's official party, Movimiento V República or MVR. My attempts to analyze Chavismo were essentially descriptions of MVR's organization and ideology. However, in early 2003, a colleague invited me to present a conference paper discussing Chavismo as an example of populism. This was an unfamiliar concept to me, and as I explored this academic literature, I was introduced to a set of ideas that gave me extraordinary understanding of what was happening in Venezuela. I began to see that Chavismo went well beyond the confines of MVR and that most of the action was taking place outside the party. This was a populist movement, and the party played only a minor role in the larger workings of this different kind of organization.

I also began to see the potential for studying the concept of populism, one that has been particularly vexing for social scientists. By treating populism as a discourse or worldview – as a set of fundamental beliefs subconsciously expressed and shaped by language – I could understand how Chavismo had transformed Venezuelan politics, what had given rise to the movement, and what its implications were for politicians and policymakers. It also seemed to challenge or at least elucidate the dominant rational-choice approach to political science that my colleagues and I used, highlighting an additional set of ideas or meanings that were essential for understanding political behavior. But the concept needed clarification and had never been quantitatively measured or treated in significant comparative perspective. I decided to write a book about Chavismo and populism that would allow me to do this.

Most of the data in this book have been collected since then. In June–July 2004, just prior to the presidential recall election, my students and I conducted the survey of members of Bolivarian Circles found here in Chapter 6. The data on the government's social programs (Chapter 7) were collected during July 2005. In spring and summer 2006 I conducted the cross-national analysis of populist discourse that provides much of the comparative data in this book. Finally, in August–September 2007 I cooperated with the Latin American Public Opinion Project at Vanderbilt University in conducting the first version of the AmericasBarometer in that country, a source of some of the data found here in Chapter 7 on the government's social programs and later in the Conclusion.

The recent emergence of other populist movements in Latin America that are strongly linked to Chavismo (including the one led by Evo Morales and the indigenous Movimiento al Socialismo in Bolivia, and the PAIS Alliance of Rafael Correa in Ecuador) makes my earlier decision seem prescient. Populism is becoming a catchphrase again among academics, policymakers, and journalists. However, much of the old conceptual confusion still prevails, and the potential for the discursive concept of populism to enhance our scientific understanding of politics – not just in Latin America or developing countries, but in the advanced industrial democracies as well – is largely unrealized. I hope this book will shed light on these other movements and provide a template for expanded approaches to the study of political institutions and ideas.

Acknowledgments

Portions of this book have been published elsewhere, and I wish to acknowledge these institutions for providing copyright permission to reproduce some of the data here. A Spanish-language version of Chapter 5 was published in a volume edited by Carlos de la Torre and Enrique Peruzzotti (*El retorno del pueblo: Populismo y nuevas democracias en América Latina*. Quito, Ecuador: FLACSO). Portions of this same chapter were published in an article in *Latin American Research Review* that I coauthored with David Hansen, one of my undergraduate students and now a graduate student in economics at Stanford University. And the cross-national analysis of populist discourse in Chapter 3 was published in *Comparative Political Studies*.

I give special thanks to Kurt Weyland, who invited me to participate in that crucial conference panel of 2003. He provided additional comments on other parts of this book, especially the cross-national description in Chapter 3. My gratitude also goes to Dan Hellinger for suggesting that I study Chavismo at the grassroots level, advice that led to my study of the Bolivarian Circles. He provided ongoing support for other phases of the research, particularly the study of the Missions, and his compelling criticisms forced me to temper some of my early thinking about populism. María Pilar García-Guadilla of the Universidad de Simón Bolívar in Venezuela provided advice and material assistance for the studies of the Circles and social programs, and her criticisms of my initial findings regarding the Circles helped me reformulate the version seen here. Her students were some of my best sources in Venezuela, especially Ana Maldonado. Special thanks also to Jennifer McCoy for comments on early drafts of the Circles and Missions studies. Ken Roberts read an early draft of the analysis of Venezuela's party system breakdown in Chapter 4. David Smilde provided comments on multiple portions of this manuscript while convincing me that there was a need for additional scholarly work on Chavismo. David Hansen, coauthor of the original study of the Bolivarian Circles, looked over the draft of Chapter 6 and gave his permission to reproduce much of our original data. And two anonymous reviewers made suggestions that greatly improved the manuscript; my sincere thanks to them for giving it such a careful reading.

Many of my colleagues at Brigham Young University (BYU) have looked over portions of this book or given feedback on the original prospectus, as well as tremendous encouragement during my early years as an academic. These include Ray Christensen, Scott Cooper, Jay Goodliffe, Darren Hawkins, Wade Jacoby, Quin Monson, Dan Nielson, and Ken Stiles. I am extremely grateful for their patience. And, of course, my deepest gratitude is to my wife, Eliza, who looked over several versions of the entire manuscript. Her work made it possible for this book to be written, and I consider it her book as much as mine. Our young children, Andrew, Edward, and Lucy, were very patient with me when I had to spend evenings and some weekends away from them. I hope they will be proud of the results.

Particular efforts at data collection in these chapters benefited from the advice and help of numerous colleagues and research assistants. These include, in addition to many of those already mentioned, Kent Burggraaf, David Coon, Moises Costa, Jorge de Azevedo, Emily Ekins, Laurie Evans, Gary Hatch, Dave Jackson, Eric Lynn, Icce Mejía, David Olave, Jeff Richey, Guillermo Rosas, Aaron "Bruce" Russell, Anne Sidwell, Matt Singer, Richard Sudweeks, Julia Velicev Story, Elizabeth Zechmeister, and, above all, Lili Cruz and Mayavel Amado.

Several survey datafiles used in this book come from generous institutions and friends. I would like to thank the Center for Political Studies at the Instituto de Estudios Superiores de Administración (IESA) in Caracas for making available the databases of the Baloyra-Torres survey, the CIEPA/DOXA survey, and the RedPol survey. I am also grateful to José Enrique Molina for early access to the 2000 World Value Survey in Venezuela, as well as the questionnaire of the Baloyra-Torres survey. Special thanks to Damarys Canache, who provided me with the datafile for her 1995 Venezuela Public Opinion Survey (hereafter simply the Canache survey), and to Ruth Collier and Jay Seawright for making available some of the data from their 2003 survey. Additional data in this book come from a set of interviews that I conducted with leaders of the major political parties in the fall of 1999, May 2000, and February 2003. All but the latest interviews (February 2003) were carried out under a promise of confidentiality and are referenced using codes rather than names; however, interview transcripts or copies of notes are available from me on request.

Research for this book has been funded by various sources, including the College of Family, Home, and Social Sciences at BYU, the BYU David M. Kennedy Center for International and Area Studies, and the BYU Department of Political Science. The study of the Bolivarian Circles particularly benefited from funding by the BYU Department of Communications. Some of the preliminary work on this book was funded by several grants from programs at Duke University, including a Mellon Foundation dissertation research travel

Acknowledgments

grant from the Duke-UNC Program in Latin American Studies; a Tinker Foundation Dissertation Research Travel Grant from the Duke Center for Latin American and Caribbean Studies; a summer travel award from the Duke Program on Democracy, Institutions, and Political Economy; and dissertation research travel awards from the Duke University Graduate School. Part of this work was also supported by the National Science Foundation through a Dissertation Improvement Award (Grant No. 9905823). As always, however, any opinions, findings, and conclusions or recommendations expressed in this book are mine and do not necessarily reflect the views of these supporting institutions or my colleagues.

1

Introduction

> The provision for recall referendum is ... giving shape to a new democratic model in Venezuela, not the old democracy of the elites.
>
> Hugo Chávez, June 2004[1]

On 3 June 2004, Venezuela's National Electoral Commission (Consejo Nacional Electoral, or CNE) announced that a recall election would be held against President Hugo Chávez in August.[2]

The announcement marked a significant victory for the opposition after years of tumultuous, polarizing conflict. Earlier, in April 2002, a violent clash between opposition demonstrators and government supporters in Caracas precipitated a military coup that removed Chávez from power for 36 hours. Subsequent efforts at reconciliation failed, and for two months the opposition led a devastating national strike that paralyzed the oil industry and much of the private sector. Finally, in May 2003, after negotiations sponsored by the Organization of American States (OAS), representatives of the government and the opposition signed an agreement committing both sides to a legal, nonviolent solution and opening the way for the presidential recall.

The recall process formally began with a signature drive by the opposition from 28 November to 1 December 2003. The effort generated an overwhelming response in favor of the recall, with 3.4 million signatures collected,

---

[1] From his speech on the evening of 3 June, accepting the results of the recall petition drive. Accessed at http://www.gobiernoenlinea.ve.

[2] The following account draws from multiple sources, especially the Comprehensive Report by The Carter Center, "Observing the Venezuela Presidential Recall Referendum," published in February 2005 (The Carter Center 2005b), and reports on the election by Gutiérrez (2004), McCoy (2005), Kornblith (2005), and Hellinger (2005), as well as my own observations and campaign literature that I collected. Totals for the UBEs and electoral patrols are taken from Chávez's speech at the close of the campaign. Information on the structure of the Comando Maisanta, as well as Chávez's 3 June speech, was downloaded from the presidential Web site http://www.gobiernoenlinea.ve.

well beyond the 2.5 million required by the constitution. The process nearly stalled after the CNE took five months to verify the signatures and then, in a controversial decision, found irregularities in over 900,000 of them. After violent demonstrations by members of the opposition and earnest efforts by the Carter Center and the OAS, the CNE and opposition agreed to allow a new "repair" period at the end of May in which affected citizens could reaffirm their initial signatures. At the completion of this new process, the CNE accepted that sufficient signatures had been collected and made its announcement.

The opposition's hard-fought victory was short, however. On the evening of 1 December, Chávez appeared on television and gave a speech that reclaimed the moral high ground. He publicly accepted the CNE's decision and affirmed his movement's unwavering support for democracy, then defiantly called on his supporters to organize and defeat the opposition. He baptized their effort the *Campaña de Santa Inés,* naming it after a historic battle from the Federal Wars in the nineteenth century when the Federalist forces defeated the conservative oligarchs following a brilliant tactical retreat. The acceptance of the CNE's decision was a replay of that retreat, and the people would again triumph over the conspiring forces of the opposition. Chávez recited passages from *Florentino y el Diablo*, a Venezuelan folk ballad in which a cowboy named Florentino is challenged to a singing duel with the Devil; Florentino courageously accepts the challenge and eventually defeats the Devil through his perseverance and wit. Chávez asserted that the coup-mongering leaders of the opposition were the Devil, and behind them was the biggest devil of all, George W. Bush. The government of the United States was "the black hat, the black horse, and the black banner, the real planner and driving force of all these movements that have attacked us." Florentino – Chávez and the people – would answer their challenge and win.

The response to Chávez's call was extraordinary. During the next two weeks, Chávez passed over his regular party apparatus that had been losing popular support and created a new campaign organization, the Maisanta Command, led by key figures in the government. The command was named for a guerrilla fighter from the turn of the nineteenth century who was purportedly a grandfather of Chávez and one of his personal heroes. The Command organized a separate grassroots structure of over 8,000 precinct committees known as Electoral Battle Units (Unidad de Batalla Electoral, or UBE), many of them constituted by Bolivarian Circles that had organized during the previous three years. These committees coordinated the work of nearly 120,000 "electoral patrols" (*patrullas electorales*), each made up of approximately 10 voters, that sprouted from community organizations associated with the movement. Over the next two months the electoral patrols carried out neighborhood voter education and registration drives, posted campaign literature, organized rallies, and kept a scrupulous count of voters on election day. The campaign made massive use of print and electronic media campaigns built around a highly consistent set of slogans and images related to the themes of Santa Inés and *Florentino y el Diablo*. Banners and balloons labeled "NO" (a negative vote would retain Chávez) festooned highways, walls, and government buildings across Venezuela. The government's advertisements repeatedly emphasized the successes of its new social programs and the purported ties of the opposition to the old party system and the Bush administration.

The opposition's campaign was a pale shadow of the government's, and it seemed to falter and lose its momentum from the start. Many in the opposition were lulled into a false sense of security by the success of the initial signature drive and early polls indicating low levels of approval for Chávez. Their umbrella organization, the Democratic Coordination (Coordinadora Democrática, or CD), failed to offer a clear program for policy change or select a replacement candidate (if successful, the recall would require a new open election), thereby fueling uncertainty about their unity and their capacity to govern. They took weeks to choose their own campaign command, ultimately a committee of 13 heads of parties and nongovernment organizations (NGOs). And they failed to carry out any grassroots organizational effort, relying instead on television-style campaigning that belied their claims to popular support. As the election approached, their own polls indicated that support for the recall was slipping and that Chávez was gaining ground among undecided voters.

By election day, the turnaround for Chávez and his movement was complete. Nearly 10 million Venezuelans cast their vote, an extraordinary 50 percent increase in turnout from the presidential elections of 2000. Chávez scored a resounding victory, with 5.8 million votes (59 percent) to the opposition's 4 million (41 percent). He and his movement would remain in power until at least 2006.

This account of the recall election of 2004 raises several questions that are often voiced about "Chavismo," or Chávez and the movement that supports him in Venezuela. Let us consider just a few of them.

First, in the recall campaign and especially in the two years that led up to it, we see the polarization of an electorate in what was once regarded as one of the most stable representative democracies in Latin America. From 1958 to 1998, Venezuela had a peculiar democratic regime known as the Punto Fijo system, named for a pact signed by key political actors during the democratic transition of 1958. This pact committed all parties to respect the outcome of subsequent national elections while implementing a set of redistributive economic development policies fed by the nation's oil wealth. Although the system that emerged was characterized by the predominance of a few hierarchical, disciplined parties that largely monopolized access to oil rents, it enjoyed a high level of peaceful electoral competition and regular turnover that made Venezuela an apparent model of democracy. The country was a striking contrast with other nations in Latin America that experienced electoral fraud and violence, polarization between parties of the right and left, and periods of military rule (Blank 1973; Levine 1973, 1989; Martz and Myers 1977; Merkl 1981, 127–8; O'Donnell 1992, 37; Kornblith and Levine 1995).

With the rise of Chavismo this exceptionalism ended. Venezuela was transformed into a polarized party system with two camps that saw each other as enemies in a cosmic struggle. The opposition made frequent recourse to nonelectoral means to challenge Chávez, while the government chiseled away at the civil liberties of its opponents and openly used public resources to win elections. Many political institutions that previously had some shred of autonomy (or at least offered proportional representation to the different parties) were turned into organizations allied with Chávez's views that frequently excluded or ruled against the interests of the opposition. Yet, throughout this conflict, both sides continued to frame their goals and tactics in terms of democratic principles, and they ultimately hewed to minimal procedural standards that gave elections a degree of democratic legitimacy. What explains this "unraveling" of pluralistic norms and institutions, especially in a country such as Venezuela, where they seemed so firmly entrenched (McCoy and Myers 2004)?

Second, we cannot help but be impressed by the mobilizational capacity of Chavismo. In a matter of two weeks, the government was able to call out and organize as many as 1.2 million activists for its recall campaign. Even if the government's estimates of campaign organization were inflated, the number of grassroots activists was clearly much higher than that of the opposition. What impresses us is not just the number of activists, but also their dedication and willingness to set aside competing goals in order to support Chávez. What explains this extraordinary capacity for mobilization and organization?

Third, of course, the recall campaign raises the issue of Chávez's international ambitions and his growing conflict with the United States. This is most evident in his rhetoric linking the opposition with Bush and the purported efforts of the United States to extend its capitalist imperialism. Already by 2004, Chavismo had become part of a broader international conflict involving other Latin American and world leaders in a kind of anti-liberal-democratic front. In large measure, Chávez had acquired Fidel Castro's mantle of authority as leader of the radical left in Latin America. What fueled the animosity of Chávez and his allies toward the United States and capitalism?

Finally, we encounter Chávez's extraordinary, inflammatory rhetoric. Although made particularly famous for English speakers in his 2005 speech at the United Nations (UN) General Assembly comparing Bush with the Devil, his discourse emerges here with its demonization of the opposition and its exaltation of the government's project as the embodiment of the popular will. His words evoke comparison with the Manichaean discourse of other historic leaders – Juan Perón's famous 1946 campaign speech proclaiming the "liberation" of the Argentine people and urging them to choose "either Braden or Perón" (Perón n.d., 60), Getúlio Vargas's depiction in Brazil of the choice between "the nation's existence and the situation of chaos," or Arturo Alessandri's warnings that the options in Chile were "either Alessandri as

President or the Revolution" (Drake 1999, 65). Is this rhetoric erratic and irrelevant – window dressing for opportunistic leaders with authoritarian ambitions – or something more consistent and significant for understanding the movement?

Together these questions highlight the fact that Chávez and his movement represent an extraordinary transformation of Venezuela's political system with ramifications for the entire region, if not beyond. For some scholars and policymakers, Chavismo is the greatest threat to representative democracy in the region and the greatest challenge to U.S. interests in Latin America since the end of the cold war (Noriega 2007); for others, Chavismo embodies hope for social justice and an end to the legacy of colonialism in Latin America and the rest of the developing world (Dossani and Chomski 2007). Yet, most of us are still a little unsure of what exactly the movement *is*. Is Chávez merely another military caudillo or a democratic revolutionary? Is his movement the product of a yearning for democracy, a reaction to economic policy failure, or an inevitable response to the challenges of globalization in an oil-based economy? Is his government reproducing old patterns of clientelism and top-down forms of political organization or opening society to participatory forms of democracy? In short, how should Chavismo be *categorized*, what is *causing* it, and what are its *consequences* for Venezuela and the region? The immediate purpose of this book is to answer these three overarching questions.

The main argument of this book is that Chavismo and many of its allied movements in other countries are best understood as instances of "populism." This is a controversial word to use in Venezuela and in much of Latin America, not to mention among social scientists. By "populist," I do not mean that Chávez and his movement are demagogic, that they have shortsighted economic policies, or that they represent a particular step along the convoluted path to modernization – although Chavismo and its allies may be all of those things. Instead, I mean that they have a distinct set of political *ideas*. Populism is a set of fundamental beliefs about the nature of the political world – a worldview or, to use a more rarified term, a "discourse" – that perceives history as a Manichaean struggle between Good and Evil, one in which the side of the Good is "the will of the people," or the natural, common interest of the citizens once they are allowed to form their own opinions, while the side of Evil is a conspiring elite that has subverted this will. Wholesale institutional change – "revolution" or "liberation," although rarely full-blown social revolution – is required in order to restore the will of the people; procedural rights (especially those of the opposition) may be treated as secondary concerns or instruments. All of these ideas are expressed in a characteristic language identifiable not through a particular lexicon, but through such diffuse elements as tone, metaphor, and theme.

Populism is not entirely undemocratic. Chávez and his supporters see sovereignty resting in ordinary human beings and argue for the expression of their will through elections and other mechanisms of direct participatory democracy. But populism is not *pluralist*. Dissent is not regarded as a valued, permanent feature of politics, especially if it means disagreement with the goals of the revolution or the authority of Chávez. Herein lies one of the great paradoxes of Chavismo and other populist movements: their ability to use democratic ideals to question fundamental democratic practices. Populism represents one end of a normative dimension of politics that partially cuts across traditional procedural definitions of democracy in Venezuela and other countries. This dimension captures the political intentions of leaders and activists and helps us predict the direction in which they are likely to take their regimes.

Many scholars, journalists, and policymakers use the word populist to describe Chávez and his movement, not to mention the other historical instances to which I have compared them. In my review of about 40 academic journal articles published between 2000 and 2006 that study Chávez, I found that about half also use the word populist or populism. But none of these observers really clarify the meaning of this term or why it applies to Chávez, and they ultimately fail to say what it reveals about the unique causes and consequences of Chavismo, let alone how these relate to similar movements in Latin America or the rest of the globe. I argue that populism in the ideational sense allows us to answer all three of my research questions and sheds light on movements in other countries.

In terms of *categorization*, subsequent chapters demonstrate that the concepts of populist worldview or discourse neatly capture Chávez and his movement, as well as a few other historical and current regimes that are frequently considered populist. Chavismo is a paradigmatic populist movement whose leader and many of its followers share an antagonistic outlook that divides and polarizes Venezuelan society. Populism, moreover, is a much deeper and more consistent attribute of Chavismo than is the movement's increasingly leftist ideology. Chávez's leftist rhetoric of "twenty-first century socialism" has clearly become an important characteristic of the movement in the past few years, one that affects decisions about policy and organization as well as the kind of allies and enemies it creates at home and abroad. Yet, the movement's Manichaean discourse was present much earlier – from the very moment that Chávez and his allies emerged on the political stage – and it has remained a surprisingly strong feature up to the present.

Seeing populism as a set of ideas also helps us identify Chavismo's *causes*. Populist movements such as Chavismo are not merely the product of economic crisis, globalization, or growing demands for participatory democracy, although these factors often contribute. Rather, populist movements become successful when there is a widespread failure of government to implement rights of citizenship, particularly the rule of law, that allows citizens to characterize their governments as *corrupt*. Venezuela experienced just such a failure after the oil boom of the 1970s. Not only did traditional politicians and their parties prove incapable of preserving economic growth and equity once oil revenues declined, but they displayed gross moral weakness in repeated scandals and halfhearted attempts to punish dishonest politicians. The message of populists like Chávez is an appealing normative response to these kinds of political failures. It frames them as part of a cosmic struggle of an idealized people against their elite oppressors and gives new meaning to democratic politics and dignity to ordinary citizens. Yet, populist movements typically prove incapable of solving these underlying problems. This is because they disdain the institutional formalities and impartial bureaucracies that the rule of law requires, a pattern we see repeated in Chavismo today. Hence, populism is a recurrent problem in developing regions such as Latin America, which manifest weak property rights and high levels of corruption, while it is largely absent or relegated to the fringes of politics in advanced industrial democracies.

Finally, defining populism in ideational terms helps us better identify and appreciate the *consequences* of Chavismo. The discourse of populist movements is indeed more than rhetorical window dressing; it reflects an underlying worldview that shapes the choices of leaders and followers as they organize themselves and implement policies. Most populists sincerely believe in the virtues of folk wisdom and direct, spontaneous expressions of the popular will, and they fear the corrupting influence of professional political organization. Hence, Chavismo has tended to remain a movement rather than a single hierarchical organization, and efforts to impose unified organizational structures have prompted schisms and fierce debate among movement activists. Chavistas sometimes struggle to reconcile their reverence for the charismatic leader with their belief in popular empowerment and autonomy. Yet, populists also feel a powerful need to demonstrate popular approval and counter what they regard as a sinister, illegitimate opposition. Partly because of this belief, the Chávez government has implemented major social policies with an idiosyncratic partisan logic that often works at cross-purposes with purely electoral goals. In allocating discretionary resources, for example, the government often fails to exploit opportunities to create a patronage machine or engage in open vote-buying, and it creates programs whose rhetoric actually drives away some undecided voters.

THEORETICAL CONTRIBUTIONS

As should be evident, this is an argument with much broader implications than just an understanding of Chavismo and Venezuela. Each of the three specific research questions – categorizing Chavismo, explaining its causes, and understanding its consequences – requires that we address three similar areas of inquiry in the subfield of populism studies. And each of these, in turn, touches on general theoretical questions from the field of political science concerning the role of ideas in political behavior. In all of these areas, we will see that defining populism as a worldview or discourse adds to our understanding and points us to dimensions of politics that are often overlooked and poorly understood.

The first and most significant contribution to the broader scholarly literature is conceptual and empirical: not only to specify a particular ideational definition of populism, but to defend it on logical grounds as a superior, minimal definition of the concept, and to defend it in practical terms by showing how it plays out across countries and across time. The study of populism is fairly old but lacks consensus on basic issues of definition and operationalization. Even with the definition of populism championed here, few scholars have tried to measure populist discourse to see if it really exists, especially in any kind of comparative context (c.f. Armony and Armony 2005; Jagers and Walgrave 2007). I demonstrate the power of this definition by showing how it encapsulates well-known structuralist, economic, and political-institutional alternatives. These other definitions describe significant causes and consequences of populist beliefs and discourse, such as movement organization and shortsighted macroeconomic policies, but the attributes they describe are logical corollaries of the worldview rather than populism's defining characteristics. By placing ideas at the center of populism, we can better understand the causal mechanisms that link these other phenomena together while identifying populism's overlooked aspects.

I also demonstrate the practicality and robustness of the ideational definition through a novel effort at measurement. After applying traditional qualitative discourse analysis to the case of Chavismo, I use a quantitative technique from educational psychology known as holistic grading to analyze a much larger sample of leaders. This technique uses whole-text analysis of political speeches and turns out to have both high validity and good reliability. The resulting dataset reveals the existence of a populist discourse across different periods of time and in multiple countries and languages, and it demonstrates that populist discourse is a reasonably coherent and consistent phenomenon that can be measured scientifically.

The second contribution of this book is a better explanation for what causes populism. That is, what causes populist movements to emerge successfully at certain times and in certain places? Over the years scholars have suggested several explanations, including economic crisis, disjunctures of modernization, and dependent development, yet none of these have been tested simultaneously or with any kind of quantitative analysis. I show that all of these theories fail to get at the heart of populism because they ignore its normative underpinnings. As a discourse or worldview, populism is ultimately a way of interpreting the moral basis or legitimacy of a political system, and it makes the most sense to politicians and citizens when there is widespread violation of democratic norms, especially the rule of law – as there was in Venezuela in the late 1990s and as there is today in many other developing countries. Severe policy crises alone can reduce support for incumbents, but they cannot undermine support for constitutional orders unless they are plausibly linked to a systematic abuse of public office that can be characterized as corruption. Charismatic leaders provide essential catalysts for organizing successful populist movements (as I put it later, they help determine the supply of populism), but they have to give the right message in order to mobilize voter demands effectively. While a few discourse analysts have made similar causal arguments (de la Torre 2000), they have traditionally been reluctant to test these theories, let alone rely on cross-national empirics or quantitative data. For that matter, few studies of populism using any other definition have been willing to do so either. I test my theory against extant ones by looking at the particular case of Chavismo, where I use individual-level data and trace out causal mechanisms; and by looking broadly across countries, where I gauge aggregate patterns with a moderately sized dataset. This analysis validates the normative theory of populist movements while finding that more traditional theories lack predictive power.

The final contribution to the broader literature is a set of theories on the consequences of populism, in particular its consequences for organization and policy behavior. These are subjects that receive relatively little attention from scholars studying populism. In the case of political organization, I present a more comprehensive set of attributes that goes beyond the qualities emphasized in political-institutional definitions by tying populism to the phenomenon of social movements. One of the implications of this study is that social movements in the classical sense, and the related concept of "contentious politics" (McAdam, Tarrow, and Tilly 2001), derive as much from the worldview of movement participants as they do from participants' resource constraints. Movement organization embodies populists' advocacy of direct democracy and the virtues of ordinary citizens. Populists organize as a movement because they want to, not merely because they have to.

In the case of policy behavior, I examine theories of discretionary spending and poverty alleviation programs to show that broad choices over policy – such as how program resources will be allocated, and whether they will emphasize radical redistribution or the protection of property rights – are contingent on the outlook of the politicians and their socioeconomic context. The kinds of partisan discretionary spending programs we often associate with populist leaders are not accidental by-products of weak institutions, but consequences of a perspective that seeks a popular movement for revolutionary change. Populists and their followers want these kinds of policies and see them as evidence of the movement's power and intentions. Purely rational perspectives on political behavior that assume vote- or office-maximizing elites all too often ignore these underlying normative dimensions and thus much of what makes these spending programs so interesting and problematic.

Beyond these three contributions to the populism literature is a much more fundamental contribution to political science. This is the attempt to forge a more positivist approach to the study of "intersubjective," "thick," or "anthropological" notions of culture. This is more than just another reaffirmation of the idea that culture matters. Over the past decade or two, scholars have responded to the dominance of rational choice theory by engaging in a number of studies of the role of ideas in political behavior. Drawing heavily on the pioneering work of Weber (1958 [1946]) and Durkheim (1984), they urge us to consider the role that beliefs and motivations outside of our raw material self-interest play in our decisions. However, this rather broad effort breaks down into warring disciplinary camps that often seem irreconcilable. On one side are postmodernists, discourse theorists, and constructivists who see ideas as socially constructed and inextricably linked to language (Wendt 1999; Laclau and Mouffe 2004; van Dijk 2008); for these scholars, our shared language exerts an almost insidious influence on our thoughts and all too frequently serves as a justification for traditional social and international relations that are unethical or unjust. On the other side are rationalists or behavioralists. They agree that ideas play an independent causal role in human behavior, but they argue that human beings exercise considerable intentionality in creating their ideas, and that the objective material world strongly conditions what ideas are ultimately accepted and acted on (Goldstein and Keohane 1993).

When we study populism, we are forced to consider both approaches to the role of ideas. This is because populism captures a different level of ideas than is usually the subject of recent research. Populism is not a set of principled beliefs such as our current system of human rights norms, nor is it a set of causal beliefs such as Keynesianism or neoclassical economics, both of which are conceptualized as relatively apparent aspects of culture capturing highly articulated sets of ideas (Hall 1989; Goldstein 1993; Keck and Sikkink 1998). Populism is a deeper aspect of culture that reflects basic, interrelated beliefs about history, the nature of self and the community, and the metaphysical. It is a worldview and is expressed as a discourse.

For behavioralists especially this is unfamiliar terrain. While several studies acknowledge the existence of worldview as a level of ideas capturing our deepest assumptions about how the political world works, they leave this level largely unexamined and instead focus on specific sets of norms, ideologies, and scientific theories. Worldviews and the thick sets of ideas that they represent are all too often treated as an unchanging background that we can largely take for granted. In the few instances where they are discussed at all, there is no real attempt to categorize or measure them (Goldstein and Keohane 1993; Berman 1998). Ironically, for better guidance we must turn to the constructivists and discourse theorists who have given much more attention to these underlying sets of ideas, including especially those who study populist discourse (de la Torre 2000; Laclau 2005; Panizza 2005b). Their work here is much more advanced and provides most of the descriptive material we need to create a better definition and measurement of populism. They also provide a crucial methodological insight that the behavioralists or rationalists miss: the close link between ideas and language at this deep level. While ideologies and rhetoric may be easily separable, thought and language become almost indistinguishable when we begin to examine deeply held, unarticulated assumptions about politics. For many purposes we must treat these two concepts – worldview and discourse – as synonyms. This should not be taken as a strong endorsement of the contructivist position that our shared language is the principal cause of our ideas. Constructivists and discourse theorists too often assume what needs to be tested, namely, the dominance of language over thought and behavior. In the study of populism, I find commonalities across

Introduction

historical periods and national boundaries that hint at more natural categories and more powerful material causes than radical interpretivists are generally willing to admit. These findings tend to confirm the traditional behavioralist or rationalist approach to ideas that sees them partly as a reasoned response to our objective conditions.

Thus, in this book I adopt a perspective on the study of ideas that attempts to build bridges between behavioralist approaches on the one hand, and discourse theoretical and constructivist approaches on the other, by studying a particularly deep aspect of our political ideas. Should this be taken as a more direct assault on rational choice theory? In explicitly studying a set of ideas – populist discourse or worldview – I necessarily argue against traditional rational-choice accounts that assume purely material self-interested voters and politicians. We cannot understand Chávez and his movement, or the reaction of his opponents in Venezuela and abroad, without taking into account a fuller set of beliefs. At several points in the text, especially when I study the consequences of populist ideas for political organization and public policy, I juxtapose my predictions with those of traditional rational-choice accounts in an attempt to show that populist ideas not only exist but that they really matter for politics.

Yet, this is not a world in which interests disappear, nor is it one in which citizens and politicians operate erratically or without regard for their material constraints. The explanation I offer for populism's causes and consequences tends to contradict newer cognitive approaches to decision making. These approaches are sometimes used to explain populism by seeing it partly as a response to changing risk aversion in an environment of "losses" or impending calamity (Weyland 2003). Instead, the theoretical arguments here are better characterized as a soft or thick version of rational-choice theory (Little 1991, 41). Much of what goes on with Chavismo and other populist movements can be explained as a rough type of rationality based on nonmaterial preferences, rather than irrational behavior that subconsciously ignores or misperceives readily available information or that short-circuits the decision-making process when choices are framed a certain way. While I do not present anything resembling a formal model, I am friendly to the view that citizens and politicians can be treated as reasoning individuals in the pursuit of their political ends.

While there are several scientific reasons for making reasoning individuals the starting point in the study of populism and Chavismo, such as theoretical parsimony or the still underdeveloped state of cognitive research programs, I have an additional normative purpose in mind. Much of the scholarly literature treats populism as a failure of rationality in the fullest sense of this phrase: as a pathology of democracy, a "paranoid mentality" that afflicts citizens and politicians (especially those of the less educated lower classes) who have ceased to reason and have given themselves over to their passions (Shils 1956; Le Bon 1960 [1895]; Hofstadter 1966). Within Latin America, critics of populism have long treated it as the deception of uncultured masses by demagogic leaders rather than as a justifiable, conscious response to corruption and policy failure (see Di Tella 1965). I am not saying that any of these empirical claims are wrong or that we cannot make moral, philosophical judgments about the merits of populism and its troubled relationship to democracy. One of the purposes of this book is to analyze and test these claims. However, we need to be careful about the kinds of signals we send our audience with our choice of methods and words. The carefully delineated notions of rationality and irrationality that we use as scholars are sometimes lost once our work leaves our hands, and they play to the fears of populism's less careful critics. If we have any choice about which theoretical perspective to start with as our baseline – and I think we do – then a rationalist one is more politically productive. It sends an important signal to populists that they are taken seriously, and it sends a signal to populism's critics that they need to take it seriously.

METHODS AND OUTLINE OF THE BOOK

All of this means that this is an ambitious book. However, the case of Chavismo is such an extraordinary paradigmatic instance of populism that we would be poor scholars indeed if we failed to explore its broader implications in a variety of contexts. Readers who are more interested in understanding the particulars of Chavismo may feel put off by this comparative emphasis, but they should bear in mind that the knowledge payoff goes both ways. Our comparative excursions not only help us speak to a broader audience, but also give us greater insight into the case of Chavismo by putting the movement into a global perspective that is often missing in the study of Venezuelan politics.

Chavismo is a vast subject, and we can consider only a few aspects of the movement here. A number of edited volumes on Venezuelan politics under Chávez already draw on varied expertise and provide fine descriptions (Ellner and Hellinger 2003; McCoy and Myers 2004; Smilde and Hellinger forthcoming). Also, the potential value of this book as a reference work for policymakers seems inherently limited; Chavismo changes constantly, with new policies and new actors emerging almost daily. Much of the specific information presented here will be old news by the time the book is published.

However, I argue that by identifying the movement as an example of populism, we have a tool or a permanent template for understanding aspects that are not covered here, including those that emerge after the book is done. Thus, we do not have to describe and analyze every feature of Chavismo in order to understand the movement. We only need to provide a theoretical framework and test it in multiple ways that demonstrate its explanatory power and coherence. This approach is largely absent from recent volumes that study Chavismo, including the better edited compilations. While they provide excellent points of empirical reference for understanding Chavismo – indeed, I rely on their analyses in this book – they generally avoid a unified theoretical argument and the generalizable claims I make here.

How do I choose which parts of the movement to cover? Part of the time I am constrained by the limited availability of data. Key portions of the movement remain poorly organized, and the Chávez government jealously guards its information nowadays, at least at the highest levels. Thus, I cannot examine complete local budget allocations for the government's social programs, and I can only survey limited samples of participants in these programs and other movement organizations. At other times the selection is more deliberate. Wherever possible, I carefully choose themes and design the research to test more effectively the arguments of this book. My general approach is to wed narrow studies of Chavismo with broader comparative data, and within each of these to combine quantitative and qualitative methods. Thus, for example, I follow a qualitative study of Chávez's discourse with a quantitative study of populist discourse across 40 chief executives from different countries inside and outside of Latin America. And after exploring the causes of party system breakdown and the rise of Chavismo in Venezuela, I explore the causes of populism across a sample of 35 countries. Readers should not assume that the analyses of Chavismo are all qualitative, while the broader comparative work is quantitative. Instead, and in keeping with a growing consensus within political science, at each step of the way I employ both approaches (King, Keohane, and Verba 1994; Brady and Collier 2004; see also the special 2007 issue of the journal *Comparative Political Studies*). In a few instances, pieces of the empirical puzzle are missing and prevent us from implementing an ideal mix of quantitative and qualitative analysis and comparative versus case study methods. I acknowledge wherever this is the case.

Chapter 2 provides key background on Chávez's movement, then explains and defends the definition of populism as a set of ideas. It expands the argument summarized in this chapter that populism as a worldview or discourse provides a minimal definition encapsulating older approaches. Populism defines one end of a normative dimension of democracy that cuts across existing procedural criteria of regime categorization, allowing us to distinguish among different types of hybrid democracies. This allows us to move beyond narrow debates over whether Chavismo represents an instance of true participatory democracy or something authoritarian, and instead treat it as a case of populist democracy with a natural tendency to slide into something totalitarian.

Chapter 3 is essentially descriptive and empirical. It provides data showing that Chavismo is a populist movement in the discursive sense and that Chávez in particular is one of the most populist leaders in the world today – hence a paradigmatic case of populism. Chávez's discourse is remarkably consistent across time, much more so than his ideology or platform. The chapter shows this first by engaging in a qualitative analysis of Chávez's published interviews and speeches, and then by presenting the results of an ambitious effort to measure populist discourse in the speeches of current and historically significant chief executives from other countries.

The next two chapters use the ideational definition of populism and the previously mentioned dataset to develop and test the normative theory of populism's causes. Chapter 4 focuses on the case of Chavismo and Venezuela's party system breakdown, showing how both of these occurred in response to a crisis of democratic legitimacy triggered by economic stagnation but ultimately rooted in worsening corruption. The chapter provides qualitative data assessing its claims, emphasizing the increase in corruption in Venezuela during the oil boom of the 1970s and its perception by politicians, scholars, and citizens. And it tests this argument quantitatively by performing a statistical analysis of vote choice for Chávez in 1998. Chapter 5 then extends this theory to a cross-national analysis of populism using our comparative dataset of elite-level populist discourse. It confirms the utility of a definition of populism centered on ideas and finds that corruption is a better predictor of successful populist movements than economic performance, mass media and education, the challenges of globalization, or economic dependency alone. However, it also argues that our understanding of populism must take into account the supply of charismatic leadership in shaping populist movement success; otherwise, we cannot explain why so few countries experience populist movements at any given time.

Chapters 6 and 7 explore the consequences of Chavismo's populist worldview and allow us to bring some closure to the book by showing in detail how the discursive definition encapsulates traditional understandings of populism. Chapter 6 addresses the political-institutional perspective through an analysis of the Bolivarian Circles, a vast network of grassroots associations that constituted much of the movement between 2001 and 2004. The Circles had low institutionalization, organized as a movement rather than a hierarchy, adopted populist rhetoric and an "anything-goes" attitude, and undermined the cross-cutting affiliations typical of pluralist civil society. The chapter provides a rough theory of populist organization arguing that these attributes are not the defining attributes of Chavismo, but products of a populist worldview and the movement's charismatic leadership. Chapter 7 studies the policy consequences of populism by analyzing the Missions of the Chávez government, an ambitious set of discretionary spending programs for addressing Venezuela's social and economic problems. Through an analysis of program allocations and a survey of aid workers and recipients, it shows that the Missions reflect a unique partisan logic that excludes enemies and rewards the faithful without overt conditionality, a logic driven by the demands of populist discourse. It also explains the general leftist trend of the Chávez government that the Missions embody, arguing that the broader choice of economic approach should be seen as a consequence of populism interacting with the distribution of wealth in a given society; economic populism is a peculiar consequence of the populist worldview in certain countries and times.

Chapter 8 concludes by discussing the book's implications for policymakers and social scientists. It starts by reviewing some of the contributions to the broader literature on populism and the study of ideas in politics and explores new avenues of research. It then offers some tentative predictions about the likely direction of Chavismo.

2

Chavismo, Populism, and Democracy

> With Chávez, the people rule.
>
> Slogan in the 2000 presidential campaign

To understand Chavismo, we need to know more about the movement's origins and how it is depicted by other scholars. We also need to learn more about the basic concepts – populism, worldview, and discourse – that I will be using to describe and analyze Chávez and his movement. This chapter provides these conceptual and empirical foundations. While the emphasis of this chapter is largely on categorization, it provides the basis for and anticipates the causal arguments in subsequent chapters.

The main argument of this chapter is that the scholarly literature places Chavismo on an inadequate unidimensional spectrum of democratic procedure. Democracy, of course, is a fundamental objective for policymakers and citizens today, and in this book I employ the minimal procedural definition of democracy that many political scientists currently use: competition over ideas and candidates ("contestation"), broad participation, and at least a minimal set of rights to make these other conditions effective (Dahl 1971; Collier and Levitsky 1997). This is a definition centered on, though not limited to, the conduct of free and fair elections. Using this definition, we can classify Chávez's Bolivarian government as a semidemocratic regime headed in an increasingly authoritarian direction. But to see what really makes Chavismo distinct from other democratic regimes and from the previous political system in Venezuela, we must complement this behavioral or material dimension with a cultural or normative one that considers the moral justifications for democracy. This dimension is defined primarily by two political worldviews or discourses: populism and pluralism. By taking this dimension into account, we can not only appreciate the unique attributes of Chavismo, but better predict the government's likely procedural direction. This normative dimension is anticipated by but not developed in the current literature on democratic regime types.

A second, equally important argument of this chapter is that this normative or cultural dimension provides a minimal definition of populism. Populist ideas and language are more than just a feature of populist movements; they are the principal quality that defines something as populist. This definition is minimal in that it reduces different historical examples of populism to their common attribute and encapsulates traditional approaches emphasizing structures of modernization, economic policy, and political institutions.

I first describe Chavismo by providing a brief history of the movement from its beginnings in the 1980s until the writing of this book in 2008. I then review the scholarly literature that describes Chavismo and subsequently lay out the ideational definition of populism and this cross-cutting, normative dimension of political regimes. I conclude by applying this dimension to Chavismo and showing how it helps illuminate the differences between this movement and other semidemocratic governments in the region.

A BRIEF HISTORY OF CHAVISMO[1]

From its small beginnings in the 1980s, Chavismo has become a broad international movement with Chávez as its leader and focal point. The movement started with an organization in the Venezuelan armed forces called the Bolivarian Revolutionary Movement 200 (hereafter MBR 200 for its Spanish name, Movimiento Bolivariano Revolucionario 200).[2] MBR 200 was formally organized in December 1983 by Chávez and fellow junior officers who hoped to alter the inequities of Venezuelan society and the growing corruption of its politics.[3] Chávez and his co-conspirators were among the first cohorts of students to graduate from Venezuela's new military academy in the early 1970s, where they were inspired by a nationalist curriculum that emphasized political philosophy and the writings of Venezuelan patriots, especially Simón Bolívar. Many of them, including Chávez, had middle-class origins that sensitized them to the problems of poverty and corruption around them, and some of them had contacts with radical leftist groups outside the armed forces (Tarre Briceño 1994; Garrido 1999, 2000; Medina 1999, 17, 93–132).

---

[1] The following account draws from a variety of primary and secondary sources; for simplicity I avoid referencing any of these in the text, except for particularly recent or contentious points or for direct quotations. Sources on the early years of Chávez and his movement include books by Tarre Briceño (1994) and Zago (1992), which cover the attempted coup of 1992 and provide helpful assessments of MBR 200 and its formative years; Blanco Muñoz (1998), which contains interviews with Chávez from 1995 to 1998; Garrido (1999, 2000) and Medina (1999), which provide insider views of the movement and particularly its contacts with the old radical left before it came to power in 1998; and Marcano and Barrera Tyszka (2004), which is probably the most nuanced and detailed biography of Chávez available.

[2] The organization was originally named Bolivarian Revolutionary Army 200 (Ejército Bolivariano Revolucionario, EBR) but changed its name in the late 1980s once civilians became incorporated (Blanco Muñoz 1998; Marcano and Barrera Tyszka 2004, 101).

[3] There is some confusion about whether it first organized in 1982 or 1983. See Marcano and Barrera Tyszka (2004, 90–1).

Members of MBR 200 operated clandestinely, biding their time while they moved up the military ranks and gradually increasing their numbers while they made plans for a grand civil–military revolution. They accelerated their efforts after the armed forces were called in to repress the *Caracazo*, a massive riot in February 1989 sparked by the government's attempt to institute market-oriented economic reforms. The government's violent repression of the riots disillusioned many officers, who felt that the government had acted excessively against the legitimate interests of popular sectors, and some of them joined MBR 200. By late 1991, the movement consisted of a few hundred younger officers and a handful of civilians, as well as a few disconnected allies among radical leftist parties, particularly La Causa Radical (Radical Cause, or LCR) and the National Revolutionary Party of Venezuela. MBR 200 itself was led primarily by its small group of founding officers, among whom Chávez was clearly the principal and the most charismatic (Blanco 1998, 11; Blanco Muñoz 1998; Garrido 1999, 2000; Medina 1999).

On 4 February 1992, the members of MBR 200 put their plans into action and attempted a coup against the administration of Carlos Andrés Pérez, the president who had attempted the neoliberal reforms. Ultimately, the conspirators failed to achieve key objectives in Caracas or prompt a more general uprising, and within 10 hours they had been forced to surrender, but they unexpectedly won a second victory that changed the fate of the movement and particularly that of Chávez. At the end of the coup, Chávez was allowed to speak on television in order to encourage fellow officers to lay down their arms. In the live broadcast, Chávez willingly accepted blame for the failure of the coup but confidently asserted that change would still come – the movement had failed "for now" (*por ahora*). His bold message and his youthful, commanding presence were a stark contrast with the image presented by the tired leaders of the traditional parties; Chávez and the other conspirators became instant heroes for many Venezuelans (Naím 1993, 101–2; Tarre Briceño 1994, 123–33).

While in prison during the next two years, Chávez and the other members of MBR 200 regrouped and made plans for the future (Zago 1992; Primicias 10 February 1998, 10; Interview No. 13.1 1999). The process of political organization accelerated after 1994, when the conspirators were pardoned and released from prison. A few of the original leaders of MBR 200 had become disaffected with Chávez and chose to enter electoral politics or accept posts in the new government of Rafael Caldera, but Chávez and his closest allies maintained a defiant posture toward the political system and spent the next few years in a tailgate tour of the country, trying to build a more popular civilian movement around a grassroots constitutional project. Initially they encouraged electoral abstention as a means of protesting the current "illegal and illegitimate" regime while calling for a constituent assembly (Blanco Muñoz 1998, 179), but by 1997 there was a sizable group of civilian and military activists ready to organize around this broader project of "democratic revolution." A decision was made to create a party and participate in the national elections of 1998 with Chávez as their presidential nominee. After rising steadily in the polls in a hard-fought campaign, he won the election with 56 percent of valid votes.

Chavismo in Power

The election of Chávez and his allies was a historic event that signaled the end of the old two-party regime and instilled hope in Venezuelans from across the political spectrum. Chávez himself was still controversial, but in the year before the election his movement had grown to include a broad coalition of parties, political figures, and civic association members from all classes, many of whom received important posts in the new government. Certainly, Chávez called for an end to the old parties and the creation of a new political system – something that most Venezuelans wanted – but his campaign rhetoric seemed milder than in the years immediately after the coup, when he refused to completely renounce violence as a means of political change. His inaugural address sounded a somewhat conciliatory note that welcomed all to join in the process of change. Throughout his first year in office and a successful effort to rewrite the constitution, his approval ratings remained well over 70 percent, as can be seen in Figure 2.1, which tracks his quarterly popular approval.

The high point for the government was the creation of the new constitution, an effort that began the day of Chávez's inauguration and consumed most of the government's first year. The constituent assembly was dominated by pro-Chávez groups and effectively excluded representatives or allies of the traditional parties. The final product was controversial for its length and excessive detail, as well as for its unrealistic provisions for worker insurance and pensions, its failure to fully protect the gains of decentralization made over the previous decade, its elimination of the Senate (creating a new unicameral National Assembly), and its concentration of authority in the executive.[4] Yet, the new constitution included novel provisions for the electoral recall of public officials, including the president; enshrined the rights of minorities; created new branches of government (the Moral Authority, centered on the attorney general's office, and the Electoral Authority, centered on the CNE); and made significant rhetorical nods to participatory democracy, civil society, and popular sovereignty.

Beginning in 2001, however, Chávez and his movement experienced a decline in popularity, and the movement became increasingly radicalized and fragmented. By the first quarter of 2002, popular support for Chávez had dropped to 38 percent (Figure 2.1). A variety of factors contributed

---

[4] Constitutional changes could initially be approved with only a majority of the legislature, virtually unlimited decree powers could be granted the president by the National Assembly, single reelection would be possible for the president, and the president would now have a six-year term versus the four-year term in the National Assembly.

Chavismo, Populism, and Democracy

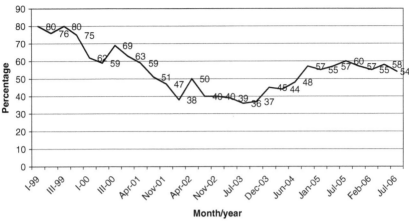

FIGURE 2.1. Levels of popular approval of Chávez, 1999–2006.
Source: Consultores 21 (2006).

to this period of uncertainty and decline, perhaps the most important of which was the need for policy direction and the subsequent choices made by Chávez. With control over the government consolidated, Chávez and his comrades faced the task of adopting substantive socioeconomic reforms to carry out the second and longer phase of their democratic revolution. While initially pursuing a relatively pro-market, fiscally conservative course, in September 2001 Chávez turned against the moderate advisers in his coalition and announced a radical set of policies entitled the Plan for Economic and Social Development (*Plan de Desarrollo Económico y Social*), a six-year strategic vision aimed at transforming the country by the end of his term in 2007. As part of this new plan, he retained the *Plan Bolívar 2000*, a controversial social assistance program that used military personnel and equipment to circumvent local governments; he began building diplomatic ties with Iraq, Libya, China, and especially Cuba, the last of which became the beneficiary of a program of preferentially priced oil shipments; and in December 2001 he decreed a set of reforms (the "49 laws") that called for land redistribution and a new public education curriculum celebrating the movement's Bolivarian ideology. Most of these policies were implemented by Chávez with little input from civil society, the new National Assembly, or even his own cabinet.

Although a wave of opposition strikes and demonstrations in December 2001 forced Chávez to roll back many of these reforms or delay their implementation, opponents and moderate supporters took them as evidence of Chávez's true leftist leanings and his dictatorial intentions. Worse still, none of his efforts paid off economically: growth and investment remained low, oil revenues were flat, and unemployment was persistently among the highest in the region. As early as the 2000 elections, many of Chávez's former co-conspirators defected from the movement to run against him for the presidency, uniting around the figure of Francisco Arias Cárdenas, one of Chávez's principal partners in MBR 200 and the coup of 1992. Business allies withdrew their support; and the press, which had mostly supported Chávez's 1998 election, began running stories about what they considered the failures and corruption of a movement that had deceived them.[5] In 2002, Chávez's closest political adviser and the architect of his earlier political successes, the octogenarian Communist activist Luis Miquilena, left the movement.

Chávez reacted to these developments forcefully, displaying the idealistic determination, fiery rhetoric, and political savvy that made him such a powerful leader. Deprived of favorable press coverage, he turned to his weekly television and radio programs to communicate with the public, and he used laws requiring that private networks broadcast special government messages to make frequent long speeches to the nation. He hardened his already bellicose rhetoric and targeted the media, business, foreign countries, and even individuals who opposed him. For example, he labeled his opponents in the 2000 election "traitors" and during the week preceding Easter of that year compared them with Judas; he eventually took to calling the four television stations that opposed him the "Four Horsemen of the Apocalypse...who trample the truth, sow terror and fear and create ghosts for our children" (Associated Press, 7 February 2003). He repeatedly reshuffled the cabinet and the vice-presidency in order to purge dissident members. Perhaps most important, in 2001 he announced the relaunching of his original organization, MBR 200, in an effort to bring the government back into contact with the people. As part of this effort, he urged supporters to create "Bolivarian Circles," small support groups in neighborhoods and workplaces across the country that would defend the ideals of Simón Bolívar and the revolution, educate fellow citizens, and promote community development. This last initiative proved particularly successful; more than 2 million Venezuelans created as many as 200,000 of these organizations. Feeling bolstered by the consolidation and rejuvenation of the movement, Chávez pressed forward with new policy initiatives.

Turning Point: The Coup and the General Strike

What nearly broke the movement was Chávez's attempt to restructure the state-owned oil company, Petroleos de Venezuela, S.A. (PDVSA). Many Venezuelans perceived PDVSA as one of the few government companies that ran efficiently, a source of pride and national wealth; Chávez and his associates, however, claimed that the company had become controlled by corrupt

---

[5] For example, Plan Bolivar 2000 reportedly resulted in some misuse of funds, and some of the public works deteriorated because of poor construction. Likewise, after massive mudslides in December 1999, there were allegations of misuse of funds and concerns about the slow pace of reconstruction.

technocrats who were allies of the old party system. After Chávez publicly fired the top managers of the national oil company during one of his television programs in April 2002, the opposition organized a series of demonstrations in favor of the old PDVSA leadership.

In Caracas the demonstrations culminated in a march of nearly 1 million on April 11, probably the largest to take place against the government since it first came to power. The protest was initially peaceful, but opposition leaders urged the demonstrators to extend their march to the nearby presidential palace and a large contingent accepted the invitation. As they approached the palace, armed groups of Chavistas tried to block them and a group of masked sharpshooters began firing into the crowd. In the confused exchange of gunfire, about 20 people were killed. Chávez's commanding officers resisted his orders to call out additional troops and proclaim martial law and instead demanded his resignation. After tense negotiations, Chávez agreed to surrender and was sent to a nearby military base, while the military leadership handed control to a civilian junta drawn from the opposition.

Chavismo might have ended there, but the interim president began issuing edicts that appeared authoritarian, and commanding officers were unable to agree on who should be leading the coup. In the meantime, reports were circulating among the general population that Chávez had not really resigned, prompting large numbers of pro-Chávez demonstrators to gather outside the presidential palace and other locations in Caracas. Segments of the armed forces that were loyal to Chávez regrouped and began retaking key government installations. In an effort to head off further civil unrest, the generals agreed to restore Chávez to power, and by April 12 he had returned to office.

After the coup Chávez and his top allies were conciliatory, but the opposition failed to respond to the government's efforts at dialogue. Consequently, Chávez resumed his inflammatory rhetoric, allowed the National Assembly to eviscerate the commission investigating the incidents before the coup, and removed the officers who had rebelled. The private media increasingly became the target of threats and violence. By the end of November, a group of dissident military officers had declared a "peaceful coup" by resigning and setting up a headquarters in the main plaza of the eastern part of Caracas, where they served as a new focal point for opposition mobilization. Despite a short upturn in approval after the coup, support for Chávez soon declined to an all-time low of 36 percent (Figure 2.1).

The polarization culminated in a two-month-long national strike that began on 2 December 2002, with organizers openly calling for the convocation of a national referendum on Chávez's continuation in office. Chávez refused to give in to their extraconstitutional demands and mobilized the army to help distribute food and other basic necessities in the poorer communities that supported him. The opposition hardened and kept the strike going until the beginning of February, when it gradually ended without having achieved its objectives. The strike left the opposition badly weakened; not only were the economic losses devastating for the private sector, but Chávez fired most of PDVSA's workforce (ultimately about 18,000 workers) and called on judges to punish the leaders of the opposition, whom he denounced as "coup-mongerers" (*golpistas*). However, the strike also sharply curtailed the government's oil revenues and left the economy in shambles. The government was forced to ration dollars and began imposing price controls to compensate for the downward spiral of the economy. While the level of opposition demonstrations was greatly diminished in the following weeks, most Venezuelans continued to disapprove of Chávez.

Consolidation and Radicalization of Chavismo

Chavismo was not dead, however, and the end of the strike actually marked the beginning of a dramatic turnaround for his movement. This new period was characterized by the movement's consolidation of control over the state and Chávez's control over the movement, as well as the implementation of a new, more comprehensive, and increasingly radical project of leftist reforms.

Moving beyond the piecemeal efforts of previous social programs such as the Plan Bolívar 2000, in late 2003 Chávez began sponsoring a series of comprehensive social programs, the Missions (*Misiones*), that provided new forms of healthcare, remedial education, basic foodstuffs, occupational training, and developmental loans for economic cooperatives, among other benefits. The quality of services and the actual scope of government support was sometimes questionable (more details on the Missions are provided in Chapter 7). Yet, the programs benefited millions of Venezuelans, allowing oil revenues to reach the poorest members of the population and make real, visible changes in their long-term well-being. The Missions were also politically significant. By covering virtually every sector of economic activity, Chávez was gradually able to create a parallel state-sponsored economy without having to make painful decisions about redistribution, thereby outflanking the private sector and most of the opposition.

During this same period Chávez solidified the movement's control over key institutions of government, particularly the judiciary and the electoral branch. In the case of the judiciary, this control was most evident in efforts to expand and administer the Supreme Court. Partly in response to rulings by the Supreme Court that exonerated leaders of the 2002 coup, in May 2004 the National Assembly passed a law (the *Ley Orgánica del Tribunal Supremo de Justicia*) expanding the size of the court from 20 to 32 justices and making it possible for the Assembly to approve new judges with a simple majority. It also allowed the Assembly to place justices under review or remove them under certain circumstances with only a majority vote. Five sitting justices resigned in anticipation of their removal under the new law, thereby allowing Chávez to appoint 17 new justices to the court and ensure a sympathetic majority (Human Rights Watch 2004; Castaldi 2006). In the case of the electoral branch, controversy centered on the government's control of the CNE. The constitution of 1999 indicated that the CNE would be a nonpartisan five-member board chosen

Chavismo, Populism, and Democracy

and approved by the National Assembly in a two-thirds vote on nominees. However, selections of CNE board members in subsequent years were routinely made by the Supreme Court rather than the appropriate legislative commission. While initially an attempt was made to balance the partisan leanings of the board, by 2005 any pretense of nonpartisanship had been abandoned and the board consisted of a majority of Chavistas.

Many of these initiatives would have been impossible without the dramatic rise in oil revenues that took place after 2002. From a low of about $20/barrel at the end of 2001, oil prices rose steadily to $30/barrel in mid-2003, then skyrocketed to over $50/barrel by late 2004 (in 2008 they passed $100). While some of the new oil boom resulted from events outside the control of the government, such as the end of the global recession in the early 2000s and the increased demand for energy in developing countries such as China and India, the government could take partial credit. Early in 1999 Chávez and his key advisers began to forge a new consensus in the Organization of Petroleum Exporting Countries (OPEC) around restricted output. While oil production in Venezuela never fully regained its pre-strike levels, the dramatic rise in oil prices largely compensated for this loss and left the government flush with funds from 2004 on.

The government's renewed sense of vision and its ability to disburse oil revenues yielded significant electoral dividends. The first evidence of this turnaround was, of course, the presidential recall of 2004. As already mentioned, early polls seemed to favor the opposition, but by the time of the election in August, the Missions were in full swing and approval of the administration had reversed its downward trend, reaching a fairly stable level of 50–60 percent (Figure 2.1). Moreover, Chávez turned away from his regular party machinery (which had failed to prevent the opposition's effort to hold the recall) and drew heavily from the Bolivarian Circles to create an entirely new campaign organization to register new voters. The result was a resounding victory for the government. We can see this turnaround not only in the public approval levels tracked in Figure 2.1, but also in the presidential election results from 1998 to 2006, shown in Figure 2.2. During the recall and again in 2006, Chávez and his movement managed to expand dramatically the overall size of the electorate, reduce voter abstention, and even increase their vote share to 59 percent of valid votes in 2004 and almost 63 percent in 2006.

Subsequent state and local elections in October 2004 (not shown in Figure 2.2) were largely a disaster for opposition parties, which failed to adopt a unified approach and lost almost all of their seats except those in the municipal governments of eastern Caracas and the governorship of the state of Zulia. Midterm congressional elections in 2005 were another loss for the opposition. After concerns were raised about the electronic voting machinery and the partiality of the CNE, opposition parties decided to abstain from the election and withdraw their candidates. The call for abstention had much of the desired effect and produced a record low turnout of 20 percent; however, the action also meant the complete takeover of the National Assembly by Chavista parties

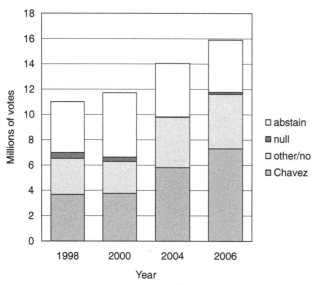

FIGURE 2.2. Presidential and recall election results, 1998–2006.
Source: CNE (2007).

and the elimination of an important platform for communicating the opposition's views to the public. In the 2006 presidential election, the results were more mixed but generally favored Chávez. On the one hand, the opposition conducted its first unified campaign, and its candidate, Manuel Rosales, the popular governor of Zulia, ran what was widely perceived as a good campaign given the odds against him. Nevertheless, Chávez won reelection handily in an election with a higher turnout than ever (74 percent). Given the popularity of the Missions and the booming economy (by now heavily stimulated by government spending), the outcome was considered a foregone conclusion.

Thanks to these successes, Chávez was able to surround himself with a new, more radical set of allies and assert ever more personalistic control over the movement and government. He pursued an increasingly leftist vision of revolutionary change he titled "twenty-first century socialism" that emphasized state-sponsored economic cooperatives, state control over key economic sectors, and new forms of community organization and local government centered on a program of Communal Councils (*Consejos Comunales*). As part of these efforts, in December 2006 Chávez announced the creation of a new, unified Chavista party, the PSUV (Partido Socialista Unido de Venezuela, or United Socialist Party of Venezuela), which all parties and other organizations would be required to join if they wanted to remain a part of the movement. At his inauguration in January 2007, he made the surprising announcement of his intention to renationalize key firms, including telecommunications and electrical firms and foreign investments in the oil industry, and to end central bank autonomy (Romero 2007b [NYT]). Shortly before this, he also announced his intent to revoke the license of the country's largest private television station, Radio Caracas Televisión (RCTV), a fierce critic of Chávez and an alleged accomplice in the attempted coup of 2002.

In the past, similar plans had been scaled back after their announcement, but this time Chávez pressed forward despite considerable international criticism and a new wave of protests at home. The government's new six-year plan for socioeconomic development, the *Proyecto Nacional Simón Bolívar*, called for more constitutional reforms, such as eliminating presidential term limits; a complete end of the private economy; and an effort to replace the United States with China as the leading customer for Venezuelan oil (Morsbach 2006; República Bolivariana de Venezuela 2007). The movement was again transformed as partisan allies such as the Communist Party of Venezuela, PODEMOS (Por la Democracia Social/For Social Democracy), and Patria Para Todos (Fatherland for All, or PPT) debated whether to subsume their organizations under the PSUV; some rebelled and found themselves marginalized, openly accused by Chávez of having lost sight of the revolutionary will of the people.

The movement also continued to attract enormous international attention from friends and foes. Like Salvador Allende's Chile in the early 1970s, Chavismo in Venezuela became a magnet for foreign social scientists and activists hoping to catch a glimpse of and even participate in the Bolivarian democratic revolution. New, sympathetic governments in Bolivia and Ecuador held their own constitutional conventions and promised radical leftist reforms that would eliminate corruption and the vestiges of colonialism, while runners-up to the presidency in Peru and Mexico promised much the same (Castañeda 2006; Seligson 2007). Chávez increasingly used international forums to speak out on behalf of foreign presidential candidates and movements he favored and to criticize the president of the United States and other world leaders who contradicted him. He dispensed enormous sums of oil revenues and donations-in-kind to bolster potential allies and promoted grandiose projects of regional integration, such as oil refineries, a new television news network (Telesur), and a regional development bank (Banco del Sur) to compete with traditional multilateral lending agencies (Lapper 2006; Shifter 2007). Chávez and his movement seemed poised to succeed Castro as a leader of the global movement opposed to capitalist globalization and U.S. hegemony.

There were some minor setbacks. During 2006, Chávez engaged in an unsuccessful attempt to win Latin America's rotating seat on the UN Security Council. And his plans for constitutional reforms were thwarted when he lost the special referendum in December 2007 by a small margin (51 to 49 percent). The results of the constitutional referendum in particular were a wake-up call for the movement that prompted internal debate and even some soul-searching by Chávez (Romero 2007). Yet, Chávez claimed that the setback was only "for now," echoing his famous phrase from the failed 1992 coup attempt. The revolution would move forward, "the battle" would continue, and Chávez would use his every resource to pursue the movement's goals (Chávez 2007).

CURRENT APPROACHES TO CATEGORIZING CHAVISMO

Chavismo represents an extraordinary phenomenon for Venezuela and most of Latin America, one that would certainly seem out of place in the advanced industrial democracies today. Chávez and his supporters respect many of the democratic norms established by the traditional parties and their leaders, such as the principle of constituting government through formally competitive popular elections, yet they consistently challenge and defy these norms in their efforts to carry out a so-called democratic (now, socialist) revolution in Venezuela. They simultaneously resist and embrace the kinds of hierarchical organizations and party penetration that characterized the old system, juxtaposing participatory democratic mechanisms with an increasingly centralized government and a hegemonic party. While the movement preaches against the corruption of the old system, it resists creating the impartial institutions that are needed to enshrine the rule of law. It condemns the imperialistic, antidemocratic policies of the U.S. government while making alliances with countries having dubious democratic credentials. And it polarizes political competition in a way not experienced in Venezuela since the 1958 transition to democracy. How should we understand or categorize Chavismo?

Venezuelanists studying Chávez and his movement tend to split along partisan lines of pro- or anti-Chávez. One side sees Chavismo as the answer to the undemocratic nature of Venezuelan politics and its failed model of economic development. Primarily scholars sympathetic to the radical left, they argue that Chavismo is embodying the popular will and creating new institutions that allow that will to be expressed while destroying the vestiges of inequality and colonialism and the particular evils of the Punto Fijo partyocracy that made democracy and economic development so shallow and problematic. They see Chavismo as one of the only credible responses to a globally hegemonic neoliberal project (Ellner 2004; Collins 2005; Lander 2005; Parker 2005). While sometimes troubled by the personalistic tendencies of Chavismo or the impracticality of particular reforms, scholars in this group tend to focus on Chavismo's strengths, arguing that its negative tendencies are necessary evils that should be endured. With careful, objective criticism, they believe, these weaknesses of the government may be overcome and the aims of its revolution fulfilled (Ellner 2001; López-Maya 2003).[6]

On the other side are those who describe Chavismo largely as an enemy of democracy and of sustainable (especially market-oriented) economic development. They focus on the negative aspects of Chavismo, such as its tendency to devalue the civil rights and societal pluralism that are at the heart of liberal democracy, as well as the personalistic tendencies of the movement and its corresponding lack of institutionalization (Coppedge 2005; Kornblith 2005; Lievesley 2005; Cedeño 2006). These scholars acknowledge the effectiveness

---

[6] Some of these allies have adopted an increasingly critical stance of the movement's hegemonic tendencies since Chávez's reelection in 2006. See, for example, López-Maya (2008b).

of some of Chávez's reforms and generally welcome the end of the old party system, but they feel that the current project is fundamentally flawed. Many of them are quite critical of the government's redistributive economic policies, which they see as unsustainable demagogic gestures reflecting Chávez's particular fascination with the revolutionary left (c.f. Naím 2004; Corrales 2006; Shifter 2006; Rodríguez 2008). For these scholars, Chavismo is an unfortunate detour from the real solutions that will ultimately be required for Venezuela and the rest of the developing world to become fully democratic and developed.

Both groups of scholars help us break away from the traditional emphasis on Venezuela's old party system and see Chávez and his movement as something new in Venezuelan politics. However, they have two flaws that prevent us from understanding Chavismo. The most obvious is their tendency to frame our choice of categories as a dichotomy rather than as a continuous scale. The debate over Chavismo is highly polarizing, and popular accounts often use extremes in their praise or criticism of the regime. Clearly, each of these views is inadequate. While Chavismo cannot be written off as an entirely negative experience for Venezuelan democracy (for example, it acknowledges the isolation and injustice confronted by citizens in the informal sector, and it holds regular, meaningful elections), it cannot be considered a particularly positive one either. Basic government services are often denied to members of the opposition, key government institutions are stacked with Chavista appointees, and new forms of corruption are rampant, to note just a few oft-cited concerns. On the democracy–authoritarianism scale the Chávez government is somewhere in between.

This weakness is partially addressed by current studies of illiberal democracy and competitive authoritarian regimes. This research claims that we must refine our understanding of democracy and look beyond the mere holding of elections when deciding if regimes are democratic. By considering the hidden ways in which authoritarian regimes can systematically bias and constrain electoral outcomes, we can introduce sharper categorical distinctions into the interval-level scales of democratic procedure that Freedom House and other organizations produce (Diamond 2002; Levitsky and Way 2002; Schedler 2002; Zakaria 2003; Schedler 2006).

This literature on hybrid democracy sees Chavismo as an emblematic case of this kind of regime. Venezuela under Chávez is a democracy in the "gray zone" (Carothers 2002), a "hybrid" regime (McCoy and Myers 2004), or a "competitive autocracy" (Corrales 2006). While still acknowledging the reality of nominally competitive elections under the Chávez government, these studies draw our attention to Chavismo's deviations from democratic procedures outside of election day. In this book I agree with this latter, more nuanced assessment and refer to Chávez's government as semidemocratic.[7]

---

[7] Some critics of Chavez argue that we should go further and classify his government as competitive authoritarian (Corrales 2006). However, Schedler (2002, 2006) argues that a regime

Yet, even this semantic solution overlooks the second and more serious problem with the current debate over Chavismo: the tendency to frame it as a unidimensional choice. Both the newer, more comparative treatment of Chavismo and the focused studies by Venezuelanists assume that the only relevant distinction is the classic one of democracy in procedural terms – of contestation and participation, plus requisite civil rights and liberties – and thus see the scholarly challenge largely as one of gauging the institutional differences between Chavismo and other governments. Chávez's allies change the terms of this debate somewhat by introducing more substantive notions of democracy into the mix – "economic" and "social" democracy arising from efforts to serve marginalized sectors of the population – but their debate is still over whether Chávez is really democratic in some behavioral sense.

Not only do most of these distinctions fail to pinpoint what really makes Chavismo different as a semidemocratic regime, but they represent only marginal improvements in these measures. We can see this by considering Venezuela's Freedom House ranking in 2006 along both dimensions measured by this organization, Political Rights (PR) and Civil Liberties (CL). This allows us to consider two of the distinctions raised in recent studies: the procedural quality of elections and the nature of the exercise of power (captured by PR) and the degree to which these institutions are accompanied by civil rights associated with liberalism (measured by CL). The data show that Venezuela is indeed weakly democratic on each count (PR=4, CL=4 or "part-free" on the 1–7 scale). Yet, Venezuela in 2006 is the same or nearly the same as Guatemala under Oscar Berger (PR=4, CL=4), Haiti under René Préval (PR=4, CL=5), Paraguay under Nicanor Duarte (PR=3, CL=3), and Nicaragua under Enrique Bolaños (PR=3, CL=3). And it is nearly the same as Venezuela during the last year under Pérez in the early 1990s, when the country was also ranked as "partly free" (PR=3, CL=3). These data reveal that there is actually little difference between the two components of these procedural democracy measures; calling these regimes "illiberal democracies" is inaccurate, because they were not highly democratic in terms of either their elections *or* civil liberties. More significantly, though, the data group together several regimes that are clearly different in quality. All of these other countries had relatively moderate pluralist governments at the time these measurements were taken and were never considered by journalists or scholars to be in the same category as Venezuela under Chavismo, despite their common failure to fully achieve procedural democratic standards.

This is not a criticism of the Freedom in the World Index or other attempts at quantifying procedural democracy, all of which draw on valid, reliable indicators of fundamental components of democracy. I accept and reaffirm these distinctions as an appropriate minimal definition of democracy and emphasize that we cannot consider Chávez's Bolivarian government to be fully

should be classified as competitive authoritarian when it achieves a 5 on the Freedom House scale of Political Rights. As of this writing, Venezuela was still a 4.

democratic without stretching the concept. But introducing finer distinctions along the same behavioral dimension can never capture the significant, *qualitative* difference between other semidemocracies and Chavismo. What is this missing dimension?

POPULISM AND THE NORMATIVE DIMENSION OF DEMOCRACY

The missing dimension is that of culture or ideas, specifically the normative framework that motivates and legitimates citizens' and elites' choices concerning democratic institutions. In his analysis of hybrid democratic regimes, Diamond states the problem this way:

> We may not have enough information now to know whether electoral administration will be sufficiently autonomous and professional, and whether contending parties and candidates will be sufficiently free to campaign, so as to give the political opposition a fair chance to defeat the government in the next elections. Regime classification must, in part, assess the previous election, *but it must also assess the intentions and capacities of ambiguously democratic ruling elites*, something that is very hard to do. (2002, 22, emphasis added)

To better predict the direction in which democratic regimes are likely to head, Diamond urges us to go beyond the material attributes or procedures that characterize regimes and identify their "intentions and capacities." Assessing the intentions of political leaders and their activists means identifying a very different set of attributes than behavior. It implies a cultural aspect of politicians and citizens: the set of meanings they attach to democracy, or the beliefs they have about what politics should be and what democracy is for. This includes causal beliefs about how the world operates but also normative ones about how the world *should* operate. This normative dimension can reinforce democratic procedures – we may all see competitive elections and universal suffrage as means for adjudicating different viewpoints – or it may work against those procedures if, as happens in the case of Chavismo, we envision democracy as the means of expressing and achieving a unified, moral, popular will. But it is not reducible to the raw material aspects of electoral procedure or even its substantive outcomes.

The particular ideational or normative dimension that best identifies the intentions and capacities of regimes such as Chavismo is that of *worldview* and *discourse*. Specifically, Chávez and his allies have a *populist* worldview, or a Manichaean outlook that identifies Good with a unified will of the people and Evil with a conspiring minority, and they convey this set of ideas with a characteristic language – a discourse – full of bellicose, moralizing rhetoric emphasizing the recent subversion of the political system. This contrasts with a *pluralist* worldview or discourse, which adopts a pragmatic tone reflecting fundamental beliefs about the inevitability or even desirability of differing viewpoints in a democracy, as well as the virtues of an institutionalized democratic order. Each of these worldviews/discourses emphasizes different justifications for democracy that potentially take this regime type in different directions.

The terms "worldview" and especially "discourse" require some explanation and contextualizing, but the effort is worthwhile because it helps clarify some of the social science debates that we necessarily address when we talk about populism and what I call the normative dimension of democracy. As popularized by political philosophers and some of the early social scientists who studied the role of ideas in politics, a worldview is a set of fundamental assumptions about how the political world works. It includes not only norms, or moral prescriptions for behavior, but also a cosmology and an ontology – a sense of how the universe operates and who the real actors in it are (Goldstein and Keohane 1993, 8).[8] As used here and as popularized by postmodernists and discourse theorists, "discourse" is not a reference to instances of speech or written text, but is a technical term describing any distinct language that subconsciously expresses – and, in the postmodernist view, shapes or constitutes – our fundamental assumptions (Alker and Sylvan 1994; Dryzek and Niemeyer 2008). Like a gigantic Freudian slip, a discourse reveals our underlying beliefs without our knowing or really intending it, and our audience recognizes and responds to it in much the same intuitive way. To use a typical postmodernist example, the neutral, dense language of this book helps identify it as an academic work rather than a political tract or a journalistic narrative and reflects my views about the values of objectivity and the scientific method – it is an instance of scientific discourse. I use this language because I have been taught to, but I do so without stopping very often to think about the underlying assumptions that it conveys.

Both of these words get at the deep assumptions that shape our interpretation of the world. This is a crucial referent that distinguishes the concepts of worldview and discourse from the more familiar term "ideology" and ultimately makes them a better choice for understanding Chavismo or the intentions of democratic regimes. An ideology refers to a coherent set of normative and causal arguments about the appropriate course of action for government, and it is distinguished by its conscious elaboration and its applied emphasis, or program for action, which provides a set of practical policies and not merely a utopia (Mullins 1972; Gerring 1997; Knight 2006). The socialism that Chávez currently claims to espouse is an ideology, as are the classic ideas of liberalism and conservatism (Schumaker, Kiel, and Heilke 1996; Freeden 2003). Worldview and discourse are both like an ideology in that they refer to sets of beliefs that shape and provide meaning to the political actions of a believer. But unlike an ideology, they lack significant exposition and contrast with other worldviews or discourses and are consequently low on policy

---

[8] For Weber, the main world religions provide this set of fundamental assumptions quite explicitly – indeed, he uses the term "world images" to describe them (Weber 1958 [1946], 280) – but his three bases of political legitimacy (charismatic, traditional/patrimonial, and rational-legal) seem to fulfill a similar function.

specifics. A discourse, in particular, lacks the official texts and vocabulary that accompany an ideology and must be discerned through more diffuse linguistic elements such as tone and metaphor and by a search for broad themes.

If worldview and discourse refer to the same deep level of ideas, what exactly is the difference between them? In the view of behavioralists who take a more traditional approach to the study of ideas, these concepts are separate and have a clear causal relationship. Worldview describes a set of fundamental ideas in the abstract, while discourse refers only to the language in which these beliefs are actually expressed and perceived by others. According to this view, discourse is merely an indicator or a symptom of a worldview, and it is the worldview that determines behavior.

Postmodernists and their colleagues see much less distance between these two concepts, however. Discourse theorists (Alker and Sylvan 1994; van Dijk 2008) and some constructivists (c.f. Kratochwil 1989; Klotz 1995) insist that thoughts or ideas are never held in the abstract but are always stored and processed in our minds as language.[9] And because the language that we use is not created anew by each individual, but inherited as part of our socialization and gradually reshaped through a larger conversation across the community – that is, "socially constructed" – it acts as a kind of structural constraint on our thoughts and behavior (Fearon and Laitin 2000). According to this view, discourse is not properly thought of as the reflection of our worldview, but as something that causes and subsumes our worldview. What determines our behavior are the ideas-as-language that are stored in our minds.

My view is that the truth lies somewhere between these two extremes, and thus I rely on both terms in this book. On the one hand, I strongly resist the claim that language wholly determines thought or behavior, at least in the sense of language as an externally generated structure of meanings. As many political discourse analysts themselves acknowledge, if only tacitly (c.f. Milliken 1999), this strong view represents an oversimplified understanding of the relationship between thought and language. First, it is not clear how much of a limiting factor our shared language is on our thinking. While linguistic limitations create some tendencies and shape our thinking at the margins, there is considerable overlap across human languages in terms of their ability to conceive of and grapple with the world, and a remarkable capacity to understand complex, esoteric subjects even in apparently primitive languages (Newcombe 2005). Human beings are adept at finding or creating words to express themselves. Second, the argument that our shared language "constitutes" or creates our identities and accompanying roles gives too little causal force to our genetic makeup and the material world around us. Needs for companionship, drives for power, and desires for transcendence all strongly

---

[9] Other constructivists are largely neutral on this point, in part because they are assessing fairly specific, consciously elaborated sets of ideas. See, for example, Finnemore's (1998) study of norms governing the conduct of war, the development of state science bureaucracies, and international development aid.

condition our political behavior, and we ultimately respond to a world that imposes strong physical constraints on what is possible or feasible. Discourse theorists and constructivists admit that the material world impinges on our behavior, of course, but they often fail to explore this relationship and in the process overemphasize nurture over nature.

On the other hand, discourse theorists are absolutely right in arguing that we cannot easily disentangle ideas and language, especially when we get to the level of ideas captured by worldview or discourse. All ideas are effectively invisible, and we must infer their existence by looking at outward manifestations such as someone's actual words or behavior. In the case of ideas such as ideologies and scientific theories, their conscious elaboration means that they have highly specific policy associations that we can often use to trace the ideas through actions – repeated votes on a certain set of legislation, for example, or consistent participation in a certain political party or interest group – or by counting up a readily identifiable set of keywords in a text. With a worldview such as populism, these policy associations become more context specific and thwart any easy attempt to impute preferences across communities or periods of time through a study of behavior. There is no set of populist issue positions we can easily trace in a voting record; what makes any issue stance populist is the way it is broadly framed. Moreover, when we do examine instances of language for evidence of a worldview, we cannot easily apply standard content analysis techniques because these depend on specific, consistent word associations or sentence-level statements about issue positions. A discourse operates by way of diffuse linguistic elements that require *interpretation*.

Because I want to draw more attention to the overlap between ideas and language in the case of populism, and because I feel that the discourse theorists have done the best job of exploring the nature of populist language and ideas, I refer to populism as a discourse in much of this book and use the word in its fuller postmodernist sense. Consequently, I distinguish it from particular instances of talk as speech, text, or language. My argument is not an especially discourse-theoretic one, however, because I do not see language per se as the ultimate determinant of ideas and behavior, and so in many parts of the text I refer to worldview (or close synonyms such as "outlook") in order to make clear the primacy of ideas and material context over language. I do not conceive of discourse as a disembodied thing that floats around causing conflict, policy, and organization; it is human beings believing in particular ideas and using characteristic language who act.[10] But there are distinctive ways of expressing these ideas, and it is this language that we are most often forced to examine when it comes time to look at data.

Now, what do I mean by populism and pluralism, and why do I emphasize these two discourses? I will not be able to outline a complete typology of political worldviews or discourses here; most discourse analysts (including those who study populism) take an interpretivist tack that provides rich

---

[10] My thanks to both reviewers for suggesting this phrasing.

description but avoids identifying general types (c.f. Aibar 2005). For simplicity's sake, and because I think these cover most of the kinds of discourses we actually see in later chapters, I emphasize just two: populism and pluralism. Scholars have suggested at least one other. Mudde (2004) argues that populism and pluralism are actually two of three fundamental worldviews (or what he labels "thin-centered ideologies") that together constitute a typology, the other being *elitism*. Whereas populism asserts the virtue of common folk and (in the case of pluralism as well) their right to sovereignty, elitism presumably affirms the superior capacity of wealthy or educated groups such as members of the armed forces, property owners, and intellectuals, and thus their right to rule over the lower classes and direct society for the common good. However, because elitism is largely antidemocratic, and because most of the leaders studied in subsequent chapters adhere to some notion of democracy, I set it aside for most of the discussion and focus on the distinction between populism and pluralism, treating these as two ends of our normative scale.

The definitions of populism and pluralism that I gave at the beginning of this section suggest five elements that allow us to identify populist discourse more clearly in speech and text. These are a Manichaean outlook; identification of Good with the will of the people; identification of Evil with a conspiring elite; and two corollary elements: an emphasis on systemic change and an anything-goes attitude toward minority rights and democratic procedure.

Manichaean Outlook

While in ordinary times politicians and citizens display a relatively neutral, dispassionate way of seeing the world that deemphasizes the grand moral significance of political issues, in moments of crisis they are more likely to slip into an outlook that is Manichaean, or moralizing, dualistic, and teleological. Populism is just such a Manichaean outlook. It assigns a moral dimension to everything, no matter how technical, and interprets it as part of a cosmic struggle between Good and Evil. History is not just proceeding toward some final conflict but has already arrived, and there can be no fence-sitters in this struggle. As de la Torre argues, "The political confrontation is total, without the possibility of compromise or dialogue" (2000, 15). Or as Hofstadter argues in his classic description of what he calls the "paranoid style":

> The distinguishing thing about [populism] is not that its exponents see conspiracies or plots here and there in history, but that they regard a "vast" or "gigantic" conspiracy as *the motive force* in historical events. History *is* a conspiracy, set in motion by demonic forces of almost transcendent power, and what is felt to be needed to defeat it is not the usual methods of political give-and-take, but an all-out crusade. (1966, 29–30)

Largely as a consequence of this Manichaean outlook, actual populist discourse often justifies the moral significance of its ideals by tying them to revered national or religious leaders. These leaders and ideologies are not merely cited, but reinterpreted in ways that see them as forefathers, mystically connected to the populist cause. As Zúquete argues,

> [The] historical past is collapsed into the present in such a way that it transcends human linear time and creates what can be called an eternal present, a living continuity, in which past wars fought over the independence of the country, for example, are experienced as "eternal" sources of the spiritual strength of the ... people. The past is not dead but is relived in the present. (2008, 108)

In contrast to populism, pluralism avoids making any mystical connections between current issues and historical figures or global problems, and it avoids reifying history. The discourse tends to be more technical and to focus on narrow, particular issues. And it is more accepting of natural, justifiable differences of opinion.

Good = The Will of the People

For pluralists, democracy means the calculation of votes. This should be respected and is seen as the foundation of legitimate government (together with other institutions emphasized later), but it is not meant to be an exercise in arriving at a preexisting, knowable "will." The majority shifts and changes across issues. The notion of citizenship is correspondingly broad and legalistic, not limited to a romanticized subset of the population; human individuality is valued, and minority rights become an important complement to majority rule.

Within the Manichaean outlook of populists, in contrast, the Good has a particular identity: it is the will of the people. This notion of the popular will is essentially a crude version of the General Will described by Rousseau (1993). The mass of individual citizens are the rightful sovereign; given enough time for reasoned discussion, they will come to a knowledge of their collective interest; the government must be constructed in such a way that it can embody their will. This version of the General Will ascribes particular virtue to the views and collective traditions of common, ordinary folk, who are seen as the overwhelming majority (Wiles 1969, 166). Hence, the voice of the people is the voice of God – *Vox populi, vox dei*. Again, though, this is a crude version of the General Will. Believing in the rightness of its cause, populists do away with concerns over the heterogeneity of our preferences and see this popular will as unique and unified – there can be only one will of the people, or it cannot be the embodiment of Good. Thus, while populism is democratic in the sense that it assigns ultimate sovereignty to the mass of individual citizens and seeks their empowerment, it is the opposite of pluralism. It abhors differences of opinion and fails to see these as legitimate, consistent outcomes that should be institutionalized through mechanisms of compromise. The consequences for the procedures that constitute democracy can be harsh, especially if some individual or minority group presumes that it knows the will of the people and speaks for them.

Who constitutes this people in actual instances of populism? As Canovan (1999, 5) points out, populists tends to draw on the principle of majority rule, but the precise notion of who constitutes this majority varies with the context. It can be those who really do constitute a majority in a particular community – the poor, the middle class, the blue-collar laborers – or it may take a more nativistic bent and look to an idealized common man of the past as the embodiment of virtue. Taggart nicely captures this latter idea with his concept of the "heartland," which he calls the place in the collective imagination embodying "the positive aspects of everyday life" (2000, 95). It is an idealized notion of the virtuous ordinary citizen and community, one that harks back to a past unspoiled by the present.

Evil = A Conspiring Elite

Pluralism avoids a conspiratorial tone and tends not to label political opponents as Evil; it may even avoid mentioning opponents in an effort to maintain a positive tone and keep passions low. Within the Manichaean discourse of populism, however, there is always some conspiring elite minority that has subverted the will of the people. Populists must discover and identify this enemy in order to negatively constitute the people. According to Hofstadter, "this enemy is clearly delineated: he is a perfect model of malice, a kind of amoral superman: sinister, ubiquitous, powerful, cruel, sensual, luxury-loving" (1966, 31–2). The people is everything that this conspiring elite is not: pure, simple, selfless, and hard-working. The particular identity of the enemy again varies according to the context – it can be the wealthy, an ethnic group, an intellectual class, or some international political actor or ideology – but it tends to be drawn from either economic classes or ethnic groups who can be easily distinguished and who might plausibly be considered subversive oppressors of the majority.

Systemic Change

Pluralism is prone to emphasize particular issues. In the words of Laclau (2005), it is a politics of "differences" rather than "hegemony." While it advocates changes in the particulars of how government operates, it typically seeks to preserve traditional institutions, especially those undergirding democratic competition and minority rights. It is a politics of policies and reform.

For populism, in contrast, the premises just discussed have two important corollaries. The first, at least in the early stages of a populist movement, is that the subversion of the people's will requires some form of systemic change, or what Laclau (2005) calls "rupture." The old regime has been taken over by the forces of Evil and no longer serves the people; it must be remade or at least substantially modified lest the forces of Evil regroup and continue their oppression. Hence, the conflict is not over particular policies or issues, but over institutions and the system. Populists frequently couch their goals in terms of "revolution" or "liberation," but the new institutions they advocate will vary widely across historical circumstances, and the actual substance of their "revolution" is often thin. In some instances, they pointedly avoid the term because of its association with "foreign" and "subversive" ideologies such as Marxism (Waisman 1987). Movements and leaders that ascribe ultimate virtue to the folk are less likely to have consistent, intellectually refined programs of action and may reject some radical ideologies. Their targets are first the political class and the corrupt institutions of the state. And true social revolutions – those that seek to reorder property relations through widespread confiscation and government ownership – are difficult to implement without alienating many of the populists' potential constituents. Consequently, populist leaders have traditionally been objects of scorn for doctrinaire leftists who see them as duping the masses and diverting the revolutionary tide from its proper destination (di Tella 1965). Yet, populists draw heavily from a rhetoric of systemic change that has real bite, and their institutional reforms often go far enough that they anger and alienate traditionally powerful groups.

An Anything-Goes Attitude

The other corollary of populism is what McGuire (1995, 1997) calls an "anything goes" attitude. Pluralist discourse openly respects formal rights and liberties, and it treats opponents with courtesy, as legitimate political actors. It does not encourage or justify illegal, violent actions, but (as mentioned previously) demonstrates respect for institutions and the rule of law. In contrast, populism regards procedural rights associated with liberal democracy as instrumental and may violate them in order to better express the will of the people. Members of the opposition are not accorded legitimacy, citizenship, or possibly human rights, and any respect given them is a generous gift rather than a moral imperative. Furthermore, the need to change the system means that current institutions will all be regarded with suspicion. In the modern era, these are often the institutions of liberal democracy and rational or scientific discourse. Hence, populism "abhors science and technocracy" (Wiles 1969, 170), and it may be willing to bend data or crudely use it to service popular wisdom or the will of a charismatic leader.

As I suggested earlier, both populism and pluralism draw on normative justifications for democracy that make both of these discourses, in a sense, democratic. Like pluralism, populism reaffirms the sovereignty of ordinary people and provides an appealing discourse when the basic rights of large numbers of citizens are being violated. Populists defend the capacity and the right of the majority to rule. If democracy is largely characterized by, as Dahl states, "the continuing responsiveness of the government to the preferences of its citizens, considered as political equals" (1971, 1), then populism is very democratic.

Yet, the idea that populism is in the same democratic league as pluralism seems jarring. Populism is frequently portrayed as something pathological that is opposed or inimical to democracy (see Shils 1956; Hofstadter 1966; Riker 1982). Critics argue that populism is a vague set of ideas that can be used to fool ignorant citizens and justify authoritarianism and shortsighted policies (Di Tella 1965). Populism indirectly questions the procedural minimum that lies at the heart of our current definitions of democracy by undermining tolerance for opposition and questioning the inviolability of basic civil rights and liberties.

The experiences of fascism and other notorious populist movements remind us that there is substance to these concerns; populism ultimately has a kind of directionality, carrying democracy down an authoritarian or, to be more precise, totalitarian path as it imposes a uniform moral ideal on citizens. This is what we mean when we say that understanding populism (and pluralism) helps us identify the intentions of political leaders. Yet, painting populist ideas as uniformly antithetical to democracy overlooks the wide variety of populist experiences in modern democracies and risks ignoring the potential corresponding failures of pluralism. Rather than engage in polemics about whether populism is really democratic, it may be more helpful to see it as a variety of democratic discourse with significant potential weaknesses that lead it in an undemocratic direction. This approach is more likely to disarm populist critics of pluralist democracies and allow for a more honest, productive effort to remedy pluralism's own failures.

This argument is made most forcefully by Canovan (1999), who suggests that we regard populism and pluralism as two faces of democracy. Each embodies one of two general approaches to politics that she calls "redemptive" and "pragmatic." In the redemptive approach, "politics is taken to be a matter of achieving perfection or salvation in this world" and is a highly meaningful experience for its participants. It entails enthusiasm for politics, a search for power, and confidence in the ability to safely wield that power. In the pragmatic approach, politics "has no overriding purpose, except to keep order and reduce occasions for conflict by maintaining and amending the precious inheritance of rights and institutions" (1999, 8). It is "suspicious both of power and of enthusiasm," and it has "much lower expectations of what government can achieve." It emphasizes the rule of law and procedural rights above all other considerations (ibid.). Canovan claims that both approaches to politics are incomplete and imperfect. The pragmatic (pluralist) approach provides predictability and stability and is less likely to commit excesses in the name of a cause; it prevents the tyranny of well-meaning majorities. However, it can also enervate voters, foster rampant individualism and corruption, and lean so far toward the will of minorities that it becomes undemocratic in its own way. The redemptive (populist) approach to democracy can restore meaning to politics, encourage community spirit, and overcome barriers to collective action. Yet, it too has its dark side: it questions minority rights, polarizes society, weakens bureaucratic effectiveness, and stifles dissent.

Thus, seeing populism as a kind of pathology is not entirely wrong. By wedding notions of popular sovereignty to a Manichaean outlook on politics, populism comes to regard the tolerance for opposing viewpoints as symptomatic of the moral failure of the institutional order. By espousing highly idealized notions of folk wisdom, it begins to challenge experts and professionals. And by seeking to replace political institutions with some vague embodiment of the popular will, it risks creating a government without checks and balances. But populism and pluralism are approaches to democracy with a certain complementarity. Populist and pluralist discourses are inherent in every democracy and present in the minds of most democratic citizens. The excesses of pluralism, if left unchecked, can undermine the legitimacy of the system and provoke a populist response.

A Minimal Definition of Populism

At this point, readers may wonder how populism defined in this discursive or ideational sense is related to the broader concept of populism that comes up in the study of Latin American politics. In this book I argue not only that Chavismo can be distinguished by its populist discourse, but that this discourse or worldview is what defines the historical phenomenon of populism.

Populism as a kind of historical phenomenon – that is, as a movement or even a wave of movements such as Peronism, the Populist movement in the United States, or interwar nationalist movements in Eastern Europe – is a highly contested concept. A number of scholars who study populism in both the developing world and the industrial democracies rely on a roughly discursive definition like the one used here. While using a variety of labels to describe exactly what populism is a kind of – referring to it as a political "style" (Knight 1998), a "discourse" (de la Torre 2000; Laclau 2005), a "language" (Kazin 1998), an "appeal" (Canovan 1999), or a "thin ideology" (Mudde 2004) – they all see it as a set of *ideas* rather than a cluster of actions isolated from their underlying meanings for leaders and participants. The ideas are embodied in particular movements and people, but it is the ideas and the way they are expressed that allow us to characterize any organization or political actors as populist.

However, for many other scholars who study populism, particularly in Latin America, three other definitions or approaches are more common (Roberts 1995; Weyland 2001). One of these, the *structuralist* approach to populism, emphasizes its social origins and conceives of it as a set of movements associated with certain stages of development, especially the attempt at industrialization in countries located at the periphery of the world economy. According to this view, populist regimes are those using cross-class coalitions and popular mobilization to support state-led policies of import-substituting industrialization, or ISI (Di Tella 1965, 1997; Weffert 1973; Ianni 1975; Germani 1978; Cardoso and Faletto 1979). The second definition is an *economic* one that identifies populism with policy outputs – specifically, shortsighted economic policies that appeal to the poor (Dornbusch and Edwards 1991). Populist regimes are irresponsible macroeconomic agents that ignore hard budget constraints and the harsh realities of a globalized economy. And a third, *political-institutional* definition focuses on organizational aspects of populism such as the degree of institutionalization of the movement, its low esteem for existing institutions of representative democracy, its emphasis on support from large numbers of voters, and the presence of a charismatic leader (Weyland 2001; Roberts 2003).

It should be clear that these alternative conceptualizations of populism emphasize largely material aspects of politics, that is, coalitions, historical preconditions, and policies.[11] This is an incomplete account. Their approaches resemble the one currently taken to the study of democracy, in that they overlook the ideational element of politics and focus only on its behavioral attributes. By analogy, one way to dispel the current conceptual confusion is simply to argue that we must round out our definitions of populism by including a discursive component. Populism is, let us say, any cross-class coalition using shortsighted macroeconomic policy that also has a populist discourse.

However, there are several problems with this solution. The first is that, unlike in the case of democracy, there is no corresponding accepted behavioral standard for what constitutes populism. Arguably, none of the material attributes covered in alternative definitions are found in *every* populist movement; many nonpopulist leaders and parties have attributes such as cross-class coalitions, charismatic leadership, or shortsighted economic policies. Second, it is unclear why we need to impose a behavioral standard. There are no obvious political stakes here, as there are with the procedures that constitute democracy, nothing that we would codify in the charter of the OAS or make the focus of a U.S. State Department report. We do not worry about a charismatic movement or even bad economic policy in the same way that we worry about the universal suffrage and freedom of speech that constitute modern democracy.

The most serious problem with this solution is that it fails to identify the underlying logic that unites all of these behavioral attributes: ultimately, *all of these other behavioral attributes are products of the underlying set of ideas.* A populist worldview is the motivating force that lies at the heart of every populist movement and drives these behavioral characteristics (K. Hawkins 2009; see also Roxborough 1984; Laclau 2005; Panizza 2005a). For example, the presence of cross-class coalitions built around a diffuse ideology – emphasized by the structuralist definition– is a natural outgrowth of an antagonistic approach to politics that seeks to erase narrow sectoral or class-based

---

[11] To be precise, Weyland and Roberts emphasize the way in which the relationship between leaders and followers is structured, or as Weyland phrases it, populism as a "political strategy" (2001, 12). To the degree that this incorporates the underlying ideas that give meaning to or even motivate these decisions about political practice, it comes very close to the discursive definition. Weyland briefly hints at this possibility (2001, 11).

identities and reaffirm a common popular identity of the majority. Populism is not just a big tent under which many groups fit, but a space in which activists *must* include large numbers in order to justify their claims to represent the popular will. This does not mean that all cross-class coalitions are populist, but it does mean that we can better understand why this feature is common to populist movements once we understand the underlying ideas.

Likewise, many of the historical aspects of classic populism emphasized by structuralists, including its emergence in late-modernizing former colonies and its reemergence in these same countries today as they fail to confront adequately the rigors of globalization, can be seen as *causes* of populism rather than as definitional attributes. Something about these countries as latecomers to development makes them prone to populism. In subsequent chapters, I argue that this something is the lack of institutions that enshrine the rule of law, a persistent problem in many Latin American countries and other developing states.

In turn, the shortsighted policies emphasized by the economic definition can be seen as a likely *consequence* of the populist worldview. In an environment where inequality is high, exploitation is systematic, and the bulk of the population is poor – as it is in developing countries such as Venezuela – the voters who typically make up the electorate and the potential "people" are more likely to favor radical redistribution. Furthermore, the charismatic politicians who lead successful populist movements may have great disdain for traditional economic institutions, believing that economics must be subject to their political will and the demands of the people. Yet, these are only possible correlates, not inevitable outcomes. What really makes economic policies seem populist are the leaders' justifications for the policies. Presumably, even the most fiscally responsible policies will seem populist if framed the right way, while irresponsible policies may result from mere ignorance or incompetence (Knight 1998).

Finally, the organizational attributes highlighted by the political-institutional definition can also be seen as important *consequences* of populism. As in the case of economic policies, we have to ask not just how populists organize, but why they organize. Attributes such as low institutionalization, charismatic leadership, and the pursuit of large numbers of voters are natural consequences of the crisis environment that typically gives rise to populism, and they constitute sensible means for embodying the putative will of the people. Populists preach an egalitarian ethic that is incompatible with hierarchical, professional political organization; thus, they organize as a movement in order to be true to their message. Yet, as with economic populism, it is ultimately these underlying motivations and not the attributes themselves that distinguish an organization as populist. Other political organizations such as religious parties and millenarian movements have charismatic leaders and low levels of institutionalization early in their organizational life cycle, but usually we do not consider them populist.

Thus, alternative definitions are not entirely wrong. While they fail to describe unique identifying traits, they do describe important causes and consequences of the populist worldview and represent important correlates that are causally linked. But it is only when we see ideas as the core attribute of populist movements that we can identify the underlying logic of these other definitions and the very real connections among them. Hence, I define populism in terms of worldview and discourse, and I change the word into an adjective – "populist movement," "populist leader," and so on – when I want to refer to actual instances of populism. This cannot entirely eliminate our confusion, as we naturally tend to use the term populism to refer not just to a set of ideas but also to the larger set of practices of which they become a part (as in "populism in Latin America first emerges in the early twentieth century"), but I try to use these terms carefully in order to preserve as clear a boundary as possible between ideas and actions.

Populism and Charisma

The word "charismatic" has cropped up several times in this discussion of Chavismo and the concept of populism, and we need to clarify its significance. As scholars of populism have repeatedly noted, including those who advocate a discursive definition (de la Torre 2000; Laclau 2005; Panizza 2005a), populist movements are nearly always led by charismatic leaders. Such leaders claim to embody the popular will: to be unique, omniscient interpreters of what true citizens would want if only they could come together and discuss their common interests. Chávez in particular is a highly charismatic leader who attracts extraordinary devotion from many movement activists and ordinary voters (Hawkins 2003). Does this mean that charisma is an essential aspect of populism?

The concept of charisma – sometimes called charismatic "linkages" – refers to a relationship between citizens and politicians. Since at least the time of the writings of Max Weber, scholars have identified a number of politician-citizen relationships defined by the types of goods exchanged and the way in which the exchange takes place (Lawson 1980; Kitschelt 2000; Roberts 2001). Thus, a relationship characterized by the conditional or direct exchange of votes for particularistic benefits is referred to as "clientelistic linkage," and a relationship characterized by the unconditional or indirect exchange of votes for policy is referred to as "programmatic linkage" (Graziano 1975; Kitschelt 2000; Hawkins 2003; Kitschelt and Wilkinson 2007). The charismatic mode of linkage – a term that draws explicitly from Weber's definition of charisma (Weber 1958 [1946]) – is an exceptional one in which voters support a person seen as having extraordinary skills and quasi-divine character who promises radical change. They support the leader without the exchange of any particular kind or quantity of goods. Such leaders make promises and possibly keep them, but what matters most is the demonstration of the leader's character, not the content of the exchange.

Many instances of populism could be considered charismatic movements relying on a populist discourse. Indeed, all of the examples of populist leaders identified in the comparative analysis in this book are or were also charismatic leaders at the head of large, diffuse movements. This is true for historical populists such as Perón and Velasco Ibarra, as well as for current populists in Latin America (Chávez in Venezuela and Morales in Bolivia) and other regions (for example, Alexsandr Lukashenko in Belarus).

However, I agree with Mudde (2004, 544–5), who argues that there is no *necessary* relationship between populist ideas and charismatic linkages. Even within Latin America, where populism abounds, many charismatic leaders have pluralist or even elitist discourses. Examples of potentially elitist charismatics include Efraín Ríos Montt, the former military dictator in Guatemala, and Abimael Guzmán, the founder of the Shining Path in Peru, both of whom were perfectly willing to destroy the people in order to pursue their vision of national salvation. A more current example of an elitist charismatic from outside Latin America might be Vladimir Putin in Russia (Krastov 2006). Examples of pluralist charismatics include Álvaro Uribe in Colombia, a president who acquired a reputation as a tireless public servant in the country's war against leftist guerrillas. And an important example of populism without charisma would be the Populist movement in the nineteenth-century United States, a largely grassroots phenomenon with several years of political activity before it allied with the charismatic figure of William Jennings Bryan (Hofstadter 1969; Goodwyn 1976).

Instead, we should treat charismatic leadership as an important *facilitator* of populist movements. Charismatic leadership is associated with politically successful populist movements (those that manage to win and maintain power). The reason is that populist discourse produces a naturally divided movement. By itself, populist discourse leads to calls for direct, participatory institutions that border on an anarchic vision of politics, both within the government and within the movement itself. This galvanizes participation and produces an army of enthusiastic supporters, but it also makes the movement's actions difficult to coordinate and puts would-be populists at a real political disadvantage. Decisions about campaign platforms, tactics, and even overall political strategy (do we go the electoral route or storm the Bastille?) can become impossible in a movement where all members feel that they deserve a voice and active involvement in decision making. This is one of the classic challenges of any social movement.

A charismatic leader who can credibly claim to embody the will of the people creates contradictions within the populist movement, in that he demands a certain submission to his will and a suppression of activists' independent preferences. But he can also impose order. Activists may participate and propose, but ultimately the leader decides, and all must fall in line or risk ostracism. As is evident in the case of Chavismo, with its swift and coordinated effort before the recall election, this leadership greatly facilitates the work of election campaigning and everyday actions of government, particularly in the legislature, transforming the populist movement from an angry mob into a common front. We may criticize the fawning sychophants and carbon-copy radicals who eventually come to the fore in such a movement, but we have to admit that they are united.

Hence, populist movements that fail to produce a charismatic leader may prove ineffective and wither away, while those that have the lucky advantage of this kind of leadership prosper and ultimately survive (at least, as long as the leader does). This is a decisive consequence of having what Laclau calls an "empty signifier" (2005) to lead the movement, a person with a vague but appealing set of ideas and language in which followers can each read their particular views. Naturally, we tend to see only the movements that achieve this kind of success, and so hindsight gives us a rather distorted picture of the place of charisma in populism. Occasionally, however, a leaderless movement achieves a measure of success and reminds us that charisma is neither required for populist discourse to be thought and spoken nor guaranteed to come along and aid it, as we see in the case of the Populist movement in the United States and perhaps in the series of Narodnik movements in eighteenth-century Russia (see Venturi 1960, especially pp. 501–6; Walicki 1969). In fact, when we look more closely, we can see that we are surrounded by countless examples of ephemeral populist movements that fail to leave any lasting imprint and may never really get off the ground. Many protest movements fall into this category (think of ineffective consumer boycotts or small groups of citizens picketing a city council zoning meeting), as do the isolated radicals who post inflammatory statements on billboards in their yards or on Web sites. Most of these are nascent populist movements that never grow to maturity. Even as dramatic an exception as the Populist movement in the United States proves the rule of charisma and political success: in the end, the Populist Party failed to win the presidential election or a plurality in Congress, although it did win control of a few local governments and congressional seats before losing steam.

This more nuanced argument helps us understand the success of Chavismo vis-à-vis the opposition in Venezuela, and it receives additional treatment in later chapters. We cannot really understand Chavismo without acknowledging Chávez's presence, nor can we understand populism's full flowering and emergence in other times and places without seeing the side of political leadership. Charisma matters for populism in action. Yet, populism exists in a variety of lesser forms that lack the presence of charismatic leaders, and many charismatic leaders draw from nonpopulist discourses. Consequently, I leave charisma out of the definition while still appreciating the crucial coordinating role that it plays for historically significant populist movements.

CHAVISMO AS A POPULIST MOVEMENT

Seeing populism as part of a cross-cutting cultural dimension of democracy helps illuminate Chavismo and many other aspects of Venezuelan politics. In terms of categorizing or describing the movement, it highlights not just the compromising of democratic procedures under the current government, but also the extraordinary qualitative differences between this new regime and the old Punto Fijo one. With respect to causal explanation, it helps us understand what gives rise to Chavismo's success. And in terms of prediction and policy implications, it helps us better understand the lines of conflict that have subsequently emerged at home and abroad, as well as the difficulty in criticizing the undemocratic aspects of the movement.

The old Punto Fijo regime in Venezuela was essentially pluralist, with a strong tendency to value democratic institutions for their own sake and to protect (albeit imperfectly) the right of minority opposition groups to representation. The system had strong elitist elements that compromised this pluralism – evident, for example, in the persistence of clientelistic relationships between the party leaders and their activists and voters, or in the parties' reliance on highly insular national executive committees. But it showed a remarkable tendency to value organizational diversity through mechanisms of proportional representation in key institutions, to co-opt rather than exclude challengers, and ultimately to permit decentralized government and an increasingly diversified civil society (Martz 1966; Coppedge 1993, 1994). It marked a dramatic change from previous experiences with democracy that were largely elitist (during most of the nineteenth century) or populist. Thus, even at its procedurally weakest moments (such as the tumultuous years of Pérez's second presidency), the Punto Fijo system was qualitatively different from Chavismo.

This difference is clearer if we compare Punto Fijo democracy with previous democratic experiences. The most competitive participatory experience to precede the Punto Fijo democracy was the Trienio, a three-year period from 1945 to 1948, when the young Acción Democrática (AD) was given control of the government following a military coup. At that time, AD alienated its authoritarian opponents and the more democratic elements of the opposition through its self-righteous zeal and its domination of the constituent assembly of 1946 and subsequent elections. AD's hegemonic tendencies provoked a second coup that removed it from power and led to a 10-year military dictatorship. The lessons learned from that experience strongly influenced the transition in 1958 and the negotiations that led to the pact of Punto Fijo (Ellner 1999).

In contrast to the parties of the Punto Fijo system, and much like AD during the Trienio, Chavismo is essentially a populist movement. It questions dissent and urges unity to the point of creating a single unified party. Legitimate competition inside the movement, if it occurs at all, is permitted primarily at the base level rather than at the top level of government, and outside competition (especially for key national offices) is regarded as a betrayal of democracy even when conducted peacefully. Yet, despite its disdain for competitors and its occasional violations of democratic procedure, Chavismo still very seriously claims to embody democracy more than the previous regime. It can do so precisely because Chávez and his supporters have a discourse that challenges pluralist assumptions of multiple interests and the intrinsic value of democratic procedures. In their minds at least, the potentially undemocratic means are justified by their truly democratic ends of serving and exalting the will of the people.

Seeing Chavismo as a populist movement also helps us put our finger on the qualities that distinguish Venezuela under Chávez from other recent hybrid democracies in Latin America. While leaders such as Bolaños, Berger, or the transitional government in Haiti have struggled to impose the rule of law and establish democratic institutions that respect minority rights and foster peaceful competition (or, in some instances, they have taken advantage of institutional weaknesses to cynically further their own careers or parties), they essentially work within and accept this pluralist framework. In contrast, Chávez and his followers pursue an agenda of direct democracy that questions the value of representative government, professional politicians, and bureaucrats. Chavismo's most ardent followers dispute whether democratic procedures always meet democratic norms, suggesting that they can be satisfied more fully by governments that restrict some aspects of competition in an effort to better discover and honor the popular will. Yet, unlike elitists, they value and pursue popular approval and input, and they base their legitimacy on their capacity to be a government of and not merely for the people. Elections are mostly free and fair, and the CNE can be highly partisan yet sincere in its efforts to achieve an honest outcome.

Understanding Chavismo as an instance of populism also helps us identify the causes of the movement and the basis for its continued success. Chavismo originally appealed to Venezuelans who had suffered under 15 years of economic stagnation, and it continues to appeal to poor Venezuelans who benefit from the government's new social policies and the general environment of oil-induced economic growth. But Chavismo's populist discourse is ultimately a message about the corruption of the old system and its elite. Whether the enemy is the traditional parties under Punto Fijo or international capitalism under the leadership of the United States, there is an enemy and it has subverted the good of the people for its own selfish interests.

This type of message resonated among citizens who experienced firsthand the progressive decay of the Venezuelan state and the decline of what had initially been a fairly programmatic party system into something highly clientelistic and venal. Corruption was real. The founders of MBR 200 shared their fellow citizens' frustrations and had an openly anticorruption message that first became public with the coup. What made this message powerful was that it did more than condemn corruption. It offered an appealing democratic interpretation of the problem that continued to celebrate popular virtue: Venezuelans as a whole were capable of goodness; the solution was not an elitist takeover of the state, but a reaffirmation of democracy through more direct popular participation. This message was also realistic: piecemeal reform was insufficient and in fact represented a manipulation by the elite; only a wholesale remaking of the political system would suffice. And it was backed up by real potential for action: the movement was led by a cadre of officers and civilian allies who had been willing to put their lives on the line and a charismatic leader who could give the movement direction and focus. Hence, the initial appeal of Chavismo lay not merely in its potential to satisfy the material self-interest of Venezuelans, but also in its credible moral message.

Chavismo's continuing political success can be ascribed to its ability to embody this message up to the present. Chávez's bellicose language and Manichaean outlook may seem ignorant and barbaric to outsiders, and his willingness to ratchet up his discourse in moments such as 2001, when he first encountered significant defections and opposition, may appear perverse. For pluralists, the appropriate response is to pursue some kind of compromise. But to Chávez's more ardent supporters, this discourse is a token of his sincerity and a manifestation of his beliefs. Leaders and citizens who believe in the will of the people never treat opponents as equals or use soft diplomatic language, especially when the going gets rough; the stakes in this cosmic struggle are too high, and gathering storm clouds of opposition mean that they must redouble their efforts. Thus, Chávez not only delivers what he promises, but he delivers for the right reasons, consistently displaying a purity of motive and a redemptive vocation that were lacking in the later years of the Punto Fijo democracy. The inconsistencies and shifts in Chávez's cabinets and government programs become virtues for his followers, ascribed as they are to his desire to stay in touch with the voice of the people. And the takeover and centralization of political institutions are symbols of his commitment to the people rather than signs of creeping authoritarianism.

Finally, framing Chavismo in these ideational terms helps us understand the movement's consequences, particularly the polarization and brinkmanship of Venezuelan politics today. To his followers, Chávez *is* the leader of a genuine democratic revolution that will end the cycle of poverty and injustice, while opponents can rightly see him as the leader of a movement that disregards procedural rights and the pluralist spirit, if not the letter, of representative democracy. The movement's discourse polarizes the electorate because it envisions Venezuelan society as a dualistic conflict that can no longer tolerate dissent. Those who are not with the revolution are necessarily against the people – they are traitors and coup-mongers – and granting them procedural rights is a generous, even risky, proposition. In turn, Chávez's opponents reject what they perceive as a messianic, egotistical leader who is unwilling to follow the rules of representative democracy. They resent being categorized as illegitimate outsiders and fight to retain their recognition as citizens – as university students chanted in recent protests against the government, "we are students, we aren't coup-mongers" (Deutche Press-Agentur 2007) – while using every means to stop what they consider an enemy of democracy. Hence, the presence of a strong populist discourse becomes a kind of self-fulfilling prophecy that works to unravel Venezuela's representative democracy. Populists turn their opponents into bitter enemies and undermine the mutual respect that democracy requires.

A parallel conflict plays out at the international level; indeed, as we see in the next chapter, Chávez and his movement have shifted from a struggle against domestic enemies to a fight with an international capitalist elite. Chavistas came to interpret the coup of 2002 not as a tragicomedy of errors sparked by Chavismo's excesses, but as a conspiracy hatched and led by the Bush administration in alliance with domestic elites of the old Punto Fijo regime. The Bush administration, while initially mirroring the neutral stance of the Clinton administration, found itself drawn into the conflict as it responded clumsily to the Chávez government's accusations and increasingly undemocratic direction. Being largely pluralist, most U.S. policymakers and pundits failed to understand the Chávez government, and they perceived it simply as undemocratic.

We can hardly blame U.S. policymakers for this mutual misunderstanding. Even careful governments in Latin America and Europe find that a slip of the tongue or an expression of frustration with Chávez's populist rhetoric turns them into his temporary enemies. After the Mexican government of Vicente Fox supported a U.S. free trade measure during 2005, Chávez called Fox a "puppy" of U.S. imperialism and later warned him to "not mess with me, sir, or you will get pricked"; the dispute led to a withdrawal of ambassadors (BBC 2005). In early 2007, after OAS Secretary General Jose Miguel Insulza criticized the Chávez government's attempts to revoke the license of RCTV, Chávez called him "an idiot, a true idiot" and suggested that "the insipid (*insulso*) Dr. Insulza should resign" (BBC 2007). And after King Juan Carlos of Spain told Chávez to "just shut up" during the 2007 Iberoamerican Summit, Chávez responded in Caracas by saying that the king's comments represented "the explosion of 500 years of imperial arrogance, 500 years of monarchism, of outrages, 500 years of feelings of superiority" and insinuated that the king had been an accomplice of the 2002 coup (Latin American Newsletters 2007). Chávez and his movement see themselves as the bearers of the popular will in a just global cause, and in their minds, an insult to them is an insult to all peoples of the world and a revelation of the offender's lack of democratic legitimacy. Ultimately, all governments must decide which side they are on, that of Chávez and the people or that of the Evil elite.

A similar logic drives the division of the scholarly literature into two highly partisan camps. Scholars from the radical left who share Chavismo's hardened assessment of historical injustices and their legacy in the Third World are more likely to have the same Manichaean worldview. Motivated by this moralizing dualistic outlook, they feel compelled to erase the boundaries between scholarship and activism and defend the government's long-overdue democratic experiments. So-called value-free, objective science is a misleading goal that only serves elite interests. In response, other scholars wholeheartedly join the opposition as they combat a movement that threatens their families, livelihoods, and traditional democratic institutions. In this morally charged, high-stakes environment, it becomes increasingly difficult for anyone to stand on the academic sidelines and pursue objective scientific inquiry; all evidence has political implications and is either for or against the revolutionary process. Neutral critics of the government or the anti-Chavistas find themselves treated not as a loyal opposition, but as accomplices of neocolonialism on the one hand or demagogic barbarism on the other. Hence, as Smilde and Hellinger (forthcoming) lament, even after a decade of Chavismo, few scholars have undertaken empirical studies of the movement. In the struggle over populism there is no need for data and careful analysis, either because we already know that the movement represents the side of Good or because we want to avoid dignifying it and getting too close to something that embarrasses and enrages us.

Of course, this is a bit of a caricature. Many members of the opposition hew more closely to the democratic rules of the game nowadays (López Maya 2008b; Hellinger forthcoming). And Chavismo is a diverse movement, with "hard-liners" and "soft-liners" distinguished by their willingness to accept coexistence with the opposition (Ellner 2005a, 2005b, 2008). Opinion polls at elections reveal that the Venezuelan electorate is better divided into three groups than two: the third that wholeheartedly supports Chávez, the third that vehemently opposes him, and the third in between that votes for Chávez with certain reservations. Yet, the adherence of Chávez to a populist discourse drives the movement in a radical direction that polarizes democratic competition and antagonizes academic and diplomatic communities abroad. The principal line of conflict in Venezuela is no longer the clientelistic distribution of particularistic benefits, or programmatic debates over classic ideologies and broad policy packages, but the struggle between Chavismo and anti-Chavismo.

CONCLUSION

Populism understood as a type of democratic worldview or discourse is our best tool for categorizing and analyzing Chavismo. It helps us distinguish qualitatively the current government from previous democratic regimes in Venezuela, as well as from semidemocracies in other countries, and it illuminates the polarization of Venezuelan politics, academia, and the broader international community. It points to a second, normative dimension of democracy that cuts across the traditional procedural one, a dimension of populism versus pluralism that captures the intentionality and direction of procedurally democratic regimes. Populist discourse is not our only tool of categorization. Procedural understandings of democracy are also important and allow us to chart the mounting failures of Chavismo to measure up to its democratic aspirations. And as we will see in later chapters, other concepts related to the programmatic component of the movement – in particular, its increasingly radical leftism – are also helpful for understanding the content and direction of many of its policies. Yet, populism as a set of ideas is a crucial concept for understanding Chavismo, one that frequently subsumes or helps us better understand the emergence of these other attributes.

I acknowledge that an ideational definition of populism is problematic for many social scientists in the positivist tradition who may be uncomfortable with a concept that privileges ideas over hard, tangible reality. First, there are epistemological concerns. Can populism or other aspects of political culture really be measured in a way that is valid, reliable, and efficient, with results that can be easily replicated and verified by other scholars (Barry 1978; Little 1991, chapter 4; Lichbach and Zuckerman 1997)? In other words, can it be subjected to the rules of "valid scientific inferences" (King, Keohane, and Verba 1994, 38)? Second, there may be ontological concerns. Is populism really populism if it is spoken and thought but never followed? Doesn't it require *action* in order to be important or real – some physical manifestation in a movement, party, or candidate that pursues power and seeks to implement policies? Finally, there is the question of real-world importance. Even if we accept that discourse is the defining attribute of populism and different types of democracy, does it matter for politics? Do different worldviews actually have consequences for policy outputs and elections, that is, for the material and moral well-being of the community?

Regarding the first concern, one of the purposes of the rest of the book is to demonstrate that populist discourse can be measured in a way that satisfies scientific criteria; the following chapter nicely shows this by qualitatively analyzing Chávez's language and by quantitatively gauging the speeches of a larger set of chief executives from across the globe. The answer to the second question is a little more complex. In offering discourse or worldview as the defining attribute of populism and as a crucial aspect of democratic regimes, I am not claiming that real manifestations of populism can exist without some material component. The underlying set of ideas is meaningless unless believed and shared by actual human beings. However, the point made by scholars who study populist discourse is that actions alone – raising the minimum wage, calling for a constitutional convention, repressing the opposition – are not unique identifiers of populism, nor by extension are they useful indicators of the direction of a regime. As Weyland so presciently argues, we need to know whether the actions we see are "due to design or mere constraint" (2001, 11). Populist movements can engage in a wide variety of behavior that is shared by very different kinds of political organizations and leaders, such as mass protest, cross-class coalition-building, and shortsighted macroeconomic policies. What distinguishes all of these actions is their meaning for participants and onlookers.

The third question – whether a populist worldview in the end really matters for actual politics, or whether all politicians and voters respond to similar sets of preferences rooted in, say, material self-interest – is, of course, one of the grand issues that this book addresses. Populism *does* leave an imprint on important political phenomena, as we will see in later chapters. This indicates that, at the very least, we must make room in our theories of political decision making for nonmaterially based preferences. Above all, we must consider popular concerns about the legitimacy of the political system and the sense of meaning that politics provides its participants.

3

Measuring the Populist Discourse of Chavismo

> Populism is a bag into which they put everything they do not understand.
> Álvaro García Linera, vice-president of Bolivia[1]

In the previous chapter I argued that Chavismo is best understood as a populist movement, where by populism I mean a Manichaean worldview or discourse that associates the side of Good with the putative will of the people and the side of Evil with a conspiring minority. This descriptive claim about Chavismo is bold but thin on evidence; besides providing a few quotes, I have yet to examine Chávez's actual words in depth or compare them to those of other political leaders. Readers who have never heard Chávez speak may wonder if he really employs the bellicose language and moralizing that I described and, if he does, whether he uses this language consistently.

In this chapter, I move beyond this abstract defense of the ideational definition and engage in an ambitious project of measurement to show why we can characterize Chavismo as consistently populist. Since Chávez is the originator and focal point of the movement, his language is the official language of Chavismo and is what I analyze here. I start by analyzing Chávez's discourse, or his ideas as expressed through his language, using a traditional qualitative approach that examines a series of his speeches and interviews. I then develop a quantitative technique to measure the discourse of 40 chief executives from across the globe and across history. In combination, this effort not only demonstrates the effectiveness of the ideational definition, but also gives us the ability to place Chávez and his movement in comparative relief. The resulting dataset provides a crucial reference point for subsequent chapters where I analyze the causes of populism.

One of the most important questions this chapter must answer is whether or not "populist" is the most apt way of characterizing Chavismo. For years

---

[1] Quoted in *Latin American Weekly Report* (Latin American Newsletters 2006).

Measuring the Populist Discourse of Chavismo

Chávez himself resisted the label and referred to populism either as a pejorative or in terms of what we would call "economic populism." Thus, we find him in 1995 saying that populism is "those movements that appropriate the popular consciousness, their customs, their traditions and religion, in particular to use these against the people" (Blanco Muñoz 1998, 119). And in a later interview from 2002 he states, with some irony for us today, "Our attitude is not like some governments that show up with a bag full of money and start giving it out – that was populism. I am totally against that" (Harnecker 2005, 176).

Journalistic and academic accounts have actually tended to emphasize *two* key attributes in analyzing Chávez and his movement, namely, populism and leftism. While these accounts have always acknowledged Chávez as a populist (the *New York Times* and *The Economist* used the word as far back as the 1998 election), in recent years they have tended to give more attention to his leftist ideology and rhetoric as the movement has radicalized, most recently under the guise of what Chávez calls "twenty-first-century socialism." Many scholars and journalists identify Chavismo as part of a trend toward the left in Latin America that includes a number of leaders and countries, such as Luiz Ignácio Lula da Silva in Brazil, Néstor Kirchner and Cristina Fernández de Kirchner in Argentina, Tabaré Vásquez in Uruguay, and Ricardo Lagos and more recently Michelle Bachelet in Chile. Scholars have debated how homogeneous this trend is and what it means (Castañeda 2006; Cleary 2006; Corrales 2006; Schamis 2006; Seligson 2007), but all agree that Chávez and his movement represent the most extreme version of this trend in the region outside of Cuba. In fact, for many of his ardent supporters on the left, Chávez's turn to socialism is what makes his revolutionary rhetoric truly meaningful and no longer populist.[2]

This descriptive trend can be visualized in Figures 3.1 and 3.2, which indicate the frequency with which the *New York Times* and *The Economist* use the labels "leftist" and "populist" to describe Chávez, as a percentage of the total number of articles each year that mention Chávez in the headline or first paragraph. In the *New York Times*, the term leftist is hardly used during the first two years in which Chávez is in power, and preference is given to the term populist; however, in 2001 leftist becomes more common, maintaining approximately the same level until the present, while the term populist has almost disappeared since 2005. The trend in *The Economist* is even more striking. The term leftist is almost never used in association with Chávez until 2005, when it rapidly increases and eclipses the use of the term populist. In fact, the word leftist seems to substitute for populist.

---

[2] One of the most prominent exceptions to this tendency among leftist scholars and activists is Ellner (2008), who makes a more nuanced argument that explicitly draws from Laclau's understanding of populism. Ellner avoids facile labeling of Chavismo as populist in the pejorative sense, as a demagogic movement devoid of real substance. Chavismo is populist precisely because it has adopted a serious vocation on behalf of the excluded, popular sectors.

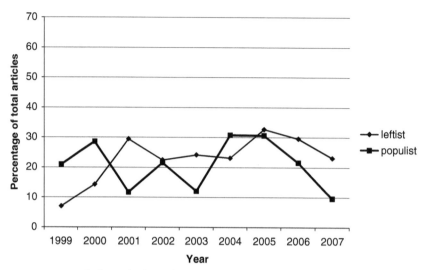

FIGURE 3.1. Labels applied to Chávez in the *New York Times*, 1999–2007.
Source: Author analysis of data from LexisNexis Academic.

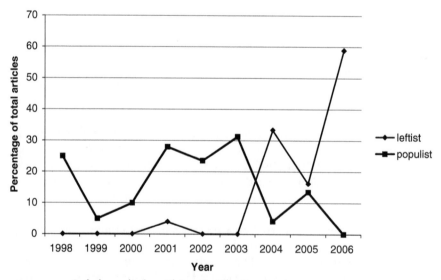

FIGURE 3.2. Labels applied to Chávez in *The Economist*, 1999–2007.
Source: Author analysis of data from LexisNexis Academic.

This depiction of increasing leftism is mostly correct, and it is not my intention to minimize Chávez's willingness to redistribute property and resources, assert state control over key industries, or develop radical participatory institutions. However, the characterization overstates what is really only a recent phenomenon in Chavismo and disregards the continuing prominence of populist language and ideas. Populist discourse runs like a river through the history of the movement, remarkably unchanged from the days when Chávez and his conspirators first came into public view, and persisting even today as it attracts less notice from journalists and scholars. If our goal is to explain how Chávez came to power or to understand his movement's effects on Venezuelan politics (many of which were felt long before the movement adopted the rhetoric and program of the radical left), then we must first understand it in terms of populism. And if we hope to understand where the movement is headed today as it adopts explicit rhetoric and policies of socialism, we must recognize the essential shape that populist discourse continues to provide the movement, as well as the potential contradictions that this creates from within. In fact, the very choice of radical leftism may itself be explained by the movement's populist worldview, as I argue in Chapter 7 when we study the consequences of Chavismo for economic policy. Chávez's discourse precedes and conditions his choices of ideology.

In saying that Chavismo is a case of populism, I hasten to add that I am not suggesting that Chavismo can be considered an example of "neopopulism," a term that gained currency in academia during the late 1990s (Roberts 1995; Weyland 1999). Chavismo is in many ways an extraordinary phenomenon in Venezuela, a country that for nearly 40 years had a political system dominated by two highly institutionalized parties. In this sense of being new, we might want to call it neopopulist. However, if we associate this label with the ideological or policy content of the movement, in particular the advocacy of neoliberalism, it is obviously inappropriate. Chavismo has a strong leftist, antiglobalization flavor and has increasingly rejected market-oriented policies (Ellner 2001). Likewise, if we associate the label of neopopulism with the unique coalition-building strategy of populist regimes during the 1980s and 1990s, one that involved a simultaneous appeal not just to the informal and middle sectors but also to the wealthy elite (Dresser 1997; Gibson 1997), then Chavismo again lands far from the mark: it has never derived serious electoral support from upper-income groups in Venezuela, relying instead on significant middle-class support that quickly vanished and a faithful core of supporters in the informal sector. Thus, Chavismo is a populism without prefixes.

A QUALITATIVE ANALYSIS OF CHÁVEZ'S DISCOURSE

To determine how well this definition of populism describes Chavismo in both the past and the present, I start by using a traditional qualitative method to look for the elements of populist discourse in a small but fairly representative sample of 10 texts by Chávez – speeches and interviews – that cover the period 1995 to 2007. As we will see, these elements are not only present in Chávez's words since he first assumed the presidency, but are also constant and fundamental aspects of his language since he was released from prison in 1994. The only significant change in this aspect of his discourse is a shift in emphasis from the domestic level to the international, which is most evident in his representation of the movement's enemies.

To increase our confidence in the analysis, the sample is drawn from a variety of contexts. First, in order to let readers see the face of Chávez that most of the people in his movement and in the country also see – and one that is generally unfamiliar to casual observers in the United States – I look at six of his speeches. Four of these are the sample of speeches by Chávez that are used in the later cross-country analysis of populist discourse. These are his 1999 inaugural address, his 2001 speech at the Summit of the Group of Three Nations (G-3) in Caracas, his closing campaign speech for the 2004 recall referendum campaign, and his October 2004 speech at the opening of a health clinic in the city of Valencia. The other two are his 2006 closing campaign speech for the presidential election and his 2007 inaugural speech, which are essential for demonstrating the continuity of Chávez's populist discourse to the present. I also briefly refer to his 1998 closing campaign speech, the full text of which is not available but which was quoted in newspaper accounts of the time.

Second, in order to let readers examine something closer to the private thinking of Chávez, I draw from three widely known sets of interviews published by authors who could all be considered friendly to Chávez. The first is *Habla el Comandante*, by Augustín Blanco Muñoz (1998), a historian at the Universidad Central de Venezuela, and was published and widely distributed during Chávez's first electoral campaign. The book is significant not only for its length – over 600 pages – but also for its coverage. It consists of a series of 15 interviews from March 1995, not long after Chávez and his co-conspirators were released from prison, to June 1998, in the middle of the campaign. The second and third sets of interviews are *Understanding the Venezuelan Revolution: Hugo Chávez Talks to Marta Harnecker*, by Marta Harnecker (2005), a Marxist scholar who works in Cuba, and *Hugo Chávez: El destino superior de los pueblos latinoamericanos*, by Heinz Dieterich (2004), a leftist academic in Mexico. Both of these are smaller texts that cover the more recent period since Chávez and his movement came to power. Harnecker's volume essentially consists of a single long interview conducted in June 2002, shortly after the attempted coup; Dieterich's volume includes two long interviews, the first from 1999 and the second from 2004, before the recall election. The style of text in these interviews is very different from that of Chávez's speeches, with longer, more detailed responses and a much less bellicose, passionate tone.

There are, of course, additional texts I could have consulted, such as the transcripts of *Aló, Presidente*, Chávez's long-running weekly television (and, earlier, radio) show. However, the current selection provides a fairly representative sample across time and contexts, and it includes the four speeches of Chávez that are used in the quantitative analysis in the next section, giving us a better sense of what it means to compare Chávez's discourse with that of other chief executives. With the exception of the Harnecker volume, all quotes reprinted here are my own translations from the original Spanish.[3]

Manichaean Outlook

To begin with, Chávez's discourse is a consistently Manichaean one combining a notion of dualism – everything should be seen in moral terms, nothing is neutral – with a strong teleological element that reifies history and perceives it as a cosmic struggle between Good and Evil that has reached its climax.

The sense of dualism is most clearly expressed in Chávez's speeches, where it seems to serve the purpose of mobilizing supporters by infusing their political choice with great moral consequences. For example, in his 1998 campaign, he declares, "In less than 8 days we make the final assault to remove the corrupt elites from power.... We are in the times of the Apocalypse. You can no longer be on the side of the evil and the side of God" (de la Cruz 1998). In his 1999 inaugural address, he argues that the country faces a crisis and that "We have two choices: either we open the way for this revolutionary force, or the revolutionary force runs over us." And in his end-of-campaign speech in 2006, eight years later, he continues to frame the electorate's choice in stark terms that go well beyond particular candidates. What is at stake is whether Venezuela becomes "a truly strong and free country, independent and prosperous" or instead "a country reduced once more to slavery and darkness." In each of these contexts the voters are presented with just two options: one Good, the other Evil. There is no gray area, no fence-sitting, no "third way," and those who fail to decide are in fact making a decision, one that benefits the forces of Evil.

In framing the voters' decisions as moral and dichotomous, Chávez frequently links these choices to grand cosmic themes. These are not struggles located merely in a few communities in the Venezuela of the present, but extensions of conflicts far beyond the borders of the country and including all peoples everywhere. Thus, Venezuelans are in "the times of the Apocalypse"; God and the Devil are themselves leading each side. The decisions will have ramifications for great issues – freedom, slavery; properity, darkness – and not just particular policies or incremental changes. Venezuelans are entering "a new era," as he declares in 2007. In some instances, the hyperbole is extreme. In the closing campaign speech for the 2004 recall referendum, he says:

All of them [the opposition] know what the whole world knows, and what all the peoples of this planet know, and above all what the peoples of this continent know, which is that this Sunday [election day] the future of the world is at stake, because we are building a path that is the alternative to the nightmare of world capitalism, the nightmare of neoliberalism.

---

[3] Harnecker's book was originally published in Spanish in 2003 as *Hugo Chávez Frias: Un hombre, un pueblo*, but I refer throughout to the English-language version.

The idea that people outside of Venezuela might not even care about the election is loudly rejected. The enemy knows what the conflict is really about; Chávez must awaken the people to this reality.

As part of this Manichaean outlook, Chávez frequently expresses a teleological worldview that reifies history, nicely encapsulated in repeated references to what he calls the "revolutionary storm" (*huracán revolucionario*) that is sweeping the country and the continent, a phrase that Chávez borrows from statements by Bolívar during the wars of independence. For example, in his speech to the G-3 summit, he declares, "Brothers and sisters, we are here face-to-face with history." And in his inaugural address from 2007, he refers to "the inexorable occurrences of history, and inside of them, we the individuals who are swept along by them." Unlike the elements of dualism and cosmic proportionality, this teological outlook is found even in his more dispassionate interviews. For instance, in his 2002 interview with Marta Harnecker he says:

> But this process has assumed its own strength. I'd make an analogy to a river, a river you can dam but not detain. If you don't give it the possibility to flow, it will tear down the dam or find its own course, but it will always flow to the sea. (2005, 103)

The current conflict and the emerging revolutionary process are part of an irresistible force that Chávez and other leaders can sustain or risk being swept aside. Chávez invites individuals such as Harnecker and her readers to become participants in this grand unfolding of events.

That said, Chávez's reification of history is a distinctively populist one. History is not an abstract external thing ("we are not watching a comet," as he says early on in *Habla el Comandante*) but the playing out of the collective will of the people. As he observes in 1995:

> *What do you mean by saying that you are just one small part of the process? Do you place the collective ahead of the individual?* Yes... I believe that what a man attempts is small when he places himself before the forces of great events. Here is where the importance of history lies.... I consider that men can place themselves, in a particular moment, in the position of protagonists that accelerate, that slow down, that give a little personal, distinctive push to the process. But I believe that history is the product of the collective being of peoples. And I feel that I have completely given myself over to that collective being. (Blanco Muñoz 1998, 28)

Thus, history is structural and seems to have a life of its own, but it only reflects the combined efforts of actual human beings who constitute the masses. This leaves open the possibility for individuals to have a place in determining its course.

Another important part of Chávez's Manichaean worldview is reflected in the use of myths, symbols, and rituals that draw from both Christian theology and great figures of recent Latin American and world history (Zúquete 2008). These enhance the movement's eternal, transcendent qualities. For example, in all of his speeches and interviews, Chávez consistently argues that "Christ is a revolutionary" who fights on behalf of the poor. As he states in *Habla el Comandante,* "God is the Christ that was crucified for fighting together with his people against an empire, the Christ that according to the Christian doctrine came down from the cross, was resurrected, and went through the world to fight on behalf of the dispossessed" (Blanco Muñoz 1998, 119). Ten years later, in the closing campaign speech in 2006, he declares, "long live Christ, the first great revolutionary of our era!" He often compares the new Bolivarian Venezuela to the biblical Lazarus, who have both been resurrected by Christ. And he makes frequent public pleas to God to bless their movement, as in the following statement from his 2004 closing campaign speech:

> I know that the majority, the great majority of us are Christian. We believe in God and we have commended ourselves to Christ, Father and Lord, our Redeemer. I am going to ask all of you that the first thing we do on that [election] day at three in the morning [when we get up to go to the polls] is to raise our supplication to Christ the Redeemer.... We are going to ask God that he continue to prepare the way through which the Venezuelan people have come traveling these past few years.

In addition to these references to God, most of Chávez's speeches and interviews contains quotes and references to Bolívar and draw parallels between present challenges and tasks and those of the revolutionary period. These include the project of hemispheric unification, the need for truly popular revolution, the revolutionary storm, key battles, Bolívar's strategies and tactics, oligarchic opposition, and above all, liberation. The movement is suffused with the language of Bolívar, who is the movement's principal hero. According to this vision of history, Bolívar is not an ambivalent democrat but a visionary leader who pursues his vision of true participatory democracy until he is overcome by events and conspirators at home and abroad.

Yet, Bolívar is not the only figure in this cosmic struggle. Chávez refers to a pantheon of great leaders and popular figures: Simón Rodríguez and Francisco de Miranda of the independence movement, Ezequiel Zamora of the Federal Wars, the early-twentieth-century guerrilla fighter Pedro "Maisanta" Pérez Delgado, Fidel Castro, John F. Kennedy, and the Venezuelan folk singer Ali Primera, among others. Chávez not only refers to these figures, their ideas, and their accomplishments, but takes great care to link them symbolically to all of his and the government's initiatives. Thus, he names most of the government's social programs or Missions after their corresponding avatar: the literacy and grade school equivalency programs for Bolívar's teacher, Simón Rodríguez; the high school equivalency program for the independence leader José Felix Ribas, who led a battalion of young students in a key victory over the Spanish forces; and the vocational training program, *Vuelvan Caras*, for the "about-face" command that General José Antonio Paez shouted to his cavalry at the battle of Boyacá during the wars of independence.[4] As already

---

[4] In 2007 Vuelvan Caras Mission was renamed Che Guevara Socialist Mission. See Chapter 7.

mentioned, Chávez named his recall campaign organization for Maisanta, and he framed the election as a replay of the Battle of Santa Inéz with its tactical but successful retreat. Chávez is especially attentive to significant historical dates and places. He never fails to plan key events on related days or to remember and enshrine new events (such as new holidays for the attempted coup of 1992), and he frequently makes televised announcements in locations with related historical significance or begins his weekly broadcasts by noting events associated with the day (Zúquete 2008).

Chávez makes these references not as empty gestures, but as an express attempt to show that these figures are part of the same cosmic struggle, and also to draw faithfully from the ideas of individuals whom Chávez sincerely considers the movement's forebears.[5] As he says in his 1999 inaugural address:

Why Bolívar? It isn't just about a merely formal, obscure repetition of any old phrase of Bolívar....It is an imperative need for all Venezuelans, especially for all Latin Americans and Caribbeans, to search in the past, in the keys or roots of our own existence, for the formula for exiting this labyrinth.

Thus, Chávez sees it as one of his duties to remind Venezuelans of their past, not merely as a pedagogical exercise or a gesture of appreciation, but so that they may understand the bond that links them together as one people.

Good = The Will of the People

In every text, from his earliest interviews to his most recent speeches, Chávez consistently expresses his belief that there is a knowable will of the people. This will is the voice of God and constitutes the Good in the cosmic struggle. Indeed, all successful, legitimate political actions must be based on or sprout organically from this will, or they are destined to failure.

The presence of this element is one of the central features of Chávez's language that distinguish it as a populist discourse. For example, in his early interviews in *Habla el Comandante*, Chávez describes history as a struggle by the people against the forces of oppression and imperialism, a struggle in which the people will eventually triumph (Blanco Muñoz 1998, 292). This united people did not previously exist, but it is now becoming aware of its collective identity:

What we do is believe in the strength of the people, in the rebellious man of Albert Camus, in that solidarity that brings the people to unity....And I believe that there is a change from the people-as-object to the people as subject of its own history, transforming itself as it discovers its potential strength. And when that "poverty-people," which is the consciousness of strength, becomes a protagonist, not even the army would dare oppose it. (Blanco Muñoz 1998, 32)

---

[5] He makes a long defense of this point at the beginning of his 2007 inaugural address.

In his 1999 interview with Dieterich he again argues on behalf of this collective conscience, stating not only that it is the only legitimate, effective basis for national development, but that it is finally being realized in Venezuela:

I believe that here the collective feeling has been reborn, and the people that was asleep has become aware of its own worth. The conscious and organized people – not the anarchic people – is the real fuel that runs the machine of history. (2004, 70)

In his 2002 interview with Harnecker, he declares that the collective conscience of the people has become a reality, and he juxtaposes this new, welcome unity with the weakness that characterized their former division and dissent:

For a long time the Venezuela people did not have a consciousness, they were divided, they did not have a common project; they were a people without hope, without direction. More than being a people, we were a collection of human beings, but then, as a result of the historical process that our country has undergone over the last few decades, a people has been formed. We are talking about awakening a giant. (2005, 157–8)

And in the second 2004 interview with Dieterich he continues to refer to "the fuel, the essential component that is like oxygen to fire: the people" (2004, 97).

Thus, the idea of a morally superior, united will of the people is an old one in Chávez's intellectual conversation. This same idea is evident in all of his speeches, albeit in shorter, catchier statements that strongly echo the slogans of classic populist movements in other countries. For example, in his first inaugural address in 1999, he declares that "The people (*los pueblos*) cannot die because the people is the expression of God, because the people is the voice of God." In his closing campaign speech of 2004, he refers somewhat more obliquely to the concept of a united will of the people with the phrase "the people of Simón Bolívar":

The valor and the conscience of the people of Simón Bolívar, the people that helped so much to carry out the revolution in South America, a people that has overthrown empires through the centuries, a people that has known how to resist, that has known how to combat, and that has known how to triumph.

In his closing campaign speech of 2006, he presents this idea as a kind of populist catechism that equates people, country, and the ultimate victory in the cosmic struggle:

Here we are, the Bolivarian Venezuela. We are the majority, we are happiness, we are Victory, we are the people made Victory, we are Victory made the people, we are Venezuela made Victory.

And in his 2007 inaugural he reaffirms a statement found in many of his speeches and interviews: that "The people is the protagonist of all of this, it must be the people."

Chávez explicitly links his intellectual understanding of the will of the people to Rousseau's *volonté general*, as well as Bolívar's conception of democracy (which was also influenced by Rousseau). Thus, in his first inaugural address he proclaims:

As Rousseau said, and as Bolívar said in the quote I gave at the beginning, "Let us convoke the popular sovereign so that it may exercise its absolute will ... the only sovereign here on Earth ... in the land of Venezuela is the people, there is no other. That is the universal and elementary principle."

Likewise, in his 2004 interview with Dieterich, he argues:

Jean Jacques Rousseau said that for there to be a people, from the sociological point of view, the group of people that inhabit a common territory must have a common identity and come to know it, based on their common past, and that in addition they must have a future common project; if not, there is no people. (2004, 112)

And in his 2007 inaugural he cites the following quote from Bolívar, one that Chávez mentions in many of his speeches and interviews as a justification for calling on the people to engage in constituent assemblies, referenda, and the new institutions of participatory democracy:

Nothing ... is in greater agreement with the popular doctrine then to consult with the nation as a whole regarding the chief points on which are founded governments, basic laws, and the supreme rule. All individuals are subject to error and seduction, but not the people, which possesses to an eminent degree the consciousness of its own good and the measure of its independence. Because of this its judgment is pure, its will is strong, and none can corrupt or ever threaten it.

This will of the people is seen in hegemonic terms. Especially in his speeches but also in his interviews, Chávez rarely refers to justifiable differences of opinion positively, except perhaps in the limited way in which he may disagree with his interviewers regarding points of theory, history, or strategy. Hence, the Venezuelan people were previously "divided," "a collection of human beings" rather than a single people with a united consciousness, and thus without "hope" and "direction." The idea that dissent might be inevitable or even positive is a rare one; a true people is ultimately one in purpose. If differences do exist, as of course they will, history will iron out these differences until the good of the people is collectively known and achieved.

The opposition poses a particularly vexing problem for this element of Chávez's discourse. Its continued existence (and at the time of some of these interviews, it was a growing threat) suggests that a sizable plurality of the people do *not* agree with the aims of the revolution and are remaining firmly outside its camp. Chávez rationalizes the opposition's existence with his belief by arguing that those who disagree with the goals and premises of the revolution are deceived; they have been led astray by corrupt leaders who do not have the good of the people at heart. We see this in the following appeal that Chávez makes to the opposition in his 2006 close of campaign speech:

Measuring the Populist Discourse of Chavismo

I ask the Venezuelan population that is going to vote against me, which exists and which I, we, of course, recognize, we recognize the right they have to vote against Chávez, we recognize their right and we want each and every one of them to participate as well. But once and for all I am going to ask them to not let themselves be manipulated by the lackeys of imperialism that already manipulated them once on 11 April [the 2002 coup] and led them to the slaughter, and afterwards those who were responsible washed their hands just like Pilate and then, the majority of them, left the country.

For Chávez, the existence of the opposition is the result not of valid differences of opinion but of manipulation. The implied hope is that one day these followers will learn the truth and return to the fold.

Evil = A Conspiring Minority

For Chávez, the will of the people is always seen as juxtaposed against, indeed subverted by, the efforts of a conspiring minority that pursues its own interests at the expense of the whole. This element is present in both the interviews and speeches. Chávez talks frequently about "enemies," "corruption," "the oligarchy," "counterrevolutionary forces," "coup-mongerers," "the lackeys of imperialism," "the nightmare of world capitalism," and "savage neoliberalism," but almost never simply "the opposition" or "those who disagree with us." He literally demonizes opposition leaders by calling them the Devil, "Pontius Pilates" who openly betray their own supporters and then walk away, while those who leave the Chavista movement are "traitors" or "Judases" who have turned their backs on the people. And in none of the speeches analyzed here does Chávez ever dignify his challengers by referring to them by name. Instead, he uses terms such as "frijolitos" (a colloquialism that could be translated as "pipsqueaks") or "petty *yanquis*." Sometimes Chávez is more conciliatory and inclusive, particularly in the years preceding and including the inauguration of 1999, and again after the coup of 2002, but even in these moments there are clear references to enemies of the people's will.

The notion of who constitutes this evil minority clearly changes, and it is here that we see the most significant shift in Chávez's populist discourse. It evolves from a narrow one of the old party elites (up to about 1999), to one that includes most of the domestic opposition, and, after the coup and national strike of 2002–3, to the idea of an international conspiracy led by the imperialist United States. For example, early in *Habla el Comandante* the references are very particular and tend to include certain individuals (such as former presidents Carlos Andrés Pérez and Rafael Caldera), the political parties, or simply the existing Punto Fijo regime embodied in the constitution of 1961. References are made to neoliberalism and capitalism, but as fairly impersonal ideas that (at that time, at least) Chávez critiques simultaneously with Marxism. Likewise, in his 1998 closing campaign speech, Chávez declares that "The rotten elites *of the parties* are boxed in, and they will soon be consigned to the trashbin of history" (de la Cruz 1998, emphasis added). In his 1999 inaugural, one of his most conciliatory speeches (and one of the few times in any of his speeches that he mentions "my opponents"), he refers to "the tragic political model" of Punto Fijo and "savage neoliberalism" – although he tempers the latter reference by emphasizing his openness to private ownership and investment – and declares that it would be treasonous to broker deals with the traditional elites.

Soon the tone becomes more conspiratorial and encompassing. In the 2001 speech to the G-3 summit, he refers again to "inhumane" neoliberalism and celebrates the government's successful efforts to "peacefully tear down the old, rotten political structures of the twentieth century." In the Harnecker interview, just months after the coup, he refers to "the oligarchy," "the counterrevolutionary forces," "the existing power structure" (2005, 32), and now "coup-mongerers" (p. 179), the last of whom he sees in a conspiratorial light. Thus, he asserts that "the coup is evidence that we are on the right track because the oligarchy, the counterrevolutionary forces, were counting on the failure of the revolutionary project, or their ability to push it off course, to neutralize it" (p. 108).

The most definitive change comes after the coup and the two-month-long national strike as Chávez and the other leaders of the movement begin to interpret these efforts at destabilization as a conscious effort led by the U.S. government and its allies in Venezuela. Thus, in the 2004 Dieterich interview there are still passing references to the "creole oligarchs that utilize the military as Cerberus [the three-headed dog that guards Hades] to assail against their own people and care for the grotesque privileges of the dominant elites on the continent" (2004, 81). But much more attention is now paid to "Washington and its intelligence units...the CIA that moves throughout the continent trying to avoid, precisely, the union amongst ourselves" (p. 88). An entire section of the interview is dedicated to showing the U.S. role in Latin America's lack of regional integration and progress since the days of independence. Chávez even blames the United States for the breakup of Greater Colombia in the early 1800s and the famous 1828 assassination attempt on Bolívar. In short, "The first great obstacle [to regional unity] that comes to my mind, and I believe it is one of the most powerful, is the hegemonic power that up until now the United States oligarchy has exercised in all of America" (p. 113).

Similar strong references to this unfolding international conspiracy are found in the 2004 closing campaign speech and the speeches from 2006 and 2007. I refer here to just the 2006 closing campaign speech. In this speech Chávez calls his current and former opponents "irresponsible, lying, unpatriotic, without any sense of responsibility or honor," but then urges his audience to always bear in mind the real force behind the opposition: the United States:

Don't anyone forget that we are facing the very Devil himself. Sunday, 3 December in the ballot boxes we will face the imperialist government of the United States of North

America. That is our real adversary. It isn't these has-beens (*bates quebrados*) here, these lackeys of imperialism.

In reinterpreting the past struggle, Chávez is carried away in a grand vision that forces him to stretch historical fact. All of Venezuela's postindependence history becomes a continuous fight against the United States, a fight that still continues:

> During three hundred or more years we were a colony of colonial Spain [sic], and during the last two hundred years we were a North American colony. Venezuela began to liberate itself from the North American empire eight years ago on 6 December 1998, and in these eight years we have complete freed ourselves.... Now the empire returns to try to reconquer Venezuela.

Thus, Chávez reminds his supporters that great successes have been achieved but that the cosmic struggle is only now achieving its full, true dimensions. By showing them these dimensions and the nature of the enemy, he helps them see the universal significance of the revolution in which they participate and motivates them to give their all.

The Need for Systemic Change (Revolution)

The logical consequence of Chavismo's Manichaean outlook is a constant emphasis on systemic change, which in this instance appears as a rhetoric of revolution. Insofar as the existing system is the product of a conspiracy against the people, one that has its roots hundreds of years ago in Spain's colonization of Venezuela, that system must be destroyed and rebuilt. "We have said it repeatedly," says Chávez in 1995, "this cannot be solved in a piecemeal fashion" (Blanco Muñoz 1998, 115). Only a full-blown revolution can liberate the people. Indeed, as Chávez emphasizes, such a revolution is inevitable; the challenge for Chávez and those in the movement is to push along this task, to facilitate rather than be found working against it.

The content of Chavismo's revolutionary program has changed considerably over time and, even with its current emphasis on classic socialist objectives of economic transformation, has a certain improvised feel; the government's most recent six-year plan (the *Proyecto Nacional Simón Bolívar: Primer Plan Socialista*) is all of 45 pages long, one-third the length of its previous nonsocialist plan from 1999. Yet, Chávez has consistently emphasized systemic change and the concept of revolution since at least the founding of MBR 200 in 1982. As Chávez makes clear in *Habla el Comandante,* the decision to include the word "revolutionary" in the organization's name was an intentional one that came after extended discussion among the conspirators (Blanco Muñoz 1998, 58–9). His interviews in *Habla el Comandante* are replete with historical analyses that link current injustices all the way to the colonial past, analyses that demonstrate that only a complete overturning of the existing order in all its aspects – political, economic, and social – will solve the problem. This is the reason why Chávez and his fellow conspirators insist on the need for a new constitution and why, immediately after the coup, they advocate a popular boycott of regular elections until this more fundamental goal can be achieved. When they finally organize MVR and participate in the presidential election of 1998, they do so with the clear understanding that their immediate task is the calling of a constituent assembly and, with a new political system in place, the subsequent creation of a new socioeconomic order.

This rhetoric of revolution is particularly strong in Chávez's first inaugural address, even with the speech's conciliatory overtones. "This is the opening of the door to a new national existence," asserts Chávez. "Let us take up with courage and valor the task of providing a channel for the Venezuelan revolution of our time, or the revolution will pass us by." Thus, the revolution is reified and made a part of the teological, dualistic vision animating the movement. Chávez claims to take seriously the concept of revolution. What at the time he calls the movement's Bolivarian Alternative Agenda is not a mere set of reforms, but a "project" for wholesale change that begins with the call to a constituent assembly, a call that Chávez repeatedly emphasizes. "The only name this can have is REVOLUTION," he declares in capital letters.

This emphasis on revolutionary change continues unabated during the first years of government, even as key goals of the initial program, such as the constituency assembly and the reconstitution of government branches, are accomplished. In his 1999 Dieterich interview as the constituent process concludes, Chávez continues to speak of the need for a fundamental break with the past and its illegitimate order (2004, 39). In his speech to the G-3 a year after the new constitution was passed, he refers to the successful efforts to "peacefully tear down the old, rotten political structures of the twentieth century by means of the revolutionary constituent process," and he urges a similar change in international affairs in order to achieve the original Bolivarian vision of political and economic regional integration (and the emphasis is on the former). With political control increasingly consolidated by 2002, Chávez then uses the revolutionary rhetoric to frame the government's increasingly grand socioeconomic reforms such as the Missions. An entire section of the Harnecker interview is dedicated to defending the success of the revolution and pointing out the directions in which it must still go in terms of social and economic reform. Likewise, in his ribbon-cutting speech of 2004, Chávez uses the new health clinic as a symbol for the government's efforts at radical change:

This [clinic] is part of a strategic project. As you know, the revolution would have no meaning if it did not return to the people what belongs to the people, what the people were denied by the anti-Bolivarian and unpatriotic oligarchy for so long, for all these centuries... "health, life, [and] happiness to the highest degree possible," as Simón Bolívar said in Angostura.

As the presidential election of 2006 draws near, Chávez again renews this rhetoric of revolution. He signals that the first phase of the revolution is complete. "Now Venezuela is free," he declares in the closing campaign speech.

"We have freed Venezuela from the jaws of neoliberalism." The people can commemorate their repeated political successes against the oligarchy and U.S. imperialism, as well as dramatic improvements in health, education, and general well-being. Yet, more is needed. After the election, "another era will begin, another revolutionary era." "We are committed to continue deepening the Bolivarian Revolution," Chávez says, "to continue destroying the old vices of corruption, inefficiency, bureaucratization; and opening new paths through which the new man will travel." He calls for a whole new society with new individuals to be created over the next decade and a half. Hence, the content of the revolution evolves over time (Chávez would argue that it follows a longer strategic plan), but the emphasis on systemic change remains almost an obsession of Chávez's vision and rhetoric.

An Anything-Goes Attitude

Finally, while Chávez's revolution is peaceful and democratic in the sense that it technically follows democratic procedure, his Manichaean outlook fosters a strong anything-goes attitude toward the opposition that allows the spirit of the procedure, and occasionally the procedure itself, to be violated. If such rights are extended, they are seen more as privileges or acts of mercy to an undeserving "other" than as basic rights that belong to fellow citizens.

Again, to be clear, the government goes to some length to follow Venezuelan law and international norms regarding democratic procedure and basic human rights. It respected the need for free and fair elections and, until at least the case of RCTV, largely maintained freedom of expression for members of the opposition. During its early years, initiatives to redistribute private land and threats to nationalize industries or close media outlets either were never carried out or were executed only gradually, typically with compensation. Likewise, observer missions from the OAS, the Carter Center, and the European Union gave their seal of approval to every national election from the recall referendum to the presidential election of 2006. While Chávez and his conspirators often equivocate regarding the use of violence to carry out the revolution – in these speeches and interviews, Chávez often says that "this movement is peaceful, but not disarmed," and he justifies his own attempted coup in 1992 as a "rebellion" with popular motives – the movement's leadership has conscientiously followed the electoral path.

Nevertheless, there have been clear violations of electoral procedures and basic civil liberties. To name just a few of the most salient examples, Chavistas freely used their control over electoral rules to their advantage in the election to the Constituent Assembly in 1999 and again in local and legislative elections of 2005,[6] and international observers have since registered strong

---

[6] Under the highly majoritarian rules of the elections to the constituent assembly, 60% of the vote translated into over 90% of the seats for MVR and its allies. Moreover, after election rules had been established that specified nonpartisan candidacies, supporters of the Patriotic

objections to these practices as well as to the government's repeated use of public resources for its campaigns (c.f. EU EOM 2006a, EU EOM 2006b). Government funding was painfully apparent to my assistants and me in the recall election of 2004, when buildings ranging from state universities to police posts were draped with banners and balloons supporting the NO campaign. The entire list of those who had signed the recall petition was subsequently uploaded to the Internet by government supporters and used by state agencies to fire employees and deny services, such as the issuance of new voter registration cards, to members of the opposition.[7] During this period of the recall, the government sponsored enormous voter registration drives that expedited the issuance of voter registration cards and citizenship papers to large numbers of Colombian immigrants who met only minimal legal requirements. Especially when passions were high during the 2002–4 period, armed groups of Chávez supporters occasionally attacked buildings and persons associated with the opposition, and journalists, editors, and their equipment were frequently harassed and threatened (Committee to Protect Journalists 2004, 2005). Today the government continues to use threats of violence, legal intimidation, selective access to foreign currency and newsprint, targeted dispensing of advertising revenues, and limited access to government data and news releases to punish news media that fail to present favorable coverage (Inter American Press Association 2008). And during the 2009 elections for municipal and state offices, the government used criminal charges to prevent some opposition candidates from running or campaigning effectively.[8]

More important for our present purposes, we can see evidence of this anything-goes attitude when we look beyond the government's actions and consider the way that Chávez and his supporters frame their behavior. Some of the Chavistas I interviewed in 2003 justified the kinds of actions previously mentioned by arguing that opposition leaders "had it coming to them," that those leaders were saboteurs and coup-mongerers who did not know how to behave like a responsible opposition; the opposition was lucky that Chávez and the government had shown so much restraint and respect for democratic procedure. As one Chavista party leader said in recalling threats and aggressive

Pole published a cheat sheet indicating which candidates were Chavista. For later national and local legislative elections, the government established a hybrid electoral system similar to that of Germany that mixed first-past-the-post rules and proportional representation with seat compensation to ensure proportionality; however, the government then created new, small parties to run different slates in the proportional representation lists – the so-called *morochas*, or "twins" – so that they could win majorities under both tiers.

[7] At first called the *Lista Tascón* because of its association with a prominent Chavista congressman, Luis Tascón, this eventually became known as the Maisanta database because of its systematization by the government's campaign command during the recall election. The history of the database and its political uses is now widely acknowledged; one of the best accounts of the database and its uses by both the government and opposition can be found in Hsieh et al. (2009).

[8] For a more extensive critique of the government's democratic shortcomings, see Human Rights Watch (2008).

acts that she and other government officials had personally received from the opposition, "No democratic government has had to endure what we have had to" (Interview 13.3 20 February 2003).

Two particular statements in the Harnecker (2005) interview provide examples of this kind of framing in Chávez's own speech. In the first, Harnecker praises the government's treatment of the media after the 2002 coup as remarkably restrained in light of their undemocratic behavior. Chávez assents to this view and portrays the government's response as one of patience and democratic moderation, but he argues that the time to get tough may have arrived:

I don't understand how it is possible to write a new constitution during the information age and not put in place procedures that allow for some control over opposition media. It seems to me that these companies are totally undemocratic, I mean, a press corps that is not objective, does not help the country, encourages destabilization, and supports the coup. I don't think I have been to any other country with such a libertarian approach to the press.

The term "truthful information" was inserted into the constitution. That was passed after considerable debate.[9] The media and their political representatives couldn't block that phrase from being included. On the other hand, the Supreme Court issued a statement last year in which they upheld the constitutional principle of truthful information, affirming that the media are obligated to respect that constitutional principle. We are now working on a legal project – one of the things they have been trying to stop – called the Law of Media Content, which, once approved, will establish much more detailed norms and rules to develop that constitutional clause about truthful information....

... We have tried to establish dialogue, to influence them through a range of procedures, but without a doubt we have not managed to do so. Lately, what has happened is that they have shown us they have no interest in moderation, in staying within their constitutional limits. They are putting up fierce resistance with the support of the international community, including the OAS.

We know there are a lot of people who are complaining: "You have to be tougher on the media, you have to get them to fall in line." At this point I think the only path left open to us is coercion, in the judicial-legal sense. (2005, 145–6)

Chávez thus justifies the qualifications of media freedom in the new laws as constitutional, popular measures that are inherently democratic; if the majority of the people choose them after deliberation, they are legitimate. And such measures presumably only serve to enhance the realization of the popular will by providing Venezuelans with "truthful" information and media that behave with moderation. The media's subsequent recourse to international institutions

---

[9] Article 58 of the 1999 Constitution declares in part, "Communication is free and plural and obeys the rights and responsibilities that the law indicates. Every person has the right to timely, truthful, and impartial information, without censorship, in accordance with the principles of this Constitution, as likewise to response and rectification when they are directly affected by information that is incorrect or disturbing." Although the article reflects contradictory approaches to freedom of the press and freedom of speech throughout Latin America, controversy at the time centered on the term "truthful."

is not a right, but an unconstitutional nuisance and a demonstration of their immoderate behavior that makes them deserving of legal sanctions.

The second instance comes when Harnecker asks Chávez how the post-coup process of dialogue is advancing. As already noted, this process was initiated by the government with encouragement from international organizations but eventually failed, largely as a result of the opposition's unwillingness to accept the legitimacy of the Chávez government. Again, however, Chávez suggests that the positive results of this dialogue constitute generous concessions by the government rather than a reconciliation of equally valid viewpoints and actors who both made mistakes:

I do think the dialogue has made progress and has had some results. Of course, as you said, there are some sectors that refuse to participate in dialogue.
 ...But you know, their approach really doesn't make sense. It would be understandable if someone refused to participate in dialogue because their rights had been trampled on. But since nothing like that has happened and we have made it more than clear, with both words and deeds, that we are committed to dialogue, this indicates that they don't have a solid reason for opposing dialogue and that we are talking about an obsession with defending privilege....
 No one can deny that we have had attitudes that one would call conciliatory, to put it that way: changes in the directorship of PDVSA, changes of government ministers, new policies, dialogue sessions; the Anzoátegui consensus[10]; the decision to transfer resources to state governments; respect for human rights in the case of the conspirators of the coup. (2005, 153–4)

Chávez remains incredulous toward the claims of the opposition. No one has violated their rights, and their reactions to the government's overtures are the result of an irrational "obsession with defending privilege" rather than justifiable grievances. This leads Chávez to redefine what should be basic rights. Note particularly the way he mentions the transfer of fiscal revenue (to then-opposition governors) and the extension of due process to the leaders of the coup. Both of these are required by law, but Chávez sees them as conciliatory gestures that opposition groups have failed to reciprocate.

Examples of this perspective can also be seen in Chávez's closing campaign speech from 2004. In the following part of the speech, Chávez goes to great pains to remind voters of the procedure they need to follow and the importance of adhering to election rules, such as not engaging in proselytism or wearing campaign colors while waiting in line. Yet, Chávez shows a kind of ambivalence toward these rules:

Another thing I want to make clear, I've been hearing out there and someone said that you have to go vote with red clothing on [the campaign color for Chávez]. That's not how it is. In the first place you know that no one can go with a "NO" T-shirt, because you can't do any campaigning in the lines at the polls. So no one should go with one of our T-shirts, because they could be taken out of line and have their vote invalidated.

---

[10] An agreement with governors from across the country.

And besides, since the vote really is secret, don't anyone think that there is a need to go with a red T-shirt, no.

Now this is very important, very important, because the vote is secret and besides, you know that sometimes we have to use camouflage. It isn't a good idea for an army to be presenting itself openly everywhere, no. There are places where, maybe, the people prefer to go vote without anyone knowing that they are Bolivarian, and that's true for a variety of circumstances.

On the one hand, Chávez admits that such procedures are important because they ensure the secrecy of the vote and uphold the rules of the game. Yet, he also suggests that observance of these rules is strategic, or instrumental. The Chavistas are a popular army struggling against an implacable, sinister enemy; they must go to the polls hidden, lest the opposition use the Chavistas' innocent enthusiasm as an excuse to question the outcome of the election and persecute or disenfranchise them.

None of this analysis is meant to deny the fact that Chavistas have suffered their own insults and injuries at the hands of the opposition. During the national strike, for example, the national headquarters of MVR was destroyed by a mob, and in the period before the recall election was announced, sectors of the opposition blocked roads and beat suspected members of the opposition in organized demonstrations. In the hours after the coup, some Chavista leaders were rounded up by the police and others were threatened by their neighbors. Members of the opposition also used the government's lists of petitition signatories to fire their own workers. Many members of the opposition see *themselves* as the only legitimate embodiment of Venezuelan values and nationhood. But the fact remains that Chávez and the members of his movement have shown a consistent willingness to bend democratic procedures in the pursuit of their cause, and the way they justify this behavior seems to stem from their populist outlook.

CHAVISMO IN COMPARATIVE PERSPECTIVE

The preceding section demonstrates the consistency of populism in Chávez's words; basic elements manifest themselves across several different kinds of texts and throughout the period that Chávez has been in the public eye. This suggests that Chávez's language really is a discourse in the postmodernist sense of the term: a distinctive way of talking that expresses an underlying set of assumptions about the world. However, we lack any ability to say just how populist this discourse is in comparison with that of other politicians from other countries. This opens us up to two criticisms. On the one hand, it may be that all politicians sound like Chávez, frequently making references to dualistic cosmic struggles, the will of the people, and political enemies. Is Chávez's discourse really that populist when we compare it to that of other leaders? Does it represent something rare and distinctive? On the other hand, it may be that *no one* sounds like Chávez, and that what I call a populist discourse is based on narrow observations of Chávez's idiosyncratic rhetoric – it is Chávez's discourse, not populist discourse. Do these elements exist in other historical contexts and across other countries and regions?

These questions get at a problem that afflicts the study of populism more generally. Discourse analysts have traditionally been reluctant to apply their concepts to any kind of extensive cross-national or cross-time measurement; those who are more empirically oriented (and there are several; see, for example, de la Torre 1997, 2000, and the various interpretivist studies in Panizza 2005b) limit themselves to case studies or comparisons of a few leaders, usually from the same country. But proponents of nondiscursive approaches to populism have also failed to provide tools for reliable measurement. Many of them rely on single-country or single-movement studies, and where populism is measured in cross-national studies of Latin America or radical right-wing populism in Western Europe (c.f. Conniff 1982, 1999; Betz 1994; Taggart 1996), the populist label is often applied by fiat rather than justified through any kind of empirics.[11]

Two recent studies break this mold by offering quantitative measurements of populist discourse. Armony and Armony (2005) use a computer-based technique to measure populist language in a large number of speeches by two Argentine presidents. And Jagers and Walgrave (2007) perform a human-coded content analysis of television programs by five Belgian political parties. Both studies find significant differences in the discourses of these leaders and parties that confirm common scholarly depictions. Yet, while these studies reaffirm the scientific validity of defining populism in terms of ideas, they are limited in scope and have natural methodological limitations I refer to later.

The Technique for Measurement

The method I use to measure populist discourse is a form of textual analysis known as "holistic grading." I use textual analysis rather than a traditional survey technique primarily because of accessibility. It is almost impossible to survey chief executives while they are in office, let alone as large a set of chief executives as I consider here; in contrast, texts such as speeches are readily available, not just for current world leaders but also for historical figures of the distant past. Textual analysis also tends to respect the culturalist origins of the concept of populist discourse. Discourse analysts often object to studying what they consider a highly intersubjective concept using individually subjective measures such as opinion surveys. If certain discourses reflect latent aspects of any culture that are activated only at certain moments, then (so the argument goes) the presence or absence of these views in a survey response may not mean very much. A study of speeches or similar texts sidesteps this problem by considering long statements of ideas that were widely communicated

---

[11] An exception is Kitschelt (1995), who measures right-wing populism by considering survey data on both ideological extremism and the willingness of centrist parties to accept extremists as coalition partners.

and accepted in a known political context. Long texts also allow us to complement quantitative measurement with qualitative assessments of specific language and themes, like that in the first half of this chapter.

Unlike standard techniques of content analysis (either human coded or computer based), holistic grading asks readers to interpret whole texts rather than count content at the level of words or sentences. It is a pedagogical assessment technique that is widely used by teachers of writing and has been extensively developed by administrators of large-scale exams, principally Educational Testing Services and the Advanced Placement exams they administer for the College Board in the United States (White 1985). Unlike analytical grading, which tries to break a text down into its parts and then combine the scores of each of those parts (as a content analysis does), a holistic approach works by assessing the overall qualities of a text and then assigning a single grade without making any intervening calculations. It is a scientific technique for textual interpretation. The first step is to design a rubric, or a simplified guide for evaluating a text that identifies the rough qualities associated with different types or grades. The second step is to train a set of graders in the use of the rubric, using not only the rubric itself, but also a set of sample or "anchor" texts that exemplify each type or score described in the rubric. Finally, the actual grading is conducted using two or three graders per text, with tests of intercoder reliability calculated along the way. Analyses of student writing that use holistic grading have been found to have high levels of intercoder reliability, with correlations typically between $r = .70$ and $.80$, comparable to those of subjective types of human-coded content analysis.[12] The costs are often not much greater than those of machine-coded objective exams, especially when the costs of preparing the exams are taken into account (Britton, Martin, and Rosen 1966; Coffman 1971, 293–5; Cooper 1977; White 1985). Perhaps more importantly for our purposes, research shows that small numbers of graders (two or three) and texts (three or four per student being assessed) have high reliability that improves only marginally with additional graders and texts (Sudweeks, Reeve, and Bradshaw 2005).

There are two reasons for using holistic grading to measure populist discourse. First, we cannot gauge a broad, latent set of meanings in a text – a discourse – simply by counting words. Because the ideas that constitute the underlying worldview are held subconsciously and conveyed as much by the tone and style of the language as by the actual words, there is no single word or phrase distinct to populist discourse or a particular location in the text where we can usually go to find the speaker's "statement on the issue," as we could using party manifestos to measure political ideology (see Budge et al.

---

[12] Psychometricians now generally acknowledge the inadequacy of correlation coefficients for measuring intercoder reliability, as they fail to indicate actual agreement (Ebel 1951; Tinsley and Weiss 1975). Consequently, recent studies use much more sophisticated techniques for assessing reliability of holistic testing. They find similar, positive results (c.f. Sudweeks, Reeve, and Bradshaw 2005).

2001; Wüst and Volkens 2003). This means that the text must be interpreted by human coders, who can quickly perceive broader, more complex patterns of meaning. Newer computer-based techniques of content analysis offer to solve the problem by generating word distributions whose broad patterns reveal something about a text (Quinn et al. 2006), but in practice these require considerable interpretation of the resulting distributions by the researcher. Holistic grading makes this process of integration more transparent. Second, while it is possible to use human-coded content analysis at the level of phrases or sections of text, these techniques are extremely time-consuming and unsuitable for the kind of cross-country analysis we need in order to generate large-N comparisons. In contrast, holistic grading requires no special preparation of the physical text and proceeds fairly quickly once the texts are available, and it allows us to compare texts in multiple languages without any translation as long as coders speak a common second language they can use in training and in reporting the results.

My assistants and I began by devising a rubric that captures the core elements of populist discourse. We did so primarily by drawing on the literature on populist discourse, but also by reading the speeches of several Latin American politicians that seemed to be widely regarded as populist and comparing these with speeches of leaders who were considered more pluralist. These included speeches by Chávez and several other Latin American leaders. A copy of the rubric is found in Appendix A; it essentially juxtaposes the elements of populism discussed earlier with their pluralist counterparts, and also includes labels and a grade scale for readers.

I next recruited and trained a set of native speakers of the languages of each country. All of these were undergraduate students at my university, many without a political science background. The training familiarized the students with the discursive definition of populism and the use of the rubric, including an analysis of anchor speeches that exemplified different categories of populist discourse.[13] I then had the students perform the actual coding, which they did by reading each speech, taking notes for each of the elements of populist speech in the rubric (as a check on their work and also as a way to find relevant quotes), and assigning an overall grade. For the sake of speed and in order to use a more holistic approach, which requires having an anchor text for each potential grade, I had readers use a simple 3-point scale of 0 (nonpopulist or pluralist), 1 (mixed), or 2 (populist). For practical reasons, the graders worked alone and on their own time rather than in a single group exercise.

The research proceeded in two phases. In the first, I analyzed the speeches of 19 current presidents (as of fall 2005) of Latin American countries, including

---

[13] The anchor texts included an international speech by Robert Mugabe of Zimbabwe (generally graded a 2), an international speech by Evo Morales of Bolivia (also generally graded a 2), a campaign speech by James Harper of Canada (graded a 1), and an international speech by Tony Blair (graded a 0). Of course, none of these anchor texts were included in the subsequent analysis.

Chávez, as well as those of a few historical chief executives in that region. In a few cases where changes in power took place during the study (e.g, the election of Morales in Bolivia), I considered both chief executives. The readers researched and selected four speeches for each executive, one from each of four categories I describe subsequently. Most of these were available on government Web sites, and I reviewed and approved the final selections. Two graders were used for all speeches, and each speech was read by the same two graders, both of whom spent no more than 30–45 minutes on each speech.[14]

In the second phase, I considered an additional 16 countries outside of Latin America. These countries were drawn from several regions, including Western and Eastern Europe, North America, Asia, and Africa, and I considered the current chief executive as of approximately March 2006. This phase was more challenging because it required training another 35 readers, 2 or 3 from each country. For a better check of intercoder reliability and in order to avoid problems with attrition, I tried to recruit three readers per country, although in some cases (noted in Table 3.2) I ended up with only two. The analysis used the same speech categories and coding procedure as in the Latin American study.[15] As in the Latin American phase, all graders were native speakers of the language and read the speeches in their original language. Readers located the speeches themselves (again, usually from government Web sites), but in this case most of the final selections were approved by two student assistants. Grading again took 30–45 minutes per speech.

The four speeches selected for each leader were a campaign speech, a ribbon-cutting speech, an international speech, and a famous speech. For comparison, I later analyzed a larger, random selection of speeches for a subset of these leaders that I report subsequently. Our general rule was to select the most recent available speech within each category that met certain standards of length (1,000–3,000 words).[16] In the case of campaign speeches, we considered the most recent presidential or parliamentary campaign and gave preference to the closing campaign speech or some other given to a large public audience rather than a party meeting. In the case of the ribbon-cutting speech, we gave preference to nontelevised speeches before small crowds and used dedications of monuments or public infrastructure. For the international speech, we selected speeches before audiences of foreign nationals, ideally in other countries or international organizations. And for the famous speech, we contacted the press office of the chief executive or his party and asked them to recommend a well-known speech that was among the chief executive's best; frequently, they recommended the executive's inaugural speech or the

---

[14] In some of our later diagnostics, we were able to reduce this time considerably by dispensing with note-taking. See Appendix B.
[15] No changes were made to the text in the table of the rubric, but labels for including identifying information and overall comments – the labels found on the copy of the rubric in Appendix A – were added to the sheet.
[16] The specific selection criteria for these four categories are available on request.

most recent report to the nation. My purpose in using these particular four categories was to test the consistency of the discourse while ensuring that my assistants and I had not overlooked key classes of speeches. I expected that the famous and campaign speeches would have a stronger populist discourse than the ribbon-cutting or international ones, because they represented contexts where there were large audiences and an appeal to the nation as a whole.

Reliability of the Technique

The first question is whether this technique of measuring populist discourse generated data that are consistent across graders, or reliable. Because the analysis proceeded in two parts with very different sets of graders, I calculate several measures of covariation and agreement.

In the first phase of the analysis (the Latin American study), which included a total of 85 speeches, each coded by the same two graders,[17] the level of reliability is high and gives us great confidence in the method. The Pearson correlation coefficient between the two sets of scores is $r = .79$ for all individual speeches and $r = .87$ for the average scores for each president ($N = 24$). Alternatively, I calculate a Spearman's rho of .70 for the individual speech scores, which is high enough that we can reject the null hypothesis of no relationship between the two coders at the $p < .000$ level. The content analysis literature generally regards these levels of covariance as high (Neuendorf 2002, 143). The level of agreement, which tells us if the coders actually had the same scores rather than simply moved in the same direction (Tinsley and Weiss 1975), is also quite strong. In the first phase of the analysis, the two graders assign exactly the same grade 78 percent of the time; if we calculate agreement as any time in which the graders are within one grade of each other, then there is 100 percent agreement. In order to account for the possibility of agreement due to chance, I also calculate Cohen's kappa, a statistic that adjusts the percentage of agreement by taking into account the size of the original scale and the actual observed agreement; the resulting scale ranges from 0 to 1. The kappa statistic for this first phase of the analysis is .68, a level generally regarded as substantial (StataCorp 2003, 208).

The level of reliability in the second phase of the analysis is not quite as high but is still encouraging, especially given the large number of graders, their lack of experience in political science, and the small number of speeches they each had the chance to read. We cannot calculate covariance figures for the data in this phase because I used a different set of graders for each country and often had three graders rather than two. However, we can calculate the level of agreement. If we consider agreement to exist when all three readers give exactly the same grade, then we have only 70 percent agreement in this

---

[17] While 92 Latin American speeches were coded in the first phase of the analysis, as indicated in Table 3.1, some of these were speeches by Brazilian presidents that were coded by other readers in the second phase.

second phase. If instead we consider agreement to exist when two readers give the same grade and a third reader differs by no more than one point, then we have 86 percent agreement. The kappa statistic for this data is .44, indicating a moderate level of agreement, although this figure is somewhat reduced by my inability to weight the calculation for the ordinal nature of the scale.

Readers may wonder about the sample sizes for each chief executive (four speeches) and whether this is really enough to generate a representative measurement. One way of testing this is to look at the variance of our results. Tables 3.1 and 3.2 report the standard deviations from the average score of each leader, which, as can be seen, are not very large. By comparison, a leader with all scores identical but one (for example, with scores of 2, 2, 2, and 1) has a standard deviation of 0.50, while the maximum possible standard deviation (associated with a set of scores of 2, 2, 0, 0) is 1.2. Few if any of the leaders in the set have a standard deviation over 0.50, and many have considerably lower ones. Thus, there is remarkable consistency within these small samples. The one outlier is Yushchenko in Ukraine, with a standard deviation of 0.85, a result that makes sense in light of the extraordinary circumstances of his election.[18]

To increase our confidence in these results, I analyze an additional large, random sample of speeches by two leaders in the set, Lázaro Cárdenas and Lula. These samples include 42 speeches for Lula and 60 speeches for Cárdenas. The results of these large, random samples are described in Appendix B and are very similar to the initial analysis of just four speeches; in fact, the difference in means and the difference in standard deviations between the two different sampling techniques are not statistically significant by common standards. This indicates not only that a small, carefully measured sample yields reliable measures for each chief executive, but also that the discourse of each chief executive is consistent. This finding reaffirms the argument of discourse analysts that populist discourse reflects a latent, subconscious set of ideas that political elites cannot readily fake.

Descriptive Results

The next question is what the average scores are for each leader, and in particular how Chávez compares with these leaders. Tables 3.1 and 3.2 present the results of these two phases of the quantitative exercise. The first positive

---

[18] Yushchenko ran for the presidency in 2004 at the head of Our Ukraine, an opposition coalition. The contest was bitter and tainted by accusations that the government, with Russian assistance, had masterminded an attempt to kill Yuschenko by poisoning him. After an initial vote marred by electoral fraud, Yushchenko and other opposition figures led a broad protest movement, the Orange Revolution, and the Ukraine Supreme Court overturned the election results. Yushchenko won in the new round of voting. During the campaign and the subsequent Orange Revolution, Yushchenko took a bold, defiant stance against the government, but since coming to power, his language has lost some of its populist overtones. For complementary accounts of the Orange Revolution, see Kuzio (2005) and Way (2005).

TABLE 3.1. *Average populism scores for Latin American chief executives*

Country	Chief Executive	Average Populism Score	Standard Deviation	Number of Speeches
Venezuela	Chávez	1.9	0.25	4
Ecuador	Velasco Ibarra	1.7	0.58	3
Bolivia	Morales	1.6	0.71	4
Argentina	Perón	1.5	0.71	4
Brazil	Vargas (1930–45)	1.0	0.54	4
Brazil	Vargas (1951–4)	0.9	0.57	4
Argentina	Menem	0.8	0.50	4
El Salvador	Saca	0.6	0.25	4
Mexico	L. Cárdenas	0.6	0.43	4
Paraguay	Duarte	0.5	0.50	3
Ecuador	Palacio	0.4	0.14	3
Peru	Toledo	0.3	0.29	3
Dominican Rep	Fernández	0.3	0.50	4
Mexico	Fox	0.3	0.50	4
Brazil	Lula	0.3	0.29	4
Uruguay	Vásquez	0.3	0.50	4
Argentina	Kirchner	0.2	0.29	4
Costa Rica	Pacheco	0.2	0.29	3
Panama	Torrijos	0.2	0.29	3
Bolivia	Mesa	0.1	0.25	4
Chile	Lagos	0.1	0.25	4
Guatemala	Berger	0.0	0.00	3
Nicaragua	Bolaños	0.0	0.00	4
Honduras	Maduro	0.0	0.00	3
Colombia	Uribe	0.0	0.00	4

Speech Category	Average Populism Score	Standard Deviation	Number of Speeches
Campaign	0.58	0.67	12
Ribbon cutting	0.28	0.48	19
International	0.37	0.62	19
Famous	0.37	0.62	19
Average (all categories equally weighted)	0.40	0.60	

finding is that Chávez is one of several leaders with this kind of discourse. Among these are a few other current chief executives, including Evo Morales in Bolivia, Lukashenko in Belarus, Victor Yushchenko in Ukraine (at least when he first came to power), Mahmood Ahmadinejad in Iran, and, interestingly, George Bush in the United States. These results likely fit the expectations of scholars and the public. Morales is an important ally of Chávez and leads a popular indigenous movement for revolutionary change that has similarly

TABLE 3.2. *Average populism scores for non–Latin American chief executives*

Country	Chief Executive	Average Populism Score	Standard Deviation	Number of Speeches
Belarus	Lukashenko	1.7	0.27	4
US	Bush	1.2	0.32	4
Iran	Ahmahdinejad	1.2	0.58	4
Ukraine	Yushchenko*	1.1	0.85	4
Philippines	Arroyo*	0.5	0.41	4
Russia	Putin	0.4	0.50	4
UK	Blair	0.3	0.50	4
Ghana	Kufuor	0.2	0.32	4
Norway	Stoltenberg	0.2	0.33	4
Mongolia	Enkhbayar	0.1	0.17	4
Bulgaria	Stanishev	0.1	0.17	4
Canada	Harper*	0	0.00	3
Finland	Halonen	0	0.00	4
South Africa	Mbeki*	0	0.00	4
Spain	Zapatero*	0	0.00	4
Sweden	Persson	0	0.00	4

*Only two graders participated

Speech Category	Average Populism Score	Standard Deviation	Number of Speeches
Campaign	0.61	0.67	15
Ribbon cutting	0.32	0.58	16
International	0.27	0.52	16
Famous	0.57	0.72	16
Average	0.44	0.62	(all categories equally weighted)

polarized the population since his election in 2005; Lukashenko has long had a strongly nationalistic outlook and a rapport with poor voters, especially in rural areas; Ahmadinejad was elected president of Iran on an anticorruption platform that celebrated the virtues of ordinary "revolutionary" Iranians and is another close ally of Chávez; and Yushchenko came to power at the head of a popular, pro-democracy movement, the Orange Revolution. In a moment, I explore the results for Bush.

This group also includes several key historical Latin American presidents who are usually considered populist. Perón in Argentina, Velasco Ibarra in Ecuador, and to a much lesser degree Vargas in Brazil have discourses very similar to that of Chávez and incorporate all of the elements identified in our rubric. The similarities were great enough that I suspect modern populists in Latin America consciously borrow from the language of these historical figures – some of them, such as Perón, are mentioned in current Latin American populist speeches – and that within countries with a long history of populism there is considerable continuity in the discourse.

What are some of these continuities and differences? Typically, while all of these leaders include the basic elements listed previously, the specific groups they mention or the claims they make vary according to context. For example, the people for Morales is frequently rural and defined in racial terms (indigenous coca farmers), while for Chávez, Perón, and Ibarra it is simply the poor. Looking at enemies, Morales focuses on the struggle against a racial elite (the descendants of European settlers and their international allies), while Chávez and Perón describe a more traditional class-based or partisan oligarchy, and Yushchenko and Lukashenko target a political class (the government and opposition candidates, respectively). All of the current populists in our sample include an international level in their speeches that focuses on the United States, George Bush, international capitalism, and/or (in the case of Lukashenko) the European Union as enemies of the people, while historical populists make more limited mention of international enemies or focus on something more vague, such as capitalism (or in the famous case of Perón in 1946, a particular U.S. ambassador). And although populist leaders often appeal to a stock set of historical figures and ideas that are shared across countries and occasionally regions, the specific names and ideas that give these movements their cosmic proportions (Bolívar, Gandhi, the pope, God) vary widely.

Another important finding is that what Chávez and these other leaders say is fairly unusual. While the more recent emergence of leaders such as Correa in Ecuador and Daniel Ortega in Nicaragua (none of whom could be analyzed here) suggests a new wave of populism in Latin America, as of late 2005 and early 2006 we found only two clear current examples of populist discourse in Latin America (Chávez and Morales) and potentially four in our sample of 16 countries outside of Latin America (Lukashenko, Ahmadinejad, Bush, and Yushchenko). Two of these four non–Latin American cases – Lukashenko and Ahmadinejad – were not originally in the sample and were included only after we realized that the sample had too little variance for the causal analysis we hoped to perform later. If we exclude these cases, then only one out of every seven leaders in either sample had a strong populist discourse.[19] Thus, Chávez stands out as one of the most populist leaders in Latin America and in the rest of our global sample.

Where populist discourse *is* more common in the data is precisely where it was expected: the famous and campaign speeches. As the data in Tables 3.1 and 3.2 indicate, these categories are nearly twice as populist as the international

---

[19] The Latin American sample is basically the entire universe of cases in this region, and this overall result should be seen as representative. To choose cases for the second, non–Latin American sample, we used a decision rule that seems unlikely to be correlated with populism, namely, we considered countries for which a sizable population of undergraduate students was available to work as readers at my university. Thus, the overall descriptive results here may be representative as well.

and ribbon-cutting speeches. This pattern manifests itself in both samples, although it comes across more strongly in the non–Latin American one.[20] This has special implications for the few instances of missing data, which in most cases is the campaign speech. The strong overall average for this category of speeches suggests that in these instances, the actual average score for the leader may be higher.

What about some of our negative findings? Two leaders who are sometimes considered lukewarm populists and allies of Chávez do not in fact seem to have a populist discourse. These are Kirchner in Argentina and Lula in Brazil. Kirchner uses populist language very inconsistently. His campaign speech is the only one with a fairly strong populist discourse (graded approximately a 1). The speech frequently hints at a popular will and a notion of a romanticized common man, and it has a Manichaean quality that features limited cosmic proportionality and bellicosity – including brief mentions of heroes such as José de San Martín, Bolívar, Mariano Moreno, and the Peróns – as well as a sense of dualism. And it mentions a clear set of enemies, mostly former politicians from the 1990s. However, both graders of his speeches agreed that these elements were not used with the same consistency and power here as in speeches by Morales or Chávez, where cosmic proportions are routinely and frequently applied to even the most mundane issues. More important, Kirchner's three other speeches are all consistently graded as zero and are largely devoid of populist elements. The language he uses in his election campaign is not the same as the language he uses at other times. This characterization contradicts that of some scholars and journalists who apply the label populist to Kirchner (c.f. Castañeda 2006; Roberts 2007), but other scholars engaging in more detailed analysis and having more familiarity with the Argentine case tend to reaffirm my finding (c.f. Schamis 2006; Levitsky and Murillo 2007). They note that Kirchner was pragmatic in his economic policies and had fewer resemblances to traditional populists or even newer ones such as Chávez, except for some programmatic affinities (for example, an emphasis on social justice, redistribution, and a clear willingness to confront the International Monetary Fund) and a tendency to centralize power at the expense of the party system and some institutions of accountability; in other areas, such as human rights and the judiciary, Kirchner made some remarkable improvements.[21] To this we would add that his discourse is more shallow and inconsistent than that of a historical populist such as Perón. Kirchner is a halfhearted populist at best.

With Lula our finding is less controversial; while acknowledging his affinities with Chávez and other populists of the left, most scholars and journalists

---

[20] If we consider the two samples separately, the difference between the campaign speeches and either the ribbon-cutting or international speeches is statistically significant at the $p < .05$ to $p < .10$ level in both samples (one-tailed test); however, the difference between the famous speeches and either the ribbon-cutting or international speeches is generally not significant.
[21] Castañeda (2006), in fact, acknowledges as much and calls Kirchner an "ambiguous" case.

nowadays tend to place Lula in the "reformed" left camp (c.f. Castañeda 2006), as someone who has moved away from the radical stance of his younger years. Likewise, we failed to find *any* speech during his years as president that is strongly populist. His speeches since 2002 are analyzed much more thoroughly in Appendix B, which considers over 40 besides the 4 studied here and finds nearly identical results. Lula tends to focus on narrow issues and avoids any kind of cosmic proportionality or mention of historical figures. He consistently emphasizes consensus and negotiation and, while briefly criticizing some individuals or opposition groups (former president Cardoso and wealthy Brazilians), he avoids characterizing them as evil. He does briefly mention the popular will in some of his speeches, reminding the audience of his own working-class origins and telling them that he understands their needs. But he is rarely confrontational and lacks bellicosity. Thus, his present discourse is more consistently populist than Kirchner's, but it is only a mild form of populism at best.

Two historical instances where we found a surprising absence of strong populist discourse are the speeches of Lázaro Cárdenas and Carlos Menem. Cárdenas is the second leader included in the extended analysis in Appendix B, where we consider about 60 of his speeches in addition to those analyzed here and again find nearly identical results; this gives us great confidence in these findings. Cárdenas, president of Mexico from 1934 to 1940, is routinely considered a classic populist in older academic studies, most of which emphasize his expropriation of U.S. oil companies in 1938, his land redistribution and pro-labor policies, and his charisma (Knight 1998, 236; Conniff 1999). However, Cárdenas's language in these speeches is only moderately populist, and none of his speeches ever scores higher than a 1. This includes the speech he delivered shortly after the oil expropriation, which we used as his famous speech, as well as all of the speeches analyzed in Appendix B. Thus, he is more populist than a leader such as Lula, but not as strongly populist as someone like Chávez or close contemporaries such as Perón. These results may reflect an accident of historical timing. Cárdenas represented a consolidated revolution, and while his speeches include strong, frequent references to a General Will and a romanticized people that are tinged with socialism ("the proletariat," "the workers," "complete emancipation of the people," etc.), as well as a strong sense of cosmic proportionality, they are largely devoid of parallel references to a conspiring elite or a notion of dualism. Instead, Cárdenas emphasizes consolidating or institutionalizing the gains of the Mexican Revolution and the need to adhere to the rule of law. These pluralist aspects may help explain the relatively positive reception that Cárdenas received from world leaders, especially the administration of Franklin Roosevelt in the United States, which gave a rather measured response to the Mexican expropriation.

Menem is a noted neopopulist of the 1990s. During the decade when he was president, scholars debated whether he and a few other politicians in his generation represented a new kind of populism, one that relied on pro-market reforms and cross-class coalitions that included wealthy entrepreneurs

(Roberts 1995; Weyland 1996). However, Novaro (1998) argues that Menem's notion of the people was more inclusive than that of Perón, emphasizing a "democratic us" versus an "authoritarian them" that easily allowed most Argentines to feel a part of the people and minimized the tendency of his discourse to polarize politics. Our analysis agrees with this latter view and takes it further. All four of Menem's speeches express a kind of Manichaean discourse that frames issues as stark, morally weighty choices and offers a bold vision for a new future for Argentina, often coupled with references to great figures and movements. For example, in the international speech he talks about "creating a new State, on solid moral foundations" and "transforming the world into something more humane," and he insists that the moment for change is "now or never." Likewise, his ribbon-cutting speech (the inauguration of a new fish cannery) waxes eloquent with references to God and the Bible and their lessons for the appropriate model of economic development. But these speeches rarely express any notion of a romanticized popular will or mention a conspiratorial elite. Thus, Menem's discourse is redemptive but lacks the core elements of populism, and I treat him as a charismatic, pluralist leader rather than a populist one.

One last finding that I should comment on is the apparently high level of populist discourse in the speeches of Bush. Bush draws from most of the elements listed in the grading rubric: he presents issues in a broad, moral, dualistic framework that ascribes cosmic proportions to his topic ("Either you are with us, or you are with the terrorists"), speaks about a common people that represents the good (Americans and friends of liberal democracy everywhere), and describes a conspiring threat that embodies evil (fundamentalist Islamic terrorism). Critics of Bush would also argue that he displays a disregard for the rule of law and the accuracy of his data – an anything-goes attitude – in defense of what he perceives to be a just cause.

That said, I suggest that it is probably not helpful to consider Bush's discourse as populist, although it can certainly be considered antagonistic. His language is not about rectifying past injustices suffered by the people at the hands of an oppressive elite. His cause is the defense against a common external enemy – in this case, the threat of fundamentalist Islamic terrorism – rather than any so-called revolution or liberation. Nowhere does he call for radically reforming the political and economic system that governs liberal democracies and the United States. He certainly urges changing or reforming key constitutional rights and the provisions of international law in the fight against terrorism, but he never claims that institutions such as the U.S. Constitution or the United Nations are the product of a subversive Islamic cabal, nor does he publicly demonize Muslims for supposedly undermining American values. Instead, in these texts he reaffirms a pluralist notion of religious and racial tolerance.[22]

---

[22] In a similar vein, some scholars have been reluctant to call parties and politicians of the radical right populist because of the way in which they sometimes defend rather than seek to overthrow the political system. If particular radical right parties really are trying to defend

The fact that our coders failed to make this distinction suggests that our training could have been more careful. These elements of populist discourse (especially the need for systemic change) are clearly stated in the rubric, but they were not emphasized enough in our workshops with the graders. This is more likely to affect the results of the second, comparative phrase of our study, where the training and experience of the graders were more condensed and there was more potential to misunderstand this point; specifically, it would tend to bias the results upward. Fortunately, if we look at the actual results, we see that the total number of highly populist leaders in this second phase is a small proportion of the total, and the difference between the two phases of the analysis is quite small (the unweighted average of the four speech categories is 0.40 in the first phase versus 0.44 in the second), all of which suggests that this kind of measurement error is an insignificant problem outside the case of Bush. When I return to the data later, I leave all of the scores unchanged and include Bush in all of the graphs, but I omit Bush from any statistical analyses.[23]

In summary, this comparative, quantitative measurement of populist discourse in speeches by chief executives from across the globe reaffirms our main argument. Chávez's language is not just that of Chávez or a repeat of what we would essentially find in any chief executive's speeches. It has distinctive elements that the theoretical literature identifies with populist discourse, and it shares these elements with a subset of world leaders who are generally also considered populist. In fact, Chávez's discourse stands out as one of the most highly populist in the sample.

CONCLUSION: WHY POPULISM AND NOT LEFTISM

This chapter has argued that Chavismo fits a definition of populism as a worldview or discourse. Since at least 1994 through early 2007, Chávez has consistently expressed a Manichaean vision of history equating the side of Good with a putative will of the people and the side of Evil with a corrupt, conspiring elite (seen initially in limited domestic terms but increasingly in global ones). Chávez also advocates the need for system change (revolution) in order to exalt the people, and he tends to assume an anything-goes attitude toward democratic procedure and minority rights. This discourse is not an idiosyncratic feature of Chavismo. An additional cross-national quantitative analysis finds that a few other world leaders who are frequently considered populist, both contemporary and historical, use remarkably similar language conveying similar ideas. Yet, Chávez stands out as one of the most populist

---

a system on behalf of the people, then I agree with this distinction, but many radical right parties also talk about the need for systemic change.

[23] The one other instance of this measurement error is probably Tony Blair's famous speech, an antiterrorism speech that was rated as moderately populist (a 1). It manifests rhetorical elements similar to those found in the Bush speeches. However, Blair's other speeches were all rated as zero, so the potential bias is slight.

leaders in our larger comparative sample, making his movement a paradigmatic case of populism for comparative analysis.

What then can we say about Chavismo and its leftism, the other quality that has attracted so much more attention among scholars, journalists, and policymakers? While scholars and journalists are now very familiar with Chávez's radical leftism, many may be less aware of the early ideological content of his speeches. If we glance back at the same texts used in the discourse analysis of Chávez, we find that Chávez has consistently critiqued neoliberalism and certain aspects of capitalism, such as its emphasis on individualism, but that the movement's early ideology was not socialist. In early interviews after the coup, Chávez declared that he was "neither Marxist nor anti-Marxist" (Blanco Muñoz 1998, 116), and he freely criticized both orthodox Marxism and the communist experiments of the twentieth century. In their stead he and the other members of MBR 200 offered the ideas of Venezuelan revolutionary thinkers as more appropriate solutions for the country's failed democracy. This program, known as "The Tree of Three Roots," was based on the writings and lives of Bolívar; Simón Rodríguez, Bolívar's tutor and an early revolutionary thinker; and Ezequiel Zamora, the liberal leader in the Federal Wars of the 1870s. The program emphasized the ideas of revolution, constructive military involvement in democratic politics, the Bolivarian dream of regional integration, nationalism and cultural independence, and the pursuit of social justice.

Documents discussing these ideas continued to be widely discussed and disseminated within the movement after it came to power in 1998 (Caponi 1999; Dirección Nacional de Formación y Doctrina 1999a, 1999b), and Chávez drew heavily on them and the experiences of these leaders through the recall election of 2004 (e.g., the *campaña de Santa Inéz* and Maisanta). It is significant that in all of the speeches from this period that I examined, the word "socialism" is never mentioned. Likewise, in the Dieterich and Harnecker interviews, this word is spoken only in passing, in response to questions from his interviewers. Instead, Chávez always identifies himself with the original Bolivarian Alternative Agenda first issued in 1995 and consistently uses the phrase "democratic revolution."

Between 2004 and 2006, of course, this rhetoric changes dramatically. The 2006 closing campaign speech and the inaugural address are both steeped in language of the Marxist left. The revolutionary agenda is now "twenty-first century socialism," and Chávez revels in the label. "No one, nothing can take us away from the path to Bolivarian socialism, Venezuelan socialism, our socialism." The old party colors of yellow (with a touch of red) have now become "red reeeeed" or *rojo rojito*. The platform includes increasingly radical proposals such as renationalization, new forms of local government reminiscent of the Paris Commune of 1871 (Romero 2007a), and a unified, ostensibly participatory party that sounds uncannily like the Communist Party of Cuba. In the closing campaign speech he announces, "This is the century of the new man, the true man, the new woman; the century of peace;

the century of justice; the century of socialism." Chávez still cites Bolívar and others from the old pantheon of heroes, but he now also quotes Marx and, in defending his inclusion of a Communist in the new cabinet, declares that "I too am a Trotskyite." Both speeches feature emotional tributes to Castro and the Cuban Revolution, perhaps the most powerful of which is a new rhetorical flourish at the end, where he concludes with the Cuban revolutionary slogans, *"hasta la victoria siempre; patria o muerte – venceremos."*

Most of these changes are familiar to anyone reading a major international newspaper between 1999 and 2007, and they clearly accompany the changes in the government's policies. Yet, this shift in ideology and rhetoric has two attributes that we must recognize. The first is its timing: the shift to the socialist left represents a dramatic, *late* change. The potential was always there (as I will argue again in Chapter 7 when we study the government Missions), and with hindsight we can claim that Chavismo was headed in this direction. Chávez had significant contacts with Marxist doctrine and the left during his youth (Marcano and Barrera Tyszka 2004), and again when MBR 200 began reaching out to civilian revolutionary movements (Garrido 1999, 2000; Medina 1999). But the radical leftist qualities of the movement cannot explain Chavismo's rise to power, its policies for the first five or more years in government, or its ability to polarize Venezuelans. These other events transpired and these trends emerged long before Chávez became openly leftist. In contrast, the populist discourse of Chavismo has always been present and continues to accompany the new socialist language and goals that Chávez has adopted. It is this discourse and its underlying worldview that best help us understand the movement and are most worth studying in comparative context.

The second attribute is the *coexistence* of a populist discourse with socialist rhetoric. Chávez's ability to combine these two suggests that socialism and populism are not mutually exclusive. This may take readers by surprise, because a long-standing assumption in the academic literature on populism is that populism and doctrinaire socialism – or, for that matter, any defined ideology – are incompatible. For these scholars, populism is by definition vague and imprecise in its programmatic content and rejects prior limitations on the will of the people or the leader who typically embodies that will (c.f. Di Tella 1965). Up to a point, this is true. Populism's nativism and celebration of folk wisdom make it wary of intellectual exercises or foreign ideas (which would certainly include classic socialism), and a movement such as Chavismo with a powerful charismatic leader may be especially reluctant to accept constraints imposed by an established ideological tradition or its intellectual spokesmen. In the concluding chapter of this book, I explore some of the contradictions that undermine Chávez's attempts to forge a lasting socialist movement. Yet, it is incorrect to assume that populism is completely incompatible with ideology, socialist or otherwise. Political worldviews and discourses such as populism represent a different level of ideas than an ideology; they are mostly empty boxes that can hold different types of programmatic content. Hence, as I reemphasize in later chapters, populism can be on the ideological right or left. Chavismo's original ideology of the Tree of Three Roots may not have been as sophisticated and well developed as socialism, and Chávez's current socialist vision is clearly imprecise, yet Chavismo did have an ideology and continues to have one today. The real question is which of these, ideology or discourse, should be our focus here. Because populism remains a more consistent feature of Chavismo, and because so many of the movement's features ultimately seem to derive from its underlying discourse, I retain this as the ultimate focus of the book. This is not to say that leaders' beliefs never change or that an ideology cannot transform a worldview, but in the case of Chavismo this transformation has yet to occur.

4

Party System Breakdown and the Rise of Chavismo

> The rotten elites of the parties are boxed in, and soon they will be consigned to the trashbin of history.
>
> Hugo Chávez, 1998 closing campaign speech

> [The constitution] must die, and with it the disastrous political system that it gave birth to during these past forty years.
>
> Hugo Chávez, 1999 inaugural address

What causes populism? In the next two chapters I shift from describing Chavismo and populism to explaining their causes. By this, I mean not the existence of populism in the abstract, in the sense of providing some kind of intellectual history or a genealogy of ideas, but the more social scientific question of why large numbers of citizens, activists, and even elected officials would embrace a movement with a populist discourse. Because of the nature of the data at hand, I present the theory in two parts. In this chapter, I focus on the breakdown of Venezuela's traditional party system and the accompanying rise of populist movements, especially Chavismo. This gives us an opportunity to explore the *demand* side of populism and demonstrate that widespread corruption is probably the most important condition for the emergence of populist movements. Then, in the following chapter, I move beyond the case of Venezuela to consider Chavismo in a comparative cross-national context. That perspective gives us a better opportunity to test the interaction of corruption and policy crisis, and it lets us say more about the possible factors affecting the *supply* of populism in any country. However, these latter factors are secondary ones that do not vary significantly in the case of Venezuela, and in this chapter I refer to them only in passing. In both chapters, I show how an understanding of populism as a set of ideas gives us crucial insights into the origins of successful populist movements.

While populism could be dismissed as a chronic problem in some Latin American countries (de la Torre 2000), in Venezuela it represents more of a puzzle. Until the 1990s, Venezuela's party system was considered highly institutionalized, with control over government alternating between relatively stable pluralist parties (Mainwaring and Scully 1995). In fact, fully 74.4 percent of respondents in the 1998 RedPol national survey agreed with the statement that "parties are necessary for democracy." Why then did voters abandon their traditional parties for one of the most populist leaders in the hemisphere? Part of the answer is that Chavismo was neither the first nor the only movement of its kind in Venezuela. The emergence of other independent, charismatic movements during this period, in particular the weakly populist one of Rafael Caldera in 1993, shows that Chavismo was only the most extreme expression of a trend that began a few years earlier. The breakdown of the party system and the rise of Chavismo were not sudden. Yet, this answer still begs the question of why the breakdown occurred and why Venezuelans were so eager to embrace poorly institutionalized radical leadership when they had other options available.

Over the past decade, this question has given rise to a sizable scholarly literature that suggests at least three explanations for the party system's breakdown and (with somewhat less attention) the successful emergence of Chavismo. These are a *deepening of democracy* argument that emphasizes the growing incompatibility of Venezuela's "partyocracy" with the increasing sophistication and democratic values of average Venezuelans; a *structuralist* argument that focuses on the changing nature of social cleavages and political technologies, especially in an era of economic globalization; and an *economic voting* argument that focuses on policy performance and Venezuela's economic crisis.

This chapter argues that none of these explanations is entirely correct. While each highlights important changes taking place in Venezuela over the past few decades, none of them fully appreciates the normative or ideational dimension of politics that populism forces us to consider. Venezuelan voters were deeply concerned about the crumbling moral foundations of their political system in its day-to-day operations, captured in frequent popular references to the concept of "corruption" that became widespread after the first oil boom of the 1970s, and populist discourse was a logical response to the resulting crisis of democratic legitimacy. None of the other changing material conditions of Venezuelan politics – the growing modernization of society, the effects of globalization on a rentier state, or the ongoing economic crisis – could have singlehandedly created the conditions for a successful populist movement. It was the underlying violation of the rule of law that created this space.

In order to make this argument, I first contextualize the breakdown in Venezuela and describe the broader emergence of charismatic and occasionally populist movements that begins in the early 1990s. I then critique existing explanations for the breakdown and present my own, which emphasizes corruption and the nature of populist discourse. Finally, I test this explanation qualitatively and quantitatively by analyzing the shifting pattern of actual corruption in Venezuela during the Punto Fijo regime and its perception by average Venezuelans and politicians; and by conducting a multivariate, individual-level analysis of survey data from the 1998 election. Data are drawn from secondary sources on Venezuelan politics and primary sources of economic indicators, as well as from five key national opinion polls: the 1973 Baloyra-Martz survey (Baloyra and Martz 1979), the 1983 Baloyra-Torres survey (Instituto Gallup 1983), the 1993 CIEPA/DOXA survey (Institute of Political Science 1993), the 1995 Canache survey (Canache 1995), and, above all, the 1998 RedPol survey (Red Universitaria 1999).[1] Additional data come from interviews with leaders of the major political parties that I conducted in fall 1999, May 2000, and February 2003.

THE RISE OF POPULIST MOVEMENTS AND THE BREAKDOWN OF THE PARTY SYSTEM

This chapter attempts to address both the rise of Chavismo and the accompanying collapse of the old Punto Fijo system of representative democracy, particularly its dominant two-party system. While the rise of Chavismo is most truly the subject of this book, the collapse of the party system has attracted the most attention from scholars of Venezuelan politics over the past 15 years. Even today, studies continue to focus heavily on the weaknesses and eventual failure of the Punto Fijo system, giving relatively little attention to the corresponding rise of Chávez (c.f. McCoy and Myers 2004; Coppedge 2005; Dietz and Myers 2007; Morgan 2007).

However, the two subjects are closely intertwined. Chávez and his movement played a crucial direct role in the final destruction of the traditional party system, because without their zealous efforts to carry out the Bolivarian revolution, the party system and the old institutional order could not have been eliminated so completely and quickly. Scholars studying recent party system breakdowns in Venezuela and other countries have frequently emphasized this voluntaristic aspect of the process (Levitsky and Cameron 2003; Coppedge 2005; Tanaka 2005; Dietz and Myers 2007). These two subjects are also related in a less direct, more profound way. Presumably, the perceived problems of the old Punto Fijo system were also what made Chavismo such an attractive option to Venezuelans; both phenomena were caused by something

---

[1] The Baloyra-Martz survey was carried out by the firm DATOS, C.A., in October 1973 and had a nationwide sample of 1,521 (Baloyra and Martz 1979, 195). The Baloyra-Torres survey (known as the BATOBA survey) was carried out by Gallup in 1983 and had a nationwide sample of 1,789 respondents (Instituto Gallup 1983). The CIEPA/DOXA survey was directed by the Institute of Political Science and Public Law of the University of Zulia, Venezuela, in June 1993 and had a nationwide sample size of 1,500 (Institute of Political Science 1993). The Canache survey was conducted by researchers at the Center for Economic and Social Research of the Andrés Bello Catholic University from January to March 1995 and had an urban sample of 897 residents of Caracas and Maracaibo (Canache 2002, 2). The RedPol survey was carried out by DATOS, C.A., on behalf of a Venezuelan social science consortium, the University Network of Political Studies (Red Universitaria de Estudios Políticos), in November 1998 and had a nationwide sample size of 1,500 (Red Universitaria 1999, 9).

similar, and any theory that explains the breakdown of the party system must also be able to say something about what emerged to take its place. Thus, both subjects are addressed in this chapter.

Before moving on to a description of these twin transformations of Venezuela's political system, I should explain why I talk about Venezuela's *party* system decline rather than the larger decline of its representative democracy. While many studies of democratic breakdown in Venezuela continue to focus on the party system (see Dietz and Myers 2007; Morgan 2007), the more recent trend is to acknowledge the breakdown of something larger: of its entire system of representative democracy (see McCoy and Myers 2004; Coppedge 2005). This system began with the pact of Punto Fijo and was eventually enshrined in a series of interrelated institutions, beginning, of course, with the Constitution of 1961, created shortly after the transition to democracy in 1958. Parties in Venezuela were only one strand of the larger web of institutions that held together the Punto Fijo system, including electoral rules, presidential–legislative relations, and tripartite consultative procedures (Crisp 2000).

This criticism contains important truths and resonates with my broader argument that Chavismo and its control of the state represent a major shift from pluralist to populist democracy. In focusing on the party system, we risk losing sight of the forest for the trees. However, Venezuela's Punto Fijo system was one with strong corporatist institutions and consociational roots that naturally placed parties at its center, making it what Coppedge (1994) calls a "partyarchy" or what Venezuelans frequently called a *partidocracia*.

To begin with, the parties played important symbolic functions in the struggle for democracy, first in the three years of failed democracy from 1945 to 1948, then again during the resistance to the military government from 1948 to 1958, and finally in the transition to a democratic regime at the end of that period. The parties and their leaders, particularly Rómulo Betancourt of AD, Jóvito Villalba of the personalistic Unión Republicana Democrática, and Rafael Caldera of COPEI, were key participants in the negotiations leading to the pact of Punto Fijo. The realities of electoral politics meant that these parties assumed a predominant role in democracy after the transition. Only parties ran for office and occupied government, especially in an era when radical participatory institutions were largely unheard of in Latin America (or when parties *were* the radical institutions). Perhaps most important, the parties' privileged access to oil revenues eventually gave them tremendous insularity from and bargaining power vis-à-vis other actors in civil society. Once in power, they used these state resources to create clientelistic relations with constituents that allowed them to co-opt or marginalize new political actors. Together these factors meant that the parties in Venezuela came to occupy the real positions of power in their democracy.

Venezuelans themselves understood this reality. Surveys from this period consistently ask about attitudes toward the party system together with attitudes toward democracy, and popular attitudes toward the parties were always highly correlated with attitudes toward other key institutions of democracy.

Thus, more than in many other Latin American countries of the era, the unraveling of Venezuela's representative democracy is essentially a story of the breakdown of the party system.

Caldera and the 1993 Election

What makes Venezuela's party system breakdown particularly puzzling is that the traditional parties were replaced not by a new set of pluralistic institutionalized ones, but by a series of movements led by charismatic, frequently populist leaders. Readers are already familiar with the case of Chavismo, but the trend was visible at least five years earlier in the 1993 election of Caldera, and it remains evident in the consistent role that independent candidates and electoral movements have played in the opposition to Chávez. The emergence of these leaders reinforces the point that not just a quantitative change occurred in the party system (in that the traditional parties lost electoral significance), but also a qualitative transformation from pluralistic competition to an alternative mode driven by populist discourse.

The first evidence of this transformation was the 1993 election of Caldera. Caldera was one of the founders of COPEI and a highly regarded former president (1969–73). In a move that surprised and devastated his colleagues, he abandoned his old party for the 1993 presidential elections and founded a new party, Convergencia (Convergence), built largely around his personality. Caldera was disillusioned with the younger generation of leaders that he had mentored, and he insisted that COPEI's machinery was dominated by opponents who would never allow him to win the nomination in a fair contest (Interview v01b.01 18 1999; Interview v20.01 1999; Interview v01d.01 1999). He probably also realized that COPEI's backing would be a liability in the antitraditional-party atmosphere that prevailed.

Caldera was the early favorite and won the election with a bare plurality of the vote in a four-way race.[2] Some scholars and politicians attribute Caldera's success to a televised speech from the floor of Congress on the day following the February 1992 attempted coup (Interview v18c.01 1999; Interview v06.01 1999). In the speech, Caldera censured the undemocratic means of the coup plotters but argued that the coup was a response to fundamental problems with Venezuela's political and economic system that required wholesale institutional change:

It is difficult to ask the people to sacrifice themselves for liberty and freedom when they think that freedom and democracy are incapable of feeding them or containing the exorbitant cost of living; when democracy and freedom have been incapable of putting an end to the terrible blight of corruption (which in the eyes of all the world is consuming our institutional order). This situation cannot be hidden. A military coup in any form is censurable, but it would be foolish to think that this one is only an escapade carried out by a few ambitious men who, working alone, launched something suddenly

---

[2] Caldera won with approximately 30% of the vote. Claudio Fermín of AD received approximately 24%; Oswaldo Álvarez Paz of COPEI, 23%; and Andrés Velásquez of LCR, 22%.

and without realizing what they were getting into. There is a whole context, a deep problem, a grave situation in our country, and if that situation is left unaddressed, destiny holds great and grave consequences for us. (Tarre Briceño 1994, 162–3)

Caldera's speech was one of the few in either chamber of Congress and the only one by an elder statesman to sympathize with the motives of the conspirators or acknowledge the fundamental problems of the political system. It immediately received an overwhelmingly positive response from the public that probably helped convince him to run again for office. Caldera also brought a record of honesty and administrative efficiency to the campaign. Voters and politicians from all parties regarded his previous term in office as one of the best since the democratic transition in 1958. This credibility not only helped him win the election but also allowed him to govern during the difficult years that followed the tumult of 1992 and 1993 (Egaña 1999, 24; Interview v16.1 1999). And last but not least, he transmitted a populist campaign message that emphasized his understanding of the common people and his pledge to ameliorate the perceived excesses of neoliberal economic reform (Poleo 1993, 8; Interview v19.01 1999). He was anticorruption and antiparty – or, in his own words, "supra-party" (Zeta 1993, 16).

Caldera was not an isolated phenomenon in 1993. At least two of the three other candidates who opposed Caldera – Claudio Fermín of AD and Oswaldo Álvarez Paz of COPEI – were party outsiders or lesser lights in their parties, chosen largely because of their popularity among the voters, not because they were favored by national party leaders (Nolia 1993; Zeta 1993, 16, 20; Interview v06.01b 22, September 1999). The fourth candidate, Andrés Velásquez of La Causa Radical (Radical Cause, or LCR), represented a challenger new-left party with a clear program for systemic change.

The campaign style and reputation of Caldera were matched by a low level of institutionalization in his new party, Convergencia. In a 1997 survey of Latin American legislators by the University of Salamanca (administered when Caldera was in office), 66 percent of the respondents from Convergencia said that they owed their election "to the popular following of their party leader," the second highest level for any party in Latin America (Alcántara Sáez 1997). The party won only 13.9 percent in the concurrent congressional election, and Caldera had to govern through a coalition with the leftist Movimiento al Socialismo (Movement to Socialism, or MAS) and later through a congressional alliance with AD. Partisan identity with Convergencia was never high among voters, reaching less than 4 percent in 1993.[3] The party virtually disappeared once Caldera ended his term, its share of the vote dropping to 2.5 percent in 1998 and just 1.1 percent in 2000.

---

[3] The 1993 CIEPA/DOXA survey asked respondents two questions about partisan sympathy: which party they sympathized with or belonged to, and which party they leaned toward if they were independent. Tellingly, the survey did not bother to ask voters if they identified with or felt sympathetic to Convergencia– only AD, COPEI, MAS, and LCR. However, a total of 4.1% answered "other."

Caldera's administration had its successes, most notably the return to some political normalcy and the "pacification" of the Bolivarian movement. He pardoned Chávez and his fellow conspirators in the hope that they could be persuaded to accept the democratic route to power, and all of them did so in various forms over the next few years. Yet ultimately, his movement failed to last. Age was a factor; Caldera was 83 when he finally left office and no longer in a position to continue exercising effective leadership of his new party. But he also lost the voters' confidence by failing to deliver on key campaign promises. The economy never really rebounded during his term, and in 1996 he was forced by a series of banking and fiscal crises to implement the very sorts of neoliberal reforms he had vilified during the election campaign. Most important of all, he reneged on promises to carry out constitutional reform and root out corruption. His own administration became embroiled in scandals involving family members and key advisers, and toward the end of his term he forged a legislative alliance with AD that discredited his administration. After initially challenging the Punto Fijo system, he failed to undermine or replace it.

Chavismo and Politics Post-Caldera

Where Chavismo represents something new is not so much in its campaign rhetoric or in its weakly institutionalized organization, but in the consistency of its message and its efforts to destroy the Punto Fijo system. Unlike Caldera, Chávez and his allies maintained their populist discourse after entering office and pursued the radical institutional change promised in their campaign, first by overseeing the creation of a new constitution that closely reflected the participatory, egalitarian ideals of their movement (ratified in December 1999) and then by holding new elections to reconstitute national and local governments in July and December 2000. As new developments unfolded, some of them initially unfavorable to the movement, Chávez demonstrated his skill and vision by exploiting them to further rid the political system of its traditional remnants while radicalizing the movement's organization and policy initiatives.

Although most of Chávez's opponents lacked his populist discourse, nearly all were charismatic leaders of poorly institutionalized movements. Both candidates who fared well at some point during the 1998 elections ran as independents: Irene Saez, a popular mayor of a Caracas municipality, and Henrique Salas Römer, a governor who founded a new party, Proyecto Venezuela (Project Venezuela), that largely failed to endure beyond the 2000 elections. The one who was clearly a machine candidate from a traditional party – Luis Alfaro Ucero, AD's candidate and secretary-general of the party – never rose above single digits in the polls, and Saez lost the voters' confidence after she accepted COPEI's endorsement later in the campaign. Venezuelans made it clear that they wanted a strong leader who could be trusted to carry out radical change, not one linked to the traditional party bureaucracies.

This trend toward electoral movements persisted in the 2000 elections, in which Chávez was elected for a six-year term under the new constitution. At least three independent candidates ran unsuccessfully against Chávez: Claudio Fermín and Antonio Ledezma, two former AD leaders and Caracas mayors who had by now left their party, and Francisco Arias Cárdenas, the former associate of Chávez and co-conspirator from 1992. All of the candidates were supported by ad hoc committees that could not really be considered parties because they failed to offer slates of candidates for any other government office (c.f. Duarte 2000). And the pattern was maintained through the presidential election of 2006. The chief opposition candidate, Zulia governor Manuel Rosales, was another former AD politician who left the party in 2000 to found his own organization, Un Nuevo Tiempo (A New Time, or UNT). After losing the election, his organization struggled to maintain its visibility.

A NORMATIVE EXPLANATION

What explains the breakdown of the party system and the rise of populist movements during the 1990s? Existing studies of these profound political changes fall into roughly three schools of thought. Earlier in the 1990s, *partyarchy* and *the deepening of democracy* were seen as the overarching concerns. According to a wide range of moderate and radical critics, Venezuela's corporatist system and its dominant political parties were preventing the political participation of new social groups and failing to keep up with the growing political efficacy of the population. Unless the government and the parties were decentralized and civil society was given a greater independent voice, popular dissatisfaction would continue to grow and threaten the democratic system (Hellinger 1991; Coppedge 1994; Kornblith 1994; Kornblith and Levine 1995; Crisp and Levine 1998; Rey 1998; Levine and Crisp 1999; and Buxton 2001).[4] A second set of explanations falls into the *structuralist* or *macrosociological* camp. These studies focus on the devastating combination of a historically weak state and an oil-based rentier economy in a context of globalization and new political technologies. Rentier economies that develop in countries such as Venezuela, with low bureaucratic autonomy and capacity, have traditionally experienced entrenched authoritarian governments and political cultures that make representative democracy difficult to achieve (Coronil 1997; Karl 1997). Lately, these problems have been aggravated by the decline in traditional economic sectors brought about by globalization, as well as the spread

---

[4] As noted in Chapter 2, some of these scholars today fall on very different sides of the Chavista/anti-Chavista divide. Those more favorably inclined toward Chávez are more likely to have been advocates of radical participatory democracy, while those who criticize Chávez today are more likely to have been proponents of limited forms of government decentralization and party reform. Despite these differences, both sides emphasize the centrality of democratic institutional reform for alleviating Venezuela's political crisis and see this need rooted in an increasingly modern society.

of technologies that make mass-based organizations less essential for political parties (Roberts 2003). Finally, with the ascent of Chávez, *economic voting* has become a preferred explanation for the breakdown in Venezuela, albeit sometimes with cognitive twists. Venezuela's prolonged economic crisis (in terms of both aggregate growth and the distribution of economic opportunities within the population) drove voters to opt for desperate solutions. The repeated failure of the parties to reform themselves and propose effective policies resulted in their rejection at the polls and their replacement by new, more radical movements (Canache 2002; Weyland 2003; Naím 2004; Coppedge 2005; Dietz and Myers 2007).

While all three of these explanations have some basis in reality, we can fully explain the breakdown of the party system and the rise of populist movements such as Chavismo only once we acknowledge the distinct qualities of populist discourse. I argue that the rejection of the traditional party system and the choice of a populist movement were calculated responses to *normative* concerns, specifically a crisis of legitimacy rooted in the breakdown of the rule of law and the perceived corruption of the political system. Prolonged policy failures contributed to undermining this legitimacy, but they became the basis for a successful populist appeal only once they were linked to deeper moral failures of the political class.

Because this is one of the central insights of this book, I will lay out a detailed abstract version of this argument before examining the evidence from Venezuela. As some of the earlier studies of party system breakdown in Venezuela recognize (Canache and Kulischek 1998), the breakdown and the subsequent rise of Chavismo represented a crisis of legitimacy. "Legitimacy" describes the deepest level of support that citizens can have for their government and the politicians who constitute it (Easton 1975). To be precise, it is the normative component of our support for government, "the capacity of the system to engender and maintain the belief that the existing political institutions are the most *appropriate* ones for the society" (Lipset 1981, 64, emphasis added). Scholars typically see legitimacy as an attribute of the political system, especially the constitution and the formal institutions of government, although it can also describe particular politicians and groups. When we accept the possibility of opposing candidates holding office, we recognize their moral right to participate in politics despite any disagreements we have over issues and personalities; when we no longer recognize that right – when we see it as illegitimate – we prevent opposing candidates from running, revoke their legal identity, or throw them in jail.

The legitimacy of any political system is based partly on the policy performance of government (Linz 1988; Lipset 1994). Hence, particularly bad policy failures such as those that occurred in Venezuela can undermine this legitimacy, generating calls for fresh ideas or new faces. This, however, is not really a crisis of legitimacy. Legitimacy is ultimately a normative attribute of the regime, and only significant moral failures can weaken this legitimacy enough for it to become a true crisis. A policy failure that can be seen as a moral failure generates demands not just for new policies, but for replacing the system and for creating new rules and actors.

While we can imagine a variety of moral failures of politicians and institutions, the ultimate failure in modern representative democracy is to violate the rule of law, and in particular to systematically violate the rule of law for selfish purposes. The rule of law is the principle that no one is above the law, or that there should be "a government of laws and not of men."[5] This principle is not unique to democracy, but it has special relevance to democratic legitimacy. As O'Donnell (1999, 2001, 2004) emphasizes in his work on the rule of law and its relationship to democratic theory, democracy is premised on the belief that all people meeting certain minimal standards are citizens entitled to a basic package of rights (see also O'Donnell, Schmitter, and Whitehead 1986, 7–8). These standards are broadly inclusive and ignore the distinctions of wealth, lineage, or education that matter in traditional societies. They are based on our sense that all human beings share some fundamental worth and rational capacity, or *agency,* Agency not only entitles us to have a say in how our lives are run (and the obligation to accept the consequences of our decisions), but also implies that the institutions surrounding us are legitimate to the extent that they respect our fundamental worth and enhance our capacity for choice. One expression of these beliefs is the process of constituting government – what O'Donnell refers to as the "regime" – under the principle of "one person, one vote." Democratic government is legitimate in modern liberal societies because it relies on free and fair elections that weigh the opinions of all citizens equally. However, the principles of agency and citizenship also extend to the application of the law during that long period of time between elections – in O'Donnell's words, from the regime to the "state" and "society." Citizens' spheres of everyday life (society) operate in an environment that the government builds and maintains by creating laws and regulations and enforcing them (the state). Applied to these realms, agency and citizenship mean equal respect for all citizens' civil rights, especially due process, and the use of universalistic criteria in policy design – in other words, the rule of law. A government qualifies as democratic not merely because of its respect for civil rights and liberties during elections, but also because it upholds the rule of law and the rights of citizenship between elections in its daily operation.

Although the rule of law might be weak for a variety of reasons, such as natural disasters and international economic crises, what undermines democratic legitimacy is the widespread, selfish violation of the rule of law by one's own political leaders. Most often we refer to this as corruption. Corruption is defined as the "abuse of public office for private gain" (Seligson 2002, 408). That which is held jointly by the community and used for the collective good, or at least in ways that the community widely agrees on (for example, using means-tested criteria), is instead used by public officials for themselves or for

---

[5] An oft-cited phrase found in the 1780 Constitution of the Commonwealth of Massachusetts, First Part, Article XXX.

interests that fail to meet the community's standards. Corruption is not the exact opposite of the rule of law; to be so, the concept would also have to include anarchy, the prerogative of monarchs and other autocrats, and crimes by citizens against citizens, among other attributes. But it is the *intentional* violation of the rule of law by public officials for their *private gain*, and thus captures the kind of violation that could become an egregious affront to democratic norms and a clear target for populist discourse.

To be clear, the word corruption has several related meanings that vary in breadth. Current empirical studies of corruption tend to measure only the narrowest one. These studies – the corruption perception indexes of Transparency International and the World Bank's Governance Matters division, and the "experienced corruption" measured in mass surveys (Seligson 2006) – have become common in the past decade and reflect the increased appreciation for problems of democracy in daily practice (IMF 1997; World Bank 1997). They take a behavioralist approach that emphasizes specific lists of formally or legally corrupt practices, such as bribery, nepotism, and the diversion of funds for partisan purposes. Such practices are examples of corruption and serve as good indicators of broader trends, but they are limited in scope. Corruption can also include conscious *legal* failures by public officials to live up to the normative ideals of the community, including favoritism in constituency service, writing legislation to favor campaign donors, and simple negligence. And in common parlance it refers to something fairly *systematic* and *widespread*. When people complain that "the government is corrupt," they usually mean more than the abuse of office for personal benefit by particular officials; they instead refer to the failure of an entire system of institutions to uphold higher ideals.

Corruption is necessarily perceived as subjective; the possibility exists that citizens will overlook or justify corruption that benefits them, or that what some cultures perceive as corrupt may be seen as a normal practice in others. Yet, current measures of corruption indicate that these subjective experiences are usually grounded in something fairly objective. Corruption perception indexes use what might seem to be the shakiest of all indicators – the perception that certain kinds of practices take place – and still achieve very reliable results across time and across component studies, results that correlate in meaningful, consistent ways with other independent indicators such as per capita GDP (Kaufmann, Kraay, and Mastruzzi 2005). More concrete indicators from mass surveys that ask about respondents' personally experienced corruption show similar results (Seligson 2006).[6] Thus, widespread complaints about corruption usually mean more than personal disagreement with politicians or anger over bad policy outcomes, while the general absence of complaints can probably be attributed to an objectively clean system.

---

[6] For more analysis of the association between corruption percention indexes and economic growth, see Mauro (1997), Chong and Calderón (2000), Acemoglu, Johnson, and Robinson (2001), and the debate between Kurtz and Schrank (2007) and Kaufmann, Kraay, and Mastruzzi (2007).

This (finally) is where populism enters in and where we can see why a leader such as Chávez has such a strong appeal. Populism is an especially well-suited response to problems of widespread, systematic corruption and enjoys distinct advantages over other discourses. To begin with, populism's Manichaean outlook means that it strives to restore or re-create the legitimacy of democratic government in the face of the state's perceived corruption. Populists may not always use the word corruption in their speeches (although, as we have seen in the case of Chávez, they often do), but their central argument is essentially about this phenomenon: popular government has been undermined by a conspiring minority that subverts the will of the people to its own selfish interests. Corruption in this broad normative sense not only exists and is reprehensible, but is part of a grand design and an imminent threat to all that the people hold dear. It represents the deeper struggle between the forces of Good and the forces of Evil in history. Thus, populism is both a causal argument about the causes and consequences of policy failure and a normative tool for interpreting or framing the problem. It arises when we perceive that policy failures represent systematic moral failures and not just passing troubles.

Populism's democratic flavor makes it an especially hopeful, flattering response to policy failure and corruption and provides it with a special advantage over elitism. Populists such as Chávez fiercely assert the virtue of common folk and their right to rule; the solution to the problem is always more popular participation. Ordinary citizens – the majority – are basically good, and it is a narrow elite that is subverting their will; with effort, the people can act on their better natures and overcome this enemy. Of course, whether or not populist governments deliver on their promises for better policy and honest government is another matter, and it is here that elitism offers its most seductive appeal. Elitism seeks to resolve policy failures and corruption by affirming the superior capacity of ruling groups such as the armed forces or intellectuals. It implies that corruption is a result of popular participation gone awry – of too much democracy rather than not enough. However, elitism is not a particularly flattering response to crisis for most citizens, and it ultimately struggles for legitimacy. Societies today have adopted liberal values and broad conceptions of human rights that eventually force ruling classes to subject themselves to elections, thereby reopening the door to populism or pluralism.

Populism also has an advantage over pluralism because it makes a call for action: for real, practical efforts to renew and change the political system and/or renovate its leadership. Not only does it offer an aggressive plan, but it overcomes the self-interest and free riding that ordinarily prevent collective action. For the populist, unity is not just crucial but natural once citizens search deeply and decide what they really support: the Good of the people or the Evil minority. Loyal opposition and coexistence are inappropriate responses to the conscious moral failure of a political class and the institutions that uphold them; such behavior can only mean acquiescence. Instead, citizens must actively identify and pursue evildoers in order to rescue the system and reaffirm themselves as moral agents.

In contrast, pluralism sees fundamental institutional reform as largely unnecessary, celebrates sectoral differences and mechanisms of compromise, and tries to show respect for political opponents. Pluralism is the discourse of the political market. Much as with market economics, it sees an invisible hand adjudicating the (often selfish!) behavior of political interests and turning them to the public good. Pluralism tends to *assume* competition and limited opportunism rather than providing a program to *create* or *restore* them; the principal directive that pluralist democratic theory provides is to multiply interests and give them free play. Obviously, pluralists recognize the need for institutions to uphold the rule of law, but these are seen as features for maintaining a level playing field rather than as tools for creating one. As O'Donnell (2001, 2004) and others (Carothers 2006) wistfully note, pluralism struggles to resolve or even acknowledge the kinds of political market failures that are endemic in many developing countries, where corruption and rent-seeking behavior are ingrained and where programs to create the rule of law are typically superficial and short-lived.[7]

A QUALITATIVE ANALYSIS

If this argument about the normative basis of successful populist movements is correct, then existing explanations for Venezuela's party system breakdown and the rise of Chavismo have an important grain of truth. Economic policy failures were serious potential threats to the legitimacy of the Punto Fijo system of partyocracy because they showed that it was no longer capable of addressing Venezuelans' basic material needs despite the country's evident oil wealth. Particular democratic institutions such as top-down party organizations and narrowly circumscribed corporatist institutions tarnished the democratic qualities of both the regime and the state, although the following data suggest that popular demands for participatory versions of democracy were never that great. And long-term changes in the structure of the economy and campaign technologies certainly made it more difficult for the parties to craft

---

[7] Note, however, that populism is not necessarily the best response to crises of procedural legitimacy, the classic problem of democratization. Democratizing discourses can be either populist *or* pluralist; the choice depends on the perceived corruption of the previous system. Corrupt authoritarian regimes arouse popular revolutionary responses. Classic cases of social revolution such as Mexico in 1910, Cuba in 1959, and Nicaragua in 1979 exemplify this mode. In contrast, an authoritarian but legalistic system that respects the rule of law is unlikely to engender a pluralist response because there is relatively little corruption to fight against. Much of the legal code and the bureaucracy – perhaps even the constitution itself – can be preserved, and the former authoritarian regime may accept the legitimacy of democratic competition and compete in the new system. This outcome is epitomized by "pacted" democratic transitions from bureaucratic authoritarian regimes in Uruguay, Brazil, and Chile in the 1980s, where the democratic opposition felt more constrained to respect military prerogatives and was less inclined to revamp the system once in power (O'Donnell, Schmitter, and Whitehead 1986; Linz and Stepan 1996). Linz and Stepan (1996, 70–1) anticipate this argument in their discussion of transitions from sultanistic regimes.

policy solutions and to maintain their old personal ties with voters. In the end, though, most Venezuelans would not have supported the dissolution of the old political system by populist challengers unless they could reasonably interpret these other failures as evidence of widespread corruption and the moral failure of their elite.

Evidence for Existing Explanations

With its concern for legitimacy, the argument for *deepening democracy* taps into the discourse of populism and its rhetoric of corruption and moral crisis, concepts that figure prominently in the normative theory I have offered. And the breakdown of the party system correlates with recent social changes and emerging political activism. Venezuela experienced steady improvement in many indicators of socioeconomic development during the past few decades. Between 1960 and 1998, life expectancy increased from 60 to 73 years; the percentage of the population living in urban areas increased from just above 60 percent to over 85 percent; and between 1970 and 1998 illiteracy dropped from 24 percent to 8 percent (World Bank 2007). Partly as a result of this process of modernization, Venezuela experienced the rise of a more autonomous civil society during the late 1970s and 1980s, including new neighborhood associations, an environmental movement, and independent labor unions (García 1992; Ellner 1993; Buxton 2001). Many of these organizations were the chief advocates of government decentralization in the late 1980s (Martín 2000; Mascareño 2000). And while general support for democracy possibly declined somewhat in the early 1990s, between two-thirds and three-fourths of the population expressed high levels of support during the decade and a half before Chávez's election (Canache 2002, 63–7).

However, the deepening of democracy argument has two significant flaws. To begin with, it goes too far in its depiction of the political values of Venezuelans and other Latin Americans. Despite real changes in Venezuelan society during previous decades and significant shifts in attitudes among important segments of the population, general support for democracy was still only average for Latin America and failed to achieve the high levels found in countries such as Costa Rica or Uruguay, let alone in most of the advanced industrial democracies (Canache 2002, 66–70). When asked what was the most important problem the country faced, survey respondents throughout the 1980s and 1990s rarely mentioned the need for democratic reforms (Table 4.2). And by the time of Chávez's election, the bulk of Venezuelans had only low or moderate levels of the postmaterialist values that some scholars associate with new movements for participatory democracy (c.f. Inglehart 1990, 1997; Offe 1985). According to data from the 1995–7 World Values Survey, conducted in the year before the election, Venezuelans had only moderate levels of the "survival/self-expression" dimension of postmaterialist values and ranked almost dead last on the second, "traditional/secular-rational" dimension (Inglehart and Baker 2000, 29). Together these data suggest a population that was still comfortable with traditional representative government or even the corporatist forms of democracy that already existed in Venezuela.

The deepening of democracy explanation also fails to coincide with the actual political behavior of most Venezuelans and particularly their support of charismatic leaders. If the argument were true, larger numbers of Venezuelans would have joined and supported organizations that espoused participatory decision making and government decentralization during the 1980s and 1990s, especially autonomous secondary associations and the newer, more deliberative parties that emerged during this period, such as La Causa Radical (López-Maya 1997; Buxton 2001). Venezuelans were fickle in their support for these kinds of candidates and parties and seemed to have been guided mostly by the prospect of overcoming political or economic crisis when deciding for whom to vote. They began abandoning the traditional parties in 1993, less than three years after the decentralization reforms were implemented and before their full effects were even felt. Most of the parties that voters did support, in particular Caldera's Convergencia and Chávez's MVR, were electoral vehicles that selected their candidates with the advice and consent of their charismatic leaders. And most voters and activists barely opposed Chávez's efforts to roll back decentralization reforms even as late as 2007, when he asked for extraordinary decree powers that virtually did away with the National Assembly for 18 months.[8] While important constituencies for democratizing reforms existed in Venezuela – including within Chavismo, as we will see in Chapter 6 – most ordinary Venezuelans generally failed to endorse parties that actually *practiced* internal democracy, and only a limited core of activists became involved in the new institutions of direct democracy fomented by the Chávez government (López Maya 2008a; Hawkins 2008).[9]

The *macrosociological* or *structuralist* explanation is corroborated by important social and technological changes. Despite the gradual improvement in many indicators of development, the country's efforts to diversify its economy beyond the oil sector were ultimately stymied by ineffective government intervention and increasing competition from abroad. Union density (the percentage of the labor force that belongs to unions) dropped from over 25 percent in 1988 to less than 15 by 1995, and the percentage of labor in the informal sector increased from about 32 percent in the late 1970s to over 50 percent by 1999 (Wibbels and Roberts 1999; OCEI 2002). These latter changes had a particularly profound effect on AD, which relied more

---

[8] Chávez and MVR did support constitutional provisions to encourage participatory democracy in 1999, but many of these were interpreted selectively and to the detriment of traditional civil society organizations (Salamanca 2004). The eventual defeat of Chávez's constitutional reforms in December 2007 might be seen as a popular reversal of this trend, but this was a very large package of reforms that included significant, controversial attempts to alter the nature of the democratic regime – and it lost by only a narrow margin.

[9] The clear exception here is the Communal Councils, which attracted as many as 8 million participants by late 2008. However, the Communal Councils are unique in terms of their high level of government funding and political functions. See Hawkins (forthcoming), López Maya (2008a), and García-Guadilla (2007b).

TABLE 4.1. *Union density in Latin America*

Country	1982	1998	Change	Percent Change
Argentina	42	22	−20	−47
Bolivia	25	9	−16	−65
Peru	21	6	−15	−73
Venezuela	26	14	−12	−47
Uruguay	21	12	−9	−43
Colombia	9	6	−3	−36
Mexico	25	22	−3	−11
Honduras	8	6	−2	−30
Ecuador	11	9	−2	−21
Costa Rica	13	12	−1	−9
Chile	12	13	1	8
El Salvador	4	5	1	28
Dominican Republic	12	14	2	19
Brazil	15	24	9	57

Source: Roberts and Wibbels (1999).

than any other party on its alliance with the national labor federation, the Confederación de Trabajadores de Venezuela (CTV). Indeed, survey data show that the urban informal sector became one of Chávez's chief bases of support (Canache 2004). At the same time as these socioeconomic transformations, new campaign technologies emerged that reduced politicians' need for grassroots party organization. Television and political consultants were first used successfully by Pérez in his 1973 presidential campaign (Interview v03b.01 8 October 1999). As early as the mid-1980s, party leaders began advocating the use of opinion polls to sound out voters on the issues (for example, COPEI had an ongoing relationship with the market research firm Consultores 21). And in the 1990s, polls became an instrument of candidate selection, with leaders in all parties – including MVR – using them to justify the selection of candidates made by party leadership (Interview v07.02 23 November 1999; Interview v12.01 13 December 1999; Interview v00.01 26 November 1999).

However, this theory becomes less satisfying once we look at the evidence beyond Venezuela. Table 4.1 presents data on union density in 14 Latin American countries in 1982 and 1998, a key indicator of the strength of the class cleavage. As can be seen, all countries that suffered breakdowns of their party systems did experience significant declines in union density: Peru, Venezuela, and (a more recent potential case of breakdown) Bolivia all had a nearly 50 percent reduction in union density prior to the breakdown of their party systems.[10] Yet, not all countries that experienced declines in union

---

[10] Ecuador, another recent case of potential party system breakdown and populist movements, had a much smaller decline in its union membership, but only because the level of union density was low to begin with.

membership also had a breakdown of their party system, and the timing of union decline and party system breakdown varies widely. For example, Argentina and Uruguay had large declines in union membership without a collapse like the one seen in Venezuela. And while Venezuela's breakdown took place at approximately the same time as its decline in union membership, Peru's occurred a few years after its decline in unionization started in the mid-1980s, and the current breakdown in Bolivia came fully 10 years after its union membership bottomed out. If the table included data from the 1970s, Chile would probably also stand out as a case of declining union density without party system breakdown. Union membership declined significantly under the military government of Augusto Pinochet, yet during and after the subsequent transition to democracy, most of the traditional parties quickly reconstituted themselves. Some other factors must have come into play.

Finally, the *economic voting* explanation resonates with important trends; indeed, of the three explanations mentioned here, it is the one best supported by quantitative studies of aggregate and survey data (c.f. Canache 2002; Coppedge 2005). Venezuela's economic crisis during the 15 years before the rise of Chávez was prolonged and severe, even by Latin American standards. Despite occasional upturns in world oil prices, by the late 1990s per capita oil revenue was about one-fourth of what it had been during the first oil boom (Ministerio de Energía y Minas, various dates). The government attempted to find other sources of income, but between 1984 and 1997 it had to reduce its per capita spending by about 25 percent (IESA 2002). As a result, by 1990, real per capita GDP was lower than it had been since the transition to democracy in 1958, and over the subsequent decade it largely failed to grow. Unemployment fluctuated considerably over this period, but from 1983 to 1998 it averaged 10.1 percent, in contrast with 5.9 percent during 1970–82; at the same time (as already mentioned), employment in the informal sector dramatically increased.

All of this makes the economic voting argument a potentially good explanation for the breakdown of the party system; however, this argument is much less effective in explaining the precise choice of leadership that followed. Why did voters prefer Chávez over other candidates, most of whom were also independent, and many of whom (such as Salas Römer, Sáez, and Arias Cárdenas) had reasonable track records in municipal and gubernatorial office? Economic theories overlook discourse, treating political behavior as a kind of instrumental choice geared to justifying an exogenous cost–benefit calculation of material interests. As we will see later, the discourse of the Chávez government had unique consequences for areas as diverse and significant as political organization and public policy, and it stands to reason that rational voters anticipated these consequences and selected candidates based not only on their prospective economic performance but also on the ideas that motivated their choice of policy. Certainly a more institutionalized, pluralist candidate would have been less risky and would have focused more carefully on the economic policy and institutional reforms that a narrowly materialistic perspective on the crisis warranted. Populist leaders such as Chávez are often vague about their economic policies, demanding a blank check for revolutionary reforms that may diverge from the interests of some voters, as Chávez's reforms did with his gradual turn to the left. What is it about this discourse that an economic voter would have found appealing?

The best attempt to grapple with this choice of a radical leader is the cognitive-psychological explanation offered by Weyland (2003). In a critique of simple economic voting approaches to Chavismo and the breakdown of Venezuela's party system, Weyland applies Kahnemann and Tversky's prospect theory (1979, 2000), which argues that individuals confronting situations of loss become more risk acceptant than individuals confronting potential gains. Weyland suggests that in analogous fashion, voters confronting prospective losses – such as an economic crisis – seek "alternative leaders" rather than an existing party (Weyland 2003, 837). Because Venezuela's economic crisis was especially severe and prolonged, voters became highly risk acceptant and were more willing to support a radical outsider such as Chávez than the experienced political insiders that they had previously favored; in fact, the more radical the alternative, the more appealing he or she became.

This cognitive twist on economic voting arguments is a helpful contribution to the debate because it forces us to confront the positive content of Chavismo. Voters did more than reject the old party system; they chose a particular replacement with extraordinary qualities. However, as we will see in the quantitative analysis that follows, this particular argument also fails to hold up under closer empirical scrutiny. The cognitive explanation ultimately misses the unique quality of populist discourse and the noneconomic roots of Venezuela's crisis of legitimacy.

Evidence for the Normative Explanation

In contrast, both the breakdown of the party system and the rise of Chavismo can plausibly be traced to broad systematic corruption in Venezuela – corruption in both the behavioral and subjective senses. Like citizens of many countries in Latin America, Venezuelans have confronted significant levels of petty corruption and a "weak state" (Karl 1997) since as far back as the colonial era (Pérez Perdomo 1995; Rey 1998). Even after the transition to democracy in 1958, bureaucratic graft, kickbacks on government contracts, nepotism, and rewards to party faithful were endemic. Under Punto Fijo, the judiciary did not always work quickly or fairly and was highly partisan, and government agencies and poverty programs sometimes failed to deliver services efficiently or with equity, tending instead to become part of clientelistic networks that rewarded citizens based on partisan support (Coppedge 1993; Pérez Perdomo 1995; Cupolo 1998; Rey 1998).

Yet, the first three democratic administrations after the transition of 1958 – those of Betancourt (AD), Raúl Leoni (AD), and Caldera (COPEI) – were generally regarded as competent and honest. They came to power on the heels of a discredited military government that engaged in the most egregious forms of corruption and had witnessed and struggled against the excesses of even earlier authoritarian regimes. Betancourt in particular was well known as a staunch critic of corruption (Pérez Perdomo 1995, 14). Much of the petty corruption at the time was seen as a minor, even acceptable practice for Venezuelans, and what we would today consider questionable procedures (such as the provision of public works to partisan clientele) were conducted under tight party discipline with ostensibly ideological objectives.

All of this began to change in the 1970s. The extraordinary revenues of the first oil boom and the lax attitude of the first Pérez government opened the doors to corruption on a scale not seen since the worst days of the old authoritarian regimes (Karl 1997; Rey 1998). Corrupt practices became more venal – truly corrupt – shifting from the well-meaning clientelism and credit-claiming activities of the parties to mere personal enrichment. The types of corruption became grand, implicating the highest officials and vast swaths of public administration and society in billionaire schemes involving government concessions, procurement, currency exchange regimes, and government loans (Rey 1998, 114–15). And finally, corruption went unpunished. Subsequent administrations proved incapable of or unwilling to address severe problems even as they became increasingly noticeable. While all candidates raised the issue of corruption in their campaigns beginning in the 1978 presidential race, once in office they did little more than conduct a few high-profile investigations and arrests, usually without any subsequent convictions.

The increase in corruption corresponded with the rise of increasingly diverse, activist media in Venezuela toward the end of the 1980s, with multiple new outlets and a strong sense of their role as political actors and defenders of democracy (Mayobre 2002). Journalists made corruption a cause célèbre, giving constant coverage to major scandals and the judicial proceedings that followed, such as the *Sierra Nevada* scandal of the first Pérez administration (involving kickbacks on the government purchase of a freighter); the intromissions of President Jaime Lusinchi's (1984–8) secretary and mistress into government decision making; the gross abuse of funds by high officials in the exchange rate agency RECADI of the 1980s; and the failure of the Banco Latino in 1994, which implicated government officials and precipitated a nationwide banking crisis. Multiple quasi-scholarly books documented its extent, with sensationalistic titles such as (in English) *How Much to Buy a Judge?* (Ojeda 1995), *LatinoMafia: History of the Corruption of the System* (Pantín 1997), *RECADI: The Great Scam* (Beroes 1990), and the highly regarded, three-volume work *The Dictionary of Corruption* (Consorcio 1989, 1992).

As a result of this increase in corruption and the amount of coverage it received, the problem of corruption became a "reified villain" for average Venezuelans (Márquez 2003, 209). The public often complained about it and by the early 1990s considered it one of the country's most significant problems (Templeton 1995; Zapata 1996). Thus, corruption became not just an objective problem, but a subjective one. We can see this trend more clearly by considering answers to the question "In your opinion, what are the most important national problems right now?" which was asked in slightly different ways in several key national surveys from the early 1970s to the late 1990s. The data are summarized in Table 4.2 with response categories related to corruption in boldface.

As of 1973, before the end of Caldera's first term and the beginning of the oil boom, data from the Baloyra-Martz survey indicate that corruption was still nowhere on the public agenda. Designers of the survey never bothered to include corruption in the list of response categories, and few if any respondents (who were unaware of the categories being used) indicated corruption either – only 6.6 percent gave an answer ("other") that could not be coded using the categories in the survey instrument; most responses referred to the economy. In the Baloyra-Torres survey of 1983, this situation seems to have changed and we have our first hint that corruption is becoming an issue. Using a nearly identical open-ended question with the same number of response categories as in 1973, most respondents again mention the economy, but now 2.6 percent mention "the government" and another 1.5 percent "corruption." By the time of the Canache survey in 1995, corruption has become a significant concern.[11] In this survey, responses to the "national problem" question are coded more loosely into 39 categories. The economic category is again the most significant set of responses, and in second place is "personal security." But close behind are several responses regarding corruption and political crisis: "corruption" receives 8.3 percent and "moral crisis" receives 1.7 percent; these plus a few related categories ("political crisis," "politicians," "crisis," "administration of justice," "government," "government irresponsiveness," some of these not shown) together account for almost 18 percent of responses. Finally, in the 1998 RedPol survey, corruption becomes one of the most significant issues for voters. The "national problem" question is asked somewhat differently in this survey, making it more difficult to interpret the results.[12] Nevertheless, nearly 53 percent of respondents mention corruption, making it the second highest response in the survey, in a virtual tie with an economic category, "unemployment."

Critics may question whether these growing perceptions reflected reality. Were public fears simply being stoked by increasingly independent media and

---

[11] The 1993 CIEPA/DOXA survey failed to include this question. However, it did include a question that asked whether "democracy can be fixed" and, if so, "what needs to be fixed first." Of the respondents who felt that democracy could be fixed and gave some answer (about 62%), "corruption" was the top response, receiving 17% of the total 1,499 responses. Bear in mind that the question's wording probably elicited responses biased toward political rather than economic concerns.

[12] Although it uses similar wording, it shows respondents a list of 15 categories and then asks respondents to choose 3. The survey datafile indicates only whether a category was mentioned and not the order of the respondents' answers. Thus, we cannot be certain whether corruption is the top priority for the individuals who mentioned it.

TABLE 4.2. *Responses to "country's most important problem"*

Survey	1973 Baloyra-Martz	1983 Baloyra-Torres	1995 Canache	1998 RedPol
Question	"In your opinion, what are the most important national problems right now? ... And which of these is the most important national problem?"	"What do you believe is the most important problem in the country right now?"	"In your opinion, what is the most important national problem right now?"	"As you see it, what is the most important thing the next government should do?"
Format	Open-ended response; worker categorizes response using prescribed list	Open-ended response; categorized later by the survey author	Open-ended response categorized later by the survey author	Closed-ended response; respondent chooses three from the list; no ranking
No. of categories	13	13	39	15
Corruption a category?	No	Yes	Yes	Yes
Categories and percent mentioned (categories with less than 1% of responses not shown)	Cost of living 37.6	Unemployment 26.5	Economic crisis 28.3	Reduce unemployment 53.3
	Unemployment 17.8	Economic situation 16.9	Crime 18.2	**Fight corruption** 52.9
	Education 9.7	Cost of living 13.9	Inflation 9.8	Improve education 49.2
	Other 6.5	Foreign debt 9.3	**Corruption** 8.3	Improve hospitals 41.4
	Crime 6.3	Devaluation 5.5	Education crisis 4.8	Combat inflation 33.7
	Lack of food 5.4	Crime 5.3	Poverty 3.9	Improve quality of life 20.0
	Housing 4.1	Education 4.2	Monetary crisis 3.9	Guarantee human rights 9.1
	Poverty 3.4	**Government** 2.6	Unemployment 3.5	Increase wages 7.4

Survey	1973 Baloyra-Martz		1983 Baloyra-Torres		1995 Canache		1998 RedPol	
	Agriculture	2.8	Housing	2.5	Political crisis	3.1	Promote decentralization	6.9
	Abandoned children	2.2	**Corruption**	1.5	Crisis	2.2	Reform constitution	6.5
	Oil nationalization/ prices	1.2	Health, hospitals	1.2	Socioeconomic crisis	2.0	Reduce public employees	5.5
	Health/hospitals	1.1	Poverty	1.1	**Moral crisis**	1.7	Deport undocumented immigrants	3.3
					Politicians	1.2	Promote private business	2.9
					Health crisis	1.0	Protect environment	2.1
							Privatize public firms	1.7

Note: Categories related to corruption are in boldface.
Source: Author's own calculation, based on the surveys noted in the table (Baloyra and Martz 1979; Institute of Political Science 1983; Canache 1995; Red Universitaria 1999).

by politicians eager to distinguish themselves from competitors? A few of the politicians I interviewed (almost all of them from COPEI) contended that these perceptions were in fact exaggerated and responded to the frustrated expectations of citizens with a rentier mentality, not to the demands of entrepreneurs hungry for the rule of law and better protection of property rights. The real problem was the decline in oil revenues after the extraordinary highs of the 1970s and the cutback in government largesse (Interview v06.01 1999; Interview v20.01 1999; Interview v01c.01 1999). Indeed, early survey data and historical evidence indicate that the line between public and private was still a little unclear in Venezuela (Pérez Perdomo 1995). Other well-known survey data reaffirm the unrealistic demands of Venezuelans for a paternalistic state that would distribute the country's supposedly vast mineral wealth. Most Venezuelans at the time believed that their country was rich; that this wealth should have been distributed among all citizens; that if Venezuela had been run well, the wealth would have been more than enough for everyone; and that once the corrupt government was removed, the country would again become rich (Zapata 1996, 161–2).[13] Perhaps no government could have satisfied these demands over the long term and avoided being labeled as corrupt.

Nevertheless, three facts argue against this interpretation. First, standard corruption perception indexes show very high levels of corruption in Venezuela during this period. Of course, we lack any replicable quantitative data on corruption during the earlier years of the Punto Fijo regime that could give us a solid reference point, but by the mid-1990s, when the first of these cumulative indexes was being constructed by Transparency International and the World Bank's Governance Matters division, Venezuela was consistently found near the bottom rung of countries. From 1996 to 1998 the country scored in the lowest quintile of the scale in both indexes, and in 1998 it ranked 77th out of 85 countries in Transparency International's index, the most corrupt country in Latin America after Paraguay and Honduras. As I have already indicated, of course, this measure alone is imperfect because it primarily incorporates subjective assessments.

Second, there is now generally wide agreement in the academic literature that corruption *was* rampant and constituted a growing problem by the 1990s. Scholars were initially slow to recognize the existence or consequences of corruption in Venezuela and, like other skeptics, tended to dismiss it as the product of popular paranoia and overzealous journalism. Early academic works analyzing the institutional failures of the Punto Fijo regime barely mentioned the word (see Coppedge 1994; Kornblith and Levine 1995; McCoy et al. 1995; Crisp and Levine 1998; Crisp 2000). Yet, by the late 1990s and especially after the accession of Chávez to power, the mainstream academic literature began to acknowledge the reality of corruption and, more rarely, cite it as a

---

[13] This widely known syllogism is generally attributed to Alfredo Keller, an associate of sociologist Roberto Zapata and fellow founder of the Venezuelan public opinion firm Consultores 21.

Party System Breakdown and Chavismo

cause of party system breakdown. Particularly detailed analyses of corruption were carried out by Templeton and Pérez Perdomo in the volume edited by Goodman et al. (1995), and Rey gives a historically rich chronology in the volume by Canache and Kulishek (1998). More recent but sketchier references to the system's widespread corruption can be found in McCoy (2004, 275) and Ellner and Hellinger (2003). The clearest mention to date, that of Coppedge (2005), suggests that corruption was a significant cause of the breakdown that arose out of the objective policy failures of the Punto Fijo regime.[14]

Finally, the politicians from the traditional parties themselves acknowledged corruption as one of the principal weaknesses of the old party system. One of the questions I asked in my interviews in 1999 was why respondents thought the party system had broken down. While leaders of COPEI were less likely to admit the significance of corruption (as indicated previously), most leaders of both traditional parties saw corruption as a major cause of the breakdown. Interviewees told a story similar to the one already presented, arguing that Venezuela's first three post-transition governments were relatively honest and effective, but that subsequent governments became increasingly tolerant of venal behavior that reached alarming proportions (Interview v16c.01 1999; Interview v01d.01 1999). They claimed that starting in the late 1960s, the parties began to forsake their ideological roots and became largely "pragmatic" (Interview v01d.01 1999) – electoral machines with little concern for the party program beyond continuing support for democracy, pursuing "power for the sake of power" (Interview v18c.01 1999). Ideological debate and training largely ceased, and the parties' youth organizations were allowed to languish as early as the 1960s (Interview v16d.01; Interview v18c.01 1999; Interview v19.01 1999). New generations of party activists were increasingly attracted by economic opportunities rather than because of their idealism, and the most able young reformers were prevented from moving very high in the party ranks (Interview v01d.01 1999; Interview v01c.01 1999; Interview v06b.01 1999; Interview v16c.01 1999).

These politicians offered a variety of explanations for the decline in the parties' programmatic zeal, including the opportunities for rent-seeking within the Venezuelan state, the parties' top-down structure and lifetime appointments of party executives, the divisive experience of ideological debate in the 1960s, and the early achievement of the parties' original program of democratic and economic reforms.[15] Yet, the important point is that they saw the

---

[14] Coppedge's analysis of the connection between the economic crisis and the breakdown of the party system is excellent. Unfortunately, he gives only secondary emphasis to corruption and never offers it the same thorough empirical treatment that he does the economic crisis. He also never makes it clear why a movement like Chavismo would be so well suited to address the crisis, that is, why its populism would make it particularly appealing to Venezuelans.

[15] Specifically, according to interviewees, the parties' clientelistic structures and statist economic policies were partly to blame; they created easy opportunities for enrichment and patterns of rent-seeking behavior that undermined the need for programmatic messages (Interview v06.01 1999; Interview v01d.01 1999; Interview v01c.01 1999; Interview v16c.01

collapse of their parties rooted not just in a sense of policy failure driven by outside events or the parties' incompetence, but in the "ethical failure" of their political class to combat real failures of their political institutions (Interview v18c.01 1999).

A QUANTITATIVE TEST: VOTE CHOICE IN 1998

The preceding data give a sense of the aggregate correlation of key variables at the national level in Venezuela, together with qualitative, individual-level evidence from political elites and voters indicating that the breakdown of the traditional party system and the rise of Chavismo were normatively motivated responses to the violation of the rule of law. Furthermore, we know from the analysis of discourse in Chapter 3 that Chávez consistently responded to these political failures with strong condemnations of the old party elite and calls for deep institutional reform. However, did concerns about corruption make voters appreciate and value the populist discourse of Chávez? Or was a vote for Chávez driven primarily by isolated considerations of economic performance, structural changes, and the lack of truly democratic institutions? Let us now look more carefully at the individual level of the voters to see if we can better substantiate these causal mechanisms.

To do this, I revisit the analysis of Weyland (2003), which models vote choice during the 1998 presidential election using the results of the 1998 RedPol preelection survey. As mentioned earlier, Weyland's analysis emphasizes a cognitive, nonrational mechanism for the choice of Chávez, which suggests that Venezuelans were more willing to support a radical leader because they were in the "realm of losses" induced by a prolonged economic crisis and hence were more risk acceptant. My dependent variable is expected vote choice, measured with a sequence of two questions that ask respondents if they plan on voting in the election and for whom they will vote. As mentioned in Chapter 2, respondents' expected turnout (74.8 percent said they would vote and had some candidate preference[16]) was higher than the actual turnout in the election (59 percent of registered voters, including null ballots),

---

1999; Interview v07.01 1999). The parties' top-down structure was also a problem. Party leaders in the executive committees remained ensconced in lifetime positions that prevented younger reformist elements from winning power (Interview v01d.01 1999; Interview v16c.01 1999; Interview v06b.01 1999; Interview v01c.01 1999). Party leaders also preferred to avoid the divisive experiences of ideological discussion that previous party congresses had provoked and possibly found it difficult to relate to younger generations with newer ideologies, such as liberation theology or the ideas of the new left (Interview v18c.01 1999; Interview v16c.01 1999; Interview v16d.01 1999). Finally, the parties' old program was completed. Their ability to successfully stimulate economic growth and implement their original programs of democratization and state-led development from 1958, culminating in the nationalization of the oil industry in the 1970s, left many party leaders without any relevant vision for change (Interview v19.01 1999; Interview v16d.01 1999).

[16] Another 9.4% of respondents said they would vote but had no preference.

but within this group the preferences concerning presidential candidates were roughly similar to those in the actual election.[17]

In order to test the economic voting argument, I include several variables from Weyland's original model. These are prospective and retrospective economic assessments, both pocketbook and sociotropic; socioeconomic status and education; two measures of issue positions regarding privatization and state interventionism; and satisfaction with existing democracy. The only change from Weyland's model is that I disaggregate the measures of prospective economic assessments into their three response categories ("better," "the same," and "worse") by turning the responses into three dummy variables, where 1 means the respondent gave that answer and 0 means he or she gave a different answer; "don't know/no answer" becomes the reference category. I initially did this to increase the number of observations in the model, from about 900 in the original model to over 1,300. As we will see, though, disaggregating these responses also allows us to examine Weyland's cognitive argument more closely.

In order to test the structuralist argument, I include two other variables from Weyland's original model that partially get at the effects of globalization and a weak, rentier state on voting behavior. These are *Education* and *Class*. However, in order to perform a more meaningful test of the structuralist argument, I run an additional version of the model with a variable called *Informal* that interacts education, housing, and union membership. Specifically, it considers three variables: one measuring the response to a question asking "Do you belong to a trade union, labor confederation, or other association?" (1 = yes and 2 = no); another recording the type of dwelling of the respondent (recorded without comment by the interviewer and used to construct the *Class* indicator); and another indicating the level of education of the respondent. Respondents are coded 1 if they do not belong to a union or a similar association, have no more than a grade school education, and live in either public housing or improvised structures; otherwise, they are coded 0.[18]

Finally, in order to test the normative theory of populism and present a more standard vote-choice model, I include several sets of variables not considered by Weyland. To gauge candidate assessment and simultaneously measure the effects of Chávez's populist discourse on the vote, I consider answers to the survey question "What in your opinion is the chief characteristic that the next President should have?" Each of the 14 possible responses is coded as a dummy variable, with 1 indicating that the characteristic was mentioned.

---

[17] Among respondents who said they would vote and had some preference, Chávez was first with 48.0%, followed by Enrique Salas Römer with 37.7%, Luis Alfaro Ucero with 10.1%, and Irene Saez with 2.5%. This compares with totals in the actual election of 56.2%, 39.9%, 0.4%, and 2.8%, respectively.

[18] A version of the model with these three variables considered separately tends not to have as large or significant an effect. In addition, union membership in isolation is actually a factor that increases the probability of voting for Chávez. Thus, Chávez receives support both from union members and from nonmembers who are poor and less educated.

Five responses are directly relevant for the final model: "be honest," which indicates leadership qualities associated with the populist message; "be independent," "be young," and "be a man," which refer more vaguely to the candidate's capacity to institute change and could be taken as support for either the cognitive theory or my own; and "have successful experience as a public functionary," which better embodies a pluralist response with its respect for existing institutions.

To gauge issue stances, and again to measure more directly the effects of populist discourse on the vote for Chávez, I consider two other sets of questions. The first set is drawn from the question mentioned previously regarding what the respondent considers "the most important thing that the next government should do" and is thus mostly a measure of issue salience. While several responses touch on economic issues (specifically, "reduce unemployment" and "combat inflation"), two others capture more clearly the unique moral aspects of populist discourse, particularly in Venezuela during this period: "fight against corruption" and "reform the constitution." The drive for a constituent assembly and the creation of a new constitution figured prominently in Chávez's campaign and were widely seen as radical means of altering the failures of the Punto Fijo system; today the new constitution remains an important Chavista symbol of this victory of the people.[19] Responses are again coded as a series of dummy variables, with 1 indicating that the issue was mentioned. The second set includes questions on actual issue positions. Besides the economic issues in Weyland's original model (privatization and state intervention), these questions ask whether PDVSA should remain state-owned and what, if any, constitutional reform should be carried out. I recode the first question so that 1 indicates leaving PDVSA as is, 3 indicates privatizing the oil company, and 2 indicates "don't know," which I consider the neutral category. I leave the second question as is, with higher values indicating increasingly radical reform (1 = none, 2 = reformed by Congress, 3 = reformed by a constituent assembly).

---

[19] Constitutional reform or even the creation of a new constitution is not inherently populist, and some recent constitutional reforms in Latin America have been enacted by presidents who were by all accounts not populist, such as in Colombia in 1991 (under César Gaviria) and in Bolivia in the mid-1990s (under Gonzalo Sánchez de Lozada). Indeed, in Venezuela, discussions about constitutional reform had been part of the national political debate since at least the 1980s, with the establishment of the Presidential Commission for State Reform under Lusinchi (COPRE 1989). However, in Venezuela, any efforts at constitutional reform were quickly abandoned by the traditional parties, and the demand for a constituent assembly became one of the key platform planks of Chávez and his fellow conspirators as early as the 1992 attempted coup. As the quote at the beginning of this chapter suggests, the old constitution was seen by Chavistas as the foundation of the Punto Fijo system and the embodiment of its corruption. Chávez's eventual reform strategy – press early for a constituent assembly, use new elections to win firm control of government, press forward with socioeconomic reforms – has since been imitated by both Evo Morales and Rafael Correa. Thus, while it would be a mistake to always and only associate constitutional reform with populist movements, it would also be a mistake not to associate constitutional reform with Chavismo's brand of populism in the late 1990s.

Unfortunately, few questions in the survey get directly at the deepening of democracy argument. The question regarding "the most important thing that the next government should do" does include three related responses that each touch on this argument. These are "promote decentralization," "guarantee respect for human rights," and "protect and restore the environment," issues frequently associated with postmaterialist values and the push for democratic reform in Venezuela during the 1980s and 1990s (Inglehart 1990, 1997; García 1992; Mascareño 2000). All of these are again coded as dummy variables. An additional question asks whether or not the respondent has "participated with other people in the solution of some problem in your *barrio* or neighborhood" (1 = yes, 0 = no). This provides a behavioral measure of whether the respondent actually participates in grassroots efforts that have democratic potential. While these questions tap into the issue of decentralization, none of them specifically gauges postmaterialist attitudes or feelings about the potential merits of participatory democracy, and they should be considered halfway measures at best.[20]

In the model, I also control for partisan identity by using the response to two questions: which party the respondents are members of or sympathize with and which one they lean toward if they call themselves "independent." Because weak partisan attachment usually has the same effect on vote choice as strong attachment, I combine the two responses into a single dummy variable for each party, with a positive response indicating identification with the party. I include only responses for the traditional parties – AD, COPEI, MAS, PPT, and LCR – and omit those for the personalistic Convergencia, Proyecto Venezuela, and MVR, for which partisan sympathy was almost certainly driven by candidate preference rather than any institutional identity (sympathy with Proyecto Venezuela and MVR is essentially a proxy for vote choice). Furthermore, I combine the responses for PPT and LCR into a single category in order to avoid statistical problems with the small number of observations in each (seven for PPT, five for LCR), because these parties were the product of a very recent split and both still overwhelmingly supported Chávez in this election.

Together these variables represent a well-specified vote choice model and give us a good chance of testing all four of our key theories in Venezuela. For greater comparability with Weyland's results, all of the models are run using multinomial logit rather than multinomial probit. While this goes against the current wisdom in the vote choice literature (Alvarez and Nagler 1998; Lacey and Monson 2002), the difference between the two techniques turns out to be very slight. Rerunning the models using multinomial probit fails to alter the

---

[20] The survey includes an additional question asking whether the respondent prefers "a democracy like we have" or "a dictatorship," but this presents a false dichotomy that reveals little about attitudes toward different kinds of democratic reform. Another series of questions asks about preferences concerning various regime types, but it uses a rather unorthodox list of options ("social democracy," "communism," "socialism") whose precise meaning is unclear.

direction of the coefficients or dramatically affect their statistical significance, and a Hausman test shows that the Independent of Irrelevant Alternatives assumption largely holds in this model.[21] To facilitate interpretation, the baseline category in all specifications of the model is the expected vote for Chávez. As in Weyland's model, the other three outcomes are Salas Römer, other candidates, and abstention, the last of which combines those who are not voting, don't know who to vote for, or don't give an answer. Breaking down the abstention category does not significantly affect the results for Salas Römer. While I provide results for all three choices in the tables, I focus the discussion on the results for Salas Römer because this comparison is the most relevant one for our different theories.

Results: Candidate Attributes and Issues

In order to explore the data more thoroughly and reduce the large number of variables in the full specification of the model, I perform two initial analyses considering the set of candidate attributes and the set of issue responses in isolation. Indicators that are statistically significant here (at $p \leq .10$) are included in the full model later.

Table 4.3 contains the results for issue responses (salience and issue positions). Let us begin with Model 1, which considers only the issue salience question. Each entry for this model indicates 1 of the 15 possible responses to the question regarding "the most important thing that the next government should do." The first column summarizes how many respondents mentioned the issue and gives us a general sense of salience; readers should bear in mind that respondents could mention three issues, so the numbers total more than 100 percent. In order to assess which of these issues had partisan relevance, in the second column I report the results of a multinomial logit regression with vote choice as the dependent variable. In this set of results, as in all that follow, negative coefficients indicate that the variable increases the probability of voting for Chávez, while positive coefficients indicate that the variable increases the probability of choosing that particular alternative (Salas Römer, another candidate, or abstention).

The first result worth noting in Model 1 is that *Fight Corruption* is the only strong issue with at least a moderately significant relationship to vote choice. Not only do respondents mention this task the second most often,

---

[21] The Hausman test is run by dropping each of the possible vote choice categories and then comparing the new logit models with the original one with all categories. When dropping either the Other Candidates or Abstention responses in the fully specified model, the difference is not statistically significant by common standards ($p < .26$ and $p < .15$). When the Salas Römer category is dropped, however, the difference is significant at the $p < .09$ level. Thus, there is some slight justification for using a probit estimation. Again, though, because the coefficients and standard errors for the Chávez–Salas Römer comparison end up largely unchanged when I run the probit estimations, I retain the logit version for greater comparability with Weyland's model.

TABLE 4.3. *Multinomial logit of vote choice (issues)*

Variable	Percentage Who Mentioned	Model 1 Salas Römer	Model 1 Other Candidate	Model 1 Abstention	Mean Response Salas Römer	Model 2 Other Candidate	Model 2 Abstention
Issue Salience							
Reduce Unemployment	53.3	−0.14 (0.20)	−0.04 (0.30)	−0.45* (0.22)	−0.11 (0.26)	0.04 (0.35)	−0.33 (0.28)
Combat Inflation	33.7	−0.15 (0.21)	−0.18 (0.30)	−0.81*** (0.22)	0.01 (0.26)	−0.06 (0.35)	−0.44 (0.28)
Fight Corruption	52.9	−0.43* (0.20)	−0.27 (0.30)	−1.01*** (0.22)	−0.27 (0.27)	−0.00 (0.36)	−0.66* (0.29)
Promote Decentralization	6.9	0.35 (0.30)	0.81* (0.41)	−0.72* (0.35)	0.49 (0.37)	0.92* (0.47)	−0.29 (0.41)
Improve Education	49.2	−0.30 (0.20)	−0.03 (0.28)	−0.50* (0.22)	−0.11 (0.26)	0.07 (0.33)	−0.40 (0.28)
Improve Hospitals	41.4	−0.28 (0.20)	−0.16 (0.29)	−0.54* (0.22)	−0.15 (0.26)	−0.05 (0.35)	−0.21 (0.28)
Reduce Public Employees	5.5	−0.36 (0.33)	−0.60 (0.51)	−0.81* (0.35)	−0.27 (0.38)	−0.33 (0.54)	−0.75* (0.43)
Reform Constitution	6.5	−1.74*** (0.36)	−1.82** (0.57)	−1.50*** (0.33)	−1.39** (0.43)	−1.46* (0.68)	−0.95* (0.39)
Promote Private Business	2.9	0.11 (0.40)	0.11 (0.59)	−0.41 (0.45)	0.45 (0.48)	0.53 (0.61)	0.20 (0.52)

(continued)

TABLE 4.3. (continued)

Variable	Percentage Who Mentioned	Model 1 Salas Römer	Model 1 Other Candidate	Model 1 Abstention	Mean Response	Model 2 Salas Römer	Model 2 Other Candidate	Model 2 Abstention
Privatizate Public Firms	1.7	−0.93* (0.53)	−31.80*** (0.37)	−1.34* (0.56)		−0.87 (0.71)	−33.53*** (0.55)	−1.19 (0.77)
Guarantee Human Rights	9.1	−0.12 (0.27)	−0.31 (0.42)	−0.33 (0.28)		0.17 (0.33)	0.02 (0.47)	0.11 (0.35)
Improve Quality of Life	20.0	0.09 (0.22)	0.11 (0.33)	−0.40* (0.24)		0.13 (0.29)	0.11 (0.39)	−0.07 (0.31)
Deport Undocumented Immigrants	3.3	−0.27 (0.40)	−0.08 (0.55)	−0.58 (0.40)		0.10 (0.48)	0.25 (0.68)	−0.01 (0.49)
Protect Environment	2.1	−0.15 (0.46)	−0.54 (0.81)	−0.26 (0.47)		−0.49 (0.64)	−0.03 (0.77)	0.23 (0.55)
Increase Wages	7.4	−0.05 (0.29)	0.08 (0.40)	−0.65* (0.33)		−0.05 (0.35)	0.04 (0.45)	−0.52 (0.39)
Issue Position								
Privatization					2.2	−0.05 (0.13)	0.07 (0.16)	0.22 (0.14)
State Intervention in Economy					1.3	0.05 (0.13)	−0.01 (0.19)	0.25* (0.13)

Variable	Percentage Who Mentioned	Model 1			Mean Response	Model 2		
		Salas Römer	Other Candidate	Abstention		Salas Römer	Other Candidate	Abstention
Constitutional Reform		0.50 (0.49)	−0.80 (0.73)		2.1	−1.28*** (0.11)	−1.30*** (0.14)	−1.10*** (0.12)
Privatization of PDVSA				1.58** (0.54)	1.1	0.49* (0.29)	−0.44 (0.48)	−0.95*** (0.29)
Constant						2.40** (0.85)	1.87 (1.16)	1.17 (0.89)
N	1500					1,263		
Chi²	18,118.21***					1,4011.01***		
Pseudo R²	0.03					0.10		
Log likelihood	−1915.34					−1,483.61		

Unless otherwise indicated, entries are logit coefficients (robust standard errors).
*$p < .10$; **$p < .01$; ***$p < .001$.
Source: Author's calculation, based on the 1998 RedPol survey (Red Universitaria 1999).

but respondents mentioning corruption are more likely to prefer Chávez. The second result is that the salience of economic issues, while very high across the electorate, is not something that distinguishes the choice of candidates; both Chávez and Salas Römer supporters are equally likely to see *Reduce Unemployment, Combat Inflation, Improve Quality of Life*, and *Improve Hospitals* as important tasks for the next government. Together, these results provide initial support for the normative explanation. Most citizens perceive the economy as a significant policy challenge, but it is the perception of corruption as an important problem that makes them more likely to vote for Chávez.

A small set of less salient issues also has an impact on vote choice. The strongest is clearly *Reform Constitution*, which is a statistically significant predictor of vote for Chávez even though only 6.5 percent of respondents mentioned it as an important issue; these respondents overwhelmingly favor Chávez. Given the strong link between the push for a constituent assembly and Chávez's populist discourse in the 1990s, this seems to provide additional support for the normative argument. The other partisan issue is *Privatize Public Firms*, which has marginal statistical significance but is unlikely to have substantive significance in our full model because of the very low frequency with which it is mentioned by respondents (less than 2 percent).[22] Importantly, none of the issues associated (loosely) with the concern for deeper democracy – *Promote Decentralization, Guarantee Human Rights*, and *Protect Environment* – plays a strong role in distinguishing among the candidates. Not only are these issues unimportant for most Venezuelan voters generally, but they fail to affect the choice of Chávez over Salas Römer.

Model 2 in Table 4.3 combines these salience responses with a few others on specific issue positions, that is, questions that ask what the government should do rather than which issues are important. As the summary statistics for these additional variables indicate, Venezuelans tended to be slightly against privatization (the modal response by far is "privatize industries that work poorly," but a large minority resist any privatization); strongly in favor of greater state intervention (most respondents mentioned healthcare and education as top priorities in a follow-up question); evenly divided on the way to conduct constitutional reform, but with about two-thirds preferring some kind of reform versus no reform at all; and overwhelmingly against privatizing PDVSA. How do these new indicators correlate with vote choice? We already know from Weyland's analysis that privatization and state intervention generally are not partisan issues in this election, and these results are repeated here; voters for

---

[22] The sign on this coefficient indicates that voters most concerned about privatization were actually more likely to vote for Chávez. These voters were almost entirely in *favor* of privatization. This surprising result may reflect the initial support that Chávez had among some supporters of neoliberal reforms, who saw his strong leadership and stance against the old party system as the only solution for the country's economic problems. Indeed, despite his rhetoric and his later turn to the left, the actual substance of Chávez's economic policies was fiscally conservative during his first years in office.

both candidates are distributed about the same across these issues. However, we do find our first economic issue that divides the electorate: *Privatization of PDVSA*. Those few voters who favor privatizing PDVSA tend to be stronger supporters of Salas Römer, although the correlation is less than perfect and not substantively large because of the small number who favor this policy overall. Thus, economic issue positions generally remain minor factors explaining the choice of these two candidates. In contrast, *Constitutional Reform* again shows up as a strong predictor of vote choice, despite the relatively low salience of the issue for the electorate. In other words, while only a few voters see constitutional reform as the most important issue of the day, a large number of voters favor it, and most of these prefer Chávez.[23] Alternative specifications of the model (not shown here) suggest that *Constitutional Reform* largely absorbs the explanatory power of *Fight Corruption*, as can be seen in the diminished coefficient for this variable in the second model. This suggests that the problem of corruption and the need for constitutional reform were closely related in voters' minds.

Now consider the results of the question on candidate attributes, listed in Table 4.4. Again, the table indicates the actual frequency with which certain attributes were mentioned, followed by the results of a multinomial logit showing which attributes were associated with vote choice. As was the case with the question on the most important issue, respondents were asked to mention three attributes, so the numbers total more than 100 percent. In this instance, several attributes stand out for the frequency with which they were mentioned, with the clear first choice being *Honest*, followed by several attributes associated with administrative capacity. Thus, we again see a response associated with the problem of corruption showing up high on the list. Furthermore, this attribute is one of the only frequently mentioned ones that is associated with vote choice, albeit somewhat weakly. Four of the other attributes associated with a vote for Chávez – *Young, Man, Authoritarian,* and *Independent* – are mentioned with much lower frequency. The last candidate attribute that stands out – *Experience in Office* – is, of course, the primary one favoring Salas Römer. This result makes sense in that Salas Römer was the only leading candidate with prior governing experience, and it hints at the greater influence of pluralist discourse on the voters who preferred him.

Results: Full Model

With the findings of these preliminary analyses in mind, I now present the results of two different specifications of the full vote-choice model (Table 4.5). The first specification contains all of the variables described in the previous section, minus any issues or candidate attributes that were not statistically

---

[23] The fact that issue position fails to cancel out the effects of issue salience reflects the fact that some voters who prefer reform by Congress still see this as an important issue and vote for Chávez.

TABLE 4.4. *Multinomial logit of vote choice (candidate attributes)*

Variable	Percentage Who Mentioned	Salas Römer	Other Candidates	Abstention
Honest	79.7	−0.47* (0.23)	−0.07 (0.31)	−0.65** (0.23)
Well Prepared	52.5	−0.16 (0.20)	−0.23 (0.24)	−0.33* (0.20)
Intelligent	38.1	−0.15 (0.20)	−0.47* (0.26)	−0.56** (0.20)
Democratic	22.1	0.02 (0.22)	0.15 (0.27)	−0.34 (0.22)
Young	13.2	−0.87*** (0.26)	−0.51 (0.31)	−0.64** (0.24)
Good Administrator	41.1	0.01 (0.20)	−0.30 (0.25)	0.00 (0.19)
Experience in Office	11.3	1.14*** (0.27)	0.43 (0.36)	0.49* (0.29)
Independent	7.8	−0.48* (0.29)	−0.71* (0.42)	−0.67* (0.29)
Man	6.2	−1.23*** (0.37)	−0.96* (0.48)	−0.31 (0.28)
Woman	0.5	0.08 (1.04)	0.92 (1.07)	−0.70 (1.30)
Authoritarian	7.8	−0.65* (0.29)	−0.82* (0.41)	−0.61* (0.29)
Tolerant	2.3	0.01 (0.48)	−1.31 (1.06)	0.31 (0.44)
Kind	6.8	−0.17 (0.32)	−0.08 (0.38)	0.04 (0.29)
Party Leader	2.9	−0.31 (0.44)	0.21 (0.47)	−0.45 (0.42)
Constant		0.44 (0.49)	−0.57 (0.60)	0.80* (0.48)
N		1,500		
LR chi^2(42)		105.62***		
Pseudo R^2		0.03		
Log likelihood		−1,905.34		

Unless otherwise indicated, entries are logit coefficients (robust standard errors).
*p < .10; **p < .01; ***p < .001.
Source: Author's calculation, based on the 1998 RedPol survey (Red Universitaria 1999).

TABLE 4.5. *Multinomial logit of vote choice (full model)*

	Model 1			Model 2		
	Salas Römer	Other Candidates	Abstention	Salas Römer	Other Candidates	Abstention
Socioeconomic Controls						
Education	0.17* (0.08)	0.10 (0.12)	−0.08 (0.09)			
Class	−0.18* (0.10)	−0.19 (0.17)	−0.12 (0.11)			
Informal				−0.56** (0.17)	−0.44* (0.26)	−0.08 (0.17)
Economic Voting						
Sociotropic Retrospective	−0.26 (0.16)	−0.50* (0.25)	−0.28 (0.17)	−0.26 (0.16)	−0.51* (0.25)	−0.30* (0.17)
Sociotropic Prospective (better)	−0.17 (0.24)	−1.20** (0.42)	−0.75** (0.26)	−0.17 (0.24)	−1.19** (0.42)	−0.74** (0.26)
Sociotropic Prospective (same)	0.11 (0.26)	−0.28 (0.36)	−0.35 (0.26)	0.13 (0.25)	−0.28 (0.36)	−0.39 (0.26)
Sociotropic Prospective (worse)	0.63* (0.26)	0.41 (0.37)	0.26 (0.26)	0.62* (0.26)	0.40 (0.37)	0.26 (0.25)
Pocketbook Retrospective	−0.41*** (0.12)	−0.28 (0.18)	−0.27* (0.13)	−0.42*** (0.12)	−0.28 (0.18)	−0.26* (0.12)
Pocketbook Prospective (better)	−0.12 (0.25)	−0.20 (0.35)	−0.35 (0.25)	−0.11 (0.24)	−0.20 (0.35)	−0.34 (0.25)
Pocketbook Prospective (same)	−0.03 (0.28)	−0.17 (0.36)	−0.48* (0.28)	0.01 (0.28)	−0.14 (0.36)	−0.47* (0.28)
Pocketbook Prospective (worse)	−0.14	0.23	0.09	−0.12	0.25	0.09

(*continued*)

TABLE 4.5. (continued)

	Model 1			Model 2		
	Salas Römer	Other Candidates	Abstention	Salas Römer	Other Candidates	Abstention
	(0.33)	(0.44)	(0.30)	(0.33)	(0.44)	(0.30)
Issue Positions						
Constitutional Reform	−1.11***	−0.90***	−0.94***	−1.11***	−0.90***	−0.93***
	(0.12)	(0.17)	(0.12)	(0.11)	(0.17)	(0.11)
Privatize PDVSA	0.49	−0.42	1.04***	0.50*	−0.42	1.04***
	(0.30)	(0.59)	(0.29)	(0.30)	(0.59)	(0.29)
Satisfaction with Democracy	−0.35***	−0.48**	−0.13	−0.37***	−0.49**	−0.16
	(0.10)	(0.16)	(0.11)	(0.10)	(0.16)	(0.11)
Issue Salience						
Fight Corruption	−0.28*	−0.17	−0.45**	−0.26	−0.15	−0.44**
	(0.16)	(0.26)	(0.17)	(0.16)	(0.26)	(0.17)
Reform Constitution	−1.37***	−2.10**	−0.74*	−1.32***	−2.07**	−0.75*
	(0.37)	(0.77)	(0.31)	(0.37)	(0.78)	(0.31)
Privatize Public Firms	−0.76	−30.98***	−0.65	−0.76	−33.98***	−0.70
	(0.77)	(0.88)	(0.76)	(0.76)	(0.86)	(0.76)
Candidate Attributes						
Honest	−0.34	0.20	−0.44*	−0.33	0.21	−0.40*
	(0.21)	(0.36)	(0.21)	(0.21)	(0.36)	(0.21)
Young	−0.66**	−0.23	−0.51*	−0.73**	−0.28	−0.52*
	(0.26)	(0.41)	(0.24)	(0.26)	(0.41)	(0.24)
Experience in Office	1.20***	0.52	0.73*	1.17***	0.51	0.73*
	(0.27)	(0.40)	(0.30)	(0.27)	(0.40)	(0.30)

Independent	−0.55*	−0.66	−0.76*	−0.56*	−0.66	−0.78*
	(0.30)	(0.49)	(0.34)	(0.30)	(0.49)	(0.34)
Man	−1.23**	−0.99*	−0.19	−1.27**	−0.99*	−0.22
	(0.44)	(0.50)	(0.31)	(0.44)	(0.49)	(0.31)
Authoritarian	−0.43	−0.22	−0.32	−0.43	−0.22	−0.33
	(0.30)	(0.46)	(0.32)	(0.30)	(0.46)	(0.32)
Political Participation						
Neighborhood Activism	−0.42**	−0.08	−0.64***	−0.47**	−0.13	−0.67***
	(0.16)	(0.26)	(0.17)	(0.16)	(0.26)	(0.17)
Partisan Identity						
PIDAD	1.82***	4.84***	1.73***	1.78***	4.81***	1.74***
	(0.43)	(0.45)	(0.43)	(0.43)	(0.45)	(0.43)
PIDCOPEI	0.60	2.80***	0.74	0.58	2.78***	0.74
	(0.52)	(0.59)	(0.54)	(0.53)	(0.60)	(0.54)
PIDMAS	−1.77**	−1.24	−1.42**	−1.88***	−1.31	−1.28**
	(0.55)	(1.15)	(0.50)	(0.54)	(1.13)	(0.48)
PIDPPTLCR	−2.60**	−1.24	−1.09*	−2.55**	−1.18	−1.11*
	(0.88)	(0.96)	(0.57)	(0.84)	(1.00)	(0.56)
Constant	5.14***	4.13**	4.24***	5.16***	3.82**	3.65***
	(0.93)	(1.38)	(0.94)	(0.70)	(1.22)	(0.71)
N	1,327			1,333		
LR chi² (78)	3,188.95***			3,707.82***		
Pseudo R²	0.24			0.24		
Log likelihood	−1,311.40			−1,320.32		

Entries are logit coefficients (robust standard errors).
*$p < .10$; **$p < .01$; ***$p < .001$.
Source: Author's calculation, based on the 1998 RedPol survey (Red Universitaria 1999).

significant predictors in the above analyses. The second introduces *Informal* while eliminating two correlated socioeconomic indicators, *Education* and *Class*.

Despite the inability of economic issue measures to explain vote choice in the previous partial models, in both of these models assessments of economic performance and prospects are clearly important predictors. The key economic voting indicators from Weyland's model – pocketbook retrospective and sociotropic prospective, and to a lesser degree sociotropic retrospective – remain statistically and (as we will see) substantively significant.[24] Yet, views about the salience of privatization are no longer statistically significant once we control for a wider range of variables. And while views about PDVSA privatization are still statistically significant, the small number of respondents favoring privatization reduces the substantive significance of these results. Together these results reaffirm the economic voting argument that policy performance mattered for vote choice and the vitality of the political system in Venezuela; those respondents most affected by poor economic performance were more likely to vote for the most radical candidate, even if their views about specific policy solutions were relatively unimportant.

The one important change from Weyland's findings occurs in the disaggregated sociotropic prospective assessment indicator. Respondents with a negative prospective assessment were much more likely to vote for Salas Römer, while those with neutral or positive assessment were about equally likely to vote for either candidate or to vote slightly in favor of Chávez. These results suggest that it was not so much the optimism of Chávez voters that motivated them to vote for him over Salas Römer, but the *pessimism* of the Salas Römer voters that motivated them to vote for their candidate. (A favorable prospective assessment did matter among Chávez supporters, but mostly for reducing abstention.) The most straightforward interpretation of this finding is that by the time of the election, as opinion polls showed Chávez in a clear lead, his opponents thought it was likely that he would win and radically transform the economy; many of these voters chose Salas Römer not so much because they liked the candidate but because they feared the alternative even more. This interpretation coincides with the fact that in the actual election, the inevitable drop in actual turnout (versus what respondents indicated in the survey) tended to work against Salas Römer more than it did against Chávez – his supporters were not as enthusiastic about him as Chávez supporters were about their candidate. These data support an economic voting argument, but it is not the sophisticated cognitive one that Weyland offers. Chavista voters were not especially risk acceptant in comparison with those for Salas Römer, even though they clearly perceived that the economy was doing worse.

The variables capturing the normative theory and its emphasis on populist discourse also do an excellent job of predicting vote choice. Views about

---

[24] The coefficient for sociotropic retrospective is significant at the $p < .11$ level in Models 1 and 2.

constitutional reform remain statistically significant and, in the case of issue positions, substantively very significant. *Fight Corruption* achieves moderate levels of statistical significance in this model and is in the expected direction. *Satisfaction with Democracy* remains a very good predictor even after controlling for perceived economic performance, suggesting again that concerns about the political system stem from more than just a poor economy. And as for candidate attributes, four of the six remain strong or borderline predictors of a vote for Chávez, including especially *Honest. Experience in Office* remains an excellent (negative) predictor as well. Thus, issues and attributes associated with Chávez's populist discourse help explain an important part of his appeal.

As for our control variables, partisan identity is a very good predictor of vote choice; identification with COPEI and especially AD predicts a vote for Salas Römer, while identification with MAS, PPT, or LCR predicts a vote for Chávez. While not necessarily confirmations of our theory, the findings do undermine claims that voters were making their choice based largely on an irrational reaction to economic performance; there is a clear directionality to the vote that can be traced to partisan identity and/or the ideological stances that traditional parties embodied, factors that cut across respondents' other material concerns.

The structuralist and deepening of democracy explanations fare about as well as they can, given our limited number of predictors. *Informal* is an excellent predictor of vote choice and is slightly better than either of its two component indicators, *Education* and *Class,* which are moderately significant but in the right direction. Given the large number of respondents who fit into this category of citizens disadvantaged by globalization and neoliberal reforms (around 540 in this model specification), this variable probably has a large effect on vote choice. Thus, there seems to be some merit to the structuralist argument that support for Chávez was rooted in long-term socioeconomic shifts. The deepening of democracy explanation is not really given a fair test here because of the limited number of useful indicators, but respondents who participated in neighborhood improvement efforts were more likely to vote for Chávez than for Salas Römer or to abstain; this effect achieves modest statistical significance. That said, none of the related measures of issue salience were strong enough to merit inclusion here in these combined models.

In summary, the results of an expanded vote choice model give at least some support to all four theories of party system breakdown and the rise of Chavismo. Support is clearest for the economic voting argument (noncognitive) and for my own theory emphasizing the normative bases of populism, and is necessarily more modest for the structuralist and deepening of democracy arguments. But which of these is the *best* explanation? This is a difficult judgment to make based on the results of this model. While the Pseudo R^2 (around .24) is fairly high for a vote-choice model using survey data, we cannot be certain that we have fully measured the effects of each of these different causal factors. This is especially true of the structuralist and deepening of democracy arguments, where we really only have one indicator each. It is also essential to bear in mind that these theories are somewhat complementary; it is not that Venezuelans' rejection of the party system and their preference for Chávez were driven by *either* economic performance *or* corruption, but that policy failures *in a context of* widespread corruption made a populist discourse appealing. Thus, we should probably be testing for interaction effects.

We can address interaction effects quickly: there are none at this individual level. Appendix C presents the results of a series of analyses of possible interaction effects and fails to find any that are statistically significant, whether between my own indicators and those of the economic voting, structuralist, or deepening democracy arguments. With some of these indicators, the problem is that we are only looking inside one country at one point in time. This is especially so for the economic voting indicators. At the time of the survey (1998), perceptions of economic crisis were widespread; in fact, in the question about salient issues, fully 71.9 percent of respondents mentioned unemployment and/or inflation, the top two economic issues, and in the retrospective question about the country's economic performance, 69.1 percent said that the economy was "worse" and only 3.8 percent said "better." Hence, we do not have a great deal of variation on our key measures of economic evaluations, and any interaction effect is likely to be small. A similar logic holds for indicators of the deepening of democracy argument, where there are very few Venezuelans who see issues of decentralization, human rights, or the environment as salient. To really test for these effects, we need to explore populism in a comparative context that allows more variation in policy crisis. For the structuralist argument, however, these results are more definitive. Here we have significant variance across the sample (about half of the respondents are coded as belonging to the informal sector, and large pluralities or small majorities see corruption as an important issue or honesty as a key candidate attribute), so we cannot use the excuse that we are only looking at a snapshot of data. The null results here suggest that problems of sectoral decline are not perceived as tied to the corruption of the political system.

In contrast, a side-by-side comparison of these theories yields more insights. Table 4.6 presents expected probability changes for several sets of variables associated with each of the explanations tested in the full models. I calculate these by considering a baseline vote probability for all of the variables using their average values, then comparing this with the expected probabilities when each of the four sets of variables is set at their lowest possible values while all other variables are left at their averages.[25] Hence, the differences indicate

---

[25] As can be seen, this baseline probability is nearly identical to the actual values among survey respondents, with over 37% predicted to vote for Chávez. This includes those who plan on abstaining; if we exclude these and consider only those with a candidate preference, the expected probability of voting for Chávez is over 48%.

TABLE 4.6. *Estimated probabilities of voting for Chávez*

Choice	Given Average Values on All Indicators	Given Low Values on:							
		Normative Indicators		Economic Voting Indicators		Structuralist Indicators		Deepening of Democracy Indicators		Partisan Identity Indicators	
		Percentage	Difference from Average	Percentage	Difference from Average	Percentage	Difference from Average	Percentage	Difference from Average	Percentage	Difference from Average
Chávez	37.4	10.8	−26.6	23.2	−14.3	30.9	−6.5	29.3	−8.1	31.7	−5.7
Salas Römer	29.3	48.8	19.5	42.6	13.3	38.8	9.6	35.6	6.3	36.4	7.1
Other candidates	10.7	0.7	−10.1	6.7	−4.1	3.3	−7.4	2.8	−7.9	3.1	−7.6
Abstention	22.6	39.7	17.1	27.6	5.0	26.9	4.3	32.3	9.7	28.8	6.2

Source: Author's calculation, based on the 1998 RedPol survey (Red Universitaria 1999).

the contribution of each basket of variables to the overall vote for Chávez.[26] All values are calculated using the coefficients from the model specification with *Informal*. For the normative argument I consider the issue responses for corruption and constitutional reform and the candidate attributes of *Honesty* and *Experience in Office*; for the economic voting explanation, the four groups of sociotropic and pocketbook assessments as well as the coefficients for privatization issue salience and PDVSA privatization; for the structuralist argument, *Informal*; and for the deepening of democracy argument, *Neighborhood Activism*. Finally, I include an additional set of predicted values when key party identity indicators (those for MAS, LCR, and PPT, all of which supported Chávez) are set at zero.

In interpreting the expected probabilities, the best approach is to compare the change in probability from the average expected one; this difference is highlighted in boldface in the table. Assuming that the model is fully specified (and we should bear in mind that it probably is not), we can say that the normative theory picks up on the set of variables with the largest effect on the vote. If none of the respondents mentioned related attitudes or issues (*Fight Corruption, Honesty, Constitutional Reform, Reform Constitution, Experience in Office*), they would be almost 27 percent less likely to vote for Chávez than for another candidate or simply to abstain, and would be nearly 20 percent more likely to have voted for Salas Römer. The economic voting theory has the next highest results: if all respondents perceived the economy positively, they would be almost 15 percent less likely to vote for Chávez and over 13 percent more likely to vote for Salas Römer. This is enough to have decided the election but not nearly as great as the effect of indicators associated with the normative theory. Finally, *Informal, Neighborhood Activism*, and the measures of partisan identity each explain a small share of Chávez's expected vote, between 6 and 8 percent for each.

Interestingly, the indicators associated with the normative theory affect not only the choice of Chávez over Salas Römer, but also of Chávez over abstention. The difference in outcomes here is dramatic, with an increasing probability of over 17 percent that voters will abstain if issues and attributes related to honesty, corruption, and constitutional reform are eliminated – three times greater than for any other set of variables except *Neighborhood Activism*, which also has a moderate effect. Thus, the factors associated with

---

[26] For most sets of variables (the economic assessments, issue positions, *Informal*, and party identity), setting their values at zero is a valid way of indicating their effect or its absence. However, for two sets of variables – issue salience and candidate attributes – setting one or more of the variables at zero requires that we redistribute their values to other response categories, as all respondents who gave an answer would have had to pick a different response if they did not choose the one that interests us. I do this by increasing the values of other response categories (in this case, all issue salience responses besides *Fight Corruption* and *Reform Constitution* and all candidate attribute responses besides *Honest* and *Experience in Office*) weighted according to their initial proportion of responses. This correction yields only minor adjustments in the expected probabilities.

the normative theory help explain not only why voters opted for Chávez over other candidates, but also why they turned out to vote.

CONCLUSION

This chapter presents and tests an explanation for the breakdown of the traditional party system in Venezuela and the rise of Chavismo that draws on the concepts of populist worldview and discourse. Normative concerns – a crisis of legitimacy rooted in concerns over widespread corruption – weighed heavily in voters' considerations about whom to support in the crucial 1998 election. Significant policy failures such as long-term economic decline helped drive voters' choices, but these alone did not push large numbers of Venezuelans to entertain such radical alternatives. The underlying inability of Venezuela's Punto Fijo system to preserve the rule of law and honor principles of citizenship made it possible for Chávez and other leaders to interpret these policy failures as manifestations of a cosmic struggle between the people and the elite.

This analysis also questions cognitive approaches to understanding Venezuela's party system breakdown and the emergence of populism. First, some issues *do* matter for the 1998 election, especially corruption and constitutional reform; the choice of Chávez was not merely an emotional response to economic stress. Second, very specific candidate attributes associated with populism (or pluralism) figured strongly in voters' choices; the voters were not merely motivated by markers of radicalism and independence. Finally, when we look more closely at the economic assessments that seem to motivate Venezuelans to vote for Chávez or other candidates, there is relatively little irrationality. Voters for Chávez tended to be those with negative assessments of the economy, making him a reasonable choice in light of Chávez's clear questioning of previous attempts at market-oriented reform and Salas Römer's defense of market principles and his association with elite interests. In contrast, voters for both Chávez and Salas Römer were about equally likely to be among those with high expectations for future economic performance; thus, most Chávez voters were not wildly optimistic. Voters for Salas Römer were much more likely to be among those with pessimistic outlooks, but this can be interpreted as an attempt to forestall the changes that they feared would come with a Chávez victory, and it fails to reveal unusual levels of risk acceptance among Chavistas. All of these findings reaffirm a more straightforward concept of economic voting in 1998 and give us confidence in the rationality of Chavistas.

This explanation is still incomplete. In particular, the connection between the breakdown in the rule of law and the emergence of these movements is rather loose. Caldera was only a minor populist and a pretty inconsistent one at that, and the successful full-blown populism of Chavismo emerged several years after the corruption of Venezuela's political system became a salient issue. Part of this problem of timing may arise from the interaction of corruption with policy failure, the argument being that the early corruption of the state could only bring down the Punto Fijo system once other policy problems became evident. I find some evidence for this argument in the next chapter, which considers the correlation between populism and corruption in a much larger set of countries. However, a more important part of the explanation is the challenge of finding charismatic leadership, which I discuss in the conclusion to the next chapter.

5

The Causes of Populism in Comparative Perspective

> Let us teach government to those who robbed our country.
>
> Evo Morales, campaign speech in 2005
>
> Enough with these spoilers of the fatherland! A fight to the death against corruption!
>
> Rafael Correa, campaign speech in 2006

In this chapter I move beyond the case of Chavismo in Venezuela to consider the causes of populism in the aggregate, across multiple countries and regions. This comparative perspective reveals causal mechanisms that a single-country case study or an individual-level analysis within that country cannot. While individual-level analysis may be needed to avoid the ecological fallacy (inferring individual-level attributes from aggregate outcomes; see Robinson 1950), and while case studies allow us to explore causal mechanisms and temporal sequencing (Brady and Collier 2004; D. Hawkins 2009), aggregate, multi-country analyses help us discern omitted variables and say something more generalizable (King, Keohane, and Verba 1994, 30). An aggregate-level analysis is especially appropriate when making causal claims that connect institutions or systemic phenomena, such as the rule of law, economic performance, and populist movements, all of which are more than the sum of individual attitudes and behaviors.

The analysis in this chapter is necessarily limited; given our dataset on populist discourse, we can only examine a narrow snapshot of recent history for a modest number of countries. This creates a challenge for us as we try to measure a relatively volatile phenomenon like populist movements.[1] Yet, the panel data here give us some empirical leverage by allowing us to better identify

---

[1] As noted in Chapter 3, and as should be obvious from a cursory glance at the history of any of the countries examined here, populism is never a permanent feature of government. Thus, a better question to ask is why some countries have more populist movements than others over time. My thanks to one of the reviewers for pointing this out.

necessary and facilitating conditions, which should be present in whatever cases of populism are found in the dataset.

The results of this analysis largely reaffirm those of the previous chapter, providing support for my argument that populism has strong normative components responding to crises of legitimacy and corruption. Using relatively simple quantitative analyses, I show that the level of populism in elite discourse has a strong correlation with perceived corruption and a fairly strong but less conclusive correlation with experienced corruption in a multinational sample of chief executives, especially when the corruption is accompanied by economic policy failure. A few other hypothesized causes, such as economic performance and labor union decline, also have strong associations with populism when considered alone, but most of these effects wash out once we control for corruption.

To be sure, I find that the correlation between corruption and populism is imperfect. Several countries with high levels of corruption in recent years lack populist leaders, a fact suggesting that widespread corruption is at best a necessary but insufficient condition for the emergence of populist movements. In the conclusion to this chapter I go beyond the different factors affecting the demand for populism and say something about its supply, especially the nature of the charismatic leadership that successful populist movements depend on. The analysis here is somewhat more speculative because of our lack of long-term data on populist movements, but taken together, these components of supply and demand bring us closer to a sufficient explanation for the rise of Chavismo and similar movements.

The starting point for this comparative analysis is the cross-national data on populist discourse among chief executives presented in Chapter 3. After briefly reviewing this data, I present a sequence of bivariate scatterplots that tests each of the principal theories of populism. These theories are economic voting (measured in terms of GDP growth averages), mass society (media access, media freedom, and school enrollment), modernization (labor union density and size of the informal sector), dependency (foreign direct investment combined with commodity exports as a percentage of GDP), and my normative explanation (corruption). Because of the modest number of observations (around 35), much of the weight of the analysis has to rest on these correlations rather than on any multivariate regression; however, toward the end of the chapter, I present a series of ordinary least squares (OLS) regressions that juxtapose some of these key indicators with corruption in order to determine if they capture some residual effect or possibly have a stronger effect than corruption. Some of the text here overlaps the theoretical discussion in the previous chapter on Chavismo, but I nearly always draw from a different set of authors that allows us to expand our horizon beyond Venezuela and better contextualize this particular case.

TESTING THE PRINCIPAL THEORIES OF POPULISM

The following sequence of bivariate analyses tests the major theories of populism. In order to be more thorough, I have broken down or separated a few

Causes of Populism in Comparative Perspective 133

subtheories that are sometimes considered together in the literature, such as mass society and modernization theory. For each theory I present one or more scatterplots that display the correlation between each variable and the level of populist discourse in our set of 35 country executives. Examining these theories with simple scatterplots lets us look more closely at particular cases and identify unusual patterns. To avoid letting the shape of the distribution play tricks on our eyes, each scatterplot also includes the line describing the best linear fit between the two variables, along with two other lines indicating the associated 90 percent confidence interval. That is, we can say with 90 percent confidence that the actual linear relationship has a slope and a *y*-intercept that fall somewhere between the upper and lower lines indicated on the graph. In one instance where a quadratic function clearly has a better fit (Figure 5.5), I produce this line instead.[2]

The data on populism come from the measurement of populist discourse in Chapter 3, specifically, the average populism score in Tables 3.1 and 3.2. By way of reminder, this dataset was generated through a holistic grading of speeches by chief executives (presidents and prime ministers) from across the globe, but especially Latin America. Approximately four speeches, each from four different categories (campaign, ribbon-cutting, international, and famous speeches), were graded for each chief executive. The speeches were graded as 0, 1, or 2, where 0 represents the absence of populist discourse (and usually, given the largely democratic selection of cases, the presence of pluralist discourse), 1 the presence of moderate or inconsistent populist discourse, and 2 the presence of consistently strong populist discourse. I then calculated the unweighted mean over all speeches for each chief executive. With two exceptions (Carlos Mesa and Morales in Bolivia), each chief executive represents a different country. Most of these chief executives were elected in the early 2000s, although a few of them (Chávez in Venezuela, Lagos in Chile, Lukashenko in Belarus, and Tony Blair in the United Kingdom) came to power earlier, during the middle or late 1990s. The analysis in Chapter 3 also included a small set of historically significant presidents in Latin America (Lázaro Cárdenas in Mexico, Velasco Ibarra in Ecuador, Perón in Argentina, Menem in Argentina, and Vargas in Brazil), but these are omitted here because of the lack of key explanatory indicators for these leaders. This leaves us with 35 observations and limits the generalizability of my findings to the present.

The resulting dataset provides an imperfect but fairly wide range of variance on our dependent variable. While most of the chief executives have scores of less than 1 (and several have scores of 0), a handful have scores well over 1 and seem to represent strong populists. These include Chávez (a score of 1.9), Lukashenko (1.7), Morales (1.6), Mahmood Ahmadinejad in Iran (1.2), George Bush in the United States (1.2), and Viktor Yushchenko in Ukraine (1.1). As mentioned in Chapter 2, the high score for George Bush is somewhat

---

[2] I ran all of these scatterplots with both a linear fit and a quadratic fit. Only where the quadratic line fell noticeably outside the 90% confidence interval did I opt for showing this form instead.

misleading, as it represents an antagonistic discourse devoid of references to a conspiring elite or the need for liberation or revolution; it is a reaction to an international security threat. Rather than drop Bush from the analysis, I use parentheses to distinguish this observation in figures or tables, and I generally leave it to readers to reinterpret the results. However, all tests of statistical significance, fitted lines, and the concluding regressions exclude Bush from their calculations.

The analysis here includes most of the theories discussed in the previous chapter, including economic voting theory, structuralist theory, and, of course, my normative explanation. The only theory not included is the argument that populism responds to growing citizen demands for greater democracy. This theory is somewhat peculiar to Venezuela, although versions of it are hinted at by proponents of radical participatory democracy in other Latin American countries today. In any case, as data in the previous chapter foreshadowed, a comparison of our populism data with measures of postmaterialist values from the 1995 and 2000 waves of the World Values Survey fails to find any positive relationship between postmaterialism and populism. If there is any relationship at all, it seems to be a negative one, with higher levels of postmaterialist values leading to *lower* levels of populism. This negative relationship is strongest along the "survival" dimension rather than the "traditional/secular" dimension.[3] Thus, while support for populists such as Chávez may initially be high among individual proponents of democratic reforms (we saw some evidence for this in Venezuela), countries with populist leaders do not have particularly high levels of postmaterialist values.

Economic Voting

The first argument is the familiar one of economic voting: populist movements are driven by repeatedly bad economic performance, especially when this performance is repeated across governments from prominent parties. Ironically, while this argument is referred to by some of its critics (de la Torre 2000) and plays a prominent role in the study of Chavismo and the breakdown of Venezuela's party system (Canache 2002; Weyland 2003; Coppedge 2005), few comparative scholars of populism make this a key part of their theories. Certainly there is a kind of economic logic to the modernization and dependency arguments that I discuss later, but these focus more on the long-term inability of late-industrializing economies to satisfy the rising expectations of their citizens than on the immediate impact of exceptionally low economic

---

[3] The correlation between our measure of populist discourse and the survival dimension is $r = -.30$ ($p < .15$), and that between populist discourse and the traditional/secular dimension is $r = -.31$ ($p < .06$). I measured the two dimensions by rerunning Inglehart's factor analysis (Inglehart and Welzel 2005) and then creating an index for each based on the factor loadings. For most countries I used the 2000 wave of the survey, although for a few (those with chief executives elected earlier), I used the 1995–7 wave.

performance. Where the concept of economic voting figures somewhat more prominently is in analyses of charismatic leadership, which routinely tie the emergence of charismatic leaders to moral and policy crisis (Willner 1984; Madsen and Snow 1991; Merolla, Ramos, and Zechmeister 2006). However, studies of charisma often include both democrats and authoritarians, making it unclear how generalizable their findings are to the emergence of populism.

To test the economic voting argument in comparative perspective, I calculate average growth in real per capita GDP for 2-, 5-, 10-, and 20-year periods for each country. This is a simple mean without any weighting, where annual growth is calculated as a percentage change in the raw, unlogged GDP from one year to the next; a more sophisticated version of this indicator, which regresses logged per capita GDP on year, yields nearly identical results. I consider various lengths of time because existing theories are unclear as to how long a decline has to persist in order to undermine support for political institutions. Short periods of severe decline should matter, but longer periods probably have a stronger effect on the government's legitimacy. With two exceptions, data for GDP are taken from the World Bank's World Development Indicators database. The two exceptions are Russia and Belarus, where World Bank data are unavailable before about 1990. Rather than drop these important cases, I fill in the missing data with rough estimates from Brooks and Wohlforth (2000/2001).

As the graphs in Figure 5.1 indicate, there is a rough relationship between economic performance and populism that emerges as the time period becomes longer, but the correlation is not very strong and the linear trends are not really discernible until we consider the longest period possible. For the shortest periods of economic performance (2 years and 5 years), there is virtually no visible or statistically significant association ($r = -.15$, $p < .41$ and $r = -.22$, $p < .21$, respectively). While Belarus (one of our most populist countries) has extremely low levels of growth in the short term, Ukraine has fairly high levels of growth in the 2–5 years before Yushchenko's election, and most other highly populist countries have economic performances that fall in between. Venezuela in particular is right in the middle, with a slight overall improvement in the economy during the 2 years before Chávez was elected, and flat economic growth in the slightly longer 5-year period. Several cases of low or nonexistent populism such as Argentina actually have worse records of economic performance without a noticeably populist leader.

As we look at the longer 10- and 20-year periods, which typically cover at least two terms of the chief executive, a stronger correlation emerges between growth and populism among the most populist countries. In the 10-year period the correlation is still somewhat faint ($r = -.27$, $p < .12$), but in the 20-year period it becomes larger and more statistically significant ($r = -.39$, $p < .02$). Venezuela clearly shifts to the side of economic decline, demonstrating the long-term stagnation of the economy mentioned in the previous chapter, and Ukraine becomes a clear case of net economic losses. Still, two of our strongest instances of populist discourse, Bolivia under Morales and Iran

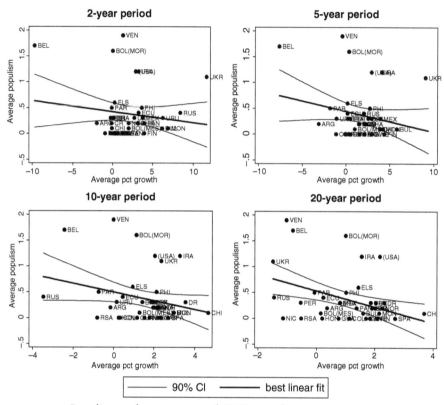

FIGURE 5.1. Populism and average annual GDP growth.
Sources: Author's populism dataset; World Bank (2007); Brooks and Wohlforth (2000/2001).

under Ahmadinejad, are not well explained by this indicator and have relatively solid trends of growth in comparative perspective. Bolivia's reputation for poor growth during this period seems somewhat exaggerated when we consider the actual data (basically neutral over the two decades before the election of Morales), and Iran's long-term growth average is actually fairly strong. And as we will see again with other indicators in this chapter, there are still a few country cases having poor records of economic growth that lack any evidence of populist discourse at the time of our analysis (Nicaragua and South Africa in particular).

Thus, economic voting theories of populism are only partially supported once we look cross-nationally. Long-term economic growth is a strong predictor of the emergence of populism. This confirms and clarifies our individual-level findings in Venezuela from the previous chapter, which demonstrated a strong relationship between personal (pocketbook) economic experience and support for Chávez but a somewhat weaker relationship between perceived aggregate (sociotropic) performance and support for Chávez. I speculated that this inconsistency was due to the lack of variance in perceived aggregate performance; in a country such as Venezuela with significant economic decline, most citizens were bound to see aggregate performance as negative, so this could not explain much of their vote choice. As we move beyond Venezuela to a set of countries where national economic performance varies more widely, we are able to discern a stronger association with populism, suggesting that economic performance does matter at both the individual and aggregate levels. Yet, economic decline is neither a necessary nor a sufficient condition, and short-term performance seems not to matter at all.

Mass Society

The next theory of populism is both one of the oldest and one of the newest: that of mass society. Although not used in the context of Chavismo, versions of mass-society theory have been applied to a variety of recent populist leaders in Latin America and Western Europe, and the theory sometimes figures in accounts of populism rooted in the modernization argument. It essentially emphasizes the ignorance and susceptibility of average citizens to demagoguery and propaganda, especially in countries that combine a modern, urban context and sophisticated media technologies with a poorly educated citizenry.

The oldest versions of this theory are cognitive psychological ones that see the support for populists as a kind of mass hysteria or "contagion" fed by the susceptibility of average citizens to rumor and political showmanship (Le Bon 1960 [1895]; Freud 1989 [1922]). Individual citizens might be rational, but in groups they seem to lose their capacity for critical judgment. They are easily impressed with simple emotional messages that are frequently repeated.

Today mass-society theories emphasize the impact of modern electronic media on the ability of populist leaders to create a charismatic bond with citizens. They argue that radio (in the populist period of the interwar years) and, more recently, television (among so-called neopopulists) enhance the potential for populist leadership by creating a forum in which leaders can forge a personal, emotional bond with large numbers of followers at a distance (Conniff 1999, 9–10; see the studies in Skidmore 1992, especially de Lima 1992). These media create a false intimacy that would otherwise be impossible in large, modern societies. The strongest versions of this theory treat electronic media as a sufficient condition for populism – television summons populist leaders and encourages ordinary politicians to act in a more populist way. The most sophisticated versions of the theory place less stock in the direct impact of the technology and instead argue that it is the technology combined with the increasingly competitive, sensationalistic quality of modern media that creates this potential (Mazzoleni, Stewart, and Horsfield 2003). According to this version of the theory, which was developed to study new cases of populism in the advanced industrial democracies, tabloid journalists seek out and magnify the image of photogenic politicians in order to attract a larger audience, especially when journalists see themselves as activist guardians of democracy. This kind of coverage facilitates the emergence of a populist leader, but then hastens his downfall if the populist leader fails to moderate his message or follow democratic principles once in power, or if the media simply lose interest and move on to newer political phenomena. The populists who survive longest are those who actually take control of the media, such as Silvio Berlusconi in Italy and Slobodan Milošević in Yugoslavia, two leaders mentioned in these studies; Chávez would also seem to fit this pattern.

If mass-society theory is correct, populism should be correlated with the increasing availability of new forms of electronic media in countries with low levels of citizen sophistication. To test this idea, I consider three indicators: the availability of television sets (a crucial component of media "demand"), media freedom (an important aspect of media "supply"), and the level of enrollment in secondary education. To avoid problems of endogeneity (for example, a successful populist who curtails previously high levels of media freedom), wherever possible, all indicators are measured in the year the chief executive first came to power.

The availability of electronic media is measured as the percentage of the population with a television set, using annual data from the International Telecommunications Union's (ITU) World Telecommunications database (2006 version). Media freedom is measured using the "freedom of the press" indicator from Freedom House, which is created as part of their annual expert survey of Freedom in the World and runs on a scale from 0 to 100; I reverse this scale for ease of interpretation so that 100 is the highest level of freedom. I consider the level of media freedom in addition to the availability of electronic media in order to get at the quality of media available to citizens; even when media access is high, according to this theory, countries with low levels of media freedom should not be permissive environments for the emergence of new populists.[4]

I measure levels of enrollment in secondary education using data from the World Bank's World Development Indicators. Education enrollment covers the net percentage of the eligible population; this statistic is slightly more intuitive than the gross percentage (which can exceed 100 percent), although the dataset omits six countries (Chile, Costa Rica, Honduras, Paraguay, Russia, and Uruguay), none of which dramatically skew our results. I consider secondary education rather than literacy or primary education because basic intellectual skills are presumably insufficient to generate a highly sophisticated electorate, and because the levels of basic educational enrollment and attainment are very high across all 35 countries in our dataset; typically, over 80 percent of the population is literate in these countries, and primary school

---

[4] Measures of media market liberalization or the number of media providers would also be helpful indicators of quality, but these are not available for the entire set of countries in the populism dataset.

Causes of Populism in Comparative Perspective

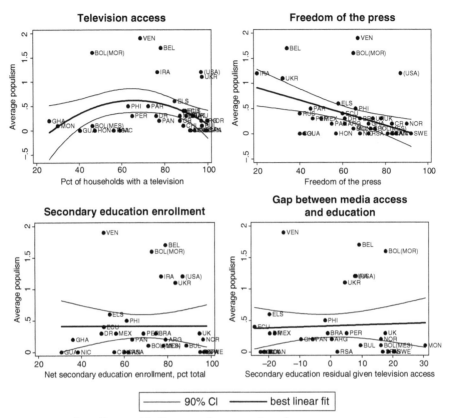

FIGURE 5.2. Populism and indicators of mass society theory.
Sources: Author's populism dataset; World Bank (2007); Freedom House (2007); ITU (2006).

enrollment is close to 100 percent.[5] Tertiary education enrollment is another possible indicator because it gets at these higher cognitive skills, but results for this indicator (not shown here) turn out to be virtually identical to those for secondary education.

The relationship between the level of populist discourse and each of these country-level indicators is presented in Figure 5.2. These bivariate results generally fail to confirm the mass-society theory. Consider first the measures of telecommunications access. The availability of television sets has no direct linear relationship to the presence of populist discourse ($r = -.06$, $p < .75$).

---

[5] There is in fact a slightly *positive* correlation between literacy in 1990 (the year with the most complete coverage in the World Development Indicators) and populism ($r = .17$), suggesting that populism is more likely in countries with higher levels of basic educational attainment, but this is not statistically significant at standard levels ($p < .40$). Bear in mind that this latter calculation excludes most of the advanced industrial democracies because they no longer report literacy data.

The most populist countries are not those with the greatest access, but those with medium levels of access. In fact, this is the one instance where a quadratic function yields a noticeably different fit than a linear one, and hence I opt for showing the curvilinear 90 percent confidence interval in this first graph. At the risk of reading too much into these data, we could argue that the incidence of populism has a roughly curvilinear relationship with television access that seems to peak at around 70 percent. This seems to be a better validation of traditional structuralist theories than it does of mass-society theory, in that structuralist theories (both modernization and dependency, as we will see in the next sections) have generally argued that populism is most common at intermediate stages of economic development or in the transition to modernity.

In the case of press freedom, the data are even less supportive. The level of press freedom clearly goes in the opposite direction of what recent, sophisticated versions of mass-society theory would predict ($r = -.43$ at the $p < .01$ level), with populism becoming more likely with *decreasing* levels of press freedom. Some of the most populist regimes in our sample – Lukashenko in Belarus, Yushchenko in Ukraine, and Ahmadinejad in Iran – emerged under significant media repression. This suggests that populism is more often a reaction to political or other problems that are associated with media repression than it is a consequence of permissive tabloid journalism, and that it requires relatively little press freedom to emerge.

Finally, looking at levels of education, I also fail to confirm a relationship between voter sophistication and populism ($r = .00$, $p < .99$). As Figure 5.2 indicates, most of the highly populist countries have at least moderately high levels of secondary education enrollment; only Venezuela's is low. While these data cannot tell us about the quality of education in these countries and whether it facilitates the kind of critical thinking that presumably wards off populism, low levels of education do not seem to be an essential condition for the emergence of populist leaders or even an important facilitator. In fact, none of the least educated countries in the dataset currently have populist leaders in power. This coincides with the individual-level results from Venezuela in the previous chapter: Chávez's supporters were on average slightly less educated than those of Salas Römer, but there was considerable variance within both groups that made education a weak predictor of support for Chávez. Support for populism was not primarily a reflection of ignorance and media manipulation in Venezuela, and it does not appear to be so at the global level either.

None of these results strongly supports mass-society theory. However, the real argument of this theory is an interactive one claiming that high levels of media access *in combination with* low levels of education make populations susceptible to populism. A few countries in our dataset do fall into this category of high media access/moderate to low education. Although levels of secondary education and television access are strongly correlated overall ($r = .54$, $p < .003$), several countries have lower levels of secondary education enrollment than we would expect, given their high levels of media access. Tellingly, most of these (particularly El Salvador, Mexico, Brazil, and Colombia) are in Latin America, a region known for its incidence of populism. Perhaps it is these educational underachievers that show the strongest tendency toward populism in our dataset.

In order to capture each country's gap between education and media access, I calculate the residual values of a regression of television access on net secondary education enrollment. High numbers indicate higher than expected levels of television access (or lower levels of education), while low numbers indicate lower than expected levels of television access. The last graph in Figure 5.2 then compares this statistic with our populism data. As can be seen, these new data still fail to vindicate mass-society theory. There is no discernible pattern between populism and the gap between education and media access; the overall correlation of these two indicators is only $r = .05$ at $p < .82$, and the linear trend is essentially flat.

In short, the data do not confirm the predictions of mass-society theory. Generally speaking, popular ignorance coupled with media access and/or media freedom is neither a necessary condition for populism nor a sufficient one. In fact, in the case of media freedom, the pattern may run in the opposite direction, with greater levels of media freedom producing lower levels of populism. The few countries that do combine high media access with relatively low education are not necessarily populist, nor are the most highly populist countries the ones with the greatest educational deficits.

Structuralism: Modernization

Outside of Venezuela, the structuralist approach to populism comes in two versions that emphasize very different causal mechanisms. The first is an offshoot of modernization theory that emphasizes the cultural and economic disjunctures of modernization, particularly the ability of societies undergoing rapid industrialization and urbanization to foster new political identities and satisfy the growing material expectations of citizens. Populism is regarded as a political phase of development and not as a permanent feature of these countries; if late-developing countries can catch up with the modern industrial societies, populism will disappear. The second of these theories is dependency theory, which will be discussed in the next section.

The oldest modernization theories (those of di Tella 1965 and Germani 1978) focused on the problems of modernization in late-industrializing societies. They argued that urbanization and cultural change during the first half of the twentieth century outpaced the ability of these societies (especially Latin American ones) to industrialize and provide either economic benefits for the lower and middle classes or the political and social institutions (such as labor unions) needed to instill new identities and create a functioning modern society. Thus, late modernization generated a "revolution of rising expectations" (di Tella 1965, 49) and acute forms of normlessness (Germani 1978; Conniff 1982, 11). Into this gap entered populist movements, which offered themselves as benefactors of the poor by celebrating new identities that valued poor workers as full citizens and by instituting models of state-led industrialization that fostered growth and created jobs. The leaders of these movements often came from the disgruntled sectors of the middle class and had an anti–status quo outlook (di Tella 1965). They created labor unions and peasant organizations to buttress the new political and economic orders and gave these organizations preferential access to social programs and the benefits of labor legislation. Their economic policies fostered the emergence of new sectors of industrialists among the middle class (or among segments of the upper class willing to ally with them), thereby making the populist coalition a winning cross-class majority.

Obviously, much of Latin America and the rest of the developing world moved beyond this stage of development in the late twentieth century, with some countries never having achieved significant growth in manufacturing, and with others achieving growth and then experiencing crises in their state-led economies during the 1980s and 1990s (Roberts 2000). A few of the newly industrialized countries succeeded in industrializing and catching up with the wealthy industrial nations, but many other developing countries failed to get past the initial stages of state-led industrialization (Haggard 1990).

Consequently, newer structuralist approaches to populism emphasize the reemergence of these older problems of modernization in laggard countries as they confront challenges of globalization, debt crises, and the exhaustion of state-led industrialization (Roberts 1995; Oxhorn 1998). These scholars see domestically owned manufacturing shrinking in the face of foreign competition, and they point to the decline of (already limited) union membership and the old labor-mobilizing parties in these countries. Where manufacturing has increased – in the *maquila* assemblies and among multinational corporations – it is less amenable to unionization, the promotion of workers' rights, and job stability. Welfare benefits and basic state services have been rolled back and privatized, leaving significant gaps in coverage and quality. Large groups of citizens are once again bereft of state protection and shorn of the jobs and labor organizations that provided them with identity; they feel disenfranchised by governments that apparently ignore their interests. Consequently, populist movements have reemerged to offer new "popular" identities and a variety of policies to redress basic material needs. This populist reaction was initially a neoliberal one that built on widespread rejection of the failures of state-led industrialization (Roberts 1995; Weyland 1996), but the failure of neoliberal policies to generate equitable growth in employment and wages means that, more recently, populism has shifted to the left. Until a new matrix of sustainable economic policies, political institutions, and cultural identities is achieved (Garreton et al. 2003), the populist cycle is likely to persist.

If this newer version of the modernization argument is true, we should see populism today in countries with low or significantly declining levels of welfare provision and union density and increasingly large informal sectors. Unfortunately, testing this argument is difficult because of the lack of complete

Causes of Populism in Comparative Perspective   143

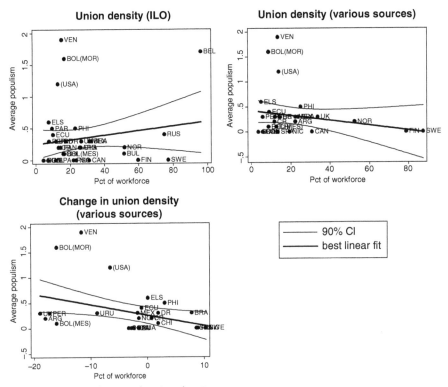

FIGURE 5.3. Populism and union density.
Sources: Author's populism dataset; Roberts and Wibbels (1999); Kuruvilla et al. (2002); Ebbinghaus and Visser (2000); ILO (1997).

datasets for most of our countries. There is no unified measure of welfare provision across more than a few countries, and data on the informal economy are scarce and frequently lack uniformity. Union membership data are available for multiple countries across regions, but even these data are unavailable for all of the countries in our populism dataset, and they are collected by different organizations using slightly different measures. Consequently, we have to take the following results with a grain of salt.

Figure 5.3 contains three scatterplots comparing our populism measure with indicators of union density: the absolute level of union density as calculated by the International Labor Organization (ILO 1997); the absolute level of union density in the late 1990s, as measured by various sources (Roberts and Wibbels 1999; Ebbinghaus and Visser 2000; Kuruvilla et al. 2002); and the change in union density over the previous 15-year period, using the latter sources. The ILO dataset offers greater consistency across countries and has greater coverage, but it lacks any time series; the other sources provide us with a time series but have more questionable comparability and omit some of the countries found in the ILO dataset.

The graphs suggest that union density may be related to populism. Consider the two that use data from various sources. These correlations are not only in the right direction, but the second of these is actually fairly strong and statistically significant ($r = -.41$, $p < .05$, as opposed to $r = -.23$ at $p < .28$ for the first one). Countries with the lowest union density or the greatest declines tend to have greater levels of populism. That said, this is obviously not a perfect predictor. To begin with, there are several countries with low levels of union density or dramatic declines in union membership and no populism at the time of this analysis, such as Peru (under Toledo), Argentina (under Kirchner), the United Kingdom (under Blair), and Bolivia (under Carlos Mesa). Two of these countries *did* have populist leaders in recent times (Fujimori in Peru and especially Morales in Bolivia, the latter of which is actually included in the graph), suggesting that we may have a necessary but insufficient condition.

When we consider the larger ILO dataset, the relationship is messier. We find a clear outlier, Belarus, that had a rather high level of unionization at the time its populist leaders came to power and another partial outlier, Russia, with a very high level of unionization given its (moderate to low) level of populist discourse. Although we lack data on Ukraine, we can guess that levels of union density were still fairly high in this country at the time of Yushchenko's accession, making it an outlier as well. These and other new cases dramatically shift the previously strong negative relationship to one that is vaguely in the wrong direction and no longer statistically significant ($r = .17$, $p < .37$), suggesting that low levels of union density may not even be necessary conditions for populism. We must qualify all of these observations, however, because with the exception of Belarus, these measures of union membership come from several years before the emergence of the leaders in our populism dataset (the 1990s rather than the early 2000s). Given the likely downward trend in union density in most of these countries today, particularly the former Communist countries, a more complete time series of union density would possibly confirm the initial limited correlation between union density and populism. Thus, there may still be some truth to this structuralist argument.

Figure 5.4 compares populism with a different set of indicators testing the structuralist argument: levels of informal sector employment using data from the ILO (specifically, the Key Indicators of the Labour Market v.5). These results are less favorable but also much less definitive than those for union density. The first graph shows small/medium enterprise employment in Latin America using comparable (harmonized) definitions; identical data for other countries are unavailable in this series. We can see that there is almost no relationship between the size of the informal sector and the incidence of populism ($r = .16$, $p < .53$). However, this series omits about half of the countries in the populism dataset and hence captures only a narrow range of variance in informal employment (the lowest levels of informal employment in Latin America would be moderate or high for many of the advanced industrial democracies and former Soviet countries). Hence, the second graph compares levels of informal sector employment using each country's definition rather than the

Causes of Populism in Comparative Perspective

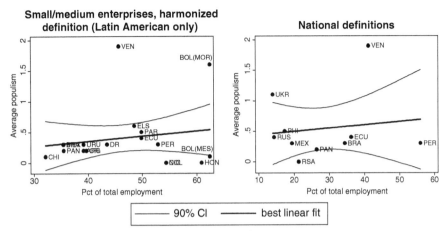

FIGURE 5.4. Populism and informal sector employment.
Sources: Author's populism dataset; ILO (2007).

ILO standard; this set of countries goes beyond Latin America. These numbers are not highly comparable across countries (in practice, they may vary as much as 15 percent, depending on the definition used), and they produce a smaller number of observations (N = 10). Perhaps not surprisingly, they again fail to demonstrate a strong relationship (r = .13, p < .71).

While not conclusive, these data reaffirm the possibility of a relationship between the negative aspects of globalization and populism that is like the modest one found in the previous chapter. A decline in union density and absolute low levels of union density may be associated with higher levels of populism. However, populism and informal sector employment are not strongly related. Neither set of variables can be tested across our full set of countries.

Structuralism: Dependency

The second structuralist explanation for populism is dependency theory. Although dependency theory in its heyday was not primarily a theory of populism, it did offer an explanation for populism's emergence in the early and mid-twentieth century that shared important similarities with the modernization argument. Dependency theorists were initially ambivalent toward the emergence of populist leaders in Latin America (Frank 1967; Cardoso 1975; Ianni 1975; Weffort 1978; Vilas 1992/1993). The most radical among them saw populism as a distraction from the truly revolutionary solutions that were needed for dependent development. In countries on the periphery of capitalism, all of which needed to overcome the entrenched legacies of colonialism (namely, an elite class that used its economic privileges to maintain an exploitative system of commodity exports), populism provided only half a solution. The policies of state-led industrialization adopted by classic populists such as

Perón and Vargas did foster economic development, raise standards of living, and mobilize the lower classes, but they achieved these goals without eliminating the power of elites to halt reforms through undemocratic means. The state and the capitalist economic system were essentially left intact. For the most radical dependency theorists, the bureaucratic-authoritarian reaction of the 1960s and 1970s and the rollback of populist, state-led development were a vindication of their prescriptions for something more revolutionary.

Whether dependency theorists' characterization of populism is really accurate is something we can dispute; it tends to adopt the pejorative use of the term as "populism is anything that fails to deliver a *real* revolution," and it disregards the strong populist discourse of at least a few Marxist revolutionaries. However, if we set aside these problematic foundations and assume that the dependency perspective on populism is correct, then we should find that populist leaders emerge primarily in countries engaged in the kinds of trade that create and reinforce backward development, especially commodity trade controlled by multinational firms. Commodity trade epitomizes the relationship of dependency: an economically underdeveloped country that produces raw materials in exchange for the manufactured goods of the industrialized core. Yet, commodity trade is only an incomplete indicator, and we would like to know something about the quality of the economic relationship: how much value-added processing takes place, how diversified the export basket is, who owns the export industries, and how those industries are regulated by the host government. Some dependency theorists claim that industrialization and increased manufacturing exports can perpetuate or deepen dependency when carried out without proper state controls (Cardoso and Faletto 1979). Fuel exports like Venezuela's exemplify this vagueness. They clearly involve commodities, ones with potentially pernicious effects on the rest of the economy and the polity (see Karl 1997 and Ross 2001). But in most of the less-developed countries in our dataset, oil and gas production is now owned or even carried out by the state, and these oil-exporting countries have tremendous bargaining leverage in international politics because of the increasing global demands for energy and the limited number of suppliers, particularly when the oil-producing countries coordinate production levels through cartels such as OPEC. In order to have a more accurate measure of dependency, then, we should also try to account for the nature of foreign involvement in the industry, which I do by also considering inflows of foreign direct investment (FDI). Countries with high levels of commodity exports *and* FDI are much more dependent on their economic relationship with the industrialized countries. They not only rely on relatively unprocessed goods, but they do so with a greater level of foreign control over the extractive industry and all the attendant possibilities of enclave economies, repatriation of profits, and interference in domestic politics.

Figure 5.5 compares levels of populism in our 35 cases with the percentage of GDP constituted by commodity exports (food, agricultural raw materials, ores and metals, and fuels, namely, natural gas and oil), multiplied by the level

Causes of Populism in Comparative Perspective   147

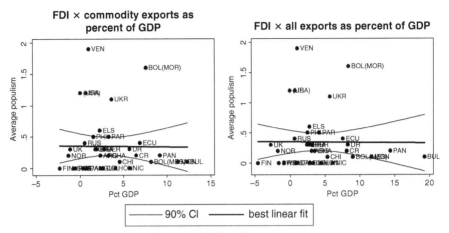

FIGURE 5.5. Populism and indicators of dependency.
Sources: Author's populism dataset; World Bank (2007).

of FDI as a percentage of GDP. High scores for this indicator mean that there is both a high level of commodity exports and a relatively strong (mathematically positive) presence of FDI (a country such as Mongolia falls in this category); numbers close to zero mean that there is little commodity trade or that FDI is relatively low (the case for Venezuela, with moderately high commodity trade in oil and gas but lower inflows of FDI); and negative numbers actually indicate the opposite of dependency, with a significant outflow of FDI and moderate to low commodity trade (such as in Norway and the United States). Data come from the World Development Indicators series. Values are averages for the 10 years prior to the year in which the leader was elected.

The data generally fail to demonstrate any relationship between dependency and populism, and the scatterplot shows essentially a flat line ($r = -.19$, $p < .27$). With the exception of Bolivia (which has a potentially high level of dependency), all of the countries with the highest levels of populism (Venezuela, Belarus, Iran, and Ukraine) fall roughly in the middle of the scale of FDI × commodity exports, while countries that do have high levels of FDI and commodity exports (Mongolia, Bulgaria, and Panama, for example) are among those with the lowest current levels of populism. In other words, the most populist countries either have low levels of FDI, export largely manufactured goods or services, or simply produce little for trade.

One response is that we have simply not measured dependency very well with our indicators of trade and investment. In particular, we are missing the fact that some of the manufacture and service exports included in these totals represent low-value-added assembly in sectors with little government regulation – sweatshops where local workers never serve as technicians, managers, or engineers. This is exceptionally difficult to gauge cross-nationally, but we can test this argument by considering a much more generous indicator of dependency: FDI × the share of GDP constituted by *all* exports, whether those are commodities or otherwise. This indicator of dependency clearly includes countries that lack anything remotely like dependent economic development, such as the smaller countries of the industrial "core" that rely heavily on trade (e.g., most of the Scandinavian countries in the dataset), but it singles out the absolute minimum that a country must have in order to be meaningfully dependent: without some international trade in the mix, we are simply witnessing a case of homegrown exploitation and poverty. The second graph in Figure 5.5 compares this indicator with our measure of populism. If it captures at least a set of necessary conditions for populism, we should see a triangular distribution of cases with cases clustering on the lower-right side of the graph. However, no such pattern emerges. There is no statistically significant relationship between populism and trade as a percentage of GDP ($r = .11$, $p < .50$), and in fact, the position of our most highly populist countries is largely unchanged.

Thus, the dependency explanation for populism simply does not hold up. We find populist leaders in countries across a fairly wide range of commodity trade and multinational participation in the domestic economy, even when we use very generous measures of dependency. A dependent economic relationship is neither a necessary nor a sufficient condition for populism to emerge.

Corruption and Democratic Norms

The final argument, and the central one of this book, conceives of populism as a normative response to crises of legitimacy resulting from widespread systematic violation of the rule of law that citizens can construe as corruption: it requires not only some policy failure, but also a backdrop of political institutional failure that populist discourse can sensibly interpret as a violation of democratic norms. This is an argument that assumes at least a basic kind of rationality – citizens and politicians are pursuing the means most likely to achieve their political ends at the lowest cost – and thus largely contradicts theories like mass-society that assert the fundamental irrationality of less well-off citizens. It sympathizes with dependency and modernization theories' claims that modern patterns of political and economic development reflect a common historical path in much of the developing world. However, it takes issue with the excessive material focus of these arguments, claiming that we must seriously consider the moral foundations of democratic politics. Thus, it intersects at various points with all of the previously discussed theories but ultimately emphasizes a different set of causal mechanisms.

As we move beyond Venezuela to a more comparative context, the clearest proponent of this argument is de la Torre (2000), who claims that populism in Latin America is a relatively constant feature deriving from chronic problems of injustice and inequality throughout the region. In Latin America, there has always been a "duality" between the rights of citizens officially noted in constitutions, law, and public discourse and the actual rights embodied in government operations and experienced in "everyday life" (p. 117). Principles of due process, basic physical security, and the sanctity of property rights are all listed on the books, but the ineffectiveness and corruptibility of key institutions means that in practice, these are respected only for the wealthy and powerful. This unequal pattern of political inclusion creates the constant potential for populist appeals. A Manichaean discourse denouncing elite conspiracies and celebrating the eventual triumph of the popular will speaks to a real underlying problem of democratic failure in which the vast majority of citizens are poorly served by a dysfunctional or even predatory state. The only thing required for its expression is some added "economic crises, change, or insecurity" that can undermine the fragile legitimacy of existing pluralist regimes (p. 118). This pattern differs from that of the advanced industrial democracies, where rights of citizenship are generally respected for all citizens, regardless of wealth or traditional status.

De la Torre's argument is not entirely new. Other scholars of Latin America have studied and emphasized the lack of impartial, effective state institutions throughout the region and this duality of citizenship, and they provide insights into the long-term origins of these patterns and their pernicious consequences, particularly for economic development. For example, historians have long argued that Latin America's exploitative system of colonial institutions and broad patterns of inequality survived the wars of independence and persisted until the present (Stein and Stein 1970), with negative consequences for economic growth (Leff 1972; Coatsworth 1978; Adelman 1999). More recently, economic historians and proponents of New Institutional Economics have used quantitative methods to partially elucidate and confirm these patterns (Engerman and Sokoloff 1997, 2000, 2002; Acemoglu, Johnson, and Robinson 2001, 2002; Krieckhaus 2006; see Lange, Mahoney, and vom Hau 2006 for a revision of this argument). They build on a literature that sees "efficient property rights" and the rule of law as crucial components of robust capitalist economic development because of the climate these institutions create for productive investment. Merely establishing property rights for elites is not enough for sustained growth; countries that in the past failed to establish and protect property rights across the broader population – predictable and professionalized taxation and regulatory structures, accessible title and business registration, commercial and banking law, intellectual property rights protection, and so on – are unlikely to experience high levels of industrialization or sustained economic growth in the modern era (North and Thomas 1973; North 1990).

What is new about this argument when applied to populism is its linking of these long-term institutional legacies to a unique set of *political* consequences. The absence of property rights and the rule of law in many developing countries does more than undermine their economic growth; in a modern context that takes fundamental democratic rights for granted, it becomes an affront to moral sensibilities by violating principles of universality for large number of citizens. The precise mechanisms that allow these institutions to persist for so long in the face of changing democratic cultures are unclear in much of the literature, and I cannot hope to elucidate them here. But enduring inequities create the basis for a rhetoric celebrating the moral superiority of a poor majority and their natural antagonism toward a scheming, antidemocratic elite. In countries without such institutional legacies, the populist discourse fails to resonate as often or with the same intensity. Moral crises of the political system tend to be shorter-lived and less intense, taking place against the background of largely functional state institutions that confine problems to specific elected officials and policies; they rarely ever become crises of legitimacy. Thus, the chronic "political instability" of many modernizing countries in the developing world (Huntington 1968) can be traced not merely to the absence of effective intermediating institutions such as political parties, but also to the persistent lack of more fundamental institutions upholding property rights and the rule of law. Without appropriate laws, an independent judiciary, a professionalized police force, and a modern bureaucracy, the economy stagnates *and* populism flourishes.

This argument helps contextualize the Venezuelan case of Chavismo, showing us that populism in that country is part of a broader problem in developing countries. While clearly aggravated by an oil economy and other contemporary factors, the interrelated problems of corruption, rentier capitalism, and the lack of the rule of law are not unique to Venezuela. Recurring populist movements in Latin America and other developing countries result from similar modes of political economy. Periodic policy failures and breakdowns in their already minimal level of governance merely serve as the spark that ignites this tinder.

In order to test this argument, Figure 5.6 compares the populism data with two country-level indicators of corruption. The first is perceived corruption as measured by the World Bank's Governance Matters division. Specifically, I use the Control of Corruption index, which is very similar to Transparency International's well-known Corruption Perceptions Index (CPI).[6] The Control of Corruption index is created by combining multiple independent surveys of ordinary citizens, businessmen (within- and without-country) and country experts (within- and without-country) by country-risk consulting firms, NGOs, and international organizations (Kaufmann, Kraay, and Mastruzzi 2006). Most of these component measures are survey questions that ask respondents either about the general frequency of certain corruption practices, such as bribery, or simply about the level of corruption in specific institutions or the government generally. To make the index more intuitive, I reverse the scale so that it effectively ranges from −2.5 to 1.5, with higher values indicating higher perceived corruption.[7] Because data are available only in even-numbered

---

[6] Data from the CPI yield essentially identical results but lack one of the key countries in our populism dataset, Belarus in the mid-1990s.

[7] A very small number of countries have higher values than this in the World Bank dataset, but they are either failed states (such as Somalia or Haiti) or highly despotic/totalitarian regimes (e.g., North Korea and Iraq under Saddam Hussein), none of which are included in our dataset of populist discourse.

Causes of Populism in Comparative Perspective

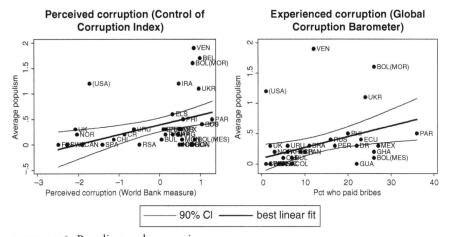

FIGURE 5.6. Populism and corruption.
Sources: Author's populism dataset; World Bank Group (2008); Transparency International (2007).

years for the late 1990s, values are taken from the year the chief executive was elected or the year before.

The second indicator is experienced corruption, as measured by Transparency International's Global Corruption Barometer (GCB). The GCB is an annual survey by Transparency International of a nationally representative set of respondents (typically at least 1,000) across a large number of countries.[8] The specific indicator I use is based on a series of questions asking "In the past 12 months, have you or anyone living in your household paid a bribe in any form to each of the following institutions/organizations?" with a list of organizations that follows. The resulting scale is simply the average percentage of respondents who answered "yes" for any of the institutions/organizations and runs from 0 to 100 (Transparency International 2007). Like the older corruption perception indices, experienced corruption measures tend to incorporate a bit of value judgment (e.g., "bribe") and thus represent a useful indicator for testing the normative theory. They are especially promising because of their greater presumed level of objectivity; respondents indicate what they or a close associate have actually witnessed firsthand, rather than their general impressions of how the government operates. However, the GCB itself is less than ideal because it has only been gathered since 2004, considers only one type of corruption (bribery), and excludes some of our key instances of populism – Belarus under Lukashenko and Iran under Ahmadinejad – and a few other leaders in the sample, leaving us with just 29 observations. In addition, the data tend to fluctuate over time more

---

[8] In many instances, these are urban samples. For more details on sampling, see Transparency International (2007).

than the familiar corruption perception indexes, perhaps reflecting the fact that a single survey is used for each country rather than an index of surveys. To ameliorate this volatility in the data, I use the average value of the GCB for each country across the entire series. In most cases this combines four annual values (2004–7), although in some it is an average of just one year of data. Needless to say, the limited time span of the data means that we cannot know the GCB for the precise year in which many of our chief executives were elected; instead, we have to accept a more proximate value, occasionally from several years later.[9]

Both graphs show a fairly strong relationship between corruption across countries and the level of populism in the chief executive's discourse. The relationship is strongest in the first graph, which measures perceived corruption. Not only is the linear correlation statistically significant and in the right direction – at $r = .41$ ($p < .02$), it is as strong as any we have considered – but the actual pattern we observe in the graph also confirms our theory in all of the most salient cases. The most populist leaders are all in countries with high levels of perceived corruption, while none of the countries at the low end of the populism scale have more than slight traces of perceived corruption. Even the variance in populism within these different groups (especially those at the extremes of the curve) corresponds moderately well with small variances in corruption; Venezuela at the moment of Chávez's first election is one of the most corrupt countries in the dataset. The relationship is weaker in the second graph, depicting experienced corruption, although the overall shape of the graph masks what is in fact a relatively strong correlation ($r = .39$ at $p < .04$). Given the imprecision in these data and the reduced number of cases, the result is encouraging. The strongest outlier here is actually Venezuela, which has lower experienced corruption than we would expect given the level of populism in Chávez's discourse. Of course, this figure for corruption comes from the mid-2000s, when Chávez had already been in office for several years.

---

[9] I also considered one other indicator, the Rule of Law index created by the World Bank's Governance Matters' Division. Like the index of perceived corruption, it combines multiple measures from other surveys and datasets that attempt to gauge the perceived quality of, in this instance, the judiciary and police force, the protection of property rights, and the control of crime. While in theory this provides us with an independent verification of the normative explanation because it taps into a different set of indicators, in practice there is little distance between many of the separate indicators used to create this index and the perceived corruption indexes. To give just one example, the Rule of Law index uses questions from the Latinobarometro about trust in the judiciary and police, while the Control of Corruption index uses questions from the same survey about whether citizens often have to bribe police and judges (Kaufmann, Kraay, and Mastruzzi 2005, 85); presumably, respondents' attitudes of trust in these institutions are at least somewhat related to the need to bribe their officials. In fact, the average annual correlation between the Rule of Law index and the Control of Corruption index ranges between $r = .92$ and .96. While it would be tempting to see this as proof of the close coincidence between the actual quality of the rule of law and citizens' perceptions of corruption, I think the two measures are too hard to disentangle and I set this indicator aside.

Data from the Latinobarometer's series on experienced corruption (a separate indicator available only for Latin America) suggest that experienced corruption in Venezuela was actually much higher in previous years, closer to the time Chávez was elected (Corporación Latinobarómetro 2007, 102); if true, this would bring this observation in line with the trend here and in the previous graph.[10] Overall, then, the results strongly suggest that widespread corruption is at least a necessary condition for the emergence of populism everywhere, not just in Venezuela. As countries pass a threshold of increasing corruption (somewhere around the middle of the scale on both measures), the likelihood of populism increases dramatically.

Thus, a comparative analysis provides support for the argument linking populism to failures in the rule of law and perceived corruption. At the same time, the previous data make it clear that corruption, like all of the other indicators we have tested so far, is an insufficient explanation; a large number of countries with high levels of perceived corruption lack any noticeably populist leader at the time of our analysis. Admittedly, some of these (such as Peru and Ecuador) have had populist leaders at other moments in their recent history, but these exceptions simply prove the point: populist movements rise to power suddenly and exit the political stage just as quickly, in many cases replaced by chief executives with pluralist discourses. Constant levels of corruption (the corruption perception indexes are fairly stable for most countries over the decade since the World Bank and Transparency International began compiling these indicators) cannot completely explain the varying presence of populist chief executives across time or their absence in many countries. Part of the problem is that we have not yet corrected for the intervening effects of policy failure; I do so in the next section. But even this additional correction fails to explain a large portion of the variance in populism across countries, and in the conclusion I take up the question of what these remaining conditions might be.

A MULTIVARIATE ANALYSIS

While these bivariate correlations shed light on the different theories of populism and show our normative explanation to be a strong contender, they only capture isolated associations. We need to test these associations while holding other factors constant, and we need to consider the interactive effects between corruption and policy failure that the normative explanation implies. Unfortunately, running a multiple regression is difficult because of our modest

---

[10] Venezuela is probably the only country in the dataset to be afflicted with measurement error of this magnitude, because Chávez is one of the earliest chief executives in the entire dataset (elected in 1998). Only Tony Blair, who first becomes prime minister in 1997, is earlier, and levels of experienced corruption in the United Kingdom seem very unlikely to have changed much over the subsequent decade. Most of the other chief executives are from the mid-2000s.

number of observations. With several of the indicators tested previously, the possible number of observations drops as low as 24, and when all of them are considered together, the remaining set of observations declines even further. Thus, rather than rely on a single regression model with all variables included and many observations missing, I calculate a series of regressions that each compares perceived corruption with a different indicator from the competing theories, culminating with a model that includes a full slate of indicators. The results (Models 1–16) are presented in Table 5.1. In each case, the dependent variable is our measure of populist elite discourse, and all models are OLS. To reduce problems of heteroskedasticity, I use a robust estimator for the standard errors. Because we know the hypothesized direction of most variables, the p-values are all for one-tailed tests, except in the case of the interaction terms, where there is no hypothesized direction.

As a baseline for comparison, Model 1 shows the results for corruption (in all models, the World Bank's Control of Corruption index) considered alone. This regression repeats the earlier results in Figure 5.6, finding a statistically significant relationship (at the $p < .01$ level) between corruption and populism that runs in the expected positive direction. In fact, in this model, the difference in perceived corruption between Venezuela and Finland (3.33, nearly spanning the World Bank's scale) is associated with a 0.63 decrease in the populism score. The association is not perfect, however; the R^2 for this model[11] is only .17, a rather modest level for a regression using a small or moderate number of country-level observations.

Models 2–6 test our indicators of the economic voting explanation by comparing the 2-, 5-, 10-, and 20-year growth averages in GDP with the corruption indicator, as well as our first interaction effect (between the 20-year average and corruption).[12] As can be seen, these results roughly parallel our earlier findings, in that the association between economic growth and populism grows stronger as we consider long growth trends; however, the increase is no longer very large once we control for corruption, and now even the coefficient for the 20-year growth average is statistically indistinguishable from zero. With the growth and corruption indicators set side by side, corruption is clearly the better predictor.

An equally striking finding is the interaction effect, which turns out to be statistically significant (at better than the $p < .10$ level) and shows that the effects of perceived corruption and economic policy failure are not entirely independent. Interpreting the results of this model requires that we calculate some predicted values. These are found in Table 5.2, which presents the

---

[11] Because these regressions use robust estimators, I cannot calculate an adjusted r-squared.
[12] Although I do not present the results here, none of the other, shorter-term indicators of growth turn out to have a statistically significant relationship to populism once I control for corruption, while corruption remains a statistically significant and large predictor. The effect of corruption, however, does diminish slightly as the period of growth under consideration increases, while the effect of economic performance increases. This fits my earlier findings and the broader literature on the relationship between corruption and economic growth.

TABLE 5.1. *Multivariate regressions on populism*

	Baseline	Economic Voting				
Variable	Model 1	Model 2	Model 3	Model 4	Model 5	Model 6
Corruption	0.192**	0.191**	0.178**	0.169**	0.13*	0.235**
	0.06	0.06	0.061	0.059	0.069	0.076
2-Year Growth		−0.02				
		0.033				
5-Year Growth			−0.023			
			0.044			
10-Year Growth				−0.041		
				0.062		
20-Year Growth					−0.087	−0.025
					0.088	0.067
20-Year Growth × Corruption						0.136*
						0.072
Media vs. Education						
Media vs. Education × Corruption						
Union Density						
Union Density (ILO)						
Union Density Change						
Union Density Change × Corruption						
Dependency						
Dependency (all exports)						
Dependency × Corruption						
y-intercept	0.389***	0.427***	0.423***	0.444**	0.47***	0.299**
	0.082	0.115	0.114	0.133	0.137	0.096
N	34	34	34	34	34	34
F	10.189	5.112	5.107	5.253	5.46	3.939
R^2	0.17	0.19	0.19	0.19	0.20	0.26
RMSE	0.473	0.475	0.476	0.476	0.472	0.462

Note: Entries are OLS coefficients (robust standard errors). All *p*-values are for one-tailed tests, except for interaction terms.
*p < .10; **p < .01; ***p < .001

(*continued*)

Table 5.1. (continued)

	Mass Society		Modernization			
Variable	Model 7	Model 8	Model 9	Model 10	Model 11	Model 12
Corruption	0.264**	0.266**	0.174*	0.208**	0.109*	0.119*
	0.091	0.095	0.101	0.071	0.054	0.062
2-Year Growth						
5-Year Growth						
10-Year Growth						
20-Year Growth						
20-Year Growth × Corruption						
Media vs. Education	−0.009	−0.009				
	0.008	0.007				
Media vs. Education × Corruption		0.000				
		0.005				
Union Density			0.002			
			0.003			
Union Density (ILO)				0.006*		
				0.004		
Union Density Change					−0.017*	−0.019*
					0.01	0.013
Union Density Change × Corruption						−0.007
						0.008
Dependency						
Dependency (all exports)						
Dependency × Corruption						
y-intercept	0.428***	0.427***	0.315**	0.196*	0.296***	0.271***
	0.098	0.107	0.094	0.132	0.082	0.067
N	28	28	24	31	24	24
F	4.98	3.223	2.054	4.311	2.271	4.208
R^2	0.24	0.24	0.14	0.24	0.23	0.26
RMSE	0.502	0.512	0.463	0.447	0.436	0.438

Table 5.1. (continued)

	Dependency			Combined
Variable	Model 13	Model 14	Model 15	Model 16
Corruption	0.219**	0.214**	0.231**	0.427*
	0.076	0.074	0.088	0.265
2-Year Growth				
5-Year Growth				
10-Year Growth				
20-Year Growth				0.059
				0.105
20-Year Growth × Corruption				0.211
				0.229
Media vs. Education				−0.004
				0.009
Media vs. Education × Corruption				
Union Density				
Union Density (ILO)				
Union Density Change				−0.014*
				0.009
Union Density Change × Corruption				
Dependency	−0.034*		−0.035*	
	0.024		0.022	
Dependency (all exports)		−0.023*		−0.051
		0.015		0.083
Dependency × Corruption			0.005	
			0.023	
y-intercept	0.476***	0.457***	0.47**	0.299*
	0.133	0.124	0.148	0.223
	32	32	32	19
	4.572	4.459	2.948	0.827
	0.20	0.20	0.21	0.36
	0.433	0.435	0.441	0.519

Note: Entries are OLS coefficients (robust standard errors). All *p*-values are for one-tailed tests, except for interaction terms.
*p < .10; **p < .01; ***p < .001.

predicted populism score for different combinations of (20-year) economic growth and corruption. As is evident, economic growth has some association with populism, but the effect varies significantly, depending on the level of perceived corruption. At high levels of corruption (one standard deviation above the mean of the dataset), an especially low level of growth is associated

TABLE 5.2. *Predicted level of populism, given corruption and economic growth*

When Growth Is...	And Corruption Is...	
	High	Low
Weak	0.80	−0.09
Strong	0.29	0.19

Note: Weak or low values are one standard deviation below the sample mean; strong or high values are one standard deviation above the sample mean.

with moderate predicted levels of populism, while high growth cuts the level of populism in half; however, at low levels of corruption (one standard deviation below the mean), the effect of growth is greatly diminished and nearly reverses itself (bear in mind that the populism scale cannot actually go below zero). The opposite is not true: even with good levels of growth, high levels of perceived corruption are still associated with increasing populism. Thus, as the normative explanation suggests, citizens' perceptions of corruption form an important background condition for populism, and economic policy failure cannot by itself produce populism.

These results for economic growth in combination with corruption turn out to be the most interesting of the set; the remaining tests all show corruption to be the best predictor and fail to yield any significant interaction effects. Models 7 and 8 (Table 5.1) consider the effects of corruption and our most meaningful indicator of mass-society theory, the disjuncture between media access and education. It shows that perceived corruption is still a strong predictor of populism even after controlling for the gap between education and media access as well as any possible interaction effects. The coefficient for this gap is not statistically significant at standard levels and is in the wrong direction now; the negative value indicates that once we control for corruption, greater disjunctures between electronic media access and education are associated with lower levels of populism. The interaction effect fails to change these results and is basically zero. In contrast, the coefficient for corruption is in the expected direction and is large (actually larger than in the baseline model) and remains statistically significant. Thus, if mass-society theory explained populism at all before, it no longer does so once we take corruption into account.

Models 9 through 12 test modernization theory by comparing corruption with our three indicators of labor union density as well as one interaction effect; I do not consider the size of the informal sector because of the small number of observations for this measure. Here the results are somewhat more mixed, but they still favor corruption as the better predictor. One of our measures of union density – the absolute level according to a mix of sources (yielding a smaller number of observations and questionable comparability) – fails to have any statistically significant relationship with populism once we control for corruption (Model 9). Another measure – the absolute level according to the ILO (with more observations and somewhat greater comparability) – is statistically significant at close to standard levels but in the wrong direction, with high levels of union density associated with greater levels of populism (Model 10). The other measure of union density, the change in union density across the smaller number of cases (Model 11), is the only indicator with a favorable result for modernization theory. The coefficient for change in union density is in the right direction and close to standard levels of statistical significance, suggesting that declining union density results in greater levels of populism; the coefficient for corruption, while still statistically significant and in the right direction, is noticeably smaller. However, the subsequent interactive model fails to display any added explanatory power, and both of these models drop a larger number of cases, including two of our crucial instances of full-blown populism. We should also wonder why populism would be correlated with the change in union density and not with the absolute levels of union density across these countries. On the whole, these results are suggestive but fail to really discount the normative explanation for populism.

The final set of models (Models 13–15) tests the two indicators of dependency theory and one of the possible interaction effects. These two indicators are the combination of FDI with the level of commodity exports as a percentage of GDP, and FDI with the level of all exports as a percentage of GDP. I consider both of these indicators since neither had a clear advantage in the original analysis. The results here clearly favor our normative explanation; corruption remains a large, statistically significant predictor across all three models. In contrast, the two indicators of dependency are statistically significant but are both in the wrong direction, with higher levels of dependency associated with lower levels of populism once we control for corruption, which is not at all what dependency theory predicts. The interaction effect here (between corruption and our first measure of dependency, based on commodity exports only) is not statistically significant.

The last model (Model 16) brings together a representative set of indicators for each of our theories. As was already mentioned, this model is far from ideal because it eliminates over one-third of our observations; the lack of statistically significant findings may not mean very much. That said, two of our indicators still have statistically significant coefficients in the direction we would predict: corruption (positively associated with populism) and the change in union density (negatively associated with populism). Our key interaction effect (between corruption and the 20-year annual rate of economic growth) is still in the right direction but is no longer statistically significant.

Together, these models provide some important, if qualified, confirmation of the normative theory. Corruption is the best predictor of populism across all of the statistical models, even when we take a large number of variables into account and lose some of our observations. In contrast, poor economic growth by itself is not a strong predictor of populism once we take corruption into account, suggesting that economic voting is not the principal cause of populism (and that perceptions of corruption are not just artifacts of policy performance). And neither economic dependency nor an unfavorable combination of electronic media access and low levels of education can predict populism, suggesting that dependency theory and mass-society theory are even poorer explanations for populism. Changes in union density have a stronger relationship with populism even after we take other variables into account, giving some credence to structuralist (modernization) theories of populism, but these results are not confirmed once we look at alternative indicators of union density with larger numbers of observations. Finally, we find evidence of a strong interaction effect between corruption and economic policy failure that fits the predictions of our theory, showing that economic growth really matters for populism only when it occurs in an environment of high corruption.

CONCLUSION: EXPLAINING THE SUFFICIENT CONDITIONS FOR POPULISM

The preceding analysis of cross-national data on populism largely confirms and adds nuance to what we learned earlier about Venezuela. Populist movements are best explained as a reaction to systematic violations of the rule of law that can be interpreted as corruption, particularly in combination with other policy failures such as economic crisis. While the economic voting and structuralist (modernization) theories used in Venezuela possibly have some explanatory power in comparative context, these effects turn out to be inconsistent or matter only when considered in combination with perceived corruption. Mass-society and dependency theories that are more common in the study of populism elsewhere have even less explanatory power. Ultimately, the ability of citizens to impute widespread and systematic corruption to their political system is a crucial precondition.

Yet, neither perceived corruption nor any of our other indicators considered in combination are sufficient conditions for the emergence of populist movements; many other countries also experience conditions of widespread corruption and policy failure without seeing populists come to power. We can see the insufficiency of our normative explanation by returning to the case of Chavismo in Venezuela. A key question left unanswered in the previous chapter is why Chávez or his predecessors became popular in the 1990s instead of much earlier, when corrupt behavior was first becoming a significant problem. There was a lag of well over 10 years between the end of the oil boom and the tumultuous second administration of Carlos Andrés Pérez that marked the beginning of the end of the party system; in fact, two decades passed between the end of Pérez's first term and the election of Chávez. The level of corruption alone seems to correlate imperfectly with the emergence and dramatic increase of successful populist leaders in Venezuela. What additional factors might account for the frequent failure of this important background condition to produce electorally successful populist movements?

One obvious response in the case of Chavismo is that populism depends not just on corruption but also on significant policy failures that can undermine the legitimacy of the political system in both normative and substantive terms. While the corruption of Venezuela's political system acquired its "billionaire" proportions early in the first oil boom, it was only after the economy declined in the subsequent decade and a half that the crisis achieved its full magnitude. The economic failure became especially acute after the mismanaged attempt by Pérez to implement market-oriented reforms after 1989 and again after the banking crisis and the new wave of neoliberal reforms under Caldera in the mid-1990s, neither of which were really causes of the decline (on the contrary, they attempted to reverse it), but did foster a sense that economic problems were tied to the incompetence and selfish scheming of the political class. Such an explanation nicely emphasizes the simultaneous rational (in the classic sense of material self-interest) and cultural bases of politics: citizens care about both, particularly when simultaneous failures in these areas can somehow be connected.

Unfortunately, this explanation still cannot account for the late emergence of populism in Venezuela. The multivariate analysis in the previous section demonstrates that the combination of corruption and long-term economic performance yields higher predictive power than corruption alone, but the amount of explained variance in these equations ($R^2 = .26$) is still low for a model with aggregate country-level data. A number of other countries that had high levels of corruption and low levels of long-term economic performance, such as Russia in 2000, Nicaragua in 2002, and Paraguay in 2003, lacked successful populist movements at the time they were analyzed.

A related answer is that the underlying failure of the rule of law becomes evident to citizens only gradually. In the case of Venezuela, journalistic exposés were first published in the mid-1980s, and survey data indicate that voters failed to pick up on the problem of corruption in their government until sometime later. Average Venezuelans had only finite resources to devote to gathering information about politics, and it probably took time – and repeated government administrations and scandals – to clarify and confirm how corrupt the system had become. Yet, failures of information cannot explain the absence of populism that we see in other countries. The corruption data examined in this chapter reflect something close to the current perceptions of average citizens. These perceptions may have lagged in the case of Venezuela (the World Bank and Transparency International indexes only go back to 1995, so we cannot be sure), but the lack of perfect correspondence between these corruption indexes and our populism dataset shows that even significant *perceived* corruption often fails to generate a successful populist response. We lack solid grounds for assuming that the time lag we see in Venezuela is merely the product of rational uncertainty.[13]

A better response is that we need to consider the conditions that govern the *supply* of populist movements. The normative theory offered here, not to mention every other competing theory that I have discussed in this and the previous chapter, analyzes only the demand for populism. While deep structural roots are crucial factors for the successful emergence of populism, an exclusive emphasis on these factors ignores the other side of the process, that of willing politicians and a political system that permits these populists to enter and compete effectively.

The supply-side factors that are traditionally considered by the comparative literature on party change and stability, including the literature on radical-right populism in Western Europe, tend to center on spatial competitive dynamics and institutional factors such as electoral rules that facilitate the entry of third parties (Kitschelt 1994, 1995; Mudde 2007). These factors are crucial for understanding the ability of programmatic parties to carve out an issue space and compete on equal terms with one another. However, they are less helpful for understanding the entry and success of populist party movements that challenge the legitimacy of the rules and do not emphasize competition on existing ideological dimensions. The issues that populists primarily compete on are questions about the form and quality of the regime rather than clientelistic redistribution or questions of policy.

In Venezuela, for example, it is true that decentralization reforms helped open up the political system to third-party challengers such as MAS and LCR, which gained significant strength and experience by winning positions in local government during the late 1980s and early 1990s (López-Maya 1997; Buxton 2001). But neither Caldera in 1993 nor Chávez in 1998 followed this path to power. Caldera had relatively little trouble running outside of his own traditional party and quickly carved out an issue space that was already filled by a number of third parties; many of these potential competitors were simply incorporated into his coalition. And Chávez and most of his associates who won seats in the 1998 election had never held significant government office. The strategy that Chávez and other recent populists in Latin America follow is to challenge the existing constitutional order through a run for the presidency, rewrite the constitution once they are in power, and call for new elections that allow them to remove the old parties. Short of outright authoritarian restraints on new challengers, institutional constraints and spatial-competitive

---

[13] We could also see this as evidence of a more methodologically challenging discourse analytical argument that evident failures in the rule of law are not *interpreted* as corruption until the right discourse emerges as a product of elite rhetoric or popular conversation that can reframe our material experiences. However, the data at the end of this paragraph indicate that even this nonrational argument cannot account for the lag we see in Venezuela. All of the indicators we have used are measures of (perceived) corruption, not objective indicators of the rule of law.

dynamics matter little for the outcome of this contest between populists and traditional political elites.

When we consider the supply side of populism, we must instead examine the factors governing the presence of a populist *leader*. I have already argued that populism is not defined by the presence of a charismatic leader; it is the ideas and language that distinguish both a leader (if one exists) and activists as populist. We can point to examples of populist movements without charismatic leaders and charismatic leaders who are not populist. Nevertheless, charismatic leadership is a likely condition for populist movements to become successful and win control of government. Mass political movements with national aspirations confront enormous collective action problems (McCarthy and Zald 1977; Olsen 1982), and these problems are heightened by a populist discourse preaching the essential moral equality of all citizens and the moral imperative of participating directly in both action and decision making. To be precise, these are not traditional collective action problems of *cooperation*; the moral argument of populist discourse provides a ready stimulus for individual participation that can override citizens' material self-interest. Rather, they are challenges of *coordination*, or of bringing together large numbers of publicly minded citizens around common strategies and tactics, especially the mundane efforts required to conduct election campaigns.

Charismatic leaders can greatly facilitate this process by providing followers with additional nonmaterial incentives and a focal point for participation, and they can speak with one voice on issues of tactics and strategy. Yet, only a leader of quasi-divine character and skills can embody the popular will. Such a role requires a demonstrably selfless regard for others and the connection to a higher metaphysical realm that can serve as an antidote to corruption and the crisis of the system. The leader must be a living example of the Good in populist discourse and a skilled politician capable of overcoming the diabolical conspiracies of the elite. He must be a champion of the people and an exemplar of folk wisdom and popular culture. And he must be sufficiently inclusive that the majority of citizens can simultaneously read their particular wills and identity into his own.[14]

Needless to say, these are fairly atypical individuals. Studies of charismatic politicians emphasize that in order to embody these attributes convincingly, leaders must become assimilated to one of the "dominant myths" of the society, perform some apparently heroic or extraordinary feat, and have outstanding rhetorical ability (Wilner 1985). A Chávez, with his sincere, consistent discourse (at least partially), articulated platform, widely recognized leadership abilities, and strong strategic skills is a rarity among politicians in

---

[14] For a similar argument about the role of charismatic leadership in marshaling populist movements, see Pappas (2008). Pappas refers to his cases as "radical mass movements," but the descriptions of his three positive cases (Milosevic, Georges Papandreou in Greece, and, coincidentally, Chávez) make it fairly clear that these are populist movements.

Venezuela. And even this rare kind of politician required a substantial share of luck to emerge on the political scene (Petkoff 2004). Small events made a big difference, such as the government's decision to broadcast Chávez's surrender on live television in 1992 (probably the key heroic feat that established his charisma; see Naím 1993 and Tarre Briceño 1994) or Caldera's decision to pardon the coup organizers in 1994. At any of these and other junctures, Chávez might have been prevented from becoming known or successful, and in 1998 a very different leader would have emerged. I am not aware of any other populist leaders of the same caliber as Chávez during this period in Venezuela; he competed mostly against halfhearted populists and pluralists with only pale shadows of his charismatic appeal.

Thus, the supply of successful populist movements depends not so much on the presence of facilitating institutions and the strategic context as on the availability of extraordinary leadership. This argument is naturally unsatisfying, because it depends on singular variables that defy generalization and testing. Social scientists dislike these kinds of causes because of their ad hoc, nonfalsifiable quality. How do we measure the supply of potential populist leaders in any country? Are they really in scarce supply, or are they prevented from emerging by structural deterministic factors that policymakers can potentially control? If a leader and his movement succeed, is this because he was sufficiently charismatic and lucky or because leadership is actually unimportant? Yet, social science theories do not have to be perfectly deterministic; on the contrary, we express concern about theories that slip into functionalistic arguments about how conditions "force" or "require" new parties or institutions to emerge (Little 1991). In this same spirit, I assert that conditions may facilitate the emergence and success of a populist leader or movement but cannot compel them to appear.

This supply-side argument *can* be tested indirectly, although not with data we currently have. Whereas contemporary snapshots of populism in the global context show an imperfect correlation between populism and corruption, if my theory holds true, there should be an even higher correlation between average populism and the rule of law *over time*. A possible way to test this would be to measure the discourse or worldview of chief executives across multiple administrations or even decades in a single country, then compare these country means across multiple countries; we should see an association between discourse and corruption that is stronger than the one measured with our single panel of data.

We currently lack precise long-term data for either of our key indicators, corruption or populism, and I leave a more precise test for future research. Yet, it is easy to see long-term patterns in Latin America that confirm this hypothesis. According to Drake (1999), Chile, Uruguay, and Costa Rica are the only countries in the region showing a distinct lack of populism during the era of mass democracy in the twentieth century. In the case of Chile, we can point to the relatively short-lived and mild experiences of Arturo Alessandri (president 1920–4, 1925, and 1932–8) and Carlos Ibañez (especially his elected

Causes of Populism in Comparative Perspective

term in office from 1952 to 1958), while in Uruguay and Costa Rica, we are hard-pressed to identify any populist president in the twentieth century at all, at least in the sense used here. By contrast, all other countries with some semblance of democratic experience feature multiple presidents and challenger parties that are widely recognized as populist. Chile, Uruguay, and Costa Rica are also the three countries in Latin American with low or modest levels of perceived corruption today, using either the World Bank data here (see Figure 5.6) or Transparency International's CPI. In 2006 Transparency International scored these countries as 7.0, 6.7, and 5.0 on the CPI, on a par with the United States, Spain, and South Korea, respectively; the next highest Latin American democracy is El Salvador at 4.0.

Even given these concerns, these two chapters provide significant contributions to theory and method. The demand-side theories examined here explain a fair amount of variance in populist movements across the globe. Unlike the previous literature on populism, these chapters test the reigning theories of populism simultaneously with more than just a few observations, both at the individual and the aggregate levels. Such a comparative quantitative analysis allows us to test normative theories more rigorously and question some of the better-known alternatives. The data reaffirm that approaching populism as a cultural phenomenon while retaining positivist methodology allows us to reduce, if not eliminate, some of our uncertainties about what causes populism.

6

Populist Organization

The Bolivarian Circles in Venezuela

> By and for the fatherland, and with President Chávez.
>
> Slogan of the Bolivarian Circles

The previous chapters demonstrate that populism understood as discourse or worldview is a distinct phenomenon that we can identify in the case of Chavismo, and that Chavismo and other successful populist movements arise as responses to crises of legitimacy rooted in the weak rule of law. In the next two chapters I begin to address a final, related question that asks what the *consequences* of populism are. That is, do politicians and citizens expressing a populist discourse also engage in unique forms of behavior that we can clearly trace to their fundamental beliefs? I attempt to answer this question here by exploring the effects of populism on political organization through a study of the Bolivarian Circles in Venezuela. In the next chapter, I move on to explore the effects of populist ideas on public policy.

This chapter and the one that follows provide valuable opportunities to show how ideas have important consequences for real political phenomena. They demonstrate that we cannot reduce basic decisions about political organization and government policy merely to the material self-interest or office maximization of politicians. However, these chapters also allow us to revisit some of the basic conceptual questions about populism and show how some of the better-known alternative definitions are encapsulated by the discursive one. Here I consider the political-institutional definition. Organizational attributes form a prominent part of this new approach to populism, which sees features such as low institutionalization, support from large numbers of voters, and low levels of organization as the primary attributes of populism. While this chapter confirms that these attributes are manifested in the heart of Chavismo, I make it clear that they are not independent features of populism, but products of the movement's worldview and, to a lesser degree, of the

---

Special thanks to my former coauthor, David Hansen, who gave comments on a version of this chapter. However, the conclusions reached in this chapter are my own responsibility.

charismatic authority of Chávez. Defining populism as discourse or worldview allows us to identify the underlying logic of these choices.

The particular set of organizations studied in this chapter, the Bolivarian Circles, were a vast network of voluntary associations that constituted the largest organized component of Chavismo during its first years in power – approximately 2.2 million Venezuelans at the peak of their activity. The Circles played a key role in the demonstrations that followed Chávez's temporary removal from power in April 2002 and were heavily involved in organizing communities, gaining access to the government's poverty alleviation programs, and campaigning for the president in the recall election. After 2004, however, they experienced a significant decline in activity and were eventually eclipsed by other government initiatives.

During the two months leading up to the presidential recall in August 2004, a colleague and I performed a study of the Circles in Venezuela (Hawkins and Hansen 2006). Using the resulting sample of survey data and a series of interviews with Circle leaders, I show here that the Circles manifested four key attributes of populist organization: low institutionalization, movement structure, disruptive tactics, and insularity within the larger civil society. To make this argument, I first critique the political-institutional approach and provide a basic theory of populist organization that links these four organizational attributes to populism's Manichaean outlook of the people versus a conspiring elite. I then review the history of the Circles and situate them within the broader movement. Finally, I present our findings on the Circles in each of these four areas of organization.

A THEORY OF POPULIST ORGANIZATION

The traditional literature is generally silent on how actual instances of populism organize. Although there are important exceptions that I note later, older scholars rarely even mention specific organizational attributes. This lack of discussion is unsurprising in the literature on populist discourse and economic populism, where the study of political organization has never been a serious concern. It is more puzzling in the modernization literature and the more recent work on populism in Western European party systems, both of which come from mainstream political science. The classic modernization scholars of populism (e.g., Germani and di Tella) and their contemporary structuralist descendants typically limit themselves to discussing the multiclass coalitions that characterize different movements. Because the composition of these coalitions varies dramatically across time and national context (Conniff 1999, 14–15), their observation fails to provide us with a consistently unique organizational attribute. Likewise, Western Europeanists such as Betz (1994) and Kitschelt (1995) focus only on the origins and success of radical-right populist parties, and they omit any attempt to determine their internal organization.

This has changed with the recent literature defining populism in political-institutional terms. In much the same spirit as this book, these studies pursue a minimal definition of populism, or a short list of core attributes that can help us identify the family to which all species of populism belong, neo- or otherwise. Unlike this book, however, political-institutional studies emphasize the material qualities of organization. They define populism as a political *strategy* characterized by (1) a direct relationship between a charismatic leader and his followers, (2) disdain for existing institutions of representative democracy, (3) an emphasis on support from large numbers of voters, (4) low levels of organization of supporters, and (5) low institutionalization (Weyland 2001; Roberts 2003).

The political-institutional approach highlights a number of attributes that potentially constitute a configuration unique to populism. As I emphasize throughout this chapter, most of these attributes are found in every historical instance of populism, including Chavismo. However, because the political-institutional approach sees these as the defining features of populism rather than as consequences of a particular set of beliefs, it fails to identify the underlying logic that unites and gives rise to them. Other than the fact that these attributes are all in some way aspects of organization, it is not clear why they appear together. For example, is charismatic leadership something that exists independent of low institutionalization, or do these reinforce each other? If an organization has all of these attributes except a charismatic leader, is it still populist? Likewise, even if an organization has all of these attributes, it is not evident that it then becomes populist. Other organizations, such as religious or labor-based parties and millenarian movements, also have charismatic leaders and/or low levels of institutionalization early in their organizational life cycle and may seek to change the political system, yet we do not necessarily consider them populist. What underlying quality makes the difference? Failing to identify the underlying logic of populist organization also means that we potentially miss other attributes that should be associated with populist movements such as Chavismo. For example, movement organization and disruptive tactics also seem to characterize many populist movements (including Chavismo), but on what grounds can we admit them to the list?

I argue that, ultimately, it is the fundamental assumptions and the accompanying language of activists and their leaders that distinguish particular aspects of organization as populist. A Manichaean worldview that leads to talk of a cosmic struggle between the will of the people and a conspiring elite also shapes preferences over certain types of organization, and it infuses those organizations with a kind of meaning that we can recognize and measure. Populists create a poorly institutionalized movement because they mistrust hierarchical forms of organization and value folk wisdom and popular participation; they employ disruptive tactics in order to express their common outrage with the system; and they emphasize large numbers to demonstrate their status as the people.

In what follows, I spell out a few observable implications of the ideational approach to populism and provide a rough theory of populist organization.

I specifically discuss four attributes: low institutionalization, movement organization, disruptive tactics, and insularity. These cover much of the terrain usually found in studies of political organization and provide us with a broadly representative set of indicators to analyze in the case of Chavismo and the Bolivarian Circles. They also happen to include all of the attributes emphasized by political-institutional definitions of populism, allowing us to see how each of these arises from populist assumptions and is thus encapsulated by the discursive definition. To be clear, my argument is not that any one of these is necessarily unique to populism; as I have already affirmed, some of them are characteristics of other kinds of organizations with other orientations. Nor should we take all of this as a claim that material interests and constraints fail to play an important role in organization; later, I reaffirm the complementary role that interests often play in shaping organizational choices. However, these common characteristics of populist organization can only be rendered sensible once we appreciate the underlying ideas that animate them.[1]

Low Institutionalization

The first organizational attribute of populism is low institutionalization. By this, I mean that the movement's constituent organizations and its upper tier of leadership have low *autonomy*, or independence from outside actors in terms of resources and decisions; that they have little *rule basis*, or codified system for making crucial decisions about goals, tactics, membership, and leadership selection; and that their organizations fail to develop *identities* that are distinct from that of the leader or the larger movement (Panebianco 1988).

Institutionalization of political organizations, and especially that of political parties, is an old concern for political scientists. Huntington (1968) regarded the development of valued political institutions such as parties as the key to stable government in societies undergoing rapid socioeconomic change. More recently, Mainwaring and Scully (1995, 2008) have argued that institutionalized parties and party systems are crucial, albeit insufficient, conditions for good governance and democratic consolidation. Institutionalized parties and

---

[1] Recent work on populist organization by Roberts (2006) represents another exception to much of the populist literature and a helpful extension of the political-institutional approach. Roberts questions the assumed affinity between populism and weak organization by noting that levels of organization actually vary across populist movements. In the case of Chavismo in particular, he argues that the movement has avoided the creation of a highly institutionalized party (MVR was neither institutionalized nor the only vehicle through which Chávez won elections) but has made significant efforts at mobilizing and organizing large swaths of Venezuelan civil society, as we see in the case of the Circles. He explains this as a response to the lack of opposition partisan organization and the strength of opposition civil society, at least circa 2003–5. Roberts's work is innovative in terms of its general approach to populist organization and its particular analysis of Chavismo. However, while there are differences in the *amount* of constituent organization, either as civil society or as a party, I suggest that there are important similarities in the *kind* of organization that also require explanation.

party systems tend to have a peaceful electoral orientation, help channel and aggregate voter preferences, enhance democratic accountability, and reduce uncertainty. These kinds of arguments have made institutionalization a key concern for the study of both democratization (see Linz and Stepan 1996; Diamond 1999) and political parties, especially in the developing world (see Panebianco 1988; Randall and Svasand 2002; Levitsky 2003).

Low institutionalization is the one attribute of organization that is widely mentioned and developed in studies of populism. Works from the classical tradition and even a few recent publications go so far as to make it a defining feature (Roxborough 1984, 9; see, e.g., di Tella 1965, 47), and it is one of the chief attributes mentioned by scholars using the political-institutional definition (Weyland 2001). However, it is not an isolated aspect of populism that emerges independently and combines accidentally with others to produce a populist movement. It is a product of a populist worldview and of the charismatic leadership that often embodies it.

With populism, the will of the people is the only sovereign voice, and one's identity as part of that people is the ultimate moral objective. This means that particular instances of popular mobilization are only means to an end. Under these conditions, it is morally suspect for any organization to acquire a unique identity and an autonomous means of action – to become valued for itself and not simply as a "consumable" instrument (Selznick 1957). Particular organizations can rarely equal, let alone stand above, the people, because they never incorporate all citizens or even majorities as active members on a permanent basis. The larger movements that do claim to embody this popular will are unstable; they require exhaustive effort and great sacrifices from their members that are hard to sustain indefinitely. Hence, smaller populist organizations never really acquire a life of their own, and the movements that do acquire this life are unlikely to endure.

A second source of low institutionalization in many populist movements is charismatic leadership (Panebianco 1988). A charismatic leader is one of the few political actors who can credibly claim to embody the popular will, becoming what Laclau (2005) calls an "empty signifier," a vague unifying referent into which individual members of the movement can read their own particular wills. When a populist movement is led by a charismatic leader, the problem of institutionalization is less likely to be a *lack* of a unified identity or capacity for decision making, because the charismatic leader provides these; rather, the problem is that members of the populist movement lack an identity or decision-making capacity *independent of the leader*. This is a different kind of low institutionalization than we would find in other organizations that merely lack cohesion and permanence. It gives the movement tremendous power to act (at least, as long as the leader maintains his popular mandate), but it undermines the identity, the autonomy, and ultimately the permanence of particular organized components of the movement, each of which becomes an instrument of the leader's will.

Movement Organization

The second attribute of populist organization is that it organizes as a movement – as a network of amateurs rather than a hierarchy of salaried specialists. Populists trade rational-legal bureaucracy for an enthusiastic army of volunteers motivated by solidary incentives and devotion to their cause. They eschew the kinds of organization and lobbying normally associated with interest groups and are especially wary of political parties.

This is probably what scholars using the political-institutional approach mean when they refer to populism's "low levels of organization." Yet, this is not an entirely accurate way of characterizing movements. Weber's work on the modern bureaucratic form of organization, defined by the use of permanent, trained personnel who are hired and promoted on the basis of merit, sometimes leads us to see nonhierarchical forms as *less* organized. However, scholars who study social movements emphasize that they are simply *differently* organized, with network-based structures that depend heavily on nonmaterial incentives and a low-cost repertoire of contentious tactics to accomplish their objectives (McCarthy and Zald 1977; Tarrow 1994; McAdam, Tarrow, and Tilly 1997). These are not empty organizational shells, but structures with high levels of individual involvement.

Scholars of populism always refer to "populist movements" whenever they describe actual occurrences of populism, but with rare exceptions (see Minogue 1969), none of them go so far as to argue explicitly that populism might *always* be associated with movements or to explain why this would be the case. Instead, the best development of this idea is found in the work of McGuire (1995, 1997) on what he calls "hegemonic movements" in Argentina.

McGuire hints at two reasons why populism has an affinity for movement organization. First, of course, movement organization is more compatible with the charismatic leadership found in successful instances of populism. Followers of charismatic leaders seek a direct connection to the leader and the vision he embodies, and they need to give their all to the cause. Bureaucratic organization weakens this connection by placing multiple layers of managers between the leader and his followers, and it undermines the voluntary spirit with salaries and other material rewards, thereby turning meaningful activism into an ordinary job. In short, professionalization breaks the charismatic bond. A movement organization, by contrast, eliminates or at least shrinks this managerial level and facilitates a direct, personal connection emphasizing nonmaterial incentives for participation. It is here that we find the reason for the direct, unmediated bond between populist leaders and followers.

Second, movement organization results from the message of popular sovereignty and participation that defines a populist worldview. Populism posits a community of morally equal citizens whose collective will is sovereign. Although this community is nativistic and exclusionary, those who belong to it see themselves as equals, and this ethic defies distinctions of rank and status as well as any specialization and division of labor. In populism, closeness to the people, not professional training, is the basis of merit. Likewise, populism sees direct citizen involvement in political decision making as an absolute good. Not only does direct democracy let government embody the popular will and avoid corruption, but it reduces the alienation and atomization that occur in modern industrial society and its political counterpart of representative democracy. Populists envision the movement as an enormous citizen assembly that is constantly in session.

Populist movements and their constituent organizations are especially wary of political parties, which are perceived not only as representatives of an old order that must be changed, but also as organizations with a strong tendency to become bureaucratized. This claim may appear to conflict with scholars' assertion that some examples of populism create strong party organizations (Roberts 2006). In fact, populist movements often do include parties, whether as an inevitable result of the need to run an election campaign with multiple candidates (especially when the law requires a registered party), as an artifact of particular ideologies and moments in history that argue for the virtue of parties as unique vehicles of popular mobilization and indoctrination (e.g., the embrace by many classic populists of Leninist party organization), or as a response to available campaign technologies and strong opposition organization (Roberts 2006). However, there is tremendous ambivalence about using this kind of organization to accomplish the movement's goals. Populist parties never feel comfortable being called a party in the pluralist sense of the word – as just another organized group that merely dissents – and as Panebianco argues, they often present themselves as "an alternative to the existing parties" (1988, 147). Moreover, they frequently come accompanied by other, nonparty organizations such as labor unions and neighborhood associations that vie for the attention of the charismatic leader or claim to incarnate the will of the people.

Populist movements that do have charismatic leaders are likely to experience considerable tension. Movement participants feel ambivalent as they try to reconcile the moral authority of the charismatic leader with their belief that all participants are equals; participants may submit to this authority but then bristle at the actual subjection it requires, attempting to carve out their own sphere of autonomous activity. One way around this tension is to accept the idea that the charismatic leader *embodies* the popular will, thinking and speaking as the people would do if only they could come together and deliberate. But people never always speak and think the same way, and inevitably the leader's will clashes with those of particular followers and organizations. Thus, populist movements are more likely than other charismatic movements to experience factions, dissent, and organizational heterogeneity.

Disruptive Tactics

A third attribute of populist organizations is that they adopt disruptive tactics displaying an anything-goes attitude. Political-institutional definitions get at

Populist Organization

this somewhat with references to the populist strategy of pursing large numbers of supporters while disdaining the traditional institutions of representative democracy, but again, they mention this strategy without fully identifying what it means or what motivates it. The explanation is that populist organizations, as well as the larger movement and its individual members, often share the Manichaean outlook of their leaders and see themselves as the unique bearers of the popular will in a struggle that will eventually eliminate the need for dissenting viewpoints. As a consequence of these ideas, members of a populist movement are more likely to treat electoral processes and procedural rights as instrumental and to view disruptive tactics of mass mobilization as an ordinary, legitimate practice.

The broader literature on political organization, especially the portion that studies social movements, has long appreciated the broad range of speech and tactics that distinguishes different types of organization. Scholars typically focus on three types of organization – parties, interest groups, and social movements – that they distinguish in terms of their organizational currency (votes vs. money and influence vs. a show of numbers) and mode of operation (c.f. Rucht 1996). Movements, in particular, are distinguished from other forms of political organization by their reliance on a "contentious" mode of politics – "the petition, the strike, the demonstration, the barricade and the urban insurrection" (Tarrow 1994, 19) – rather than on the lobbying or electoral campaigns that interest groups and parties use. Movements' reliance on contentious politics is generally seen by scholars as a response to participants' low resource base and nonhierarchical structure (McAdam, McCarthy, and Zald 1996; McAdam, Tarrow, and Tilly 1997). According to this view, disruptive tactics are the weapons of the poor and powerless, that is, groups that cannot afford or are not allowed to engage in the quietly efficient methods associated with interest group politics or ordinary partisan activity (Piven and Cloward 1977). Activists' only choice is to rely on relatively low-cost tactics and make heavy use of externally generated resources such as free media coverage and public spaces while strategically awaiting a moment of weakness in the state. The role of ideas or culture in determining this mode of operation is seen as secondary. Culture matters for movements, of course, but it enters in primarily by determining the available set, or *repertoire*, of specific tactics (does the movement plan a candlelight vigil or bang pots and pans?) and by providing the *framing* or normative justification for political action more generally. In other words, culture provides the basic fuel for popular mobilization and helps explain the way each movement markets itself, but it is not seen as connected to the meso-choice of contentious politics over less confrontational forms of collective action.

When we turn to the study of populism, however, we are forced to consider the possibility that the broad employment of disruptive tactics constitutes a natural outgrowth of the movement's Manichaean worldview. External material factors still play a crucial role in making collective action feasible, as we can see in earlier discussions of charismatic leadership and movement success; without a clear leader, coordination problems can become insurmountable and destroy the movement. Movements that are potentially based on large numbers of resource-poor activists (as they often will be when they are populist) must choose efficient means of political participation or they will find themselves without popular support or political impact. But culture is an essential factor in the decision to behave contentiously. According to this perspective, populist movements use disruptive tactics because they *want* to, not simply because these are the only tools available. Lobbying and ordinary partisan activity are manifestations of an unacceptable pluralistic outlook that accepts the legitimacy of the system and the presence of competing viewpoints and organizations; these are the tactics of professional organizations, not genuine expressions of the popular will. Compromise and passivity are symbols of corruption. The people must manifest their collective spirit and their outrage with the political system, and these demand confrontation and active speaking out by all citizens. Large-scale marches, picketing, and even riots are the authentic expressions of the people's voice.

McGuire anticipates this argument in his discussion of the "hegemonic vocation" and the anything-goes attitude of hegemonic movements. He claims that movements such as those in Argentina tend to believe in "a form of national unity in which political opposition withers away" (1995, 200). Members of the movement believe that they embody this unity. Consequently, they disregard formal institutions associated with pluralistic democracy and "try to achieve or retain power by the most expedient means at hand," including sometimes violence (ibid.). They justify these tactics as a way of dealing with an opposition that is an enemy of the unified popular will, and as a reaction to existing institutions that were ostensibly created to subvert that will.

The tendency of populist movements to rely on disruptive tactics and an anything-goes attitude toward their opposition is one of the chief reasons why we may feel reluctant to consider them democratic. Populist movements believe wholeheartedly that average people are the ultimate bearers of sovereignty; particular populist organizations publicly, wholeheartedly endorse democracy, and they may even use it as their principle of internal governance. Chavismo and other populist movements preach the gospel of popular empowerment and its incorporation into politics, and they do so precisely in polities where these have been the most absent and where the legacy of exploitation and injustice is greatest. Yet, this is not a pluralistic vision of democracy, and these same organizations may readily exclude certain groups from their definition of the people. Populist organizations place their opposition in an outsider category that can or must be denied legitimacy and citizenship.

Insularity

A fourth attribute of populist organizations is their tendency to be highly insular, or isolated from the rest of civil society. Populist organizations, whether at the level of parties or of civil society, are a kind of antisystem organization. While they may build or reinforce a dense network of relationships among like-minded citizens, they erect a wall against other organizations that fail to show their support for the populist cause. The antagonism quickly becomes mutual; older organizations that are not part of the movement feel repelled by these populist newcomers who question the very legitimacy of the system on which the old organizations are predicated. They may come to regard members of the populist movement as barbarian invaders rather than worthy, credible participants in a pluralist system.

It is rare for the populism literature, including that of the political-institutional approach, to consider organization at this systemic level, but it receives a great deal of attention in Sartori's work (1976) on parties and party systems. While his book largely emphasizes the normative innovation that modern pluralist party systems represent (specifically, the willingness to institutionalize differences of political opinion) and attempts to catalog the types of systems that belong to this broader category, he also describes a suggestive, qualitatively different type of system that he calls "polarized pluralist." This type is distinguished by the presence of one or more organizations that are unwilling to merely dissent within an existing institutional framework and instead seek to overthrow the system. Theirs is not an "opposition on issues" but an "opposition on principle" (p. 133). If these parties gain enough electoral strength, they divide the system into two opposing camps.

While populism is never mentioned by Sartori, the relevance of his typology should be fairly obvious. Populist organizations – whether parties or other groups – are based on an "opposition on principle" that seeks the overthrow of a system subverted to elite interests. They are antisystem organizations that polarize political systems. They undermine the pattern of cross-cutting affiliations that are the hallmark of pluralism by making it impossible for any person or organization to be on both sides. Old organizations either realign along this new, fundamental dimension, or they risk being torn apart from within and repressed from without. Populism never completely destroys civil society, and its participatory ethic may actually encourage the formation of new associations that increase their participants' connectedness and power. However, these will only be new forms of association *within* the movement, not across the rest of civil society. Populist organizations are good at creating what Putnam (2000) calls "bonding" social capital, but they are poor at generating "bridging" social capital; they build connections among themselves but fail to cross sectoral bounds.

THE CIRCLES AS A FORM OF POPULIST ORGANIZATION

Chavismo is constituted by a large number of organizations of varying size, degrees of autonomy from the government, and trajectories of organization. Some of these, such as the quasi-guerrilla organizations in shantytowns like 23 de Enero (Velasco forthcoming) or the old Communist Party of Venezuela, are small organizations located within a narrow sector of Venezuelan society or even a single geographic area; others, such as the Communal Councils and Urban Land Committees (Comités de Tierra Urbana) can be rather large (García-Guadilla 2007a, 2007b; López Maya 2008a). Typically, the largest organizations are the newest and most dependent on the state for financing and leadership, although many smaller organizations (such as the Bolivarian labor unions and producer associations; see Ellner 2005a) are relatively new and vie for the attention and recognition of the government.

At the intersection of these different organizations are the Bolivarian Circles. At their peak of activity, they were the largest of the organizations within the movement, incorporating hundreds of thousands of local units. Like some of the largest organized components of Chavismo, they were initiated by the state, but they also had an extraordinary level of autonomy normally found only in the smaller Chavista organizations; members had considerable control over the membership, leadership, financing, and activities of their Circles. This combination of qualities made them the focus of international attention and the hope of many proponents of radical participatory democracy across the region, who saw in them the potential for new forms of civil society and popular mobilization. These qualities also make them a particularly interesting case for testing my theory of populist organization. They are representative of a broad swath of the Chavista movement, but they are also a more genuine expression of the viewpoints and behavior of ordinary activists.

The Rise and Decline of the Circles

We can trace the beginnings of the Circles back to MBR 200 in the years immediately after the 1992 coup. In about 1995, not long after their release from prison, Chávez and his associates began encouraging the formation of what he called "Bolivarian Circles" among like-minded citizens as part of their effort to reach out to the civilian population and create a more popular movement. The Circles would study the ideas of the original military movement, including the works of key Venezuelan patriots, provide locally generated solutions to national problems, and mobilize "from the bottom up," with the eventual objective of radically transforming Venezuela (Blanco Muñoz 1998, 296–7). There are few published accounts regarding the level of popular response to this early initiative, but at least several groups formed during this time and were still active in 2004, when we conducted our survey.

After 1997, this effort at creating Bolivarian Circles was set aside after the leaders of the movement decided to form a party and participate in national elections. As part of this shift in tactics, Chávez and his associates now began to encourage the formation of "Patriotic Circles" (Círculos Patrióticos), which ultimately constituted the base-level apparatus of MVR and its first electoral campaigns (Blanco Muñoz 1998, 434–5; Dirección Nacional Político-Electoral 1998, 19; Dirección Nacional de Organización 1999, 33; Interview v03d.01 2000). MVR and these base-level organizations were intended as an electoral front for the real organization, MBR 200. However, once Chávez and his coalition were in power, and as the constituent process and new elections came to dominate the movement's efforts, MBR 200 became largely inactive and the Bolivarian Circles were forgotten (López Maya 2003, 82–3).

The Circles were called back into existence and began to assume their eventual proportions after Chávez issued the call to reorganize MBR 200 in 2001. Chávez personally initiated this effort during a speech in April of that year. The new MBR 200 would not replace or do away with MVR – it was *not* a party – but it would have the benefit of strengthening MVR (Harnecker 2005, 160–1). The Circles would be the basis of this renewed movement or, in Chávez's words, a "popular force spread out in slums, towns, countryside and cities in order to consolidate, ideologize, and reinvigorate itself, thus contributing to the Bolivarian revolution" (quoted in García-Guadilla 2003, 192). Details about the Circles unfolded slowly during the months after MBR 200 was announced. Essentially, each Circle was to consist of up to 11 members sworn to defend the Constitution, be faithful to the ideals of Simón Bolívar, and serve the interests of their community. Applications would be submitted directly to the office of the president in Miraflores, where a National Coordination was set up to administer the Circles (Comando Supremo Revolucionario Bolivariano n.d.).

On 17 December 2001, Chávez conducted an initial mass swearing-in ceremony that involved 20,000–30,000 members (Agence France Presse 2001; VHeadline 2001). The effort grew rapidly as applications poured into the new National Coordination by fax and e-mail, and within a few years the national leadership estimated a total of 200,000 Circles and 2.2 million members (Cháves and Burke 2003; Gable 2004). The Circles ended up playing a key role in the demonstrations that followed Chávez's temporary removal from power in April 2002, and for over two more years they remained heavily involved in organizing communities, facilitating access to the government's poverty alleviation programs, and campaigning for the president in elections. For a time, they represented one of the most important organized components of Chavismo.

After 2004, however, the Circles experienced a significant decline in activity as Chávez and his followers shifted their attention to newer, more concrete efforts such as the Missions and the Urban Land Committees. Already by summer 2004, state-level leaders reported that only one-third and perhaps just one-twentieth of their original members were still active (Hawkins and Hansen 2006). And by 2005, although some die-hard members remained and struggled to keep the organizations going, news reports and follow-up interviews made it clear that the Circles had ceased to be an active part of the Chavista movement (Botia 2005a, 2005b). When Chávez announced the creation of a new, unified political party after the 2006 presidential election, most of the few remaining Circles folded themselves into the new party and formally ceased to exist (Durango 2006).

A Test: The Circles as a Populist Organization

To learn more about the Circles, my colleague and I performed a survey of 112 Circle members during June and July 2004, shortly before the presidential recall election. The survey sample was based on a nonrandom snowballing technique and used a standardized questionnaire administered in four different states: Aragua, Carabobo, the Capital District (the Libertador municipality in Caracas), and Miranda.[2] The nature of the sample necessarily limits our findings, but the dataset provides us with a valuable snapshot of this part of Chavismo at its peak and allows us to test the theory of populist organization.

Low Institutionalization. The first and most obvious quality of the Circles that conforms to this theory of populist organization is their weak institutionalization and their peculiar connection to Chávez. Despite representing a form of organization that in several ways was separate from the state, the Circles also manifested a strong charismatic bond to Chávez and a belief in an overarching popular identity that undermined their capacity to become autonomous, rule-based, and valued for their own sake. Thus, they were not simply weakly institutionalized, but also had an identity and a decision-making capacity that were dependent on the leader and hamstrung by their discourse.

We should begin by acknowledging that the Circles manifested autonomy in several key areas and had a semblance of self-determined rules to guide their conduct. First, membership was voluntary in the most basic sense of being noncoerced; few Chavistas were *required* to create a Circle, and even if they felt compelled by social sanctions from their peers to create one, the choice of fellow members was their own. Thus, creating a Circle required some initiative. Second, in terms of their social objectives, our survey revealed significant independence. The members of Circles that we studied pursued a wide variety of objectives, from neighborhood beautification to elder care. In every instance, these social objectives were generated or at least selected by the membership of each Circle, not coordinated from above. Third, with regard to leadership selection, each Circle was fairly democratic and, again, independent. Out of the 100 respondents whose Circle had a leader, only one indicated that their leader had been imposed on them by higher authorities, and over half had chosen their leader through a voice vote (another third was by consensus – the leader was the one who had initiated the creation of the Circle). Finally, the Circles demonstrated almost complete autonomy in their financing. Most respondents reported that they needed very little money to carry out their activities, and only about 10 percent of their resources came from the government.

---

[2] Additional details about the sample can be found in Hawkins and Hansen (2006).

Despite these signs of autonomy and self-governance, the Circles embodied a charismatic linkage to Chávez that often compromised their independent decision making and made it extremely difficult to form a corresponding, unique identity. Consider first their attachment to Chávez. To measure the kind of political linkage that the Circles embodied, we asked very early in our survey what the respondent's principal motive was in joining his or her Circle. Respondents were nearly evenly divided between two responses: 41 percent indicated that their principal motive was "to work in some project to improve the community," and another 42 percent indicated that it was "to support President Chávez." Likewise, on at least a few occasions, members of the Circles who came out to meet us expressed their faith in Chávez in spontaneous speeches that used very religious language, and the *casas bolivarianas* that we visited (houses or offices that had been rented or donated to service the Circles in the neighborhood) always displayed posters, poetry, and other messages dedicated to Chávez. Even when their faith and affection were not expressed so emotionally, as in our interviews with some of the state-level leaders of the Circles, respondents expressed great respect for Chávez and openly acknowledged his role as a focal point for organization.

The Circles' relationship to Chávez was most evident in their support for the recall campaign. Although most of the Circles had social objectives that they had chosen independently, nearly all respondents made it clear that they were currently participating in the recall campaign and that this took precedence over their social work. For example, fully 88 percent of respondents said that their Circles participated in meetings, demonstrations, or campaigns in favor of Chávez at least a few times a month (44 percent on a daily basis). In response to an open-ended question about their principal current activity, 26 of 109 respondents mentioned some aspect of the campaign to defeat the recall and not their social mission (although, to be fair, it was clear from their answers to subsequent questions that they were still heavily involved in social work). Members often described to us how they had joined official Electoral Battle Units and electoral patrols, all of which were responsible to the state and national committees of the Maisanta Command. Campaign activity was ever-present when we conducted our interviews, and the *casas bolivarianas* that we visited had often been turned into campaign headquarters for the Maisanta Command. All of these activities forced the Circles to set aside or reduce their original social activities and objectives, if only temporarily.

Likewise, only a minority of the Circle members whom we interviewed had a unique sense of identity, and their competing identities were essentially limited to two closely related objects: Chávez and the movement. To gauge this aspect of the Circles, we included an open-ended question that asked respondents to indicate their primary partisan identity. Of the 111 responses, 57 percent gave "Chavista," "Bolivarian," or "the government/the *proceso*" (a catchphrase for the Bolivarian revolution) as their first identity, in that order. Another 25 percent mentioned "revolutionary," and only 18 percent mentioned a specific organization (such as the Circles, MBR 200, or an older leftist organization) as their principal political identity. Our survey also asked respondents with which they identified most: the national Bolivarian movement or their own Circle. Only 30 percent of respondents indicated that they identified most with their own Circle; another 26 percent indicated that they identified with both equally; and the largest portion of the respondents – 44 percent – indicated that they identified most strongly with the national movement. Finally, we asked respondents what they thought the relationship between the Circles and Chávez should be. All of the respondents indicated that the relationship should at least be a positive one. Of those who gave a more specific response, however, 51 percent felt that the Circles should be dependent on Chávez, 31 percent felt that this relationship should be one of equality, and just 18 percent felt that the Circles should occupy a position of sovereignty or superiority.

The final demonstration of the Circles' weak institutionalization is, of course, their decline after 2004. After the presidential recall, and probably in the months preceding it, the Circles experienced a precipitous decline in activity. Even at the time we conducted our interviews, state-level coordinators indicated that the vast majority of Circles were no longer active, and by summer 2005 this had become common knowledge in the public media. All of the possible reasons for the Circles' decline suggest low institutionalization, and especially low institutionalization due to populist discourse and a charismatic leader. To begin with, we know that the Circles were *not* the victims of large-scale repression such as we might have seen if the 2002 coup had been consolidated. In fact, Chávez's popularity was high during the period of the recall and the two years afterward, with levels of presidential approval well over 50 percent and with solid electoral victories throughout the period. Chavismo was clearly ascendant when the Circles were in decline. Likewise, the country was not experiencing the kind of economic catastrophe that would have kept Venezuelans engaged in desperate, time-consuming efforts to find employment and satisfy their basic needs. Times had been much more difficult during the general strike of 2002–3, with its gasoline and food shortages, and yet the Circles had survived.

Instead, the decline of the Circles seems to be associated with three other factors. First, the Circles had a difficult time competing with the government's newer organizations for poverty relief and popular mobilization, especially the Missions. As I make clear in the next chapter, these newer programs were much better financed (receiving billions of dollars in oil revenues each year), had clearer objectives, and provided important, tangible benefits addressing some of the most pressing needs of the poor, including education, healthcare, food, housing, and employment. In our follow-up interviews during 2005, some of our contacts mentioned these as reasons why they and their friends had stopped participating in the Circles (González 2005; de Juliac 2005; Maldonado 2005).

Second, conflicts over leadership and disaffection with heavy-handed attempts to impose national governmental control possibly led some activists

Populist Organization 181

to abandon the Circles in favor of other forms of Chavista organization that were newer and less corrupt (Botía 2005a, 2005b). As I discuss later, members of the Circles fought the tendency toward bureaucratization within the organization, and they were upset with national and regional leaders who tried to assert this control. According to one of our contacts, many of the other popular organizations sponsored by the government, and not just the Circles, became distanced from their national coordinating offices and pursued their activities through local networks that disregarded or distrusted the actions of the national leadership (Maldonado 2005). This frustration with movement bureaucratization was heightened by the internal primaries for city council and neighborhood association candidacies held by MVR in April 2005. In our original interview and again in follow-up interviews, some of our contacts in the Circles were clearly upset with local party leaders, who used old-style tactics to ensure the victory of their favored candidates at the expense of candidates favored by the Circles and other popular organizations (Silva 2004; Vivas 2004, 2005; Mendoza 2005).[3]

Third, Chávez simply stopped emphasizing the Circles and the new MBR 200. The Circles were largely the result of presidential initiatives – Chávez's initiatives – and these were followed by other initiatives, the latest, of course (as of early 2007), being the creation of a unified party and the Communal Councils. Chávez shared the Circle members' dislike for bureaucratization and had a constant concern for achieving his vision of popular participation. In published interviews, he often spoke of the need to stay in touch with the people (Blanco Muñoz 1998; Harnecker 2005). Indeed, this was the reason he had called for the refounding of the MBR 200 and the Circles. Thus, the Circles fell victim to the constant efforts of Chávez and ordinary activists to keep the Bolivarian movement close to the people.

Movement Organization. The Circles also manifested the second attribute of populist organization: they had a movement-like form of organization that resisted bureaucratic hierarchy, especially political parties, and were part of a broader movement that did the same. Consequently, they manifested considerable heterogeneity in the precise organizational forms they chose and often engaged in conflict with the putative national leadership. The point here is not that the Circles were unorganized, but that they were organized differently, as a movement-within-a-movement. Importantly, this structure was more than just a consequence of the Circles' charismatic attachment to Chávez. It was a direct result of their populist worldview with its emphasis on egalitarianism and participatory democracy.

To appreciate this aspect of the Circles, we must bear in mind that there was a minimal organizational template imposed by the Chávez government on would-be Circles. All official Circles needed to have 7–11 members and submit

---

[3] Partly in response to this outcry, Chávez decided to incorporate members of the UBEs into the slate of candidates for the midterm congressional elections in 2005.

an official registration form that naturally imposed certain requirements. For instance, each Circle had to choose a name and a leader, and each member provided personal information and a signature. This form was submitted to the National Coordinator's office, which set up a single organizational structure to manage the Circles across various levels of states and municipalities, a structure that was reinforced through conferences and community activities. Thus, while the members of Circles had considerable autonomy in terms of who joined and what they did, there were at least a few rules and structures they had to respect, and these tended to have a top-down, hierarchical flavor.

This neat pattern conflicted with what we found on the ground. To begin with, while the majority of our respondents belonged to Circles that followed the official template, we found several large, older Circles that clearly followed their own path. One very large Circle reported having 1,000 or more members, and a few others had up to 500 members. Some of these groups predated the official inception of the Circles in 2001 and claimed to trace their roots to the original MBR 200. When we asked members of these larger groups how they operated, we found that they often resembled a loose association of Chavistas rather than a tightly knit community organization, and we had the impression that they were not formally registered with the National Coordination.

Second, most of the Circles that we studied, including the ones following official guidelines, had numerous conflicts with the national organization and created multiple factions or divisions that gave the Circles a movement-like feel. Attempts by the National Coordination to direct the Circles caused considerable friction between them and local leaders, and parallel organizations of Circles emerged that competed for legitimacy. While still recognizing Chávez's leadership, the largest of these groups, the Red Nacional de Círculos Bolivarianos (National Network of Bolivarian Circles, or Red Nacional), consciously attempted to reproduce a horizontal mode of organization through a loose confederation of state Circle organizations divided into smaller levels of organization. As of early 2006, the Red Nacional had held three national conventions. Likewise, in certain areas of Caracas and the outlying state of Miranda, a competing parallel organization of Circles, the "Bolivarian Circles: Bolivarian Revolutionary Movement 4-F" (named for the original Chavista organization) emerged in association with military reservists and former officers.

Third, even within these alternative national groups, relations across organizational levels were often confusing and antagonistic. For example, Circles were grouped by parish, municipality, and state levels, as well as on an intermediate level known as an *eje*, or axis, encompassing several municipalities (Carreño 2004; Mendoza 2004; Silva 2004; Vivas 2004). Each of these levels of organization had a coordinating body, sometimes with a head coordinator (different labels were used in each state), who was ostensibly responsible to the membership in his or her area. Yet, few of these regional officials had been formally elected, and the sense we had from subsequent interviews was that these leaders were not widely respected by actual Circles and neighborhood activists, many of whom seemed to operate independent of regional leadership (Maldonado 2005). Aside from the act of choosing the leader of their individual Circles, members resisted the idea of adopting formal mechanisms of representation.

Finally – and this was not actually a transgression of the official guidelines, but it seems to capture some of the same spirit that I have just described – the organizational complexity and rule basis of individual Circles were exceptionally low. For their internal rules and general mission, most of the Circles that we examined relied on a small booklet (the *pequeño libro amarillo*) published by the national leadership. These rules were not very explicit on such issues as how collective decisions would be made, leadership chosen, or tasks divided. Thus, when we asked if the members had some kind of specialized role inside their Circles, only 55 percent of our respondents said "yes"; the remainder said that they did "a little of everything."[4]

While a variety of idiosyncratic factors might be coming into play here (for example, the pride that members of early Circles had in the organizations they had created and sustained since the mid-1990s or the real mistakes made by particular national leaders), one of the most obvious explanations for these discrepancies is that they reflected the egalitarian, participatory ethos of populism and the kinds of tensions that naturally arise in a movement with a charismatic leader. Members of a populist movement resist hierarchical organization and prefer direct forms of involvement that reaffirm the fundamental equality of all participants. Even when the people feel attracted to a charismatic leader who embodies their popular will, they also want to assert their sovereignty and self-sufficiency.

In fact, many of our respondents openly expressed their dislike of hierarchy and bureaucratic organization. Several of the leaders we interviewed emphasized the idea of "horizontal" organization (Mendoza 2004; Silva 2004; Vivas 2004), by which they meant a highly consensual form of decision making with little hierarchy or division of labor, and they insisted that the Circles needed to be bottom-up, with decision-making power exercised directly by average members, rather than top-down, as in the traditional parties and MVR. Other studies of the Circles have also found the concept of horizontal organization to be a prominent part of members' discourse and one of the factors that first attracted them to the Circles (Sjöö 2006).

This aversion to hierarchical organization and professional politicians and the preference for direct, participatory politics were manifested in another important area: the ambivalence of Circle members toward parties. While respondents mentioned political activity in support of Chávez and the recall

---

[4] On the positive side, the fact that 93% of the Circles had some kind of leader indicated at least a small degree of organization based on rules and a division of labor. Likewise, 79% of respondents indicated that their Circle met weekly, although it was hard to tell if this meant a formal meeting with all members present, or conversations and informal meetings between sets of members in the course of their work.

campaign as a frequent and important part of their activities, most Circle members in our sample did *not* participate heavily in other forms of political activism and interaction with the government, and they resisted being characterized as a political party or even associating with the regular Chavista political parties. In fact, only 6 percent of respondents said that their Circle had ever participated in the campaign of a candidate other than Chávez.

The mistrust of parties extended to MVR. As already noted, our interviews in 2004 and the follow-up interviews in 2005 revealed a strong dislike for MVR among the Circles' leaders. In some states, the Circles went so far as to propose alternative candidates for the local elections in October 2004 and to create new regional parties to campaign for these candidates, such as the Movimiento de Concentración Gente Nueva (Movement of New People Gathering) in Guatire-Guarenas, state of Miranda, or the Unidad Patriótica de Carabobo (Patriotic Unity of Carabobo). These partisan organizations – note the careful avoidance of the word "party" in their names – competed directly, and usually unsuccessfully, with the candidates from MVR and other traditional parties in the Chavista coalition. Within the survey itself, we asked our respondents if they were members of or at least sympathized with a political party. While 46 percent indicated that they sympathized with MVR, another 9 percent sympathized with these newer, unofficial parties and another 42 percent failed to sympathize with any party at all. As one of our interviewees affirmed, MVR and the other parties in the official coalition were a necessary evil and would one day be supplanted with a true, bottom-up organization that could embody the will of the people (Vivas 2004).

Anything-Goes Tactics. The third way in which the Circles conform to a populist mode of organization is their democratic practice. While they were openly democratic in many of their attitudes and practices, such as their internal organization, they espoused a particularly populist version of democracy and tended to engage in activities that violated the spirit, if not the letter, of democratic procedure. While some of these tactical choices can be traced to the very real poverty and political marginalization of Chavistas in their formative years, it can also be tied to a uniquely populist worldview in which Chavistas saw themselves as bearers of the popular will.

In our initial published report, my colleague and I spoke positively of the Circles' democratic qualities and attitudes. At the most abstract level, for example, the democratic attitudes of the Circle members that we interviewed were exemplary. To gauge these attitudes, we used a standard question from the 2000 World Values Survey (hereafter, WVS) that asked respondents how they felt about certain regime types (World Values Survey 2006). As the data in Table 6.1 indicate, attitudes of most Venezuelans (in the table, WVS) and Chavista voters (WVS [MVR]) were a little equivocal: only half of the respondents from either of these groups felt that the nondemocratic regimes would be "bad" or "very bad," and only two-thirds felt that a democratic regime would be "very good." In contrast, nearly three-fourths of the members of

Populist Organization

TABLE 6.1. *Attitudes toward regime types*

How would it be for our country to have the following types of government? (Numbers show percentage of total respondents)	WVS	WVS (MVR)	CB Survey
A strong political leader that doesn't have to bother with the National Assembly or elections			
Very good	17.9	18.6	7.6
Good	27.3	28.5	13.2
Bad	28.6	28.8	31.1
Very bad	20.4	19.0	45.3
DK/NA	5.8	5.1	2.8
N	1,200	452	106
Experts, not a government, to make decisions based on what they think is best			
Very good	25.6	25.2	11.3
Good	39.6	42.9	17.0
Bad	19.9	18.1	28.3
Very bad	10.0	10.8	41.5
DK/NA	4.9	2.9	1.9
N	1,200	452	106
A military government			
Very good	7.8	10.8	1.9
Good	13.9	19.5	22.9
Bad	31.4	29.0	26.7
Very bad	43.0	37.2	46.7
DK/NA	3.8	3.5	1.9
N	1,200	452	105
A democratic political system			
Very good	63.9	62.2	80.0
Good	28.3	31.4	15.2
Bad	4.3	4.0	1.0
Very bad	2.2	1.3	1.9
DK/NA	1.4	1.1	1.9
N	1,200	452	105

Circles whom we interviewed (in the table, CB Survey) felt that the nondemocratic regime types would be "bad" or "very bad," and nearly 80 percent felt that democracy would be "very good." Thus, the members of Circles that we surveyed held these abstract democratic ideals much more strongly than the average Venezuelan.

Likewise, the political methods of Circle members were remarkably peaceful. To measure this, we used a question from the WVS that asked if the respondent agreed with the statement that violence is never justified in politics. Because this particular question was included only in the earlier 1995–7 WVS, we were unable to gauge the responses of average Chavistas; however, we could compare our responses with those of average Venezuelans. We found that our respondents were much more likely to reject violent political means. While only 38 percent of WVS respondents strongly agreed with the statement that violence is never justified, fully 65 percent of our respondents strongly agreed.

The results of an additional battery of questions about political methods reinforce this initial positive characterization of the Circle members and also reveal their extraordinary level of political activism. The 2000 WVS asked respondents if they ever had or would be willing to participate in various kinds of political action, including signing a petition, joining a sabotage or boycott, attending a legal demonstration, joining an illegal strike, and taking over a building or another location. The results presented in Table 6.2 show that our respondents were essentially the same as average Venezuelans and Chavistas, with all groups equally likely to endorse peaceful political methods except legal demonstrations. The principal difference is in the degree to which they had actually engaged in these peaceful activities: 44 percent of our respondents from the Circles were willing to sign a petition and 55 percent had actually done so; fully 74 percent had participated in legal demonstrations.[5]

Nevertheless, once we delve deeper into the words and actions of Circle members, we find strong indications that this democratic outlook was populist rather than pluralist and that this had important consequences for their choice of tactics. Looking first at language, the most significant evidence comes from an open-ended question in which we asked respondents "What does a country need in order to be democratic?" (*¿qué necesita un país para ser democrático?*). This question was identical to one used by Collier and Handlin (2009) in a survey of approximately 1,400 Venezuelans in early 2003, which allows us to compare the responses of Circle members with those of the general Venezuelan population.[6] To do this, I measured the percentage of respondents who used a set of words or cognates likely to be associated with Chávez's own populist language (namely, *pueblo, popular, participación,* and *protoganismo*), as well as the percentage of respondents who used the word *libertad*, a term more likely to be associated with pluralist notions of democracy and its focus on minority rights. These are the most commonly mentioned words or phrases

---

[5] The fact that average Venezuelans and Chavistas indicated much less willingness to engage in legal demonstrations may be an artifact of timing. The 2000 WVS was conducted before the polarization of the electorate and the beginning of the anti-Chávez mobilizations; by 2004, large numbers on all sides had participated in legal (and illegal) demonstrations.
[6] A general description of the Collier and Handlin survey is found in their book, but the content analysis performed here uses part of their original dataset that they generously made available to me.

TABLE 6.2. *Democratic methods*

Tell me if you have carried out, would carry out, or would never carry out the following political activities (numbers show percentage of total respondents)	WVS	WVS (MVR)	CB Survey
Sign a request or petition			
Have done it	14.4	17.9	54.5
Might do it	65.9	68.4	43.6
Would never do it	16.3	11.9	2.0
DK/NA	3.3	1.8	0.0
N	1,200	452	101
Join a sabotage/boycott			
Have done it	1.5	1.3	0.0
Might do it	5.8	6.0	4.0
Would never do it	88.9	90.9	95.0
DK/NA	3.8	1.8	1.0
N	1,200	452	100
Attend a legal demonstration			
Have done it	7.6	10.0	74.3
Might do it	33.5	36.1	17.8
Would never do it	56.2	52.7	7.9
DK/NA	2.8	1.3	0.0
N	1,200	452	101
Join an illegal strike			
Have done it	2.4	2.7	2.0
Might do it	6.1	6.0	2.0
Would never do it	87.9	89.4	96.0
DK/NA	3.6	2.0	0.0
N	1,200	452	101
Take over a building, factory, or other location			
Have done it	1.7	2.0	1.0
Might do it	8.0	7.5	10.9
Would never do it	87.3	88.5	88.1
DK/NA	3.0	2.0	0.0
N	1,200	452	101

in both samples, accounting for over half of the responses (and sometimes as many as three-fourths) in each.[7]

The results presented in Table 6.3 show that Chavistas in general, and especially our respondents in the Circles, were more likely to have a populist

---

[7] As a check, I considered a set of words or cognates associated with output-oriented notions of democracy that are compatible with either discourse, namely, *empleo*, *salud*, and *educación*.

TABLE 6.3. *Content analysis of definitions of democracy*

Word or Phrase	Collier and Handlin Survey (percentage of respondents)				CB Survey (percentage of respondents)
	All	MVR	AD	PJ	
libertad	50.7	35.1	56.0	67.9	27.0
libertad de expresión	43.5	31.8	47.6	59.9	16.0
pueblo/participación	4.3	4.8	4.8	2.9	30.0
empleo/salud/educación	10.5	11.1	11.9	9.5	10.0
N	1,364	396	84	137	100

worldview. The pattern is clearest when we consider the use of terms associated with the pluralist outlook. In the large sample, while approximately half of the respondents from the opposition party AD and nearly two-thirds of the respondents from the opposition party Primero Justicia mentioned the terms *libertad* (freedom) and especially *libertad de expresión* (freedom of expression), only one-third of the Chavista respondents mentioned these words. Thus, Chavistas were much less likely to define democracy in terms of civil liberties. This pattern is repeated in the Circles sample, where an even smaller percentage of the sample – one-fourth – mentioned these same words or phrases.

A similar pattern emerges when we consider terms associated with populist discourse. In the sample from Collier and Handlin (2009), only about 4 percent of respondents overall used terms such as *pueblo* (people) and *participación* (participation) to define democracy. This is a relatively small proportion, although Chavista respondents tended to use these terms somewhat more often than respondents sympathizing with Primero Justicia (about 5 percent of the time versus 3 percent). The difference becomes more dramatic when we consider our respondents from the Circles: fully 30 percent of our respondents mentioned these terms, making these the most common responses to the survey question in our analysis. Thus, while members of the Circles were more likely than Venezuelans or Chavistas to espouse democracy in the abstract, they were less likely to do in terms of civil liberties and more likely to do so in terms of populist concepts.

Another piece of evidence regarding the populist worldview of the Circles comes from a closed-ended question regarding democratic tactics. This question was drawn from the 2000 WVS and asks respondents whether society needs to undergo deep change through revolution, if instead it should undergo

---

Interestingly, Chavistas and members of the opposition were all equally likely to associate democracy with substantive rights: about 10% of respondents in both samples and all three groups mentioned the words *salud*, *educación*, or *empleo*. Thus, output-oriented conceptualizations of democracy were not really a distinguishing characteristic of Chavistas or Circles members.

TABLE 6.4. *Attitudes toward social change*

Attitudes toward social change: Which phrase is closest to your own views? (numbers show percentage of total respondents)	WVS	WVS (MVR)	CB Survey
Our society must undergo deep change through revolutionary actions	12.2	16.8	41.5
Our society should be gradually changed through reforms	56.4	52.4	26.4
Our current society should be defended from any subversive force	29.1	29.0	30.2
DK/NA	2.3	1.8	1.9
N	1,200	452	106

gradual change through reform, or if it should be defended from change by subversive forces. The results presented in Table 6.4 indicate that respondents from the Circles had relatively radical views about social change. While average Venezuelans and Chavista voters in the WVS both expressed a strong preference for gradual change through reform (56 and 52 percent, respectively) and ranked revolutionary change last (12 and 17 percent), the largest proportion of our respondents from the Circles preferred deep revolutionary change (42 percent), and the next largest proportion (30 percent) preferred to defend the gains they had already made; the smallest support was for gradual reform. Thus, members of the Circles were more likely to accept the corollary of populist discourse that defending the popular will requires liberation or revolution.

This populist pattern in the words of Circle members seems to have affected their actions or behavior. My colleague and I found troubling evidence of partisan conditionality in the provision of government services and the role that the Circles played in lobbying for these benefits or participating afterward in their provision. For example, members of Circles whom we interviewed often mentioned the role they played in petitioning the government for access to resources and especially the new Missions of the Chávez government (more on this in the next chapter). While in some of these programs there was evidently no potential for conditioning benefits on political support, a few programs were run with the understanding that only people who supported the Chávez government were entitled to benefits. This pattern was clearest in the efforts to issue new government ID cards before the recall election, an activity in which many Circles actively participated as part of their work with the recall campaign. Cards were denied to many citizens who had signed recall petitions. In other programs, such as the remedial education Missions discussed in the next chapter, at least one program director made it clear to us that only those who supported Chávez were eligible to participate (Interview No. 11 2004). And during the period of the recall campaign when we first visited these Missions, students were expected to participate regularly in demonstrations that supported Chávez's campaign (Interview No. 11; Interview No. 13).

The other behavioral evidence of a populist worldview that we saw was the participation of the Circles in the recall campaign. As already noted, Circle members were generally very averse to participation in traditional political parties and were even hostile to Chavista parties such as MVR. Yet, nearly all respondents also made it clear that they were participating in the recall campaign and that the campaign at least temporarily took precedence over their social work. Furthermore, the members of the Circles whom we interviewed never once expressed any concerns about the use of state resources and facilities for the recall campaign, a practice that was evident to us during our weeks of interviews. Yet, if Chávez is seen as the embodiment of the popular will, this participation in the recall campaign becomes more sensible. While the efforts of MVR and the more traditional parties could be seen as partisan, supporting Chávez was not because he represented the will of the nation rather than that of a political faction. Thus, one leader of the Circles justified the electoral efforts as a necessary popular antidote to the increasingly corrupt behavior of the Chavista party leaders (Carreño 2004).

Insularity. The final way in which the Circles fit a populist form of organization was at the system level, in their insularity. While the Circles added to the density and plurality of Venezuela's civil society, they did so largely *within* the Chavista movement. Considering Venezuela's civil society as a whole, the Circles were part of a process that tended to disenfranchise members of the opposition and limit or at least disadvantage organizations that were not part of the movement.

On the one hand, the Circles probably enhanced the organizational density of Chavismo. To gauge membership in other associations, we asked members of Circles a standard series of questions from the 2000 WVS about whether they were members of a list of possible organizations and activities. The results of the 2000 WVS and our own survey are given in Table 6.5. The members of Circles whom we interviewed had much higher levels of membership in voluntary associations than either Chavista voters or Venezuelans in general.

On the other hand, we found that the Circles did not seem to have enhanced the kinds of cross-cutting relationships that scholars traditionally associate with pluralist civil society. In fact, we found that the Circles coexisted uncomfortably with traditional civil society organizations and were often used by the government to supplant the latter. While many Circles worked alongside other organizations in the shantytowns, there was frequent tension between the Circles and traditional NGOs that tried to maintain political neutrality or supported the opposition. Like other Chavistas, the members of the Circles tended to see opposition members as illegitimate coup-mongers and the Bolivarian movement as a true expression of the Venezuelan people. Cases

Populist Organization

TABLE 6.5. *Membership in organizations and activities*

Organization/Activity	WVS	WVS (MVR)	CB Survey
Social welfare services for the elderly, handicapped, or poor	6.6	7.3	33.0
Church or religious organization	22.9	21.5	24.5
Educational, artistic, musical, cultural activities	17.8	15.9	57.0
Unions	3.0	4.6	8.7
Community work on issues of poverty, employment, housing, or equal rights	10.3	11.3	69.2
Human rights	8.9	10.0	37.5
Environmental conservation, ecology, or animal rights	11.9	11.5	33.0
Professional organizations	9.3	9.5	31.8
Youth work (such as Boy Scouts, guias, youth clubs, etc.)	8.4	10.6	30.8
Sports or recreation	21.1	21.7	43.0
Women's organizations	5.1	6.2	28.3
Peace movement	5.8	7.7	27.2
Volunteer organizations related to health	9.8	12.2	63.2
Other	0.7	1.1	14.3
Average (not including "other")	10.8	11.5	35.8
N	1,200	452	107

were reported of the government denying funding and jurisdiction to existing charitable organizations and giving them to local Chavista ones (Peñaloza 2004, 7).

To gauge the degree of organizational insularity of our respondents, we immediately followed up on the earlier series of questions about membership by asking respondents to name the actual organizations they belonged to. This generated a smaller list because respondents belonged to organizations that carried out multiple activities and covered various issues, the Circles themselves being one of the most frequently mentioned. Based on these responses, we were able to determine the degree of closure or encapsulation of their affiliations, that is, how often a member of a Circle belonged to other organizations inside the Chavista movement. The results are shown in the histogram in Figure 6.1. We found that at least one-fifth of the respondents belonged only to Chavista organizations, and a total of at least two-thirds of our respondents belonged to organizations of which at least two-thirds were Chavista. Because these estimates are almost certainly low (if we were unsure about the identity of an organization, we coded it as non-Chavista), this suggests a fairly high level of exclusive involvement in Chavista civil society.

We find additional evidence of this insularity when we examine the kinds of news media that our respondents in the Circles relied on. In the years after

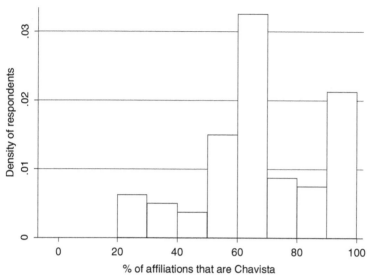

FIGURE 6.1. Histogram of organizational insularity.
Source: Author's survey of Bolivarian Circles.

Chávez was first elected, the media became increasingly polarized, with the private media – especially television – becoming open opponents of Chávez and the state media becoming a mouthpiece for the government. After the attempted coup of 2002, when the private media played an important role in galvanizing opposition marches, the government made significant investments in the state-owned media in order to provide more sophisticated programming and new venues, and it financed a large network of community radio and television stations that were mostly aligned with the government (Fernandes 2006; Hawkins 2006; Schiller 2006). Although the private media moderated their tone after Chávez's victory in the recall election of 2004, Venezuelans hoping for unbiased news at the time of our survey had few options.

Our respondents made it clear that they contributed readily to this media polarization. First, our respondents almost universally relied on state-run media as their source of news. Fully 80 percent said that they consulted primarily state-affiliated news sources, including state-owned media, community media, and members of their own Circle. Further, 82 percent of respondents claimed to watch the televised presidential talk show *Aló, Presidente* three times a month or more, and most of these said that they watched the entire program or most of it. This was an incredible act of political devotion, considering that the weekly program was known to run as long as six hours per episode.[8]

---

[8] Echoes of this polarization can be found in the 2007 AmericasBarometer. In response to a slightly different question about which television station they watch for news, 30.5% of past and present members of Circles mention a state-owned channel compared to 11.3% of the rest of Venezuelans.

Second, our respondents showed a peculiar tendency to equate community media with government-owned media. When we asked if there was a community radio or television station that they enjoyed most (about 68 percent indicated that they regularly watched or listened to community media), the vast majority indicated a Chavista outlet. This response was predictable, because community media had been heavily promoted by the government. What was more puzzling was the fact that another 35 percent said that their favorite community medium was Radio Nacional, a traditional government-owned radio station and not a community media outlet. One way of interpreting this response is that the programming of actual community media stations confuses their listeners. Because community media outlets include rebroadcasts of Radio Nacional news in their programming, listeners occasionally hear references to Radio Nacional and its journalists. However, another possibility is that Chavista listeners tend to think of community media as the people's media, in which case all government programming could be considered community media. What to outsiders would seem an inappropriate partisan bias in community and government media is in fact the principal quality that legitimated them in the eyes of our respondents.

CONCLUSION

The Bolivarian Circles largely conform to what we would expect of a populist organization. Despite their significant formal autonomy from the Venezuelan state, they not only show weak institutionalization and a strong charismatic attachment to the populist leader (attributes not unique to populist organizations), but they also have a strong movement-like organization and an aversion to permanent hierarchical organization such as parties; a language and a tactical repertoire with strong populist overtones; and a high level of insularity from other components of civil society. Not all Circle members we surveyed displayed these attributes, and in each instance we could point to sizable minorities of respondents that fell within nonpopulist modes of organization. But the dominant pattern that emerges from our study is one of a populist organization.

Crucially, this chapter shows how these organizational features are not isolated elements of populism or choices driven merely by material imperatives, but logical consequences of a populist worldview and to a lesser degree of charismatic leadership. Attributes that political-institutional theories generally associate with populism – a direct relationship between the leader and followers, low levels of organization, disdain for existing institutions of representative democracy such as parties, and others – are present in the Circles. But while these features are predictable aspects of populism, they are not really its core. We see evidence here that they emerge partly from an underlying set of beliefs that transforms these attributes into meaningful, logically consistent choices for leaders and activists.

In making this argument, I am not saying that the Circles or other organizations constituting Chavismo are entirely undemocratic. We can see populism's democratic foundations in the activism of the Circle members, their professions and actual practices of participatory democracy, and their attitudes toward democracy. Yet, populism is not pluralism. The members of Circles whom my assistants and I met demonstrated many of the negative consequences of a populist worldview or discourse, including an anything-goes attitude and an equivocal attitude toward citizenship and procedural rights for members of the opposition. The direct or participatory forms of political decision making that they advocated were often utopic and excluded large numbers of Venezuelans who lacked the resources or inclination to engage in permanent political activity. Consequently, the Circles tended to reinforce the polarization of Venezuelan society into Chavistas and opposition. Newer, better-funded forms of participatory democracy in Venezuela, such as the Urban Land Committees and Communal Councils, may ultimately involve more citizens in more permanent programs (see García-Guadilla 2007a, 2007b; López Maya 2008a), thereby instilling new hope in advocates of participatory democracy in Latin America, but these Chavista initiatives are driven by the same underlying ideas and seem likely to partake of the same vices as the Circles.

7

Populist Policy

The Missions of the Chávez Government

With Guillermo Rosas and Michael E. Johnson

> Now Venezuela belongs to everyone.
>
> Chávez government slogan in 2004

In this chapter my colleagues and I consider the consequences of populism, but in the realm of public policy. We do so by engaging in an analysis of the Missions, which were the principal poverty alleviation programs of the Chávez government after 2003. The Missions represent a significant shift in Chávez's approach to socioeconomic development as well as an enormous outlay of government resources. This analysis of the Missions is a very different topic from the study of organization and the Bolivarian Circles, but one that again reveals the distinct imprint of populist ideas on the actual conduct of politics.

The analysis demonstrates the consequences of populism in two ways. First, we show how an economic definition of populism is subsumed under the ideational one. Economic definitions link populism with shortsighted macroeconomic policies. These approaches emphasize one of populism's key consequences; however, rather than showing how policies are framed and the worldview that informs them, they focus on the raw material qualities of economic policy and their long-term sustainability. The tendency to associate populism with bad economics is not entirely wrong (we see these kinds of policies in the case of Missions and in Chavismo more broadly), but definitions of populism emphasizing economic policy put the cart before the horse, failing to appreciate the underlying ideas that drive policy choices. Statist

---

We thank the BYU David M. Kennedy Center for International Studies, the BYU College of Family, Home, and Social Sciences, the Weidenbaum Center at Washington University for grants supporting this research. Special thanks also to our research assistants: David Hansen, Laurie Evans, David Jackson, Aaron Russell at BYU and Jacob Gerber at Washington University. Finally, we thank our colleagues Brian Crisp, Jay Goodliffe, Michael Penfold-Becerra, Dan Hellinger, David Smilde for their insights. The conclusions are the responsibility of the authors.

redistributive policies such as the Missions are understandable consequences of a populist worldview in a material context of poverty and inequality. In environments of greater income and better distribution of wealth, populists may instead push policies in a rightist direction that favors macroeconomic prudence and property rights.

Second, we consider the Missions at the micro level, as a type of poverty alleviation or discretionary spending program. This topic is more specific to Venezuela and Latin America nowadays, where poverty alleviation programs have multiplied in response to economic crisis and structural reform. Scholars studying these kinds of programs generally adopt a rational-choice approach that treats them as examples of either programmatic or clientelistic policy; most critics of Chávez's public policies fall into this camp. This perspective reinforces a unidimensional view of political behavior that emphasizes the material nature of the exchange relationship between voters and politicians and largely ignores the role of ideas, particularly at the level of elites. The analysis in this chapter shows that this perspective is too narrow and that the design of the Missions can only be understood when we also bring in the fundamental beliefs that motivate and give meaning to policy choices. Chavismo's populist worldview not only informs how these programs are designed and offered to the public, but also distorts their implementation in ways that sometimes go against the expectations of rational-choice accounts. While the Missions have a number of flaws deserving of criticism, calling them clientelistic (at least in the rational-choice sense) misinterprets their political purposes and imputes a kind of patronage machinery that does not yet exist.

My coauthors and I start the chapter with a few words about the broader relationship between populism and economic policy. We illustrate these claims with a description of the Missions and their origins, which provides a helpful background for the remainder of the chapter. We then focus on the microfeatures of the Missions, starting with a brief exploration of the literature on poverty alleviation programs. This allows us to outline a set of predictions about what a populist poverty alleviation program should look like and how these predictions differ from those of traditional rational-choice models of clientelism and discretionary social spending. Finally, in order to test these predictions, we present the results of a study of some of the best-known Missions. This study starts with a standard statistical analysis of program allocations in three Missions during June/July 2005, subsequently incorporates a novel series of interviews with ministry officials and an on-site survey of approximately 140 aid recipients and workers, and finally presents a few results from the 2007 AmericasBarometer survey in Venezuela. In the end, we find that the Missions display a number of attributes that fail to confirm the predictions of the existing literature and better conform to a model that takes political ideas into account.

ECONOMIC POPULISM

Populism potentially affects economic policy at two levels: that of macro decisions about broad fiscal allocations and the overarching structure of economic governance (Will the state participate actively in creating a social safety net? Will it foster economic cooperatives, state-owned enterprises, or sole proprietorships and joint-stock companies?) and that of micro decisions about the design of specific programs (What curriculum will the government use in its literacy program? Who will administer the program? How will the government allocate resources across localities?).

Economic definitions of populism focus on the macro level of policy. They associate populism with fiscally shortsighted redistributive policies and collective ownership of the means of production (Dornbusch and Edwards 1991). There are many historical instances of this kind of populist government; some buy into radical prescriptions for a command economy and/or collective forms of ownership, while others adopt heterodox or structuralist perspectives that retain the principle of private capital and emphasize less intrusive, temporary forms of government regulation and investment. For example, the newest populist movements in Latin America are all part of the region's "turn to the left," particularly its most radical antiglobalization variants (Castañeda 2006; Seligson 2007). While nonpopulist leftists such as Bachelet and Vásquez are moderates who basically accept orthodox economic guidelines, populists such as Chávez, Morales, and Correa openly criticize the reigning neoliberal paradigm and challenge institutions such as the IMF while engaging in a variety of redistributive policies that overstimulate domestic consumption in an effort to reduce poverty; in extreme instances, the state has (re)nationalized key industries and punished the owners of capital. Classic populist movements in Latin America such as Peronism and Velasquismo, while much more openly critical of the Communist left because of its ties to the Soviet Union, also offered redistributive policies, experiments in state ownership, and an ethic of social justice that resonated with socialist programs and preempted parties of the left, although they clearly stopped short of wholesale expropriation and redistribution of assets (Conniff 1982, 1999).

As we see more clearly once we move beyond the study of Latin America, however, populist policies can also veer toward the right, favoring continued protection of individual property rights, careful control of the money supply, and the elimination of opportunities for rent-seeking. Many radical right parties in Western Europe adopt this position (Kitschelt 1995), as have most populist movements in the United States. The right populism that prevails here lashes out at poor people (especially immigrant communities and racial minorities) about as often as it condemns the wealthy "plutocrats" and "corporate lobbyists." While it sometimes emphasizes novel collectivist solutions to economic problems, such as the farmers' cooperatives and crop insurance schemes championed by the late-nineteenth-century Populist Party in the United States, it never seriously challenges the basic capitalist underpinnings of the economic system and its reliance on private ownership of the means of production. Its concerns are more with the particulars – monetary policy, corporate regulation, and deficit spending, for example.

What determines the path that populism takes? The choice depends on the interaction of populist ideas with the broader socioeconomic context and the interests it generates. In developed countries such as the United States, populist movements are associated with the owners of small to medium-sized enterprises, including farmers and the middle class (Kazin 1998). Most of the movement's followers are property owners, albeit small-scale ones. While their sense of popular outrage may lead them to demand radical changes to the system, their demands are more likely to emphasize political and cultural reforms than economic ones. This populist constituency has little to gain and much to lose by overturning the system of property rights in an effort to redistribute wealth.

In contrast, the predominance of left-populism makes sense in developing regions such as Latin America where inequality is high, exploitation is systematic, and the bulk of the population is desperate. As earlier chapters have emphasized, most countries in Latin America suffer from a weak rule of law, with corrupt judiciaries and burdensome regulatory systems that tend to favor the wealthy and those entrepreneurs who have managed to legalize themselves. Many citizens operate in a gray area of informality and black markets where property rights are tenuous or nonexistent. Under these conditions, the voters who make up the bulk of the population are poorer and more likely to demand radical redistribution that challenges private ownership of the means of production. This populist constituency has little or no stake in the current system of property rights.

This correlation between policy direction and socioeconomic context under populism is clearly imperfect. Some pluralist politicians in Latin America also enact shortsighted macroeconomic policies, as we see in the case of the disastrous heterodox reforms of Raúl Alfonsín in Argentina and José Sarney in Brazil during the mid-1980s. And Latin American populists such as Fujimori in Peru occasionally pursue fiscally prudent rightist economic policies that increase long-term growth. During his first few years in office, Chávez himself followed a fairly tight macroeconomic strategy of reduced public spending. Hence, as recent conceptual works on populism point out (Roberts 1995; Knight 1998; Weyland 2001), we should avoid the tendency to *define* populism in terms of a particular set of economic policies. The relationship is not entirely deterministic.

That said, radical redistributive policies are the most likely corollaries of populist governments in Latin America.[1] This has certainly proven to be the case with Chavismo, where the government has gradually turned to inflationary policies, price controls, and expropriations as oil revenues have grown (Rodríguez 2008). The movement's increasingly leftist policy direction – which

---

[1] In this regard, one of the chief contributions of the literature on neopopulism (Roberts 1995; Weyland 1996) is to highlight the extraordinary possibility of Latin American politicians using a populist discourse to implement neoliberal reforms. The fact that this outcome is *unusual* but not *impossible* draws our attention to the unique historical moment that the debt crisis and the exhaustion of ISI presented in Latin America, one that temporarily turned the tables on heterodox or structuralist economic policies and made them appear elitist and antipoor.

becomes clearer when we describe the Missions – was never inevitable, but given Venezuela's high levels of poverty and inequality, it was likely. The majority of Venezuela's voters and of Chávez's support coalition are not small property holders, but poor wage earners, participants in the informal sector, and agricultural tenants and workers. These groups stand to lose more and gain less by leaving the existing distribution of resources intact.

THE MISSIONS

The Missions exemplify the increasingly leftist direction of Chavismo's broad program of socioeconomic reform. They are a set of initiatives designed to achieve the Chávez government's overarching goal of eliminating poverty by the year 2021, called Christ Mission (Misión Cristo), and were initially created as part of the government's first six-year plan, the *Líneas Generales del Plan de Desarrollo Económico y Social de la Nación* (República Bolivariana de Venezuela 2001). Together they received billions of dollars in funding between 2003 and 2005, as much as 3.5 percent of GDP according to some estimates (Corrales and Penfold 2007).[2] This funding makes them the best-financed of any of the new social programs of the Bolivarian Revolution and one of the most significant poverty alleviation programs in Latin America over the past two decades. By comparison, the National Solidarity Program (Programa Nacional de Solidaridad, or PRONASOL) of the Carlos Salinas de Gortari administration in Mexico constituted about 1.2 percent of GDP each year it was in operation (Magaloni, Díaz-Cayeros, and Estévez 2007), and in 1993 the National Fund for Development Cooperation (Fondo Nacional de Cooperación para el Desarrollo, or FONCODES) of the Fujimori administration in Peru is estimated to have received 0.5 percent of GDP (Schady 2000, 292). However, unlike these other poverty alleviation programs, which are largely neoliberal in concept, the Missions aim to transform the system of economic governance from one emphasizing atomistic participation in the market to one relying on cooperatives, state coordination, and local know-how, a system the government calls "endogenous development." The Missions do not complement but often compete with the private sector, which is put at a disadvantage by the government's exchange rate regulations and is increasingly the object of active government interventions or appropriations.

Although most of the Missions were formally begun in late 2003, they evolved out of the government's previous experiences with development programs. The most important antecedent was Plan Bolívar 2000, implemented

---

[2] According to National Treasury Office figures provided by Francisco Rodríguez, approximately 672 trillion Bolivares (Bs.) were spent on the Missions during 2003; Bs. 4,462 trillion in 2004; and Bs. 3,194 trillion in 2005. At the average official exchange rate listed by the Central Bank (Bs.1,607/US$ in 2003, Bs.1,885/US$ in 2004, Bs.2,150/US$ in 2005), this translates into US$420 million, US$2.4 billion, and US$1.5 billion. Most of this was financed by presidential discretionary funds or direct transfers from PDVSA; only 8% to 24% of the funds came from the regular national budget, depending on the year.

by Chávez shortly after taking office in 1999. Plan Bolívar spent hundreds of millions of dollars on projects such as community beautification, improvements in public schools, road building, healthcare for the poor, and distribution of basic foodstuffs in street markets. The program was novel and highly controversial because it relied on regular armed forces using military equipment to administer aid (e.g., army engineers and medical personnel used military construction equipment and medical supplies). According to Chávez, the program's principal goal was to create a "civil–military alliance," explicit within the old MBR 200, that would redeem the armed forces from their participation in the Caracazo of 1989 and bring them back into harmony with the needs and will of the people (Harnecker 2005, 74–5). Academics and members of the opposition expressed concerns about the program's tendency to blur the lines separating the civilian and military realms and to bypass state and local governments; military commanders received funding directly from the executive branch and were not required to consult with local elected officials when they planned or executed projects.[3] Plan Bolivar was initially intended to run for six months (Trinkunas 2002) but was subsequently extended. After about three years, it was gradually eliminated in favor of regular government programs run by civil agencies and local governments, nearly all of which were now controlled by Chavistas. According to Chávez, the program had succeeded in its real goal of transforming civil–military relations in Venezuela (Harnecker 2005, 81–2).

Based on the lessons of Plan Bolívar and the continuing socioeconomic needs of the Venezuelan population, the government experimented with additional programs that eventually became the first Missions and the foundation for its six-year plan. One of the earliest was the Cuban medical mission sent as part of the Agreement for Cooperation (the *Convenio Integral de Cooperación entre la República de Cuba y la República Bolivariana de Venezuela*) signed by Chávez and Castro in October 2000. In April 2003, Cuban doctors were invited by the Libertador municipality in Caracas to help establish a program of popular clinics. The program was accompanied by the creation of local Health Committees (Comités de Salud), small organizations consisting of neighborhood volunteers who were encharged with caring for the facilities, staffing the clinic, and providing citizen feedback. Within months, the national government expanded the program to the rest of the country, resulting in the placement of more than 10,000 doctors. On 14 December 2003, Chávez formally instituted the program as the Barrio Adentro Mission[4] (Misión Barrio Adentro n.d.; MINCI n.d.a).

Another important early program focused on literacy. In 2000, the government made an initial attempt to eradicate illiteracy called the Bolivarian

---

[3] For arguments pro and con, see Hellinger (2003, 44), Buxton (2003, 126–7), Trinkunas (2002), Pion-Berlin and Trinkunas (2005), and Chávez's own comments in Harnecker (2005, 73–82).
[4] "Barrio Adentro" lacks a pithy English equivalent but roughly means "inside the shantytown."

Literacy Campaign, implemented by the Ministry of Education. Results of this effort were average, with only 200,000 people educated in two years. Frustrated by the slow pace of reform, the government designed a new program in May 2003, the Emergency Literacy Plan: Simón Rodríguez, which made use of the Cuban literacy program Yes, I Can (Yo, Sí Puedo, or YSP). Cuban educators were brought to Venezuela to adapt the curriculum, train Venezuelan volunteers, and provide supplies. The program, renamed the Robinson Mission, was formally initiated on 1 July 2003. The Mission had a distinct grassroots feel and drew heavily from an army of 125,000 volunteers, many of them neighborhood activists without prior teaching experience, who helped teach literacy classes while receiving logistical assistance from the military. The YSP program was adopted because of its novel technique, which built on the existing knowledge of many illiterates; because it encouraged self-help among students; and because it operated within familiar environments of houses and local buildings and drew from local volunteers, thus bringing literacy to the people and respecting their needs and outlooks (Misión Robinson n.d.). According to the government, the initial goal of teaching 1 million Venezuelans to read and write was achieved in December 2003, and by 2005 Chávez declared the country "free of illiteracy." The success of the Robinson Mission led the government to expand the program to include remedial elementary education (Robinson Mission II) and create new programs covering remedial high school (Ribas Mission) and university education (Sucre Mission) (Calzadilla 2005; Wagner 2005b; Misión Robinson n.d.).

The Missions received added impetus from two key events. The first of these was the general strike of 2002–3. The government was forced to make drastic efforts to counteract food shortages resulting from the lack of fuel and the temporary closing of supermarkets and other key points in the distribution chain. These efforts, which built on the popular markets set up under Plan Bolívar, led in April 2003 to the creation of the Mercal Mission, a chain of government-subsidized supermarkets and outdoor street markets providing subsidized foodstuffs and other household goods, often at 40 percent below regular market prices (Wagner 2005a; MINCI n.d.b).

The second event was the recall election. Once the recall became a real possibility following the government-opposition accord of May 2003, the government felt increasing pressure to deliver on its promises of socioeconomic development. It seized upon the Missions as the key vehicle for implementing these changes. Most of the initiation and expansion of the core Missions – Barrio Adentro, the educational Missions (Robinson, Ribas, and Sucre), Mercal, and Vuelvan Caras, a job training program with a special emphasis on forming economic cooperatives with government financing – took place between May 2003 and the final announcement by the CNE in early June 2004.[5] The Missions delivered enormous results and helped improve public

---

[5] Although some of the Missions technically began in April, one month before the May 2003 accord between the opposition and the government, the timing of the Missions' subsequent

opinion toward the government. In his 1 August 2004 transmission of *Aló, Presidente* just two weeks before the election, Chávez could claim 270,000 students registered in Vuelvan Caras programs, 1.25 million newly literate Venezuelans through the Robinson Mission, an additional 1.1 million students registered in Robinson's primary education program (with almost 100,000 monthly scholarships), 740,000 students registered in Ribas (with another 160,000 monthly scholarships), 45.5 million visits at Barrio Adentro clinics, and 8 million customers at Mercal stores (*Aló, Presidente* No. 200).

The Missions as they existed in early 2007 are listed in Table 7.1 along with their approximate inauguration dates. As is evident, basic programs of healthcare, education, and nutrition are complemented by a panoply of programs ranging from reforestation (Arbol) to poverty relief for single mothers (Madres del Barrio). While the Missions are extensive, it is important to note that they do not necessarily represent an increasing prioritization of social spending under the Chávez government. Absolute expenditures have gone up in tandem with increasing government revenues overall, but the proportion of the national budget dedicated to health, housing, and education has remained fairly stable, at around 25 percent (Rodríguez 2008). Rather, the Missions represent a significant restructuring of previous government social programs as part of a qualitatively different approach to economic development.

We can see this qualitative difference more clearly if we consider some basic information about the most popular Missions, particularly Barrio Adentro, Mercal, Vuelvan Caras/Che Guevara, and the educational Missions. As already noted, the educational Missions seek to provide Venezuelans who have traditionally been excluded from public or private schools with a quality education; with the exception of Sucre, none are intended to supplant regular public education. Ideally, an adult student could achieve literacy in Robinson, Phase I; acquire a grade-school equivalency degree in Robinson II; obtain a high-school equivalency in Ribas; and receive a university degree in Sucre. Most of these Missions use standardized national curricula that incorporate distance-learning techniques (usually videocassettes with a classroom "facilitator") and are usually taught as night or weekend classes (Calzadilla 2005; Jáuregui 2005; Misión Robinson n.d.); Sucre, however, is organized more like a regular university, with daytime classes and classroom instructors who have a hand in designing their own courses. Registration and materials are free for students, and one-fourth to one-fifth of all students receive a monthly need-based scholarship of about Bs160,000 (about US$80). Registration requires a written application that is reviewed by program facilitators and regional directors, who because of high demand must often decide which students to admit. Classes are offered at a variety of locations, often with more than one

---

growth coincides highly with the recall election. Mercal, for example, underwent its largest absolute increase in coverage ever – a doubling in store capacity and clientele served – between June and July 2004, whereas after the election it experienced only marginal increases (Toro 2005).

TABLE 7.1. *Missions by origin and area of emphasis*

Mission	Date of Founding (date of presidential decree)	Area of Emphasis
Barrio Adentro	16 April 2003 (14 December 2003)	Health care
Robinson	30 May 2003 (1 July 2003)	Remedial education (literacy)
Robinson II	28 October 2003	Remedial education (primary)
Sucre	10 July 2003	Decentralized university education
Ribas	17 November 2003	Remedial education (secondary)
Guaicaipuro	12 October 2003	Communal land titles and human rights for indigenous groups
Miranda	19 October 2003	Creation of a military reserve based on citizens' militias
Piar	1 October 2003	Assistance to small-scale mining while promoting environmental sustainability
Mercal	22 April 2003[a] (16 September 2004)[b]	**Subsidized food**
Identidad	3 February 2004	Distribution of new national identity cards; record keeping on aid recipients at Missions
Vuelvan Caras/ Che Guevara	12 March 2004	**Endogenous and sustainable economic development (vocational training and cooperatives)**
Habitat	28 August 2004	Housing
Zamora	January 2005	Land redistribution/reform; elimination of latifundismo
Cultura	14 July 2005	Sponsorship and dissemination of popular culture in the arts
Negra Hipólita	14 January 2006	Assistance for other marginalized groups (handicapped, drug addicts, the homeless, etc.)
Ciencia	19 February 2006	Local scientific research through collaborative efforts
Madres del Barrio	6 March 2006	Social assistance for indigent mothers and female heads of household
Arbol	28 May 2006	Reforestation and environmental education

Note: Missions studied in this book are in bold.
[a] Date at which the first Mercal stores are created. See Toro (2005).
[b] Date at which Mercal is reorganized into its present form under the Ministry of Nutrition (Ministerio de Alimentación n.d.).
Source: http://www.mem.gob.ve/Missions/index.php, http://www.unfpa.org.

classroom at each site. While some buildings are dedicated, most are facilities ordinarily used for other purposes, including public schools, military bases, universities, and rented homes. The number and location of sites are chosen by national officials, although early program allocations in Robinson seem to have been determined by the initiative of Chavista activists. Classroom instructors are part-time workers, many of them regular teachers from public schools, and those who are not government employees are eligible for a small stipend. A university degree is required for instructors in either Ribas or Sucre but not in Robinson, which has continued to rely heavily on neighborhood activists who sometimes have limited formal education. Each of these three Missions is housed under a different government ministry, only one of which is a regular education ministry: Robinson is a quasi-cabinet agency loosely affiliated with the Ministry of Sports and Education; Ribas is run by the Ministry of Energy and Mining and the national oil company, PDVSA; and Sucre is run by the Ministry of Higher Education. The programs have had significant levels of participation. According to government figures, as of late 2005/early 2006, approximately 1.5 million students were enrolled in Robinson II, 600,000 in Ribas, and 250,000 in Sucre.[6]

Except for the reliance of Robinson on classroom facilitators without traditional pedagogical training and the tendency to house classes in irregular facilities, none of these attributes of the educational Missions seem particularly radical or leftist; free public education and need-based scholarships are not new ideas. Instead, the left-populist flavor of these Missions comes through most clearly in their curricula and in the teachers' training. Although all of the program curricula include traditional subject areas such as science, math, language, and history, parts are suffused with Marxist, nationalistic language and Bolivarian philosophies of the revolution, and all of them encourage community activism and service in the government's new programs of participatory democracy, including participation in economic cooperatives.

For example, students in Ribas take a civics course each semester (originally called Citizenship Education, or *Formación de la Ciudadanía*) that is seen as an integration of all of their other coursework. In early versions of this course, topics included Bolivarian thought; the new Constitution; the government's six-year plan; and the government's program of "sovereign and sustainable Endogenous Development" (Misión Ribas n.d.c, 5). A readings packet for this course introduces itself with a discussion of the holistic quality of the students' education, a process that will teach students the "conscience and knowledge" required to build a "democratic participatory, protagonistic, multiethnic,

---

[6] According to the 2007 AmericasBarometer, conducted exactly two years later, 9.3% of Venezuelans said they were currently participating in Ribas, 6.9% in Sucre, and 4.9% in Robinson II, representing roughly 1.6 million, 1.2 million, and 900,000 adult students, respectively. These changes in number may reflect the progression of students from lower to higher programs.

multicultural" society (Misión Ribas n.d.a, 3). Students are encouraged to use their new skills and knowledge to create economic cooperatives that can participate in the government's project of Endogenous Development. And they are required to engage in a service learning and outreach program (the *componente comunitario y sociolaboral*) in which they organize Bolivarian citizen assemblies (one of several forerunners of the current Communal Councils) to discuss community problems and craft a solution with government assistance, ideally using other existing programs such as the Health Committees or Urban Land Committees (Misión Ribas n.d.b). In short, the emphasis is on education not just for the purpose of enhancing earning potential or even self-actualization, but also for understanding and participating actively in the government's project for socioeconomic transformation. Heavy emphasis is placed throughout on serving the needs and ideals of the community.

The language in the materials for Sucre is stronger and more radical. In one pamphlet by the Ministry of Higher Education for an initial orientation workshop for instructors and students (Fundación Misión Sucre 2004), readers are informed that Sucre has been created in response "to the enormous social debt accumulated over decades of 'representative democracy.'" Sucre is a "radical transformation of the current model of higher education" designed to revolutionize the academic and socioeconomic spheres of the nation and operate with the other Missions in changing society and the state and "conquering national sovereignty." In its effort to liberate the poor – "the people" – it will overturn the "forms of domination" between teacher and student reproduced in the traditional system of education. Later, readers are told that Sucre responds to a Manichaean conflict between the poor majority and a wealthy few:

For years our universities produced professionals like on an assembly line, according to the demands, requests, and directives of the centers of power. The expansion of private institutes was the distinguishing feature of the area of higher education in recent years. A segregating border was implanted on our soil: on one side the educated, on the other, *the poorly educated, the ignorant who never tried to study or be anyone in life. Exclusion was required, only an elite had the right to professional training: "the chosen."* (p. 7, emphasis in the original)

The writers further lament that Venezuelan professionals have been traditionally fashioned for and by the market, with "a conception of mankind as merchandise, evaluated in terms of his purchasing power" (p. 7). Now, with the exhaustion of its old system of representative democracy, Venezuela is experiencing a moment of revolutionary change that will overturn the neoliberal paradigm and exalt the poor.

The government's effort to replace capitalism with a new, self-sustaining economy and an egalitarian society is also encapsulated by the Vuelvan Caras Mission. Recently renamed the Che Guevara Socialist Mission (Che Guevara: Misión Socialista) to reflect the government's changing ideology, it commenced in 2004 when the government took the old vocational-technical job training program, the National Institute for Training and Education (Instituto Nacional de Capacitación y Educación, or INCE[7]), and wedded it with the new Vuelvan Caras Mission to create an entirely new ministry, the Ministry for Popular Economy (today Ministry of Popular Power for Communal Economy). The ministry was charged with carrying out a chief component of the government's six-year plan called the Clusters for Endogenous Development (Núcleos de Desarrollo Endógeno).

The Clusters are government-led and -financed strategic development projects undertaken with community participation. Reminiscent of Soviet-style economic planning, but with a greater emphasis on community governance and small to medium-size industries, they ostensibly seek to end poverty and inequality while empowering the poor, increasing national economic self-sufficiency, and decentralizing economic activity throughout the country (Ministerio para la Economía Popular n.d.a). Working in consultation with community activists and local government officials, the national government surveys potential Cluster sites with a preference for poor rural areas that are considered isolated from the traditional cores of service, manufacturing, and oil industries. Once these sites are identified, the government works to organize local citizens through assemblies and other, more permanent organizations; draws up an integrated development plan (including improved health and education services and communication/transportation infrastructure); and then executes the plan by providing workers with vocational-technical training, building the infrastructure, and purchasing initial production inputs (seeds, cattle, etc.). In many instances, entirely new industries (cacao plantations and processing plants, for example) are created.

Vuelvan Caras/Che Guevara enters the picture by providing vocational-technical training and technical assistance in organizing the economic cooperatives; by 2008, the government claimed that over 200,000 economic cooperatives had been created (SUNACOOP 2008). The Mission has since added a program of political instruction, Lights and Morale (Moral y Luces), designed to create new, "revolutionary" men and women (see Ministerio del Poder Popular para la Economía Comunal 2008). As all of these name changes suggest, the program has acquired stronger leftist overtones with time. While initially supportive of mixed economic approaches and somewhat friendly to private ownership, program documents have became increasingly socialist in rhetoric and have dropped language friendly to the market.[8]

---

[7] After 2007, the word "socialist" was added to its name, making it INCES.

[8] A ministry document from 2005 refers to "a new national-popular mixed economy headed towards Socialism of the XXI century" and states that "the elimination of private property is not what we propose" (Ministerio para la Economía Popular n.d.b). By 2008, the ministry Web site declares that the purpose of Che Guevara Mission is "to contribute to the creation of a national productive force to replace the neoliberal capitalist system with a socialist model," and there are no explicit defenses of private property or a mixed economy (Ministerio del Poder Popular para la Economía Comunal 2008).

Barrio Adentro and Mercal are also integral parts of the government's overall project of reform. They are organizationally very similar but differ substantially from the educational Missions. Because they focus more on meeting basic short-term material needs rather than solving long-term problems of human capital formation, services do not require an extended commitment after an application procedure, but can consist of a single visit to a dedicated locale that essentially has an open-door policy. Both programs use full-time employees who receive a larger salary (over $700 per month for the Cuban doctors) but still operate outside of the regular civil service regulations. Predictably, we found that workers in these programs were more dependent on the incomes they received through the Mission, and particularly in the case of Mercal, they seemed to manifest less of the idealism and autonomy that we often found in the educational Missions.[9]

Barrio Adentro remains one of the government's best-known programs. At the time of our field study in late 2005, the Mission still relied heavily on Cuban doctors who came for 18-month stints (nearly 22,000 by then), as well as a number of Venezuelan nurses or assistants (about 6,500 at the end of 2005) (Aló, Presidente No. 242, 2006); these numbers have declined considerably since then, as we will see later. The Mission originally focused its efforts on providing primary care at cheaply built clinics, visible throughout Venezuela because of their hexagonal, bare-brick design and staffed by one or two doctors who usually lived on the premises. Patients wait in line and are received on a first-come, first-served basis, although at some of the sites we visited, long lines prevented some patients from being seen before the clinic closed. Potential recipients at Barrio Adentro are generally required to provide basic identifying information before receiving services (including their name, age, national identification number, symptoms, and medical history), but our visits showed us that this was largely a formality for data collection or for help in making diagnoses. The Mission has since been extended to include additional tiers with increasingly sophisticated diagnostic and treatment centers; these were fewer in number and, at the time of our study, were only in the process of creation.

Mercal (short for Mercados de Alimentos, C.A.) is run as a semiautonomous government-owned enterprise under the Ministry of Nutrition. At the

---

[9] Here a comparison between Sucre and Mercal, our two randomly sampled programs, is illustrative. While about 64% of Sucre workers indicated that they were salaried (rather than volunteers or recipients of stipends) and only 27% indicated that this was their principal employment, 91% of Mercal employees said that they were salaried and that this was their principal employment. Mercal employees were generally also less well-to-do than the workers in the educational Missions. When asked about the type of housing they live in, about 17% of the Mercal workers reported living in the top two of the four possible categories, while 50% of the volunteers in Sucre reported the same. The figures for Barrio Adentro, which do not reflect a random sample, typically lie somewhere in between these two extremes but closer to Mercal, as 82% of the workers and coordinators whom we interviewed in Barrio Adentro indicated that their work was their main employment, but only 33% said they were salaried. Twenty-one percent indicated they lived in the top two categories of housing.

time of our study, over 209 government-owned stores operated nationwide (including 32 Supermercal stores), as well as 870 cooperative-owned locales and more than 12,000 street markets, or Mercalitos (Mercal 2006). The programs are immensely popular. According to the 2007 AmericasBarometer survey, over 71 percent indicated that they had used Mercal's services (question MIS4), and nearly 50 percent had used Barrio Adentro at least once that year (MIS1). The vast majority of these respondents expressed overall satisfaction with services, despite problematic shortages of goods and long lines (MIS2, MIS5). According to our on-site interviews and observations, customers are able to buy as much of any product as they want, but there is often rationing of high-demand products (such as meat and milk) or whenever there are concerns about reselling on the black market. When high-demand products are available, there is usually a long line of customers; in these instances, however, admittance is first-come, first-served, except for the elderly and young mothers with infants, who are allowed to move to the front of the line. No identification is required.

The leftist-populist direction of these two noneducational programs is partly evident in their official publications, although the rhetoric is not as strong as that of the educational Missions and Vuelvan Caras/Che Guevara. In one of Barrio Adentro's early documents, the program is billed as a way of achieving the government's goals of "protagonistic participation of the people," as well as the constitutional mandate for "citizen participation" and the right to good health. Decrying the "clientelistic" health apparatus of the Punto Fijo system and the reigning national medical associations (the *gremios*), the traditional "individualistic model of healing," and the deterioration of public health under the influence of neoliberalism, directors of the program offer an "integrated" system of health care. Doctors are to act as "transforming agents of the socioeconomic reality of the individual and community," placing greater emphasis on prevention and on the broader living conditions and culture of the community, and, above all, providing direct access to health care within the poorest neighborhoods (Misión Barrio Adentro n.d.). Likewise, printed information from Mercal's directors in around 2005 proclaims their goal of helping the government "establish justice, the struggle against exclusion, and a just and equitable distribution of wealth," as well as eliminating malnutrition and guaranteeing "food security and [the] right to quality of life of our people." While primarily a distributor of foodstuffs and other basic goods, it acts as a supply agent for some of the government's food banks, and it works to supply itself through local producers and cooperatives as part of its overarching goal of ensuring food security (Mercal 2005). In our visits to program locales during summer 2005 (both Barrio Adentro and Mercal), government propaganda was always posted on the walls and doors, and the packages of food at Mercal came printed with cartoon figures and text that reminded patrons of constitutional rights or revolutionary ideals.

The leftist direction of these noneducational programs can be seen more clearly in the way they operate and fit into the government's broader project of revolution. All of these noneducational Missions – as well as the educational ones – form part of a network constituting a vast parallel economy. For example, most of the Venezuelan nurses or assistants at the Barrio Adentro clinics at the time of our interviews were medical students from Sucre, as the mission had been given the task of training a cadre of Venezuelan doctors who could eventually replace the Cuban ones at Barrio Adentro clinics; Robinson classes included instruction on basic health care that was prepared and sometimes administered by Barrio Adentro workers; and Mercal stores often included pharmacies that were staffed and administered by Barrio Adentro workers and located near a Barrio Adentro clinic. Many of the Missions are associated with cooperatives organized under the aegis of the Ministry for Communal Economy and the Vuelvan Caras/Che Guevara Mission.

Crucially, this is a network that vies with and even supplants the private sector. While providing services to marginalized Venezuelans who have lacked access to basic health care, Barrio Adentro often competes with the traditional medical establishment in Venezuela; this has happened particularly as the government has gone beyond the original set of neighborhood clinics to establish larger diagnostic and care facilities and refurbish state hospitals. The dislike of the Ministry of Health and directors of Barrio Adentro for the medical associations, or *gremios*, is undisguised. The *gremios* supported the opposition and originally refused to participate in the government's new health care initiatives – hence the decision to eventually staff Barrio Adentro with medical students from Sucre rather than from traditional Venezuelan medical schools – and during the peak of inflation in 2007, Chávez went so far as to threaten nationalizing the private hospitals for charging high prices, calling their profits "the evil of capitalism" (Associated Press 2007). The private health sector is burdened by government price controls designed to offset the inflationary consequences of heavy government spending and deficits, as well as partisan rationing of foreign currency that is crucial for buying imported supplies such as medicine and surgical equipment. A similar logic plays out for owners of private supermarkets and some of the agricultural firms that supply them. Mercal often fills gaps in the distribution chain, especially in rural areas and shantytowns far from developed urban centers, but stiff price controls on basic foodstuffs have generated shortages for several years, and there is frequent government talk of punishing hoarders and profiteers. Particularly in early 2007, when shortages became acute, the government raided warehouses, intervened in firms producing key products, and nationalized others (Romero 2007c, 2007d).

It would perhaps be erroneous to see these policies as part of a well-coordinated frontal assault directly solely at undermining the private sector. Many of these changes and controversies represent piecemeal reforms and sporadic efforts to deal with the economic contradictions of government policies; the tendency of the Chávez government has been to take the politically easy route, letting the private sector alone and even ignoring it while using its oil bonanza to create new Missions and draw away customers of private industries. The most noteworthy expropriations – the electrical company of Caracas, the national telephone company, the national steel company – have been in sectors that are not directly related to the Missions. Yet, the Missions represent a clear redirection of government policy in Venezuela, one that increasingly scorns market mechanisms while celebrating the virtues of state intervention and collective ownership and management.

POPULISM AND ECONOMIC POLICY AT THE MICRO LEVEL

While the Missions exemplify Chavismo's left-populist approach to economics, they also provide us with an opportunity to witness the unique influence of populist ideas at the micro level of public policy. That is, given a set of policies, we can look more closely at decisions about program design (such as content and site allocations) to identify attributes that are explicable only in terms of the leaders' beliefs about the political world.

The Missions are a particularly good choice for this kind of analysis because they constitute what in political science jargon are known as "discretionary spending programs." These are government programs in which allocations are controlled by a small group of elected officials (typically those surrounding the chief executive) and where no one except those officials knows the resulting distribution of funds. The Missions are created and managed by Chávez and his cabinet; most of them were extracabinet or emergency programs for the first year or two of operation. They are funded primarily by revenue transfers from PDVSA, either directly or via state development banks controlled by the executive, and without any regular legislative budgetary oversight (Rodríguez 2007); until 2005, only 8 to 24 percent of funds came from the regular national budget, depending on the year.[10] Perhaps more significantly, information about the programs' distribution is extremely scarce. Although the overall accomplishments of the Missions are widely broadcast by the government, detailed information on the programs (i.e., below the state or even the national level) is rarely available on the Web, in government publications, or even at government agencies on written request. Budgets and program allocations could not be analyzed in detail by the media or opposition parties in Venezuela during the crucial early years. A few scholars have attempted statistical analyses of select program outputs (Corrales and Penfold 2007; Rodríguez 2007; Ortega and Rodriguez 2008; Penfold-Becerra 2008; Hawkins, Rosas, and Johnson forthcoming), but as is true of most academic work, their studies were slow to reach the public and had no impact during the first years of the Missions' operation. Ordinary Venezuelans could look around them and see where certain centers of government aid were located in their neighborhoods or which of their friends and family members were recipients, but the distribution of these programs was widely dispersed, with hundreds or even thousands of sites per program.

[10] Again, data were provided by Francisco Rodríguez.

Populist Policy

Thus, information about how the Missions are run brings to light what Chávez and his close associates do when they lack any institutional constraints and when they think no one is watching them. They potentially reveal the true motivations of Chavista officials, whether these are purely self-interested ones, such as a desire to maximize votes and office, or additional ideals that might sometimes take precedence over electoral considerations.

Over the past two decades, scholars of Latin American politics have engaged in several quantitative studies of similar poverty alleviation programs in the region, including the PRONASOL program of Salinas (Dresser 1991; Molinar and Weldon 1993; Magaloni, Díaz-Cayeros, and Estévez 2007), the PROGRESA program of Ernesto Zedillo in Mexico (Rocha Menocal 2001), and the FONCODES program of Fujimori (Kay 1996; Roberts and Arce 1998; Schady 2000), most of which also had significant discretionary components. The studies typically decide whether each program is *clientelistic* or *programmatic*. That is, they try to determine if the program is based on universalistic, means-tested criteria (programmatic) or instead reinforces a relationship between voters and politicians characterized by partisan conditionality in rendering services (clientelistic).[11] Most of them adopt a rational-choice perspective (some quite formally) that assumes away the influence of ideas at the level of elite behavior.

The few existing analyses of the Missions in Venezuela fall into this genre. While some approach the Missions more strictly in terms of policy analysis – asking whether the Missions actually achieve their stated goals at a reasonable cost (Rodríguez 2007; Ortega and Rodriguez 2008) – others do so in more classic political science fashion by attempting to model the causes and consequences of program allocations (Corrales and Penfold 2007; Ortega and Penfold 2007; Penfold-Becerra 2008). Both types of studies offer quantitative analyses that are generally critical of the Missions, finding that partisan determinants of allocations are strong and policy performance is moderate or weak. They conclude that the Missions "are not predominantly pro-poor, but rather, vintage clientelism and cronyism" (Corrales and Penfold 2007, 21), thereby lumping them together at one end of this dichotomy.

These studies clearly demonstrate partisan elements in Mission allocations, which we verify later. However, they overlook the possibility of an alternative, populist mode of discretionary social spending with attributes distinct from those of either programmatic or clientelistic modes in this rational-choice sense. As we look closely at the Missions, we can anticipate several of these unique influences of a populist worldview.

The most obvious influence of populism on program design is to make leaders less likely to rely on universalistic criteria in allocating resources and

---

[11] As I make clear later, this is a relatively new notion of clientelism that traditional anthropological approaches find foreign precisely because it lacks significant mention of the role of culture or ideas. For examples of this newer use of the term, see Stokes (2005) and many of the selections in Kitschelt and Wilkinson (2007).

more likely to use discretionary spending programs for partisan goals. This, of course, is not a particularly unique prediction – rational-choice accounts of discretionary spending programs argue the same – but the logic underlying this claim deserves to be laid out. On the one hand, because a populist worldview requires that the movement demonstrate large-scale support to show that it truly embodies the popular will (Weyland 2001), leaders and activists may justify targeting undecided voters and marginal districts, especially at electorally critical moments. Populists cannot content themselves with winning pluralities but must pursue large majorities and high turnout. Moreover, they see their cause in Manichaean terms, as a historic struggle between the forces of light and darkness; the forces of Evil stand at the gates, ready to resume their dark oppression and undo all of the gains made by the people. Such noble, desperate ends may justify a bit of electorally pragmatic temporizing, although this is likely to be hidden from ordinary voters and even movement activists. On the other hand, because committed populists believe that they embody and pursue the one true will of the people, and that they confront a corrupt system in which it is impossible to treat opponents as moral equals, they are more willing to engage in punitive behavior that denies benefits to all but the faithful followers of the popular will while extending tentative benefits to undecided voters who might be persuaded to join.

Needless to say, during the very time the Missions were being enacted (and it was perhaps one of the key reasons for their quick implementation), Chávez and his movement confronted a threat to their existence in the form of a potential recall election. Moreover, public support for Chávez was still at an all-time low when the recall first became a possibility (May 2003), making it all the more tempting to justify the targeting of benefits to districts where it would do the most electoral good rather than to districts that were more faithful and deserving. The survival of the Bolivarian revolution was at stake. If ever there was a time when a populist government felt justified in targeting discretionary funds, it was in Venezuela during the second half of 2003 and the first half of 2004.

Again, this is not a very bold conjecture. Fortunately, there are three additional ways in which populism should have a more distinct impact on discretionary spending programs like the Missions. First, there should be *very little or no overt conditionality in populist discretionary spending.* Studies of clientelism from the rational-choice perspective make a great deal of the presence of conditionality; in fact, they consider it one of clientelism's most basic defining attributes (Graziano 1975; Stokes 2005; see also Kitschelt 2000; Kitschelt and Wilkinson 2007). For these scholars, clientelism features a *direct* exchange of goods and services from the politician for demonstrated political support, such as a vote; ostensibly public goods are transformed into particularistic benefits that are handed out selectively, based on partisanship rather than citizenship. Given Chavismo's organizational resources for monitoring and enforcing compliance with conditional exchanges, as well as the near absence of institutional checks and balances, standard theories of discretionary spending would expect open conditionality to be rampant in the Missions. However, *populist* politicians are less likely to engage in this kind of vote-buying. In political systems like that of Venezuela, where the populist movement is a reaction to the clientelism of the Punto Fijo period with its party machines and brazen corruption, openly targeting voters (especially undecided fence-sitters) is a highly inappropriate strategy that can alienate core voters. Populist leaders must prove to themselves and others that they represent a moral, popular option that would never engage in the corrupt practices of the past (at least, not for their own selfish purposes). This is not to say that populist movements such as Chavismo are free from self-interested behavior or that their politicians always resist the temptation to misuse state revenues, especially in programs without outside monitoring; the activists and leaders of Chavismo are among the first to admit that opportunists are infiltrating the movement and that chances for enrichment are corrupting some officials. Yet, those activists rightly expect their leaders to periodically purge corrupt elements and wield their authority in ways that maintain the movement's purity. If any targeting does take place at the individual or district level among marginal voters (and as we will see, it does), populist politicians must handle it discreetly.[12]

Second, all of this makes it *nearly impossible for the populist to construct a patronage machine*. Rational-choice approaches to clientelism and discretionary spending argue that a party or movement with the superior organizational resources of Chavismo will not simply engage in ad hoc vote-buying, but will do so efficiently by creating a political machine that consciously distributes state resources in electorally maximizing ways, typically through a network of local bosses or patronage brokers (Cox and McCubbins 1986; Dixit and Londregan 1996; Stokes 2005). In populist movements such as Chavismo, however, a patronage machine cannot operate effectively without the capacity or will to use open conditionality. Although objective material conditions seem to allow it (in the case of Chavismo, a large network of organized, get-out-the-vote activists and civil society organizations), the government's discourse has tied its hands just as effectively as if watchdog agencies, the media, or opposition parties were monitoring and threatening it with punishment. Discretionary spending programs like the Missions may eventually degenerate into some form of open vote-buying as the movement spends time

---

[12] The *Lista Tascón* seems to exemplify this. While it was fairly widely used in government hiring and firing decisions in the time around the recall referendum, the construction and use of the digitial list of government opponents and supporters was largely a spontaneous affair that apparently lacked coordination from the presidency, and most government officials tried to avoid telling employees the real reason they were being fired when notices were given. When it finally became an open secret, Chávez felt compelled to speak out publicly and abjure further use of the list.

in office and becomes routinized, but this is only a looming prospect, not the initial way the movement comes to power.[13]

The third unique influence of populism is at the individual level of program participants. Even if programs are sometimes targeted at marginal districts, as they can be under populist movements, *their participants are probably core supporters*. Whatever the temporizing of the populist leadership in their aggregate-level allocations, the masses of activists and followers are likely to express a strong populist discourse that flavors every aspect of these programs. Many of the movement's leaders and rank and file replicate the leader's language, imagining themselves to be part of the true people struggling against its subversive, conspiring enemies. This is not a welcoming pluralistic discourse that makes marginal voters or opponents want to join in, receive benefits, and work side by side. The more that discretionary programs consist of a long-term association in an environment controlled by movement participants and leadership, the more fence-sitters and opponents will feel repelled by these programs and avoid participating. In the particular case of Chavismo, the movement features a strong Bolivarian nationalist ideology celebrating key historical figures; the revision of twentieth-century history (especially of the Punto Fijo era); a growing emphasis on the struggle against capitalism and globalization, with explicit use of Marxist terminology; and the celebration of Chávez as the embodiment of the popular will. As we have already discussed, these trends are particularly evident in the educational Missions, where the pedagogy includes important political components and where participation means much more than a short one-time visit. Despite the targeting of Mission locations to marginal districts, the average participant is unlikely to be an undecided voter, let alone an opponent.

This expectation again runs counter to the predictions of rational-choice theories of clientelism and discretionary spending. For these theories, the profile of individual participants should *correlate* with whatever the cross-district allocation of resources is, which in this instance is likely to favor median voters and marginal districts. This is because targeting is either the direct consequence of individual vote-buying through a machine or, where individual targeting is not feasible, a by-product of district-level allocations (a marginal district with a roughly normal distribution of voters tends to

---

[13] Critics here may point to the ostensibly large patronage machines created by figures such as Vargas in Brazil, Perón in Argentina, or Cárdenas in Mexico during the mid-twentieth century. However, the populist status of some of these figures (e.g., Cárdenas) has been disputed earlier in this volume, and it is not clear how much the more clearly populist figures from this era created meaningful patronage machines with explicit vote-buying when they first came to power. Perón in particular relied much more on his ties to organized labor, his charismatic persona, and a wide array of social and economic policies during his first years in office. The patronage machine that makes Peronism infamous today was largely a creation of post-Perón leaders such as Menem, who steered it away from its original labor-based organization to a more purely clientelistic mode of linkage (Levitsky 2003). Thus, at least Peronism seems to fit the pattern I describe here.

TABLE 7.2. *Expected attributes of the Missions*

	If the Missions Are:	
	Clientelist	Populist
Partisan criteria in the allocation of resources	Yes	Yes
Open conditionality (vote-buying)	Yes	No
A patronage machine	Yes	No
Aid recipients are disproportionately marginal supporters	Yes	No

contain a higher number of undecided voters). In a situation like the one the Chávez government confronts, and because core voters are already committed to the incumbent for normative reasons, the best choice for purely self-interested, office-maximizing politicians is to target marginal constituencies and constituents.[14]

These expectations are summarized in Table 7.2. Note again that when the table and the preceding text refer to clientelism, they mean newer rational-choice accounts of this phenomenon. The classic anthropological understanding of clientelism emphasizes a broader array of material and cultural conditions that includes inequality of status, a personal relationship between client and patron, and traditional/patrimonial forms of political legitimacy (Scott 1969; Mainwaring 1999, Chapter 9; Kitschelt and Wilkinson 2007), all of which characterize certain parts of Chavismo. The affective relationship of Chavistas to the charismatic figure of Chávez, not to mention the direct linking of citizens to the executive branch via discretionary programs, captures some of this spirit and reinforces a paternalistic relationship between Venezuelans and the state. In most classical approaches, Chavismo has what looks like significant attributes of clientelism.[15] However, in terms of current rational-choice approaches to clientelism and vote-buying, the structure of the Missions that we see in the next section is anomalous.

---

[14] In a new set of programs like the Missions, there are fewer accumulated expectations and obligations of reciprocity among voters, so allocations can more easily be targeted to undecided or marginal voters. In addition, as most of the rational-choice literature argues, a high potential for individual-level targeting and the creation of a patronage machine make it more cost-effective to target marginal voters. For more discussion of the contexts that affect this calculation, see Cox and McCubbins (1986), Dixit and Londregan (1996), Stokes (2005), and Magaloni, Díaz-Cayeros, and Estévez (2007).

[15] Bear in mind that this paternalistic relationship must constantly contend with a populist discourse that celebrates the virtues and capacities of ordinary citizens. This tension between populism and clientelism in the traditional anthropological sense has already been touched on in the previous chapter and is widely debated by analysts of Chavismo; see Smilde and Hellinger (forthcoming).

TABLE 7.3 *Data sources on the Missions*

Data Source	Robinson II	Ribas	Sucre	Mercal	Barrio Adentro
On-site nonrandom interviews	3 (14)[a]	–	–	–	7 (27)
On-site random interviews	–	–	8 (50)	12 (46)	–
Ministerial interviews	Yes	Yes	Yes	–	–

Note: Number of sites visited, with number of total interviews in parentheses. All interviews were conducted between 27 June and 16 July 2005.

[a] Because we only visited three nonrandomly selected Robinson sites, we generally do not include information about these responses.

ANALYSIS OF KEY MISSIONS

In order to determine which set of microlevel expectations best characterizes the Missions – programmatic, clientelist, or populist – we analyze five of the original programs: the educational Missions (Robinson II, Ribas, and Sucre) and the two most popular noneducational Missions (Barrio Adentro and Mercal). Field research was conducted during the summer of 2005; because Vuelvan Caras/Che Guevara was undergoing reorganization at the time of our visit, we do not consider it here. Our access to data on these Missions varied considerably, and the data are summarized in Table 7.3. Basic information about policy output and aggregate performance for all of these Missions was available from various government Web sites, especially the site for the *Aló, Presidente* television program (www.alopresidente.gob.ve). For two of the Missions (Robinson and Ribas), we were able to speak directly with officials in the government ministries; for two of the other Missions (Barrio Adentro and Mercal), we instead obtained information through on-site interviews with workers and aid recipients, primarily in the Libertador municipality of Caracas (between 27 and 46 interviews at seven or more sites for each Mission). For the remaining Mission (Sucre), we acquired data through both on-site interviews (about 50 interviews at eight sites in Libertador) and ministry-level interviews. Only the on-site interviews at Sucre and Mercal used random sampling, which limits the generalizability of some of the findings reported here. All on-site interviews were conducted under conditions of confidentiality.[16]

As a supplement to this focused fieldwork, we also consider data from the AmericasBarometer in Venezuela. The AmericasBarometer is a nationally representative sample of 1,500 respondents interviewed by the Latin American Public Opinion Project in August–September 2007. In addition to standard

---

[16] At the beginning of each interview, we explicitly informed participants that their responses were voluntary and confidential, and we took care to never ask for identifying information. Site-level interviews were always conducted individually and out of earshot of other aid recipients and program directors or facilitators. In contrast, ministerial-level interviewees were not guaranteed confidentiality.

questions about sociodemographics and partisan preferences, the survey includes a module of questions about respondents' participation in these five Missions. If respondents did not participate in one of these Missions, the survey follows up with an open-ended question (with a fixed list of responses coded by the interviewer) on why they chose not to participate. The wording of all questions referred to here and technical details about the survey sample can be found in the official report available at the LAPOP Web site (http://www.vanderbilt.edu/lapop/; see Hawkins et al. 2008), although I include the question labels from the survey for easier reference.

Finding 1: District-Level Targeting

Our first finding is that Mission allocations show a strong electoral bias at the district level. Municipal- and parish-level allocations of the Missions have some association with their ostensible means-tested criteria of poverty and education, but partisan criteria are also very strong. In particular, Mission benefits are generally targeted to *marginal* districts, although this pattern changes for at least one program.

In order to determine what criteria were used in allocating Mission benefits, we statistically analyzed key policy outputs for three of the Missions for which we were able to find data: the number of student slots by municipality for Ribas (*Ribas Slots*), the number of scholarship recipients by municipality at Sucre (*Sucre Scholarships*), and the number of Mercal stores (Type I) by parish (*Mercal Stores*). We analyzed these outputs because actual budget figures are not available. Data for the first indicator were provided to us directly by government officials, while data for the latter two indicators were found on government Web sites (http://www.misionsucre.gov.ve and http://www.mercal.gov.ve) and downloaded in July 2005.

In order to circumvent concerns about reverse causality – that is, the possibility that Mission expenditures had important effects on the electoral and social indicators that concern us – we measured all independent variables almost five years prior to the period in which we collected the Mission indicators. Our key independent variable, *Chávez Support*, is the degree of political support for Chávez in any given circumscription (municipality or parish, depending on the program we analyze). We use the percentage of the vote for Chávez in 2000 and also include its squared value to capture curvilinear (quadratic) patterns in Chávez's spending behavior in contested districts. Our key control variable for gauging the level of poverty, *Sewer*, is the percentage of dwellings that had access to a regular sewer connection (sewer line or septic tank), and is calculated as the ratio of houses in this category to the total number of houses in the municipality/parish. This control variable is an important one, because there is a modest correlation ($r = .25$, $p < .000$) between poverty levels and the vote for Chávez in any municipality. The two other control variables we include are *Population* and *Pct College*. The former is simply the total population in the territorial unit (municipality or parish) according to the 2001 Census. Data are from the Nomenclador program available from the National Institute of Statistics (INE), which provides the final government estimates from the census. Unfortunately, because these data are available only at the municipal level, in some cases we resort to preliminary parish-level estimates provided directly by Census officials at INE.[17] *Pct college* is a measure of education level that reports the percentage of the population with at least some college education; these data are also taken from the tables provided us by INE. We include this variable with our analyses of the educational Missions as an alternative way of gauging the degree to which they use universalistic criteria. Thus, we would expect expenditure on remedial education to be higher in municipalities with lower levels of education.

Since distribution of *Sucre Scholarships* is positively skewed, we consider a log transformation to normalize its distribution.[18] Moreover, though scholarships and the number of Ribas students come in integers, their sheer numbers are such that we can consider *Sucre Scholarships* and *Ribas Slots* to be continuous variables. We thus resort to OLS analysis of these variables. In contrast, the relatively small number of *Mercal Stores* makes this a dichotomous variable that requires a logit/probit specification.[19]

Table 7.4 presents estimates from three different models, one for each of our dependent variables. Consider first the models for *Sucre Scholarships* and *Ribas Slots,* whose estimates are reported in the first two columns. The first thing to note is that our control variables – *Population, Pct College*, and *Sewer* – have very mixed effects that only partly accord with claims of universality. The size of the population is clearly our strongest predictor of the allocation of Sucre scholarships and Ribas students (more densely populated municipalities receive more scholarships and have more students). This finding speaks well of the universalistic qualities of the Missions because population varies much more widely across municipalities than does either poverty or education; hence, larger municipalities tend to have more poor, less-educated people than even the poorest smaller municipalities. However, once we control for population, the level of education in the community has almost no relationship to the number of scholarships or students, and the effect of poverty is practically nil in the case of scholarships. The effect of poverty is large only in the case of Ribas enrollment (we can expect 300–400 more students in municipalities with moderate levels of wealth than in poor or wealthy

[17] The population figures in these preliminary reports are accurate for the major urban municipalities, but population counts in the more rural municipalities seem to suffer from minor nonsystematic measurement error. Using this indicator surely biases our parameter estimates downward, i.e., toward finding less of an effect.
[18] The mean and standard deviation of log scholarships are 5.15 and 0.92, respectively.
[19] The mean and standard deviation of *Mercal Stores* are 0.62 and 2.20, respectively. However, Mercal lacks a presence in 254 out of 335 municipalities. Of the 208 Mercal locales in Venezuela, 31 are located in Libertador (Caracas) and 16 in Maracaibo; the municipalities of Girardot, Caroni, Iribarren, Sucre (Miranda), Sucre (Sucre), Vargas, and San Francisco each have at least 5 Mercal locales. It is obvious that Mercal stores are distributed mostly in urban centers, and therefore population size is the best predictor of Mercal presence.

TABLE 7.4. *Model results for Missions*

	Sucre Scholarships	Ribas Slots	Mercal Stores	
			(1)	(2)
Constant	−4.574	−6.504	−9.115	−8.828
	(0.638)***	(0.695)***	(1.344)***	(0.664)***
Chávez Support	0.073	0.100	0.046	0.015
	(0.018)***	(0.019)***	(0.035)*	(0.005)***
Chávez Support^2	−6.06E-04	−9.28E-04	−2.56E-04	
	(1.52E-04)***	(1.66E-04)***	(2.79E-04)	
Sewer	1.044	4.123	−0.948	0.760
	(1.026)	(1.116)***	(1.906)	(0.392)***
Sewer^2	−0.902	−3.606	1.304	
	(0.770)	(0.838)***	(1.507)	
Population (log)	0.704	0.899	0.618	0.630
	(0.030)***	(0.033)***	(0.066)***	(0.065)***
Pct College	0.006	0.001	−0.001	
	(0.007)	(0.008)	(0.033)	
Adjusted R^2 [pseudo R^2]	0.692	0.735	[0.308]	[0.307]
F (p-value)	125.2	153.8		
	(0.000)	(0.000)		
LR chi^2 (p-value)			235.29	234.98
			(0.000)	(0.000)
Level (N)	Municipality (335)	Municipality (333)	Parish (1,066)	Parish (1,066)

Note: *$p < .10$; **$p < .05$; ***$p < .01$.

municipalities), but this is where we would expect it least, as student enrollment should be correlated more strongly with education than with wealth.[20]

In these specifications, we have also included a squared term for *Sewer* to capture a potential nonlinear effect of poverty on scholarships and student slots. The logic is that these programs should initially benefit middle-class households, as rich households are presumably wealthy enough to purchase university and high school education in the private arena, whereas poor households are only just beginning to acquire the educational credentials they need to qualify for the university or high school programs. Consequently, more scholarships per capita should be going to municipalities that are toward the middle of the distribution in terms of poverty. Be this as it may, neither the main nor the squared term of *Sewer* displays an effect parameter centered away from zero in the case of Sucre scholarships.

---

[20] Because potential participants in Ribas needed to have a grade-school education to qualify, we reran the model for Ribas enrollment with a squared term for *Pct College*, but the results were not statistically significant.

In contrast, we find that both of our indicators for Chávez support have large, statistically significant signs in both models. The combined effect of these indicators in Table 7.4 is such that we expect the distribution of scholarships and students to be at a maximum in marginal municipalities. Specifically, given the coefficient estimates, the number of scholarships and students is highest in municipalities where Chávez won about 60 and 54 percent of the vote, respectively. Municipalities with a middle level of support for Chávez are expected to receive about 100 more scholarships and to have 500–600 more students than municipalities that were strongly in favor of or against Chávez. These are large effects, given that the mean number of scholarships per municipality is about 300 and the mean number of Ribas students is about 1,800.

The model for Mercal offers a contrasting set of results that again confirm the importance of electoral factors. It should first be noted that our inferences in this case are much more precise, largely because we observe Mercal stores at the parish rather than the municipal level; thus, our number of observations increases from 335 to 1,134. Two different columns in Table 7.4 offer alternative parameter estimates. As these indicate, the location of Mercal stores is first and foremost a function of population size, just as the allocations of Sucre and Ribas were. Once we control for the effect of this variable and poverty, however, the combined effect of our two indicators of Chávez support is large and positive (linear). Specifically, a parish that is uniformly in favor of Chávez is 35 percent more likely to have a Mercal store than one that is completely opposed to him. Oddly, in this case, we find that the control variable that should matter most according to government claims – the level of poverty (*Sewer*) – has exactly the opposite association from what we would expect: once we control for other factors, the wealthiest municipalities are actually about 10–15 percent more likely to have a Mercal store than the poorest ones. This finding may be a result of the fact that our dataset covers only one aspect of the Mercal program, the Type I stores, and excludes open-air markets, which may be used more often in shantytowns. Perhaps a larger sampling of all the Mercal programs would have a clearer, more sensible relationship to indicators of need.

These partisan associations are depicted in Figures 7.1 through 7.3, which indicate the expected distribution of Sucre scholarships, Ribas slots, and Mercal stores (measured on the vertical axis) conditional on the percent of the 2000 vote for Chávez in a particular circumscription (measured on the horizontal axis). As can be seen, the relationship between partisan support and the first two measures of Mission output is an inverted-U, with expected allocations peaking at around 50 to 60 percent of the vote for Chávez. In contrast, the probability of locating a Mercal store peaks in parishes with 100 percent support for Chávez.

Finding 2: Lack of Open Conditionality or a Patronage Machine

Our second set of findings is that there was no mention of any open conditionality by site-level respondents and no evidence of any coercive apparatus for extracting votes in exchange for program services.

Populist Policy

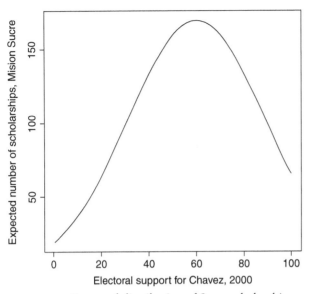

FIGURE 7.1. Expected distribution of Sucre scholarships.

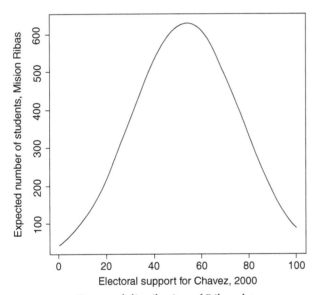

FIGURE 7.2. Expected distribution of Ribas slots.

This is clearly the case with Barrio Adentro and Mercal, whose open-door policies mean that there is no obvious way of screening aid recipients or preventing them from using facilities. In order to verify this initial impression and especially to see how it extended to the educational Missions, which had much greater potential for screening and rejecting applicants, we studied

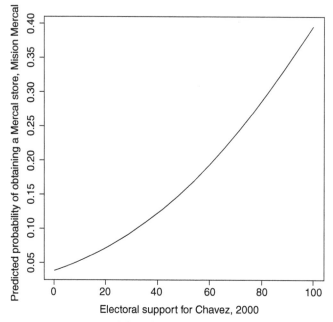

FIGURE 7.3. Expected distribution of Mercal Type I stores.

the attitudes and experiences of aid workers and recipients on the ground. Specifically, as already mentioned, we surveyed workers and recipients in the Libertador Municipality of Caracas, including random samples of about 10 workers and 40 aid recipients at the Sucre Mission and 15 workers and 30 recipients at the Mercal Mission.

In our survey, we included a module of open-ended questions asking whether any kind of partisan criteria were used to determine who received services.[21] Only 1 out of 137 respondents indicated that there was any overt conditionality. Most respondents emphatically denied that this took place and affirmed that services were available to all, opposition or pro-government. Obviously, respondents could have been trying to give the "right" answer to our interviewers, but we took great pains to ensure the confidentiality of respondents and asked this question in multiple ways. Our experience suggested that most respondents were giving us honest answers and would have admitted conditionality if it existed openly. We base this claim on two observations. First,

---

[21] We asked this question gently, toward the middle of the survey and after a set of less controversial questions about the basic structure of the Mission. Several forms of the question were possible, depending on how the conversation went, but generally the interviewer said, "It's evident that the Mission offers very valuable services. From what you know, are program recipients required to support the government? For example, do students/recipients have to participate in marches and campaigns?" If answers were unclear or evasive, the interviewers returned to the topic again with their own follow-up questions.

although interviewees initially received us with different levels of trust across sites – in some, we were first perceived as foreign spies, while in others, we were seen as possible government inspectors – we always got the same answer regarding partisan conditionality. Second, a significant minority of respondents actually thought that conditionality would be a good thing, and they seemed disappointed that it was not being used.

At the same time, as mentioned in the previous chapter, in an interview during the recall campaign one year earlier, at least one educational program director had admitted screening participants based on partisan qualifications (Interview No. 11 2004). Likewise, in our 2005 field study, a few respondents mentioned that they felt compelled to attend pro-Chávez rallies, and it was clear that during earlier periods such as the recall election, facilitators in the educational Missions had engaged in pro-Chávez propagandizing and used class time for political activism, especially in Robinson (Calzadilla 2005; Misión Robinson n.d.). However, few respondents seemed to think of this as a form of conditionality. As we will see, most of them strongly supported Chávez, and they suggested that others who had received the benefits of these extraordinary programs should feel the moral obligation to do so as well.

Our conclusion is that *screening* sometimes occurred and that, more than likely, there was some kind of *self-selection* of aid recipients and workers, particularly in the educational Missions, but that the Missions were not using any overt conditionality at the time we studied them and were clearly not part of a patronage machine. The recipients and workers we surveyed had no sense of program benefits being a quid pro quo for their participation and no expectation that they might be expelled or excluded if their partisanship wavered. In addition, recipients and workers were unaware of the kinds of political targeting that our district-level data later revealed (and we were unaware of this ourselves until we ran the statistical analysis). If conditionality was used by site directors or higher officials as part of a larger clientelistic apparatus, it could not have been very effective because it was not being clearly communicated.[22]

Additional evidence in favor of this conclusion comes from the AmericasBarometer. As mentioned, the survey included a series of open-ended questions asking nonparticipants in each Mission their reasons for not using its services. Representative responses to two of these questions (for Mercal and Ribas, MIS6 and MIS12) can be found in Figures 7.4 and 7.5. Nonparticipants almost never cite partisan concerns. Less than 1 percent of nonparticipants say that they were denied services for political reasons, and only 1–3 percent mention their disagreement with the government's politics. Instead, most nonparticipants (69 to 79 percent) emphasize the lack of need, the fact that services were unavailable (primarily Chavistas), their inability to participate, or the perceived low quality of services (primarily Chávez opponents), in that order.

---

[22] Even the site director who admitted using partisan criteria never indicated that she actually *told* potential recipients why they had been denied.

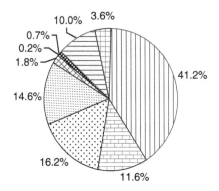

FIGURE 7.4. Reasons for not participating in Mercal Mission.
Source: Generated by the author from AmericasBarometer 2007 datafile (question MIS6).

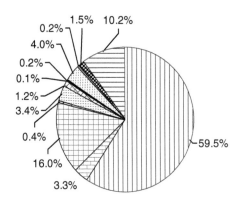

FIGURE 7.5. Reasons for not participating in Ribas Mission.
Source: Generated by the author from AmericasBarometer 2007 datafile (question MIS12).

Finding 3: Partisan Profile of Individual Recipients and Workers

Our third finding is an unusually high level of support and affect for Chávez among workers and aid recipients. First, consider the aid workers. Just as we found in the previous chapter on the Bolivarian Circles, there seems to be a high level of affect for Chávez driving workers' participation in the Missions. Nearly 88 percent of all the workers we surveyed ($N = 41$) and 91 percent of workers at the randomly selected sites ($N = 32$) indicated that they would vote for Chávez if elections were held the next day, even though the actual vote for Chávez in the 2004 recall election in these same areas of the Libertador municipality was only about 57 percent (63 percent in our randomly selected localities). When asked an open-ended question about what word or phrase would characterize their feelings toward Chávez, most of these workers used phrases indicating a strong charismatic tie, such as "love," "idol," or "I worship him" (*amor, ídolo, lo adoro*).

Of course, these results could simply be a result of patronage in government hiring decisions, especially among the fully salaried employees of Mercal. What is more telling is that these results were repeated and amplified for aid recipients. A slightly smaller 82 percent of all recipients ($N = 66$; 83 percent of recipients at the randomly selected sites, $N = 35$) indicated that they would vote for Chávez, and nearly as many of them expressed feelings for Chávez that indicated a strong charismatic tie. Not only was this level of support much higher than that found in the population as a whole, but it went in exactly the opposite direction from what we would have expected based on the district-level targeting of these programs. That is, the percentage of support for Chávez among the program recipients was actually higher in Mission Sucre (86 percent, $N = 21$), which is located disproportionately in swing districts, than it was in Mission Mercal (79 percent, $N = 14$), which is located more in core ones. Critics might argue that the level of presidential approval should have gone up in the year between the recall election and the time we performed our survey and that this increase would explain the high levels of voting intention for Chávez. Levels of approval did increase during this year, from about 50 to 60 percent (see Figure 2.1), but this is insufficient to explain the results of our survey. By comparison, in the presidential election of summer 2000, when levels of presidential approval were also around 60 percent, Chávez won only 63–68 percent of the vote in the parishes where we conducted our survey.

The small number of respondents means that we cannot put too much stock in these latter results (a *t*-test indicates that the difference between Mercal and Sucre is significant at only the $p < .30$ level). However, this pattern is confirmed when we consider the results of the AmericasBarometer. To provide a similar indicator of partisanship in the Missions, we cross-tabulate participation (questions MIS1, MIS4, MIS7, MIS10, MIS13) with affect for Chávez (C5CH), a 4-point ordinal measure of whether respondents agree with the statement that "Chávez expresses a convincing vision of the future." This

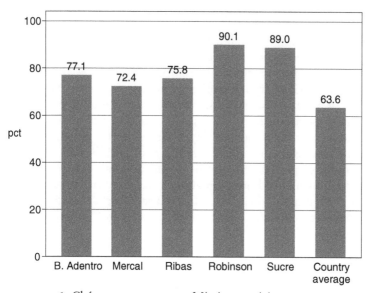

FIGURE 7.6. Chávez support among Mission participants.
Source: Generated by the author from AmericasBarometer 2007 datafile (questions C5CH, MIS1, MIS4, MIS7, MIS10, MIS13).

measure of affect is part of a four-item series designed to gauge charismatic linkages to politicians (Merolla, Ramos, and Zechmeister 2006); responses to the four items correlate very highly, so we use just one of the most representative ones here. For simplicity and greater comparability, we recode both the participation and Chávez affect measures to a dichotomous scale (participate annually/not, positive/negative confidence); doing this does not substantially alter the tests of statistical significance.

The results, shown in Figure 7.6, reaffirm that users of all of these Missions tend to be disproportionately Chávez supporters. The chi-squared statistic for each of these cross-tabulations is highly significant, showing that partisanship and participation are positively correlated. In addition, however, the relatively small number of Venezuelans who use the educational Missions tend to be much more highly Chavista than those using Barrio Adentro or Mercal. In the case of the Sucre and Robinson Missions, 89–90 percent of participants somewhat or strongly agree with the statement that Chávez expresses a convincing vision of the future. Some of these positive results of partisanship probably reflect some reverse causality, in that those who use the Missions and have a positive experience are subsequently convinced to support Chávez, particularly after experiencing several years of noticeable benefits (the survey was conducted over three years after the inception of these Missions). Unfortunately, we cannot control for this effect by using these survey data; none of the other questions in the AmericasBarometer survey provide useful instruments for an instrumental variable regression, a standard way of modeling this kind of reverse causality. However, we again note the interesting finding that the educational Missions (Robinson and Sucre, but not Ribas) are characterized by higher levels of support than Barrio Adentro and Mercal. Reverse causality cannot explain this difference in partisanship, because the educational Missions generally require greater effort and commitment by participants and do not yield greater material benefits, especially in the short term. The exception to this pattern, Ribas, may in fact prove the rule: it is probably the best equipped and financed of the three educational Missions because of its connection to PDVSA,[23] and in our interviews and on-site visits we found it to be the least ideologically charged. Together, these findings suggest that something in addition to the material output of these Missions is driving their participants' support for Chávez.

DISCUSSION

How are we to make sense of these findings? Our first conclusion is that the Missions clearly do not operate on purely universalistic criteria and are not part of a broader set of programmatic linkages between the Chávez government and Venezuelans. Although there is a moderate association between program allocations and means-tested criteria at the district level, the additional strong association with the electoral profiles of these municipalities and parishes suggests that the principle of citizenship is not fully honored by the top administrators of the Missions; allocations are based partly on partisan criteria. This revises somewhat the findings of existing studies while giving us greater confidence in their results, many of which have been based on smaller numbers of observations and fail to test for curvilinear effects (see especially Penfold-Becerra 2008).

However, these results alone do not allow us to distinguish between the expectations of populist public policy and a rational-choice approach to discretionary spending. While we could interpret our findings as a well-intentioned effort by senior Chavistas to preserve the revolution at a time when it was under a grave threat from the opposition, district-level targeting may also reflect the actions of a government that did not really believe in its rhetoric and was merely fighting to maximize its hold over offices. Such a government would also naturally target allocations where they would do the most electoral good, in this case usually in marginal districts.

We have clearer evidence for the effects of a populist worldview in our two other sets of findings. First, the Missions we studied do not seem to be using any kind of overt conditionality at the individual level. Some of the programs are structured in ways that preclude individual-level conditionality,

---

[23] One of the ministry-level officials over Sucre complained to us about the unfair advantage that Ribas had in its finances and administrative oversight because of its connections to PDVSA (Santander 2005). We could see the difference in our own visits to the cabinet-level offices of the Missions.

and aid workers and recipients were unaware of the criteria that were apparently used in making national- and state-level decisions about allocations, assuming instead that criteria were universalistic and nonpartisan. Even in the case of programs with some potential for choosing among aid recipients – the educational Missions – neither our field study nor the more recent nationally representative results of the AmericasBarometer provides any evidence of a patronage machine that openly threatens or entices voters with offers of particularistic benefits.

This absence is extraordinary. During this period there was almost no external check on how the Missions were run, no real opposition from the National Assembly, and no effective, independent judiciary or attorney general to reign in these programs.[24] There was little internal bureaucracy to impose rules and standard operating procedures (organization was a slow, ongoing affair during the time we conducted our interviews). These programs could *at least* have been used by local officials to benefit their friends and allies. Yet, even the isolated incidents of corruption that top program officials admitted to us were considered embarrassments. Specifically, in Robinson, the distribution of scholarships was poorly regulated during its first year, and problems with patronage and cronyism (*amiguismo*) surfaced; the National Coordination subsequently required an application to demonstrate need, although approval for each scholarship was still granted by the multisite coordinator. In some areas of the country at the time we conducted our interviews, scholarship awards had been suspended while these problems were ironed out (Calzadilla 2005). In short, the Missions failed to show open conditionality and machine politics where we could have most expected them, at least according to standard rational-choice theories of discretionary spending.

Second, the Missions show strong evidence of a populist discourse in the overwhelming presence of Chavistas among aid recipients and program participants. This outcome again seems to defy the logic of vote or office maximization. If circumstances indicate that self-interested politicians should target marginal districts (and the data indicate that they do), then presumably they should also target marginal voters. And if no individual targeting is feasible, then we would at least expect to find a partisan profile among aid recipients that reflects the district as a whole. What we instead find is a set of aid recipients that is unusually Chavista in comparison with the rest of the population. This finding is strongest in the program that was targeted to marginal districts most heavily, the Sucre Mission, as well as another educational program (Robinson) requiring significant investments of time and resources by participants.

While some of this partisanship is probably endogenous – the Missions are attractive, functioning poverty alleviation programs, so they really do convince participants to support Chávez – this kind of pro-Chavista demographic

---

[24] A nominally independent attorney general's office exists, of course, but it is noted for its unwillingness or inability to pursue cases involving corruption.

is also a predictable outcome in a set of programs infused with a populist worldview and discourse. Visitors to any Mission locale (including our team of researchers) are confronted with images of Chávez and the Bolivarian Revolution in posters and fliers; during our first visits, this often included recall campaign material. The revolutionary language was most prevalent in the educational Missions, where it occurred not only in government publicity but also in the very substance of the program. Students who were unsympathetic to the goals of the Bolivarian Revolution would have been uncomfortable working in this environment on a daily basis. Hence, aid recipients tended to be predominantly Chavista, and some of the highest concentrations of Chavistas were in the educational Missions.

Directors of the Missions were not unaware of this phenomenon. While emphasizing the openness of the Mission, one of the national directors of Sucre acknowledged that opponents of the revolution tended to exclude themselves from consideration as instructors. "People who aren't with the *proceso* don't participate" (Interview v19d.01 2005). With a little less self-awareness, a national director of Mission Ribas insisted that there was "at least one" anti-Chavista he knew of at the ministry level (Interview v10b.01 2005). And site directors, workers, and recipients all repeatedly insisted on how open the doors of their Mission were to government opponents. The resulting profile of participants might incline us to see these expressions of ecumenism as an effort at deception, but we see the reality less cynically. If activists believe that the Bolivarian Revolution represents the true will of the people, they may have a hard time conceiving of how any program such as the Missions could be exclusionary or, if it were, why this would be problematic. If anti-Chavistas or fence-sitters refuse to come, it is their own fault for resisting something so good. Hence, individual-level partisanship in the Missions becomes the product of self-selection rather than an open, systematic effort to buy votes.

CONCLUSION

This chapter reaffirms that populism is best defined in terms of the ideas that give meaning and direction to policies and other political behavior. At the level of macro policy, the Missions embody the strong leftist flavor of Chavismo, one emphasizing state ownership and economic planning, collective ownership and management, and policies centered on the poor. This fact should not be taken as confirmation of economic perspectives on populism, which equate the phenomenon with shortsighted macroeconomic policies; other populist movements take rightist directions favoring macroeconomic prudence and free-market solutions, as Chavismo did during its first years in power. Either path is possible, and the choice depends largely on the interaction of populist ideas with the socioeconomic context. Thus, just as we saw in the case of Chavismo's organizational attributes in the previous chapter, a populist worldview helps drive public policy down predictable paths.

At the micro level of policy design, the Missions also manifest the unique imprint of populism. Scholars who analyze poverty alleviation programs such as the Missions in Venezuela typically criticize them as cases of clientelism and vote-buying that reinforce the worst vices of traditional politics. While we cannot speak directly to other poverty alleviation programs in Latin America, we feel that the Missions could be more usefully characterized as a populist mode of discretionary spending. Partisan criteria are very strong predictors of Mission allocations across localities, but Mission participants (perhaps naively) perceive an absence of conditionality in the way that programs render services, and the Missions do not seem to be part of any patronage machine governing the distribution of aid. Individual recipients are much more likely to be strong supporters of Chávez than we would have predicted based on the partisan profile of their district. If by clientelism we mean a more traditional notion of a personalized relationship of deference, then the Missions may indeed embody some of the elements of Venezuela's traditional party system; but if we mean a more narrow, rational-choice understanding of this concept emphasizing a direct, conditional exchange of goods and services, Chavismo fails to fit the bill. This does not mean that these aid programs are praiseworthy examples of programmatic policymaking; the partisan biases in program allocations mean that these Missions are not reaching all of the people who need them, and the disproportionately Chavista profile of aid recipients is troubling. But criticisms of these programs seem more likely to gain traction and even the attention of Chavistas if they more accurately perceive the ideas and beliefs behind them.

8

Conclusion

This book began with a series of three interrelated questions about Chavismo: How can we categorize the movement? What are its causes? And what are its unique consequences for Venezuelan politics? The answers all rely on the concept of populism as discourse or worldview. Chavismo is a populist movement, and it has been since Chávez first came to prominence after the failed 1992 coup. The peculiar Manichaean outlook of Chavismo has been relatively constant since at least 1994 and easily predates (and partially explains) the movement's turn to the left in recent years. Understanding the discourse of Chavismo gives us crucial clues to its origins, helping us find these not so much in the decades of economic stagnation that preceded the election of Chávez in 1998 as in the systematic violation of the rule of law that worsened during the oil boom of the 1970s under the protective shelter of Punto Fijo democracy. The unique imprint of the movement's worldview is seen in peculiar organizational features, such as the fact that Chavismo is organized as a polarizing movement. And it is manifested in significant economic policies such as the Missions, which embody the government's leftist brand of populism and include a series of partisan features that contradict a purely office-maximizing strategy.

Seeing populism in terms of ideas does more than help us understand Chavismo, however. It forces us to reconsider our understanding of populism and ultimately helps us spell out the logic that undergirds other successful populist movements. Movement organization, shortsighted macroeconomic policy, and political strategies for bringing about late modernization are ultimately imperfect correlates of populism and make poor definitions. But they do describe likely consequences of a populist worldview and provide helpful clues to its origins. When we see these largely material qualities manifested in Chavismo, we can see them not as its defining features, but as symptoms of something deeper.

The underlying set of ideas that defines populism repeatedly proves to be a crucial cross-cutting dimension for situating and categorizing some of the most important phenomena we study in political science today. Perhaps the most important of these phenomena is regime type. Procedural elements of regimes such as electoral contestation, participation, and civil rights and liberties are fundamental to how we define democracy, and judged in these terms, Chavismo has clearly become a semidemocratic or even competitive authoritarian regime. But these procedural elements exist in a normative context that colors how they are understood and implemented by politicians and citizens, a context that ultimately helps determine the direction the government is taking. The populism of Chavismo celebrates popular sovereignty while dismissing the virtues of dissent and questioning the legitimacy of opposition. It stands in opposition to the more familiar pluralist understanding of democracy, which tries to achieve compromise among competing views and emphasizes democratic procedure as the means for achieving this compromise. The worldview of Chavismo propels the movement in undemocratic directions that distinguish it qualitatively from other partially democratic governments.

In the remainder of this conclusion, I revisit and expand on these findings. First, I briefly summarize the contributions of this book to the study of populism. I then move on to a broader discussion of the study of ideas that the book speaks to – specifically, the concepts of worldview and discourse – and use this as an opportunity to outline some directions for future research. Finally, I conclude on a note more likely to please those of us who are particularly interested in the case of Chavismo, by discussing a series of implications for Chavismo and outlining several scenarios for the movement in Venezuela.

POPULISM

This book represents an attempt to revisit the concept of populism using more creative concepts and better methodological tools. While the product of this effort is not necessarily a grand theory of populism in the old sociological tradition, it makes several contributions that help answer some of the enduring questions and debates over this concept. Let us review these in each of the three areas addressed above, namely, categorization, causes, and consequences.

Categorization

One of the key contributions of this book is in terms of categorization – defining and measuring populism. The study of populism has become complicated by multiple definitions that have elements of truth but often talk past each other. Adding to the confusion is the fact that few scholars have tried to measure populism, especially quantitatively and in any cross-national, cross-historical perspective. My goal here was to do more than just salvage the concept of populism, an objective that other scholars have admirably achieved in recent years (see Roberts 1995 or Weyland 2001). Rather, I hoped to turn the concept of populism into a more powerful instrument that could elucidate new areas of politics.

To do this, I proceeded along two tracks. The first was a logical defense characterizing the discursive approach to populism as our best minimal definition. I repeated and expanded on the argument of other scholars (Laclau 2005; Panizza 2005a), suggesting that by getting at the ideational core of actual populist movements, we could account for features of populism highlighted in the structuralist, economic, and political-institutional definitions. Older definitions point us to causal connections rather than spurious correlations. At several points in this book I spelled out these connections, showing why populist movements often occur in less-developed countries, why the discourse is sometimes linked to shortsighted macroeconomic policies favoring redistribution and deficit spending, and why actual instances of populism typically emerge as movements with low institutionalization and an emphasis on mass mobilization. Consequently, I was able to point out new observable implications, such as the origins of right- and left-populism in different modes of capitalist industrialization and current economic conditions (Chapter 7); the strong affinity between populist ideas and the tactics of contentious politics (Chapter 6; more on this in the next section); and the importance of corruption as the distinguishing factor in the developing countries that are most prone to populism (Chapter 5; again, more on this below).

The second track was an empirical one demonstrating our capacity to measure populist discourse usefully. Of all the definitions of populism, the discursive one has been the weakest empirically. Analyses of populist discourse are often limited to in-depth case studies of particular movements or discussions of theory that avoid any data at all. I try to correct for this lack of comparative data – and raise the ante for other approaches to populism – by measuring populist discourse through a novel technique of textual analysis. The result is a fairly large dataset on populist discourse with good reliability and face validity, one that can readily be expanded in future research. Traditional qualitative techniques of discourse analysis still help us understand the content of a given leader's discourse (and I use these techniques here), but the quantitative analysis allows us to situate Chávez and other leaders in a larger universe.

Causes

The contribution of this book to the study of populism's causes is fairly comprehensive. The chapters here are the first attempt to test simultaneously the different theories of populism that have accumulated over the years, a test that considers both individual- and aggregate-level evidence and ranges from a case study to statistical analysis. The results do not completely discount some of the most prominent theories, but situate them in a more comprehensive framework that sees widespread injustice and the absence of the rule of law as necessary conditions for successful populist movements to emerge. At least in my contemporary dataset, populist leaders are found only in countries with high levels of corruption, and citizens who support populist leaders (at least in Venezuela in the late 1990s) are much more likely to be concerned about corruption, the honesty and innovative capacity of their leaders, and systemic political reform. All of this supports the book's central claim that populism is a phenomenon that cannot be explained until we take into account the normative dimension of politics.

The theory provided in this book is still insufficient. The weak rule of law and the lack of property rights, often generated by a historical legacy of colonial exploitation, describe only the background conditions that create the demand for populists; the supply of populist leaders is determined by other factors. Because populism taps into deep issues of regime structure, this supply is unlikely to be affected very much by the kinds of competitive dynamics and institutionally determined barriers to entry that are so important in shaping programmatic and clientelistic party systems (c.f. Lipset and Rokkan 1967; Kitschelt 1994, 1995; Mudde 2007). Rather, it reflects a simpler problem confronted by all movements: that of finding coordinating devices that can reduce barriers to collective action. The charismatic leaders who characterize successful populist movements provide such a device, but these are rare individuals who can be prevented from emerging on the political scene by any number of minor historical accidents. Chávez himself confronted several such decisive moments along his path to success, and a different outcome at any of them would have eliminated him as a key political figure. This is a difficult argument to test and requires additional analysis of populism across longer spans of time. Historical analysis and the creation of a time series are obvious avenues for future research.

One area of populism that some readers may still wonder about, and which I should briefly address before concluding this section, is radical-right populism in Western Europe (Betz 1994; Kitschelt 1995; Mudde 2007). Technically speaking, "radical right" is not equivalent to populism, but refers to a programmatic category of parties that feature xenophobic, anti-immigration platforms with strong elements of neoliberal economic policy. Most studies of these parties are careful to separate this feature from the phenomenon of populism, treating the latter as a diffuse, nonprogrammatic aspect of their appeal that characterizes only a subset of radical-right parties. Yet, the populist parties within the radical right are probably the most salient examples of populism in Western Europe today, and readers may wonder if, by excluding them, I have somehow biased my results.

In fact, the recent experience of radical-right parties in Western Europe roughly confirms our normative argument, which links the frequency of successful populist appeals to the quality of democratic government. Radical-right populism is very rare in this region, where governance tends to be superior. The scholarly literature makes it clear that few radical-right parties of any kind have actually come to power as dominant members of parliamentary coalitions in Western Europe. Several radical-right parties have won regional governorships or seats as mayors, several others have won second place in national parliamentary elections, and a couple have been minority members of government coalitions, but none except perhaps Silvio Berlusconi's Forza Italia has ever gained control over the office of chief executive.[1] At the same time, the rule of law and the quality of democratic governance in these countries are high both in absolute terms and in comparison with most of the developing world. Far and away the worst performer on corruption perception indexes, Italy (5.2 on Transparency International's CPI in 2007), is still a better performer than all Latin American countries except Chile and Uruguay (7.0 and 6.7, respectively). Thus, the broad regional differences in the rule of law today are matched by relative differences in the incidence of populism.

When we look more closely inside Western Europe at the intraregional pattern of electoral success of the most explicitly populist parties, the data again confirm the book's argument. Of course, we cannot determine here whether any of these radical-right parties have particularly strong populist discourses; the analysis in Chapter 2 considers only a handful of European countries and examines the speeches of actual chief executives, none of whom were from radical-right parties. Yet, a few facts still stand out. First, the two most electorally successful parties that all of the literature agrees are populist, the Austrian Freedom Party (FPÖ) under Jörg Haider and the Northern League under Umberto Bossi in Italy, rose to prominence in countries that featured Western Europe's most clientelistic party systems. Italy, in particular, has a long history of (relatively) corrupt politics, particularly in the south, and even today continues to receive the lowest ratings of any European country on corruption perception indexes; the Northern League and its eventual coalition partner, Berlusconi's Forza Italia, won power during the anticorruption scandals that precipitated the breakdown of Italy's postwar party system in the 1990s. Second, in European countries with a relatively stronger rule of law, populist radical-right parties gain electoral strength only as they become more moderate, and in such cases radical party leaders frequently find themselves thrust from power by factions within their own parties. This is the case, for example, with the Danish Progress Party, whose radical founder, Mogens Glistrup, was eventually forced out of the party (Betz 1994) and whose moderate elements (such as Pia Kjaersgaard's Danish Peoples Party) enjoyed much greater success after leaving the party.

Thus, the cross-regional and within-region patterns of populism in Western Europe seem to confirm our arguments about the causes of populist movements. In a region where problems of governance and the rule of law are rather minor in comparison with those of many developing countries of the world, populism gains very little foothold and tends to remain isolated to minority parties or exists as a secondary element of party platforms. But where such problems of governance become more severe, the populist response becomes more salient.

---

[1] While some scholars characterize Berlusconi and his party as populist (Mazzoleni, Stewart, and Horsfield 2003), those who study radical-right populism tend to see his coalition partner, the Northern League, as a clearer instance of this type of party (Betz 1994; Kitschelt 1995; Mudde 2007). Unfortunately, Berlusconi was not included in my cross-national analysis of populist discourse.

Consequences

In terms of studying populism's *consequences* – showing that populism understood as a worldview really matters, and in what ways – the contribution of this book is somewhat more limited but still real. I explored only two areas in which the populist worldview exercises its unique effects: political organization and public policy, particularly discretionary spending programs. Yet, I hope to have demonstrated that the ideational definition of populism gives us insights into basic features of these two areas. For the sake of brevity, I will focus here on just political organization and set aside the effects of populism on economic policy.

In Chapter 6 I argued that fundamental aspects of social movements are linked to the populist worldview. Populists organize as diffuse movements and use contentious tactics not merely because of the resource constraints of poor, marginalized activists and the challenges of collective action, but also because of activists' self-perception. Movements are a way of putting into practice activists' moral claim to embody a democratic, popular will struggling against a corrupt, undemocratic system. Even affluent groups (e.g., chambers of commerce) and large, institutionalized secondary associations (such as labor confederations) – both of which presumably have encompassing interests and the capacity to overcome collective action problems in the pursuit of their cause – may opt for movementism rather than lobbying or electoral participation if they believe they represent the will of an unjustly treated people.

We see this point most clearly when we try to explain the behavior of Chávez's opposition during the first years of his government. This consisted of the wealthiest and best-organized segments of Venezuelan society and included nearly all of the traditional civil society: the old governing political parties (as well as most new challengers), organized labor, the national chamber of commerce, and secondary associations that emerged in the 1970s among the middle and upper classes. Yet, the opposition resorted first and foremost to sometimes violent protests and popular mobilization, even very early in Chávez's tenure, when the opposition had greater resources and electoral routes were available. Despite the urgings of friendly outsiders and intense efforts by the Carter Center and OAS to maintain a dialogue between the two sides (c.f. Domínguez and Levitsky 2003; The Carter Center 2005a), the opposition spent over a year in marches, strikes, and sometimes violent protests before agreeing to even pursue the route of a presidential recall, an option that was at least in theory available as early as the beginning of 2000.[2] Many pro-government activists have interpreted the opposition's contentious tactics as attempts by a conspiring, self-interested elite to manipulate popular sentiment, but this is a cynical interpretation that applies a double standard.

---

[2] This was really a much longer process of protest and violence. The first major opposition protests occurred in December 2001. The Carter Center and the OAS were invited to help mediate the conflict in summer 2002, after the attempted coup, and the two opposing sides reached an agreement to pursue an electoral route only in May 2003.

It seems simpler and more consistent to assume that sectors of the opposition, like many Chavistas, were motivated by a strong sense of their own moral superiority and a dogged belief that *they* embodied the true popular will, contra the ostensibly false one of Chavismo. Their choice of organization and tactics ran counter to their relative abundance of resources and was prompted by their own (right populist?) worldview.

This is, of course, a difficult argument to make without more systematic data about the opposition's language, and we should avoid painting the opposition in too broad strokes; part of the opposition's message was a pluralist one emphasizing the importance of democratic institutions (although this was not a particularly dominant theme in the first years of protests), and it had clear elements of elitism against which Chávez successfully played off. Yet, a naive early belief by the opposition that it embodied the true majority will could help us understand its initial failure to organize for regular, institutionalized, partisan activity in elections. Without the charismatic leadership that imposed order on Chavismo, the opposition's discourse placed it at an enormous disadvantage. Mass spontaneous demonstrations always feel more appropriate for populists than organizing a prolonged get-out-the-vote campaign, which requires that all activists subject themselves to a unified, coordinating organization engaged in mundane activities that implicitly acknowledge the political system's legitimacy. A charismatic leader in the opposition might have given them an equivalent figure to embody their will and coordinate activity.

This combination of populist worldview and lack of charismatic leadership cannot explain all of the opposition's inability to organize effective grassroots electoral campaigns (overconfidence, poor media strategy, and a lack of contacts in shantytowns probably also matter; see Gutiérrez 2004 and Smilde forthcoming), but it seems a likely factor. Probably the key transformation of the opposition since the recall election of 2004 is the adoption by their leaders of a much more pluralistic outlook that privileges democratic institutions and avoids polarizing confrontations with Chávez. In both their loss during the 2006 presidential election and the significant victories of the 2008 local elections, the opposition was "conspicuously conciliatory" and even willing to extend a hand to the Chávez government (Gómez 2006, 2008; Latin American Newsletters 2008a). This has gone hand in hand with greater coordination and careful electoral organization, and has allowed the opposition to increasingly take the moral high ground (López Maya 2008b).

THE STUDY OF (DEEP) IDEAS

All of the above contributions to the study of populism are valuable, yet they are also somewhat limited. Populism is just one particular set of ideas, and populist movements are just one version of mass democratic politics. In studying populism, we find ourselves speaking to a larger literature on the role of ideas, a literature that in recent years has acquired greater visibility and impact in political science. Here the book suggests a number of avenues for future study that are less apparent and thus worth pointing out, because they indicate a larger program of research.

The Near Unity of Worldview and Discourse and Its Methodological Implications

One key insight into the larger study of ideas and politics is the close link between abstract ideas and language. Behavioralists who study ideas have generally missed this important connection. This is likely because of their tendency to study very specific, consciously articulated sets of ideas: causal beliefs such as Keynesian economics, principled beliefs such as human rights norms, or programmatic beliefs and ideologies such as socialism. When we consider such consciously elaborated ideas, it makes more sense to separate the abstract ideas from the language used to communicate them, because the former are usually found in published academic treatises, while the latter can be located in political speeches and campaign publicity. For example, socialist ideology sits primarily in the pages of books dedicated to its conscious study, but Chávez's socialist rhetoric is separate from these books – informed by them, of course, and ultimately drawing on some of their language, yet still at least physically separate. But there are few books consciously laying out, let alone advocating or critiquing, a Manichaean worldview. The meanings and ideas constituting such a worldview are too deep and may not be the kinds of ideas that one preaches and adopts, even if we could make more people aware of them. They seem to be rooted in much deeper attributes of our minds – personality, for example, or long-term patterns of socialization.[3] As a result, it is normally a physical impossibility to separate the worldview from the discourse or to examine any physical instances of the worldview outside of language or the interpretable acts of others. Ideas at this deep level become relatively unified with language, and the relationship between them becomes a little messier.

Here is where the postmodernists, discourse theorists, and constructivists enter the debate. These scholars already have considerable experience in studying language as a bearer of meanings. Focusing, as many of them do, on the subtle ways in which language expresses and reinforces our hidden assumptions, and ultimately the relationships of power and dominance that they see pervading society, they have devoted much more of their attention to discourse than to rhetoric. Admittedly, many among them are antipositivists who feel uncomfortable with the idea of measurement and science generally,

---

[3] The world religions that Weber enumerates (1954 [1948]) obviously contradict this depiction of worldview because they are consciously elaborated systems of fundamental beliefs, and each of them gained large numbers of new converts at relatively specific moments in history. But Weber's subsequent discussion of the various cultures or bases of political legitimacy concerns an abstraction that is no longer in a political or religious tract, but instead a fundamental outlook that has more of the taken-for-granted quality we associate with the notion of worldview.

Conclusion

and they do not measure discourse in the sense that I do here or that most positivists would prefer. But they give us clues about how to do this kind of measurement. Because discourses lack a consistent lexicon – the underlying ideas are too poorly developed for us to create and share a unified set of terms to express them – we have to look at deeper linguistic elements of the text, such as metaphor, tone, and theme. In other words, we must *interpret* what other people say and do, an activity that requires looking for broad patterns in language that go beyond specific words or even phrases.

Aside from noting this connection between language and ideas, my contribution here is to suggest that we can make this interpretation more systematic through the use of techniques such as holistic grading. While the search for broad patterns of meanings – the elements of a discourse – requires some initial qualitative work and must ultimately depend on human coders and whole-text analysis, we can eventually systematize this process and make it more precise and replicable through the use of tools such as coding rubrics, anchor texts, and multiple graders. Thus, in an attempt to measure populism, I have come up with additional means for measuring discourse and worldview, leaving the behavioralists with less excuse for overlooking this important level of ideas. Both sides have contributed something to this effort, although in this instance the contribution seems to have come more from the postmodernists and their allies.

What else do we learn from this effort? First, looking at methodological issues, the analysis in this book offers a better sense of the criteria that should guide our choice of technique in measuring ideas. Traditional and computer-based methods of content analysis continue to have an honored place in the quantitative analysis of texts, but they are not as appropriate for studying the deep, implicit sets of ideas that a discourse represents. As ideas become less explicit and discrete – as we shift away from issue positions to worldviews – we need to rely on holistic techniques that can quickly and flexibly deal with abstract, latent aspects of speech and text. These techniques are still handled more efficiently by human coders, who are capable of seeing broad patterns of ideas very quickly and with minimal training. The behavioralist inclination to quantify things is not mistaken, but the tendency to do so in ways that eliminate human coding and error is, given our present technologies, a dead end, at least when it comes to measuring our most fundamental beliefs about the world.

Another direction for further research is conceptual. Populist and pluralist discourses have clear referents in both scholarly literature and the speeches I have analyzed here; we can be confident that these types are sound categories. But are these the only discourses that politicians and citizens use, the only worldviews that exist in modern democracy? Obviously not. In Chapter 2 I acknowledge a third discourse, elitism, but dodge the problem of really defining this discourse and providing clear examples from actual speech. And recent work by a variety of scholars suggests others: for example, Wendt's

(1999) three "cultures" of international relations or even Weber's classic bases of political legitimacy. The fact is that there are no comprehensive typologies of discourse or worldview. Discourse analysts typically eschew comprehensive typologies in favor of understanding the intricacies of how speech, thought, and action interact (c.f. Aibar 2005; for a partial counterexample, see Dryzek and Berejikian 1993). And behavioralists have not given this area enough attention to come up with labels and examples. We need to spend time looking for additional types and subsuming these under a general framework. Work here might proceed deductively, identifying different possible values and their combinations among the discursive elements that others and I have highlighted; but inductive work seems likely to bear quick fruit. The effort of my assistants and me to actually read large numbers of speeches gave us much greater insight than we imagined possible, and these speeches together with readings in the discourse analytic literature allowed us to see patterns very quickly. Perhaps more behavioralists should take talk seriously and look closely at actual speeches, including those of purported elitists (Krastov 2006) or even authoritarian leaders.[4]

Causal Theories of Ideas and Their Impact

When we look back on the results of the causal analysis in this book – on the study of why people adopt certain ideas and what impact those ideas have on their behavior – the direction of contributions goes the other way. Discourse theorists and constructivists emphasize the determining qualities of our shared language. This language and the ideas it embodies are structural phenomena – no one person creates them, only the extended conversation of our community does – and they should be seen as causally powerful, constraining, and shaping the ways in which we are able to see the world. Once our leaders or we as citizens slip into a particular discourse, we invoke a whole set of arguments that biases our subsequent thinking and propels our behavior in certain directions.

However, the findings in this book go against this strong constructivist view and support a somewhat more traditional behavioralist approach to the causal properties of ideas, which sees ideas responding strongly to material constraints in our environment and in ourselves. The book also defies the postmodernist or radical interpretivist view that culture is best thought of as a highly idiosyncratic set of meanings that changes dramatically across groups of people and resists categorization.[5] First, the consistency I find in

---

[4] Dryzek and Niemeyer (2008) recommend Q method for inductively analyzing discourse at the mass level, and I think this technique shows promise. However, it introduces its own biases insofar as researchers must still select a set, albeit a rather large one, of possible statements that can capture respondents' modes of thought.
[5] A fairer reading of much of the interpretivist literature would be that it remains wary of scholarly efforts to typologize cultures in ways that make the researcher feel superior or justify relationships of dominance. It is not really opposed to typologies and causal arguments. After

populist discourse across time and communities suggests a set of ideas and language that come rather naturally. The fact that the language of a Chávez, a Perón, and a Lukashenko should have such remarkable similarities – similarities strong enough that we can measure them using multiple coders – suggests that commonalities of human thought and experience are helping to drive the choice of language. What are these commonalities? Basic democratic ideas regarding agency and popular sovereignty are one set of logical antecedents; and the populist worldview would be impossible without the human ability and tendency to conceive of a moral, metaphysical realm.

Second, the rather high correlation between populist movements and corruption, with economic crisis as secondary factor, strongly suggests the need for a set of material conditions that make certain ideas more sensible and likely. We see this in Venezuela in Chapter 4, where I reported an objective problem of weak governance that worsened dramatically after the first oil boom. Although interpreted by media and politicians, this was a real phenomenon that had an existence independent of exposés and speeches. The material bases are clearer in the comparative analysis in Chapter 5, where we find that countries with high levels of populism all had high levels of perceived and experienced corruption. While these measures necessarily take into account a certain level of value judgment and subjectivity, they reference and correlate with actual behaviors that affect economic development and democratic stability (Mauro 1995; Seligson 2002).

Finally, in the case of Chavismo, we do find that populist ideas produce consistent patterns in organization and public policy. Yet, ideas are not a completely determinate force. For instance, they interact with a concrete socioeconomic environment to produce different directions of macropolicy, and they must acknowledge and sometimes clash with the constraints imposed by material resources (for example, the need for a leader who can overcome problems of coordination in running campaigns).

Thus, calling populist discourse socially constructed tells us little about when populist discourse will actually be accepted by citizens and turned into political action. Seeing populism instead as a relatively reasoned response to real problems – moral problems, but moral problems rooted in a material reality – generates rather strong findings with some predictive power, especially considering the small snapshot of countries we have here. This is not to say that populist discourse and the underlying set of ideas it represents are not shared meanings – different people obviously understand this set of ideas, and multiple leaders use a similar language – but knowing this tells us little about how the discourse becomes activated or accepted. As even some critics within the discourse analytic camp argue (de Ipola 1982; de la Torre 2000), the fact that a leader uses a particular discourse is no guarantee that it will be accepted or that people will follow the leader because of his discourse. To explain why

---

all, the argument that language typically reinforces relationships of dominance can itself be seen as an assertion of patterns and causality that refer to basic human instincts.

people buy into the leader's discourse and even adopt similar worldviews, we need to think of people as at least roughly rational beings who have some grasp of the objective world around them and who respond to it intentionally and consistently.

One direction for future research is to explore the consequences of worldview and discourse in other realms. This means studying not only the unique impact of the ideas, but also how they interact with aspects of the material environment. Current work on populism, particularly populist discourse, tends to emphasize its consequences for coalitions, policies, and political polarization (Conniff 1999; de la Torre 2000; Weyland 2001). These are important areas to consider further, but we might also think about exploring the unique consequences of populism for international behavior (including both security/conflict and international political economy, which for populist leaders are closely intertwined), ethnic conflict, and, of course, voting behavior (which I have touched on in Chapter 7). Much of the existing behavioralist work on ideas already takes this tack by studying the unique impact of ideas on different areas of political behavior; the trend is strongest perhaps in international relations. But thus far, it is the constructivists who have done the best job of studying the impact of fundamental ideas such as worldview or discourse on behavior (Kratochwil 1989; Klotz 1995; Wendt 1999). Perhaps a more behavioralist approach emphasizing the intersection of ideas and material constraints on reasoning citizens can add something to this discussion.

One of the most interesting areas of causal analysis – and one that the behavioralists again seem better equipped to address – is how discourse and worldview operate at the individual level. The book's data on elite-level discourse give us reason to claim that a populist worldview exists, but they cannot help us answer finer questions about the nature of worldviews and discourses among citizens. We explored survey data in Venezuela in order to model the vote choice for Chávez in 1998, but this was a model of vote choice rather than affinity for populist discourse and ideas. Sorting out programmatic effects (such as support for a relatively leftist leader) is difficult to do and may still leave us with doubts about exactly why voters supported Chávez over other candidates. Thus, finer questions remain. Are discourses such as populism latent sets of ideas and language already shared by most democratic citizens and acquired early in youth, or are they taught to us later as we interact with articulate, inspiring politicians? How much of our affinity for populism or other discourses is affected by recent experience, and how much is in fact rooted in personality or inherited traits? Does personally lived experience (pocketbook assessments) matter most, or is our affinity for certain worldviews and discourses shaped primarily by perceptions of our neighbors' experiences and those of the larger community (sociotropic)? Addressing these and other similar questions requires survey data and perhaps experimental work that allow us to see inside individuals and small groups in carefully controlled ways.

Conclusion

THE FUTURE OF CHAVISMO AND DEMOCRACY IN VENEZUELA

Since the initial writing of this book, Chavismo has taken additional steps down the path of authoritarianism and socialism that raise questions about the regime's viability and direction. By way of conclusion, it seems appropriate to address the practical implications of this book for policymakers and those concerned primarily with Chavismo and the future of democracy in Venezuela. Where are Chavismo and Venezuela headed? If our understanding of Chavismo as an instance of populism is to have real merit, it must demonstrate its utility by providing us with some clear, unique predictions and a better sense of the factors at play.

For critics of Chávez who hope to return Venezuela to a path of pluralist democracy and market-oriented development, the implications of this research are largely negative. Even if it loses power, Chavismo is unlikely to moderate its populist discourse and will probably remain a force in Venezuelan politics for the forseeable future. Moreover, the underlying weaknesses in the rule of law and Venezuela's model of economic development that gave rise to populism will not soon be corrected. The course of democracy over the next few years will be difficult. For those who support Chávez and would like to see his movement succeed in its goals of democratic or socialist revolution, the challenges are equally great and may not favor their particular vision of participatory democracy or socialist economy.

For Chavismo's critics, the economy might seem to be the determining factor right now. The growing deficit and macroeconomic mismanagement could eventually spell the government's doom, especially with the global economy entering into a severe recession and oil prices in a tailspin as of early 2009. Increasing social spending since the general strike of 2002–3 had already driven the fiscal deficit to well over 3 percent of GDP and was pushing inflation to almost 30 percent in 2008 (Latin American Newsletters 2008b). Government efforts to renationalize key industries, to redistribute agricultural lands, and to assume greater control over foreign oil investments continue to depress private investment in production, resulting in deteriorating infrastructure and basic services (c.f. Reuters 2008). Declining revenues are already undermining the government's ability to project its power internationally (Romero 2009). These indicators herald a difficult macroeconomic future even in good times with high oil prices, let alone with the sudden drop in oil prices witnessed at the end of 2008. The catastrophe could be more severe than the crisis of the early 1980s, when plummeting revenues forced the government to engage in a massive currency devaluation while sharply curtailing spending on state-owned enterprises and development programs.

Yet, the implication of the book's normative theory of populism is that Chávez's destiny is determined by much more than just the economy. At the risk of ignoring vast literatures on regime consolidation and party system stability, I suggest two or three factors that will determine Chavismo's direction and its ability to survive.

To begin with, Chavismo's survival depends critically on the credibility of Chávez's discourse. This credibility is based on Chávez's perceived honesty and sincerity, and especially on his ability to sound and really be someone who hates corruption and injustice and believes in the people.

Of course, corruption within the government remains a significant problem. Both quantitative indicators and journalistic evidence suggest that levels of corruption have remained essentially unchanged or have even grown worse in the past few years. Transparency International's CPI and the World Bank's Control of Corruption index continue to show Venezuela at the bottom of the pack in Latin America and among the bottom ranks across the globe.[6] Measures of experienced corruption, which are ostensibly more objective than corruption perception surveys, show Venezuela in a much more favorable position regionally but in a poor position compared to the advanced industrial democracies. The AmericasBarometer 2007 and Transparency International's Global Corruption Barometer 2007 find that 10–15 percent of Venezuelans indicate having to pay bribes for various government services, depending on the government officials in question. These figures are about average for Latin America and more than double those of European Union countries, and they seem to have grown in recent years (Transparency International 2007; Hawkins et al. 2008).[7] The identity of the perpetrators and the precise locus of corruption have shifted somewhat – the Missions seem less afflicted by violations of the rule of law, at least at the level of service provision, while PDVSA seems to have been largely corrupted since the layoffs of 2003 – but the overall pattern in Venezuela remains the same. The news since 2004 is full of lurid reports of kickback schemes, extortion, and outright fraud as bureaucrats and high-level officials take advantage of growing government revenues, lax controls, and a partisan environment that discourages government officials from releasing any news that might depict the government in an unfavorable light (for a few examples in the English-language print media,

---

[6] In 2008, Venezuela sank to a low of 1.9 on Transparency International's 10-point index, a drop of about 0.7 points since 1999; in this year it ranked 158 out of 180 countries (Transparency International 2008). In 2007, it received a score of −1.04 on the the World Bank's Control of Corruption measure, essentially unchanged since 2002 but lower than the −0.86 it received in 1998 (The World Bank Group 2008).

[7] Wilpert (2007) provides datapoints suggesting that perceived corruption had declined by 2005, but recent data from the AmericasBarometer, Latinobarometer, and the Transparency International GCB series all suggest that levels have rebounded since then. Transparency International's figures for the entire GCG series – the percentage of respondents who report being paid a bribe – are 12% (2007), 21% (2006), 6% (2005, the year Wilpert cites), and 9% (2004). Likewise, Latinobarometer shows a steady decline in the number of persons who report having witnessed bribery, from 27% in 2002 to 13% in 2006, but a dramatic rebound to 22% in 2007, which closely parallels the trend throughout the region and fairly consistently places Venezuela around the regional average (Corporación Latinobarometro 2007, 102). The AmericasBarometer data are mentioned earlier, and we lack any time series here. But as already noted, these figures tend to place Venezuela at the regional average for perceived corruption as of late 2007.

see *The Economist* 2006; Witt 2007; Forero 2008). Corruption is not just a problem that the opposition sees. Movement activists and sympathizers are among the first to complain about corruption in the government and urge its systematic eradication, as I heard repeatedly in interviews during 2004 and 2005 (for grudging admissions in the alternative print media, see Parma 2005 and Wilpert 2007).

Similar problems of corruption have forced out populist leaders in other countries (for example, Fujimori in Peru), but only after the leaders were personally implicated. Thus far, Chávez has managed to preserve his reputation for honesty and idealism among staunch supporters and even among most of the electorate. Results of the AmericasBarometer 2007 indicate continuing high levels of support for Chávez, with nearly two-thirds of the population expressing strong positive affect for Chávez and high regard for his performance. While corruption victimization is essentially constant across partisan categories, Chavista respondents are much more likely to agree that the government is combating corruption[8] (Hawkins et al. 2008). Chávez seems to have remained free of the excesses that plague other officials and family members, and he is among those speaking out most often against corruption in the government. He made the anticorruption drive an important part of his 2006 presidential campaign, promising in his closing campaign speech "to continue deepening the Bolivarian Revolution, to continue defeating the old vices of corruption, inefficiency, bureaucratization," and in his inaugural speech to wage a "war to the death against corruption...a war to the death against excessive bureaucracy." As long as Chávez remains committed to the goals of his movement, he has the potential to retain his legitimacy in the face of economic downturns and crisis.

The fate of Chavismo also depends on the movement's ability to work through the contradictions that populism creates for ideology and institutionalization. The populist discourse, with its emphasis on popular know-how and direct participatory democracy, tends to sow mistrust of political professionals, complex bureaucracies, and hierarchy. This makes it difficult for Chavismo to create the kind of permanent machinery – in other words, a political party – that would ordinarily be required to make it a permanent force in Venezuelan politics. While the new PSUV tries to incorporate a bottom-up organization with an emphasis on member activism, it seems painfully clear that the party is largely held together by patronage and by Chávez's charismatic authority and populist discourse.

Other populist movements such as Peronism have managed this feat by finding islands of independent organizational permanence in a sea of fluid popular support, such as labor unions (see Levitsky 2003), thereby balancing the imperatives of bureaucratization with those of their worldview. With

---

[8] When presented with a 7-point scale of responses, approximately 50.7% of Chávez opponents report that the government does nothing to combat corruption, while only 11.5% of Chávez supporters choose this answer (Hawkins et al. 2008, 54).

Chavismo, though, organized labor is not a real option because its numbers are small, partly because the oil industry is a relatively small employer (roughly 30,000 employees). Popular sector organizations are also a poor choice. Chávez has encouraged significant levels of popular sector mobilization, particularly in the realm of civil society (Roberts 2006). As Stokes's (1995) analysis of popular mobilization under the Velasco Alvarado regime in Peru suggests, these components of the movement may outlive the leader. This remains the hope of many sympathetic critics of the Chávez government (Smilde and Hellinger forthcoming). Yet, like the PSUV, instances of popular mobilization within Chavismo seem highly dependent on the charismatic leadership of Chávez as well as on access to oil revenues and deficit spending. The experience of organizations such as the Bolivarian Circles augurs poorly for the ability of Chavismo to persist without Chávez; the Circles were more autonomous and more truly grassroots than almost any of the government's current participatory initiatives, but they were never really valued for their own sake and disappeared quickly once Chávez pushed the movement in new directions. Venezuelans on the lowest rungs of the social ladder may have developed real political skills and a greater sense of their potential to exercise their power under Chávez, but Chavismo as a populist movement is overly dependent on the figure of Chávez for its rules and identity. It is hard to imagine the persistence of Chavismo without Chávez.

Chavismo also confronts the particular contradiction of its worldview and its newer leftist ideology. Radical socialism of the Marxist variety imposes a strict notion of what the revolutionary efforts of the movement must consist of: government ownership of capital in the sense of both finance (banking) and the productive base (industry); limited forms of private property; cooperative forms of business organization; new forms of urban planning and architecture; an end to old class distinctions; suspicion of traditional institutions of representative democracy; suspicion of traditional religious institutions; and so on. These are ideas with a long history, a body of official texts, and an elite corps of dedicated intellectuals. Thus, there are some nice affinities between populism and socialism, such as an emphasis on social justice, the legacy of colonialism, and the need to recapture state institutions from the elite, but there are also some significant incompatibilities.

One of the most significant obstacles that formerly prevented populist movements in developing countries from adopting Marxism was the perception of it as a foreign doctrine. The reluctance of classic populists of the 1930s and 1940s to embrace socialism can be explained in part by the (not incorrect) perception that communism was essentially a movement dominated by Stalin and the Soviet Union; this international movement was not warmly received by nationalistic leaders. Hence, AD's leaders in Venezuela shunned ties to the Communist movement (Ellner 1999); in Peru, Haya de la Torre distanced himself from the doctrinaire Communists and espoused a homegrown multiclass approach to revolutionary transformation; in Argentina, Perón offered his movement as the only viable alternative to a Marxist revolution (Waisman

1987); and even in Chile, the Socialist Party "shunned any formal international affiliations" and was "committed to nationalism and anti-imperialism" until its decisive turn to the workers'-front strategy in the 1960s (Drake 1999, 66–7).

Today, with the breakup of the Soviet Union, socialism has become a much more fragmented movement. This provides a better screen for the moderate left in Latin America by eliminating pretexts for U.S. and domestic military intervention (Castañeda 2006; Smith 2008, chapter 11), but it also legitimates radical forms of socialism within countries by making it possible to adopt versions that feel more Latin American and homegrown. Hence, Chávez can comfortably turn to Castro's Cuba for an ally and a revolutionary model at the same time that he praises patriotic heroes of Venezuela's past.

Nevertheless, much of the tension still remains. To become more fully socialist, Chávez and his lieutenants feel compelled to adopt a unified party structure that looks very similar to Lenin's democratic centralism, and bold young leaders are brought into the cabinet who promote radical policy initiatives that the population is not really sure about. The government pursues a socioeconomic transformation that looks increasingly like a real social revolution. This is a hard sell (and one of the reasons for the loss in the December 2007 constitutional referendum even as Chávez's public approval rating was riding high), one that makes Chávez and his team appear more and more like an elitist revolutionary vanguard than interpreters of the popular will. Chávez's subsequent decision in 2008 to impose many of these changes by decree (most notably the creation of superregional governors appointed by the president), as well as his continuing hard line against recalcitrant parties such as the PCV, only reinforce this impression. All of this hints at a change in discourse from "the will of the people" to "the good of the party," from a reified collective that is us to a collective that stands outside the people and that the people must honor and serve.

Thus, the fact that Chávez has maintained his populist discourse for so long, especially after adopting such a radical specific ideology, is a remarkable feat. It is not surprising that scholars and journalists wonder whether he can still be considered populist. But this is not because we define populism as any halfhearted revolutionary movement without an ideology. Rather, it is because of the very real contradiction between a specific ideology with a radical, not-always-popular message about a party vanguard and a discourse or worldview that celebrates the people's will and its unmediated expression as the ultimate repository of goodness. This is a contradiction that Chavismo will eventually have to resolve. So far Chávez has had the best of both, but it seems that the movement is reaching another moment of decision. Given the unusual strength and durability of Chávez's populist discourse, as well as his demonstrated disposition to purge allies and advisers who seem to distance him from the people, it may well be that ultimately he will pull back from a doctrinaire socialist vision and adopt yet another variation on his Bolivarian ideology.

Together these considerations yield three possible scenarios for Chavismo. The first and most likely one is *persistence*. As long as corruption is seen as something unintentional, as a serious but unfortunate by-product of Chávez's well-meaning efforts to reform the system, Chavismo will have staying power even in the face of economic crisis. Events may force Chávez from office, and he may ultimately adopt a differently ideology, but he and his movement will remain a political force to be reckoned with. The current trajectory of the movement will be more like that of Velasquismo in Ecuador or perhaps Peronism in Argentina: a powerful voice in opposition, future returns to office, continuing polarization of the party system, and, if it succeeds in permanently mobilizing some sectors of the poor, some kind of institutionalization and eventual transformation along more pluralist, clientelistic lines. Chávez will remain in many Venezuelans' political imagination as a defender of the people, despite the evident failures of his movement to achieve a new mode of productive, long-term economic growth or institutions that fully enshrine the rule of law.

Of course, there are no guarantees. Populists and their movements are often corrupted by power and succumb to the temptation for self-enrichment that their control over institutions provides. Thus, the second, somewhat less likely scenario is breakdown and *dissolution* following major scandal. If Chávez does not remain a committed fighter for popular justice and anticorruption, then he will presumably suffer the fate of charismatic neopopulists such as Fujimori or more recent populists such as Abdalá Bucaram and Lucio Gutiérrez in Ecuador, all of whom fell from grace once their complete inability or even unwillingness to fight corrupt practices became evident, and their movements essentially disappeared. Note that such a fall could take place even in a context of relative economic prosperity, although it seems most likely to be accompanied by ongoing economic decline. If Chávez experiences this kind of disgrace, he will no longer be a significant political figure, and the disillusioned members of his movement will struggle to find unity and significance.

The third and least likely scenario for Chavismo is *moderation* in the short or medium term. By this I do not necessarily mean his ideology (which I have already said may change), but rather his discourse or underlying worldview. Chávez might become more pluralist, as Lula has done in Brazil over the course of his three-decade-long political career. This path seems unlikely, however; except for brief moments following the election in 1998 and the attempted coup of 2002, Chávez has never shown a strong disposition to moderate his views. Moderation not only requires changing his fundamental assumptions about the political world but also threatens his coalition. If Chávez goes down that path, he stands to alienate radical supporters and fragment the movement in Venezuela while losing the support of international allies who have come to see him as a leader of the struggle against capitalist globalization and U.S. hegemony.

In the end, even if the unusual happens and Chavismo as a viable political movement disappears from the Venezuelan memory, the future of democracy is difficult. Successor movements from the left, center, or right must all contend with an environment where corruption abounds and the appeal of populist discourse remains high. The conditions that facilitated the emergence of Chavismo – lack of the rule of law and a set of development policies overly reliant on oil revenues – are still present. The judiciary is less independent today than it was when Chávez first came to power, the police forces have not been professionalized, and partisan criteria are still used in hiring and promotion decisions throughout the bureaucracy. While the government's efforts to expand education, provide loans to economic cooperatives, and invest in new industries represent laudable efforts to enhance the long-term productive capacity and well-being of Venezuelans, many of its popular social programs (such as the healthcare and subsidized food missions) are unsustainable once oil revenues decline or stagnate. The ultimate long-term solutions – export diversification into other high-value-added products – are not being effectively implemented; the currency remains overvalued, and government support for these industries is inconsistent or guided by unsound economic criteria. Under these circumstances, even the most highly institutionalized parties of the opposition will be tempted to adopt their own populist discourse and charismatic messiahs in their struggle for power and reform in Venezuela – and most of the parties today are not well institutionalized. The cycle of corruption, crisis, and populism seems likely to continue here, as in many areas of Latin America.

Appendix A

The Populist Speech Rubric

Name of politician:

Title of speech:

Category:

Grader:

Date of grading:

Final grade (delete unused grades):

2 A speech in this category is extremely populist and comes very close to the ideal populist discourse. Specifically, the speech expresses all or nearly all of the elements of ideal populist discourse and has few elements that would be considered nonpopulist.

1 A speech in this category includes strong, clearly populist elements but either does not use them consistently or tempers them by including nonpopulist elements. Thus, the discourse may have a romanticized notion of the people and the idea of a unified popular will, but it avoids bellicose language or references to cosmic proportions or any particular enemy.

0 A speech in this category uses few if any populist elements.

Populist	Pluralist
It conveys a Manichaean vision of the world, that is, one that is moral (every issue has a strong moral dimension) and dualistic (everything is in one category or the other: right or wrong, good or evil). The implication – or even the stated idea – is that there can be nothing in between, no fence-sitting, no shades of gray. This leads to the use of highly charged, even bellicose language.	The discourse does not frame issues in moral terms or paint them in black and white. Instead, there is a strong tendency to focus on **narrow particular issues**. The discourse will emphasize or at least not eliminate the possibility of natural, justifiable differences of opinion.
The moral significance of the items mentioned in the speech is heightened by ascribing **cosmic proportions** to them, that is, by claiming that they affect people everywhere (possibly but not necessarily across the world) and across time. Especially in this last regard, frequent references may be made to a reified notion of history. At the same time, the speaker will justify the moral significance of his or her ideas by tying them to **national and religious leaders** who are generally revered.	The discourse will probably not refer to any reified notion of history or use any cosmic proportions. References to the spatial and temporal consequences of issues will be limited to the material reality rather than any mystical connections.
Although Manichaean, the discourse is still democratic in the sense that the good is embodied in the will of the majority, which is seen as a unified whole, perhaps but not necessarily expressed in references to the will of the people; however, the speaker ascribes a kind of unchanging essentialism to that will rather than letting it be whatever 50 percent of the people want at any particular moment. Thus, this good majority is romanticized, with some notion of the common man (urban or rural) seen as the embodiment of the national ideal.	Democracy is simply the calculation of votes. This should be respected and is seen as the foundation of legitimate government, but it is not meant to be an exercise in arriving at a preexisting, knowable will. The majority shifts and changes across issues. The common man is not romanticized, and the notion of citizenship is broad and legalistic.
The evil is embodied in a minority whose specific identity will vary according to the context. Domestically, in Latin America it is often an economic elite, perhaps the oligarchy, but it may also be a racial elite; internationally, it may be the United States or the capitalist, industrialized nations or international financiers, or simply an ideology such as neoliberalism or capitalism.	The discourse avoids a conspiratorial tone and does not single out any evil ruling minority. It avoids labeling opponents as evil and may not even mention them in an effort to maintain a positive tone and keep passions low.

The Populist Speech Rubric

Populist	Pluralist
Crucially, the evil minority is or was recently in charge and subverted the system to its own interests, against those of the good majority or the people. Thus, systemic change is/was required, often expressed in terms such as "revolution" or "liberation" of the people from their "immiseration" or bondage, even if technically it comes about through elections.	The discourse does not argue for systemic change but, as mentioned previously, focuses on particular issues. In the words of Laclau, it is a politics of "differences" rather than "hegemony."
Because of the moral baseness of the threatening minority, nondemocratic means may be openly justified or at least the minority's continued enjoyment of these means will be seen as a generous concession by the people; the speech itself may exaggerate or distort data to make this point, and the language will show a bellicosity toward the opposition that is incendiary and condescending, lacking the decorum that one shows a worthy opponent.	Formal rights and liberties are openly respected, and the opposition is treated with courtesy and as a legitimate political actor. The discourse will not encourage or justify illegal, violent actions. There will be great respect for institutions and the rule of law. If data are distorted, this is either an innocent mistake or an embarrassing breach of democratic standards.

Overall comments (just a few sentences):

Appendix B

Test of the Sampling Technique

In order to further check the robustness of our sampling technique, I had my assistants score large, randomly selected sets of speeches by two Latin American presidents, Lula and Cárdenas. Collecting larger samples for all of the chief executives would have been too expensive. I selected these presidents because their discourse would be more difficult to measure (both were perceived as only mildly populist, somewhere between 0 and 1), thereby presenting us with a harder test, and because my assistants and I were reasonably certain that we had the entire universe of their speeches. We randomly selected one speech from each month of their respective terms in office, 42 speeches for Lula and 60 for Cárdenas.[1]

Because of the large numbers of speeches, I asked the graders to dispense with any note-taking or other written analysis other than a short set of comments and a grade; thus, this was also a test of a more truly holistic grading technique than we used in the previous two phases of the study, when I asked graders to compile notes on each of the elements of populist discourse. This new grading technique was much faster (typically requiring 15 minutes per speech instead of 30–45 minutes). Two native Portuguese speakers and two native Spanish speakers conducted the grading, taking about four weeks to complete the task.

Table B.1 provides the results of this analysis. In the case of Cárdenas, the level of intercoder reliability is about as high as in previous phases of the project, with 75 percent absolute agreement and a kappa of .33 (the kappa is low because Cárdenas never receives more than a 1, thereby generating a high level of expected agreement). In the case of Lula, however, the level of intercoder reliability is not quite as high. The absolute agreement is only 64 percent and the kappa is only .27. This lower reliability may be a result of having to grade "in between" speeches using our 3-point ordinal scale. Our graders indicated

---

[1] Speeches were not recorded for a few months of Cárdenas's term, and for both presidents we initially selected a few speeches that were too short and had to be dropped later.

TABLE B.1. *Analysis of random samples of Lula and Cárdenas speeches*

	Lula		Cárdenas	
	Grader 1	Grader 2	Grader 1	Grader 2
Mean	0.48	0.64	0.32	0.20
Standard deviation	0.51	0.48	0.50	0.44
Overall mean	0.56		0.24	
Overall standard deviation	0.39		0.35	
N	42		60	
Percent agreement	64.4		75.0	
Kappa	.27		.33	

afterward that many of Lula's speeches were between 0 and 1 (hence the average scores of around 0.50), thereby forcing them to make a hard decision. The fact that the *average* scores of each grader across the entire Lula sample were almost indistinguishable from each other suggests that the lack of agreement was not a problem of bias or inadequate training, but of small differences in judgment magnified by the scale.[2] We may want to modify the scale in future analyses.

The more specific question, however, is whether these results indicate that we were justified in using a small sample in our two previous phases. One indicator of the robustness of our sampling criteria is whether the average scores for Lula and Cárdenas from the first phase of our project (using different sets of graders and just four speeches) was close to the average scores from the new analysis. Indeed, the actual differences between these two phases of the analysis are not very large, only about 0.31 in the case of Lula and 0.32 in the case of Cárdenas, differences that are significant at only the $p < .12$ level and the $p < .23$ level, respectively (*t*-test with unequal variance). Given the fact that we used different sampling criteria in these two different phases (one a nonrandom sample from four speech categories that took context into account, the other a random sample from all available speeches), these similarities are actually quite striking.

The other important indicator of the effectiveness of our sampling criteria is the size of the variance in our data and especially the difference in variances across the samples. If the larger random sample yields a dramatic improvement in the variance of our estimates, we may not be justified in relying on such small samples in the cases of Lula and Cárdenas and perhaps, by implication, for the other chief executives in our first phases of the analysis. As it

---

[2] Although the difference in means is statistically significant for Lula, with a *t*-test of $p < .09$, the actual difference in scores is only 0.16. This is comparable to the Cárdenas data, where a *t*-test is significant at the $p < .07$ level but the actual difference is only 0.12.

turns out, the variances of these two samples are nearly identical and not very large. In the first sample, the four scores for Lula had a standard deviation of 0.29 and the scores for Cárdenas had a standard deviation of 0.35, while in the second, larger samples, the standard deviations are only 0.36 and 0.43, respectively. Using the Levene test for difference in variance, the difference between the earlier and later standard deviations is not significant by common standards for either president ($p < .71$ for Lula and $p < .69$ for Cárdenas).[3] Thus, even with a nonrandom sample of four carefully coded speeches, we have about the same variability in our scores as if we had graded a much larger random sample of quickly coded speeches.

---

[3] Because the distributions of scores are not symmetric, the Levene test is calculated using the median in place of the mean.

Appendix C

Test of Interaction Effects

In order to test for interaction effects between the indicators of sympathy with Chávez's populist discourse and indicators of the other, traditional explanations for the party system breakdown, I ran several new versions of Model 2 from Table 4.5 (the model using *Informal* rather than *Education* and *Class*). Specifically, I interacted *Honest, Fight Corruption,* and *Constitutional Reform* separately with (1) each of the retrospective economic evaluations (sociotropic and pocketbook), (2) *Informal*, and (3) *Promote Decentralization, Guarantee Human Rights,* and *Protect Environment*. Because all of these but the retrospective economic evaluations are dummy variables, I created the interaction measure by simply multiplying the two components; hence, a 1 indicates that both effects are present, while a 0 indicates that one or both of them are not. In the case of the retrospective economic evaluations, the resulting scale instead goes from 0 to 3, similar to that of the original economic indicator. In keeping with best practice, I include both the interaction term and the component indicators (Brambor, Clark, and Golder 2006).

Table C.1 presents results from just one of these estimations, using *Fight Corruption × Pocketbook Retrospective* as the interaction effect. As can be seen, coefficients for this new indicator are in the predicted direction (a respondent who sees corruption as a significant problem and perceives his or her economic situation to be worse over the past year is more likely to vote for Chávez instead of Salas Römer/other candidates/abstain) and seem to absorb some of the variance associated with *Fight Corruption* and *Pocketbook Retrospective* alone. But the coefficient is not statistically significant for any of these outcomes, and the overall strength of the model fails to show any improvement over the original specification (a likelihood-ratio test is significant at only the $p < .49$ level). Nearly identical results prevail for all other specifications; that is, coefficients are often in the expected direction, but few are statistically significant (never for the choice of Salas Römer), and neither is the overall improvement in the fit of the model.

TABLE C.1. *Multinomial logit of vote choice (with interaction)*

	Salas Römer	Other Candidates	Abstention
Interaction Effect			
Corruption × Pocketbook retrospective	−0.45	−0.27	−0.12
	0.30	0.47	0.30
Socioeconomic Controls			
Informal	−0.52**	−0.46*	−0.03
	0.17	0.26	0.17
Economic Voting			
Sociotropic Retrospective	−0.26	−0.49*	−0.31*
	0.16	0.24	0.17
Sociotropic Prospective (better)	−0.19	−1.21**	−0.78**
	0.25	0.41	0.25
Sociotropic Prospective (same)	0.09	−0.30	−0.42
	0.26	0.39	0.26
Sociotropic Prospective (worse)	0.60*	0.39	0.21
	0.26	0.38	0.25
Pocketbook Retrospective	−0.29*	−0.21	−0.21
	0.15	0.24	0.15
Pocketbook Prospective (better)	−0.06	−0.19	−0.28
	0.24	0.37	0.24
Pocketbook Prospective (same)	0.04	−0.16	−0.42
	0.27	0.41	0.28
Pocketbook Prospective (worse)	−0.06	0.30	0.16
	0.32	0.47	0.30
Issues			
Constitutional Reform	−1.11***	−0.91***	−0.93***
	0.11	0.18	0.11
Privatization of PDVSA	0.54*	−0.41	1.07***
	0.30	0.57	0.28
Satisfaction with Democracy	−0.37***	−0.51**	−0.16
	0.11	0.17	0.11
Fight Corruption	−0.12	−0.06	−0.40*
	0.19	0.30	0.21
Reform Constitution	−1.34***	−2.04**	−0.79*
	0.39	0.72	0.33
Privatize Public Firms	−0.77	−29.64	−0.71
	0.66	2.04E+06	0.66
Candidate Attributes			
Honest	−0.32	0.21	−0.39*
	0.21	0.35	0.21
Young	−0.72**	−0.25	−0.52*
	0.25	0.37	0.24

Test of Interaction Effects

	Salas Römer	Other Candidates	Abstention
Experience in Office	1.19***	0.55	0.72*
	0.29	0.43	0.31
Independent	−0.59*	−0.66	−0.80*
	0.29	0.53	0.32
Man	−1.31**	−1.01*	−0.26
	0.41	0.60	0.32
Authoritarian	−0.45	−0.25	−0.32
	0.30	0.50	0.30
Partisan Identity			
PIDAD	1.79***	4.86***	1.73***
	0.41	0.44	0.42
PIDCOPEI	0.47	2.73***	0.62
	0.49	0.54	0.51
PIDMAS	−1.91***	−1.33	−1.34**
	0.52	1.05	0.44
PIDPPTLCR	−2.60***	−1.16	−1.18*
	0.78	1.07	0.52
Constant	4.61***	3.64**	3.26***
	0.73	1.18	0.73
N	1,333.00		
LR chi² (78)	817.12		
Prob > chi²	0.00		
Pseudo R^2	.24		
Log likelihood	−1328.20		

Note: *p < .10; **p < .01; ***p < .001.
Source: Author's calculation, based on the 1998 RedPol survey (Red Universitaria 1999).

References

Acemoglu, Daron, Simon Johnson, and James A. Robinson. 2001. The colonial origins of comparative development: An empirical investigation. *The American Economic Review* 91 (5): 1369–1401.
2002. Reversal of fortune: Geography and institutions in the making of the modern world income distribution. *The Quarterly Journal of Economics* 117:1231–94.
Adelman, Jeremy, ed. 1999. *Colonial Legacies: The Problems of Persistence in Latin American History*. New York: Routledge.
Agence France Presse. 2001. Chávez relanza su Movimiento Bolivariano 2000 y Círculos Bolivarianos. 17 December (in Spanish).
Aibar, Julio. 2005. El retorno del general. El bussismo, la otra cara de la democracia argentina. *Perfiles Latinoamericanos* 26:199–226.
Alcántara Sáez, M. 1997. *Encuesta de elites parlamentarias 1997*. Unpublished raw data. Salamanca, Spain: Universidad de Salamanca.
Alker, Hayward, and David Sylvan. 1994. Some contributions of discourse analysis to political science. *Kosmopolis* 24 (3): 5–25.
Aló, Presidente Web site. various dates. Available at http://www.alopresidente.gob.ve.
Alvarez, R. Michael, and Jonathan Nagler. 1998. When politics and models collide: Estimating models of multiparty elections. *American Journal of Political Science* 42 (1): 55–96.
Armony, Ariel C., and Victor Armony. 2005. Indictments, myths, and citizen mobilization in Argentina: A discourse analysis. *Latin American Politics & Society* 47 (4): 27–54.
Associated Press. 2003. Chavez supporters crack down on media. *New York Times*. 7 February.
2007. Venezuela's Chavez says his government may nationalize hospitals. 3 July. Available at http://www.lexisnexis.com/.
Baloyra, Enrique A., and John D. Martz. 1979. *Political Attitudes in Venezuela: Societal Cleavages and Political Opinion*. Austin: University of Texas Press.
Barry, Brian. 1978. *Sociologists, Economists and Democracy*. Chicago: University of Chicago Press.
BBC. 2005. Chavez blasts Mexico over summit. *BBC News*. 10 November. Available at http://news.bbc.co.uk/go/pr/fr/-/2/hi/americas/4424374.stm.

2007. Chavez bid for more state control. *BBC News.* 9 January. Available at http://news.bbc.co.uk/go/pr/fr/-/2/hi/business/6243299.stm.

Berman, Sheri. 1998. *The Social Democratic Moment: Ideas and Politics in the Making of Interwar Europe.* Cambridge, MA: Harvard University Press.

Beroes, Agustín. 1990. *RECADI: la gran estafa.* Caracas: Planeta.

Betz, Hans-Georg. 1994. *Radical Right-Wing Populism in Western Europe.* Basingstoke, England: Macmillan.

Blanco, Carlos. 1998. Todos los poderes para el Constituyente. *Primicias.* 29 December, 7–14.

Blanco Muñoz, Agustín. 1998. *Venezuela del 04F-92 al 06D-98: Habla el Comandante Hugo Chávez Frías. Testimonios Violentos,* Vol. 12. Caracas: Fundación Cátedra Pío Tamayo.

Blank, David Eugene. 1973. *Politics in Venezuela: A Country Study.* Boston: Little, Brown and Company.

Botía, Alejandro. 2005a. Círculos Bolivarianos parecen burbujas en el limbo. *Ultimas Noticias.* 20 March, 20.

  2005b. Rollos palaciegos enredaron a los Círculos Bolivarianos. *Ultimas Noticias.* 21 March, 15.

Brady, Henry E., and David Collier, eds. 2004. *Rethinking Social Inquiry: Diverse Tools, Shared Standards.* Lanham, MD: Rowman & Littlefield Publishers.

Brambor, Thomas, William Clark, and Matt Golder. 2006. Understanding interaction models: Improving empirical analyses. *Political Analysis* 14:63–82.

Britton, J. N., N. C. Martin, and H. Rosen. 1966. *Multiple Marking of English Compositions: An Account of an Experiment.* London: Her Majesty's Stationery Office.

Brooks, Stephen, and William Wohlforth. 2000/2001. Power, globalization, and the end of the Cold War. *International Security* 25 (3): 5–53.

Budge, I., J. Bara, A. Volkens, and H. D. Klingemann. (2001). *Mapping Policy Preferences: Estimates for Parties, Electors and Governments, 1945–1998.* Cambridge: Cambridge University Press.

Buxton, Julia. 2001. *The Failure of Political Reform in Venezuela.* Burlington, VT: Ashgate Publishing.

  2003. Economic policy and the rise of Hugo Chávez. In *Venezuelan Politics in the Chávez Era: Class, Polarization, and Conflict,* eds. Steve Ellner and Daniel Hellinger, pp. 113–30. Boulder, CO: Lynner Rienner Publishers.

Calzadilla, Omar, National Coordinator of Mission Robinson. 2005. Interview with authors. Caracas, 14 July.

Canache, Damarys. 1995. Venezuela Public Opinion Survey. Dataset in possession of author.

  2002. *Venezuela: Public Opinion and Protest in a Fragile Democracy.* Coral Gables, FL: North-South Center Press.

  2004. Urban poor and political order. In *The Unraveling of Representative Democracy in Venezuela,* eds. Jennifer L. McCoy and David J. Myers, pp. 33–49. Baltimore: Johns Hopkins University Press.

Canache, Damarys, and Michael R. Kulisheck, eds. 1998. *Reinventing Legitimacy: Democracy and Political Change in Venezuela.* Westport, CT: Greenwood Press.

Canovan, Margaret. 1999. Trust the people! Populism and the two faces of democracy. *Political Studies* 47 (1): 2–16.

Caponi, Orietta. 1999. *La nueva doctrina*. Manuscript in possession of author.
Cardoso, Fernando Henrique. 1975. The city and politics. In *Urbanization in Latin America: Approaches and issues,* ed. Jorge E. Hardoy, pp. 157–90. Garden City, NY: Anchor Books.
Cardoso, Fernando Enrique, and Enzo Faletto. 1979. *Dependency and Development in Latin America*. Berkeley: University of California Press.
Carothers, Thomas. 2002. The end of the transition paradigm. *Journal of Democracy* 13 (1): 5–21.
Carothers, Thomas, ed. 2006. *Promoting the Rule of Law Abroad: In Search of Knowledge*. Washington, DC: Carnegie Endowment for International Peace.
Carreño, Orlando, coordinador comandante de Círculos Bolivarianos MBR-200 (4-F) Estado de Miranda. 2004. Interview with author, 3 August, Guatire.
Castaldi, Lauren. 2006. Judicial independence threatened in Venezuela: The removal of Venezuelan judges and the complications of rule of law reform. *Georgetown Journal of International Law* 37 (3): 477–506.
Castañeda, Jorge G. 2006. Latin America's left turn. *Foreign Affairs* 85 (3): 28.
Cedeño, Jeffrey. 2006. Venezuela in the twenty-first century: "New men, new ideals, new procedures." *Journal of Latin American Cultural Studies* 15 (1): 93–109.
Chávez, Hugo. 2007. Concession speech of President Hugo Chávez. Trans. Dawn Gable. 8 December. Available at http://www.venezuelanalysis.com/analysis/2978.
Cháves, Rodrigo, and Tom Burke. 2003. The Círculos Bolivarianos. *ZNET*. 30 July. Available at http://www.zmag.org.
Chong, Alberto, and César Calderón. 2000. Causality and feedback between institutional measures and economic growth. *Economics and Politics* 12 (1): 69–81.
Círculos Bolivarianos. n.d. ¿Cuál es la misión de los Círculos Bolivarianos? Available at <http://www.Círculosbolivarianos.org/inicio_anexos/mision.html>.
Cleary, Matthew. 2006. Explaining the left's resurgence. *Journal of Democracy* 17 (4): 35–49.
CNE (Consejo Nacional Electoral). 2007. Resultados electorales (Election results). Online dataset. Available at http://www.cne.gov.ve/.
Coatsworth, John H. 1978. Obstacles to economic growth in nineteenth-century Mexico. *American Historical Review* 83 (1): 80–100.
Coffman, William E. 1971. Essay examinations. In *Educational Measurement,* 2nd ed., ed. Robert L. Thorndike, pp. 271–302. Washington, DC: American Council on Education.
Collier, David, and Steven Levitsky. 1997. Democracy without adjectives: Conceptual innovation in comparative research. *World Politics* 49 (3): 430–51.
Collier, Ruth Berins, and Samuel Handlin, eds. 2009. *Reorganizing Popular Politics: Participation and the New Interest Regime in Latin America*. College Park: Pennsylvania State University Press.
Collins, Sheila. 2005. Commentary: Breaking the mold? Venezuela's defiance of the neoliberal agenda. *New Political Science* 27 (3): 267–95.
Comando Supremo Revolucionario Bolivariano. n.d. *Círculos Bolivarianos*. Pamphlet in possession of author.
Committee to Protect Journalists. 2004. *Attacks on the Press 2003: Venezuela*. Available at http://www.cpj.org/attacks03/americas03/ven.html.
    2005. *Attacks on the Press 2004: Venezuela*. Available at http://www.cpj.org/attacks04/americas04/ven.html.

Conniff, Michael L., ed. 1982. *Latin American Populism in Comparative Perspective*. Albuquerque: University of New Mexico Press.
   1999. *Populism in Latin America*. Tuscaloosa: University of Alabama Press.
Consorcio de Ediciones Capriles. 1989. *Diccionario de la corrupción en Venezuela*. Vol. 1. Caracas: Consorcio de Ediciones Capriles, C.A.
   1992. *Diccionario de la corrupción en Venezuela*. Vol. 3. Caracas: Consorcio de Ediciones Capriles, C.A.
Consultores 21. 2006. Quarterly time series on presidential approval. Data in possession of author.
Cooper, Charles R. 1977. Holistic evaluation of writing. In *Evaluating Writing: Describing, Measuring, Judging*, eds. Charles R. Cooper and Less Odell, pp. 3–32. Urbana, IL: National Council of Teachers of English.
Coppedge, Michael. 1993. Parties and society in Mexico and Venezuela: Why competition matters. *Comparative Politics* 25 (3): 253–74.
   1994. *Strong Parties and Lame Ducks: Presidential Partyarchy and Factionalism in Venezuela*. Stanford, CA: Stanford University Press.
   2005. Explaining democratic deterioration in Venezuela through nested inference. In *The Third Wave of Democracy in Latin America: Advances and Setbacks*, eds. Scott Mainwaring and Frances Hagopian, pp. 289–318. Cambridge: Cambridge University Press.
COPRE (Comisión Presidencial para la Reforma del Estado). 1989. *La Reforma en síntesis: Proyecto de reforma integral del Estado*. Caracas, Venezuela: Comisión Presidencial para la Reforma del Estado.
Coronil, Fernando. 1997. *The Magical State: Nature, Money, and Modernity in Venezuela*. Chicago: University of Chicago Press.
Corporación Latinobarómetro. 2007. *Informe Latinobarómetro 2007: Banco de Datos en Línea*. November. Available at http://www.latinobarometro.org/.
Corrales, Javier. 2006. Hugo Boss. *Foreign Affairs* 152:32–40.
Corrales, Javier, and Michael Penfold. 2007. Social spending and democracy: The case of Hugo Chávez in Venezuela. *LASA Forum* 38 (1): 20–2.
Cox, Gary W., and Mathew D. McCubbins. 1986. Electoral politics as a redistributive game. *The Journal of Politics* 48 (2): 370–89.
Crisp, Brian F. 2000. *Democratic Institutional Design: The Powers and Incentives of Venezuelan Politicians and Interest Groups*. Stanford, CA: Stanford University Press.
Crisp, Brian F., and Daniel H. Levine. 1998. Democratizing the democracy? Crisis and reform in Venezuela. *Journal of Interamerican Studies and World Affairs* 40 (2): 27–62.
Cupolo, Marco. 1998. Public administration, oil rent, and legitimacy crises in Venezuela. In *Reinventing Legitimacy: Democracy and Political Change in Venezuela*, eds. Damarys Canache and Michael R. Kulisheck, pp. 99–112. Westport, CT: Greenwood Press.
Dahl, Robert A. 1971. *Polyarchy: Participation and Opposition*. New Haven, CT: Yale University Press.
de Ipola, Emilio. 1982. *Ideología y discurso populista*. Mexico City: Folios Ediciones.
de Juliac, María Eugenia, leader of Bolivarian Circle. 2005. Interview with author. 7 May, Caracas/Provo, Utah.

de la Cruz, Alberto. 1998. Anuncia Hugo Chávez Frías: General Raúl Salazar será ministro de la Defensa. *El Universal.* 30 November. Available at http://archivo.eluniversal.com/1993/11/30/30115CC.shtml.

de la Torre, Carlos. 1997. Populism and democracy: Political discourses and cultures in contemporary Ecuador. *Latin American Perspectives* 24 (3): 12–24.

  2000. *Populist Seduction in Latin America: The Ecuadorian Experience.* Athens: Ohio University Center for International Studies.

de Lima, Venicio A. 1992. Brazilian television in the 1989 presidential campaign: Constructing a president. In *Televisión, Politics, and the Transition to Democracy in Latin America*, ed. Thomas E. Skidmore, pp. 97–117. Washington, DC: Woodrow Wilson Center Press.

Deutche Press-Agentur. 2007. Estudiantes Venezolanos piden "libertad de expresión" ante Brasil. 26 June. Available at http://www.lexisnexis.com.

Di Tella, Torcuato S. 1965. Populism and reform in Latin America. In *Obstacles to Change in Latin America*, ed. Claudio Veliz, pp. 47–74. London: Oxford University Press.

  1997. Populism into the twenty-first century. *Government and Opposition* 32 (2): 187–200.

Diamond, Larry. 1999. *Developing Democracy: Toward Consolidation.* Baltimore: Johns Hopkins University Press.

  2002. Thinking about hybrid regimes. *Journal of Democracy* 13 (2): 21–35.

Dieterich, Heinz. 2004. *Hugo Chávez: El destino superior de los pueblos latinoamericanos.* Caracas: Alcaldía de Caracas.

Dietz, Henry A., and David J. Myers. 2007. From thaw to deluge: Party system collapse in Venezuela and Peru. *Latin American Politics and Society* 49 (2): 59–86.

Dirección Nacional de Formación y Doctrina del Movimiento Quinta República. 1999a. El diseño de un partido y una doctrina progresista (papel de trabajo). Manuscript prepared for the Primera Reunión Nacional de Formación y Doctrina, 30–1 October.

  1999b. Bolivarianos: El árbol de las tres raíces (papel de trabajo). Manuscript prepared for the Primera Reunión Nacional de Formación y Doctrina, 30–1 October.

Dirección Nacional de Organización. 1999. El MVR: Instrumento de construcción de la V República. Unpublishd manuscript in possession of author.

Dirección Nacional Político-Electoral. 1998. *Comando Táctico Nacional.* Photocopy in possession of author.

Dixit, Avanish, and John Londregan. 1996. The determinants of success of special interests in redistributive politics. *Journal of Politics* 58:1132–55.

Domínguez, Jorge I., and Steven Levitsky. 2003. Peron, Pinochet and Patience. *New York Times.* 26 January, p. A13.

Dornbusch, Rudiger, and Sebastian Edwards, eds. 1991. *The Macroeconomics of Populism in Latin America.* Chicago: University of Chicago Press.

Dossani, Sameer, and Noam Chomski. 2007. Neo-liberalism and empire in Latin America today. Interview. Venezuelanalysis.com. March 21. Available at http://www.venezuelanalysis.com/analysis/2291.

Drake, Paul W. 1999. Chile's populism reconsidered, 1920s–1990s. In *Populism in Latin America*, ed. Michael L. Conniff, pp. 63–74. Tuscaloosa: University of Alabama Press.

Dresser, Denise. 1991. Neopopulist solutions to neoliberal problems: Mexico's National Solidarity Program. *Current Issue Brief No. 3.* San Diego, CA: UCSD Center for U.S.-Mexican Studies.
  1997. Falling from the tightrope: The political economy of the Mexican crisis. In *Mexico 1994: Anatomy of an Emerging-market Crash*, eds. Sebastian Edwards and Moises Naim, pp. 55–79. Washington, DC: Carnegie Endowment for International Peace.
Dryzek, John S., and Jeffrey Berejikian. 1993. Reconstructive democratic theory. *American Political Science Review* 87 (1): 48–60.
Dryzek, John S., and Simon Niemeyer. 2008. Discursive representation. *American Political Science Review* 102 (4): 481–93.
Duarte, Alexander. 2000. Política: Encuentro Nacional lanzó a Fermín para la Presidencia de la República. *El Nacional.* 20 February, p. A1.
Durango, Hernán. 2006. Congreso ideológico de Círculos Bolivarianos ratifica ingreso al PSUV. 12 December. Available at http://www.aporrea.org.
Durkheim, Emile. 1984. *The Division of Labor in Society.* Introduction by Lewis Coser, trans. W. D. Halls. New York: Free Press.
Easton, David. 1975. A reassessment of the concept of political support. *British Journal of Political Science* 5:435–57.
Ebel, Robert L. 1951. Estimation of the reliability of ratings. *Psychometrika* 16 (4): 407–24.
Ebbinghaus, Bernhard, and Jelle Visser. 2000. The Societies of Europe: Trade Unions in Western Europe since 1945. CD-ROM. Data taken from Comparative Data: Aggregate Density tables. "Net Density II."
The Economist. 2006. The sickly stench of corruption. 1 April, pp. 31–2.
Egaña, Fernando. 1999. Auge y caída de Venezuela (V): La crisis bancaria. *Zeta* 1224, 13 May, pp. 24–32.
Ellner, Steve. 1993. The deepening of democracy in a crisis setting: Political reform and the electoral process in Venezuela. *Journal of Interamerican Studies and World Affairs* 35 (4): 1–42.
  1999. The heyday of radical populism in Venezuela and its aftermath. In *Populism in Latin America*, ed. Michael L. Conniff, pp. 117–37. Tuscaloosa: University of Alabama Press.
  2001. The radical potential of Chavismo in Venezuela: The first year and a half of power. *Latin American Perspectives* 28 (5): 5–32.
  2004. Leftist goals and the debate over anti-neoliberal strategy in Latin America. *Science and Society* 68 (1): 10–32.
  2005a. The emergence of a new trade unionism in Venezuela with vestiges of the past. *Latin American Perspectives* 32 (2): 51–71.
  2005b. Revolutionary and non-revolutionary paths of radical populism: Directions of the *Chavista* movement in Venezuela. *Science and Society* 69 (2): 160–90.
Ellner, Steve, and Daniel Hellinger, eds. 2003. *Venezuelan Politics in the Chávez Era: Class, Polarization, and Conflict.* Boulder, CO: Lynner Rienner Publishers.
Engerman, Stanley L., and Kenneth L. Sokoloff. 1997. Factor endowments, institutions, and differential paths of growth among New World economies: A view from economic historians of the United States. In *How Latin America Fell Behind: Essays on the Economic Histories of Brazil and Mexico, 1800–1914*, ed. Stephen Haber, pp. 260–304. Stanford, CA: Stanford University Press.
  2000. History lessons: Institutions, factor endowments, and paths of development in the New World. *Journal of Economic Perspectives* 14 (3): 217–32.

2002. Factor endowments, inequality, and paths of development among New World economies. *Economia* 3 (Fall): 41–109.
EU EOM (European Union Election Observation Mission). 2006a. *Final Report: Parliamentary Elections Venezuela 2005*. March. Available at http://www.eueomvenezuela.org/pdf/pre_statement_en.pdf
  2006b. *Final Report: Presidential Elections Venezuela 2006*. Available at http://www.eueomvenezuela.org/pdf/MOE_UE_Venezuela_2006_final_eng.pdf
Fearon, James D., and David Laitin. 2000. Violence and the social construction of ethnic identity. *International Organization* 54 (4): 845–77.
Fernandes, Sujatha. 2006. Radio Bemba in an age of electronic media: The dynamics of popular communication in Chávez's Venezuela. Paper presented at the XXVI Congress of the Latin American Studies Association, San Juan, Puerto Rico, 15–18 March.
Finnemore, Martha. 1996. *National Interests in International Society*. Ithaca, NY: Cornell University Press.
Forero, Juan. 2008. Court case in Miami casts light on corruption in Venezuela. *Washington Post*. 24 October, p. A13.
Frank, Andre Gunder. 1967. *Capitalism and Underdevelopment in Latin America: Historical Studies of Chile and Brazil*. New York: Monthly Review Press.
Freeden, Michael. 2003. *Ideology: A Very Short Introduction*. New York: Oxford University Press.
Freedom House. 2007. *Freedom of the Press Historical Data: Global Data (1980–2006)*. Available at http://www.freedomhouse.org/.
Freud, Sigmund. 1989 [1922]. *Group Psychology and the Analysis of the Ego*. Trans. and ed. by James Strachey. New York: W. W. Norton & Company.
Fundación Misión Sucre. 2004. *Proyecto Nacional y Nueva Ciudadanía*. Caracas: Gobierno Bolivariano de Venezuela, Ministerio de Educación Superior.
Gable, Dawn. 2004. Civil society, social movements, and participation in Venezuela's Fifth Republic. *Venezuelanalysis*. 9 February. Available at http://www.venezuelanalysis.com.
García, Maria Pilar. 1992. The Venezuelan ecology movement: Symbolic effectiveness, social practices, and political strategies. In *The Making of Social Movements in Latin America: Identity, Strategy, and Democracy*, eds. Arturo Escobar and Sonia E. Alvarez, pp. 150–70. Boulder, CO: Westview Press.
García-Guadilla, María Pilar. 2003. Civil society: Institutionalization, fragmentation, autonomy. In *Venezuelan Politics in the Chávez Era: Class, Polarization and Conflict*, eds. Steve Ellner and Daniel Hellinger, pp. 179–96. Boulder, CO: Lynne Rienner Publishers.
  2007a. Ciudadanía y autonomía en las organizaciones sociales bolivarianas: los Comités de Tierra Urbana como movimientos sociales. *Cuadernos del CENDES* 24 (3): 47–73.
  2007b. El poder popular y la democracia participativa en Venezuela: los Consejos Comunales. Paper presented at the XXVII International Conference of the Latin American Studies Association, Montreal.
Garretón, Manuel Antonio, Marcelo Cavarozzi, Peter Cleaves, and Gary Gereffi. 2003. *Latin America in the Twenty-First Century: Toward a New Socio-Political Matrix*. Miami: North-South Center Press.
Garrido, Alberto. 1999. *Guerrilla y Conspiracion Militar en Venezuela*. Caracas: Fondo Editorial Nacional.

2000. *La Historia Secreta de la Revolución Bolivariana*. Merida: Editorial Venezolana.
Germani, Gino. 1978. *Authoritarianism, Fascism, and National Populism*. New Brunswick, NJ: Transaction Books.
Gerring, J. 1997. Ideology: A definitional analysis. *Political Research Quarterly* 50:957–94.
Gibson, Edward L. 1997. The populist road to market reform: Policy and electoral coalitions in Mexico and Argentina. *World Politics* 49 (3): 339–70.
Goldstein, Judith. 1993. *Ideas, Interests, and American Trade Policy*. Ithaca, NY: Cornell University Press.
Goldstein, Judith, and Robert O. Keohane, eds. 1993. *Ideas and Foreign Policy: Beliefs, Institutions, and Political Change*. Ithaca, NY: Cornell University Press.
Gómez, Elvia. 2006. Presidenciales 2006: Reconocemos que hoy nos derrotieron. *El Universal*. 4 December. Available at http://www.eluniversal.com/2006/12/04/elecc_art_98447.shtml 21.
  2008. A quien derrotamos es el hampa. *El Universal*. 24 November. Available at http://www.eluniversal.com/2008/11/24/pol_art_a-quien-derrotamos_1161550.shtml.
González, Lilliam, member of Bolivarian Circle. 2005. Interview with author. 3 May, Caracas/Provo, Utah.
Goodman, Louis W., Johanna Mendelson Forman, Moisés Naím, Joseph S. Tulchin, and Gary Bland, eds. 1995. *Lessons of the Venezuelan Experience*. Washington, DC: Woodrow Wilson Center Press.
Goodwyn, Lawrence. 1976. *Democratic Promise: The Populist Movement in America*. New York: Oxford University Press.
Graziano, Luigi. 1975. A conceptual framework for the study of clientelism. Western Societies Program Occasional Paper No. 2. New York: Cornell University.
Gutiérrez Infante, Edgardo Javier. 2004. Sí o No? Las estrategias de opinión pública y comunicación política del Referendum Revocatorio Presidencial 2004. Unpublished thesis. Caracas: Universidad Simón Bolívar.
Haggard, Stephen. 1990. *Pathways from the Periphery: The Politics of Growth in the Newly Industrializing Countries*. Ithaca, NY: Cornell University Press.
Hall, Peter A, ed. 1989. *The Political Power of Economic Ideas: Keynesianism across Nations*. Princeton, NJ: Princeton University Press.
Harnecker, Marta. 2005. *Understanding the Venezuelan Revolution: Hugo Chávez Talks to Marta Harnecker*. Trans. by Chesa Boudin. New York: Monthly Review Press.
Hawkins, Darren. 2009. Case studies. In *The SAGE Handbook of Comparative Politics*, eds. Todd Landman and Neil Robinson, pp. 50–66. Thousand Oaks, CA: Sage Publications.
Hawkins, Eliza Tanner. 2006. Community media in Venezuela. Paper presented at the XXVI Congress of the Latin American Studies Association, San Juan, Puerto Rico, 15–18 March.
Hawkins, Kirk A. 2003. Populism in Venezuela: The rise of Chavismo. *Third World Quarterly* 24 (6): 1137–60.
  2009. Is Chávez populist? Measuring populist discourse in comparative perspective. *Comparative Political Studies* 42 (8): 1040–67.
  2008. Assessing popular mobilization in the Bolivarian Revolution: The AmericasBarometer 2006. Paper presented at the conference The Popular Sectors

and the State in Chavez's Venezuela, Yale University, New Haven, CT, 6–8 March.
Hawkins, Kirk A., and David R. Hansen. 2006. Dependent civil society: The Círculos Bolivarianos in Venezuela. *Latin American Research Review* 41 (1): 102–32.
Hawkins, Kirk A., Jane Ann Patch, Adam Anguiano, and Mitchell A. Seligson. 2008. *Political Culture of Democracy in Venezuela: 2007*. Nashville, TN: Latin American Public Opinion Project, Vanderbilt University. Available at http://www.vanderbilt.edu/lapop/.
Hawkins, Kirk A., Guillermo Rosas, and Michael E. Johnson. forthcoming. The Misiones of the Chavez government. In *Participation and Public Sphere in Venezuela's Bolivarian Democracy*, eds. David Smilde and Daniel Hellinger. Durham, NC: Duke University Press.
Hellinger, Daniel. 1991. *Venezuela: Tarnished Democracy*. Boulder, CO: Westview Press.
    2003. Political overview: The breakdown of *Puntofijismo* and the rise of Chavismo. In *Venezuelan Politics in the Chávez Era: Class, Polarization, and Conflict*, eds. Steve Ellner and Daniel Hellinger, pp. 27–54. Boulder, CO: Lynne Rienner Publishers.
    2005. When "No" means "Yes to revolution": Electoral politics in Bolivarian Venezuela. *Latin American Perspectives* 32 (3): 8–32.
    forthcoming. Defying the iron law: Grassroots democracy in Venezuela. In *Participation and Public Sphere in Venezuela's Bolivarian Democracy*, eds. David Smilde and Daniel Hellinger. Durham, NC: Duke University Press.
Hofstadter, Richard. 1966. *The Paranoid Style in American Politics and Other Essays*. New York: Alfred A. Knopf.
    1969. North America. In *Populism: Its Meaning and Characteristics*, eds. Ghita Ionescu and Ernest Gellner, pp. 9–27. London: Macmillan Company.
Hsieh, Chang-Tai, Daniel Ortega, Edward Miguel, and Francisco Rodríguez. 2009. The price of political opposition: Evidence from Venezuela's *Maisanta*. NBER Working Paper No. w14923. Available at http://www.nber.org.
Human Rights Watch. 2004. Rigging the rule of law: Judicial independence under siege in Venezuela. 16 (3B): 1–24.
    2008. *A Decade Under Chávez: Political Intolerance and Lost Opportunities for Advancing Human Rights in Venezuela*. New York: Human Rights Watch.
Huntington, Samuel P. 1968. *Political Order in Changing Societies*. New Haven, CT: Yale University Press.
Ianni, Octavio. 1975. *La Formación del Estado Populista en América Latina*. Mexico, D.F.: Ediciones Era.
IESA (Instituto de Estudios Superiores de Administración). 2002. Base de Datos Macroeconómica. Available at http://www.iesa.edu.ve.
ILO (International Labour Organization). 1997. *World Labour Report 1997–98: Industrial Relations, Democracy, and Social Stability*. Geneva: International Labour Organization.
    2007. *Key Indicators of the Labour Market, version 5*. [CD-ROM file] Geneva: International Labour Organization.
Inglehart, Ronald. 1990. *Culture Shift in Advanced Industrial Society*. Princeton, NJ: Princeton University Press.
    1997. *Modernization and Postmodernization: Cultural, Economic, and Political Change in 43 Societies*. Princeton, NJ: Princeton University Press.

Inglehart, Ronald, and Wayne E. Baker. 2000. Modernization, cultural change, and the persistence of traditional values. *American Sociological Review* 65:19–51.
Inglehart, Ronald, and Christian Welzel. 2005. *Modernization, Cultural Change, and Democracy: The Human Development Sequence.* Cambridge: Cambridge University Press.
Institute of Political Science and Public Law at the Universidad de Zulia. 1993. CIEPA/DOXA survey. Dataset in possession of author.
Instituto Gallup. 1983. Baloyra-Torres (BATOBA) Survey. Dataset in possession of author.
Inter American Press Association. 2008. *Venezuela: Report to the midyear meeting.* 28–30 March, Caracas, Venezuela. Available at http://www.sipiapa.com.
International Monetary Fund. 1997. *Good Governance: The IMF's Role.* Washington, DC: International Monetary Fund.
International Telecommunications Union (ITU). 2006. *World Telecommunications Indicators Database.* Geneva: ITU. [CD-ROM].
Jagers, Jan, and Stefaan Walgrave. 2007. Populism as political communication style: An empirical study of political parties' discourse in Belgium. *European Journal of Political Research* 46:319–45.
Jáuregui, Michael, Coordinador de la Sala Situacional Nacional, Mission Ribas. 2005. Interview with authors. Caracas, 27 June.
Kahneman, Daniel, and Amos Tversky. 1979. Prospect theory: An analysis of decisions under risk. *Econometrica* 47 (2): 263–91.
Kahneman, Daniel, and Amos Tversky, eds. 2000. *Choices, Values, and Frames.* Cambridge: Cambridge University Press.
Karl, Terry Lynn. 1997. *The Paradox of Plenty: Oil Booms and Petro-States.* Berkeley: University of California Press.
Kaufmann, Daniel, Aart Kraay, and Massimo Mastruzzi. 2005. *Governance Matters IV: Governance Indicators for 1996–2004* (with appendices). Washington, DC: World Bank.
  2006. Governance Matters V: *Aggregate and Individual Governance Indicators for 1996–2005.* Washington, DC: World Bank. Available at http://www.worldbank.org/wbi/governance/wp-governance.htm.
  2007. Growth and governance: A reply. *Journal of Politics* 69 (2): 555–62.
Kay, Bruce H. 1996. "Fujipopulism" and the liberal state in Peru, 1990–1995. *Journal of Interamerican Studies and World Affairs* 38:55–98.
Kazin, Michael. 1998. *The Populist Persuasion: An American History.* Rev. ed. Ithaca, NY: Cornell University Press.
Keck, Margaret E., and Kathryn Sikkink. 1998. *Activists beyond Borders: Advocacy Networks in International Politics.* Ithaca, NY: Cornell University Press.
King, Gary, Robert O. Keohane, and Sidney Verba. 1994. *Designing Social Inquiry: Scientific Inference in Qualitative Research.* Princeton, NJ: Princeton University Press.
Kitschelt, Herbert. 1994. *The Transformation of European Social Democracy.* Cambridge: Cambridge University Press.
  2000. Linkages between citizens and politicians in democratic polities. *Comparative Political Studies* 33 (6/7): 845–79.
Kitschelt, Herbert, in collaboration with Tony McGann. 1995. *The Radical Right in Western Europe: A Comparative Analysis.* Ann Arbor: University of Michigan Press.

Kitschelt, Herbert, and Steven I. Wilkinson, eds. 2007. *Patrons, Clients and Policies: Patterns of Democratic Accountability and Political Competition.* Cambridge: Cambridge University Press.

Klotz, Audie. 1995. *Norms in International Relations: The Struggle against Apartheid.* Ithaca, NY: Cornell University Press.

Knight, Alan. 1998. Populism and neo-populism in Latin America, especially Mexico. *Journal of Latin American Studies* 30:223–48.

Knight, Kathleen. 2006. Transformations of the concept of ideology in the twentieth century. *American Political Science Review* 100 (4): 619–26.

Kornblith, Miriam. 1994. Crisis sociopolitica, nuevas reglas y estabilidad de la democracia en Venezuela: Estructura y coyuntura en la crisis del sistema politico venezolano. *Politeia* 17:11–58.

  2005. The referendum in Venezuela: Elections versus democracy. *Journal of Democracy* 16 (1): 124–37.

Kornblith, Miriam, and Daniel H. Levine. 1995. Venezuela: The life and times of the party system. In *Building Democratic Institutions: Party Systems in Latin America*, eds. Scott Mainwaring and Timothy R. Scully, pp. 37–71. Stanford, CA: Stanford University Press.

Krastov, Ivan. 2006. Democracy's "doubles." *Journal of Democracy* 17 (2): 52–63.

Kratochwil, Freidrich V. 1989. *Rules, Norms, and Decisions: On the Conditions of Practical and Legal Reasoning in International Relations and Domestic Affairs.* Cambridge: Cambridge University Press.

Krieckhaus, Jonathan. 2006. *Dictating Development: How Europe Shaped the Global Periphery.* Pittsburgh: University of Pittsburgh Press.

Kurtz, Marcus J., and Andrew Shrank. 2007. Growth and governance: Models, measures, and mechanisms. *Journal of Politics* 69 (2): 538–54.

Kuruvilla, Sarosh, Subesh Das, Hunji Kwon, and Soonwon Kwon. 2002. Trade union growth and decline in Asia. *British Journal of Industrial Relations* 40 (3): 431–61.

Kuzio, Taras. 2005. Ukraine's Orange Revolution: The opposition's road to success. *Journal of Democracy* 16 (2): 117–30.

Laclau, Ernesto. 2005. *On Populist Reason.* London: Verso.

Laclau, Ernesto, and Chantal Mouffe. 2004. *Hegemonía y estategia socialista: hacia una radicalización de la democracia.* 2nd ed. Buenos Aires: Fondo de Cultura y Economía.

Lacy, Dean, and Quin Monson. 2002. The origins and impact of votes for third-party candidates: A case study of the 1998 Minnesota Gubernatorial election. *Political Research Quarterly* 55 (2): 409–37.

Lander, Edgardo. 2005. Venezuelan social conflict in a global context. *Latin American Perspectives* 32 (2): 20–38.

Lange, Matthew, James Mahoney, and Matthias vom Hau. 2006. Colonialism and development: A comparative analysis of Spanish and British colonies. *American Journal of Sociology* 111 (5): 1412–62.

Lapper, Richard. 2006. *Living with Hugo: U.S. Policy toward Hugo Chávez's Venezuela.* CSR No. 20. New York: Council on Foreign Relations.

Latin American Newsletters. 2006. Quotes of the week. *Latin American Weekly Report.* 17 January, p 16.

  2007. Divisiveness marks Santiago summit dedicated to 'social cohesion.' *Latin American Weekly Report.* 15 November, p. 2.

2008a. Opposition figureheads. *Latin American Weekly Report.* 27 November, p. 2.
2008b. Venezuela politics: Signs of a tough contest in November. *Latin American Weekly Report.* 16 October, p. 6.
Lawson, Kay. 1980. Political parties and linkage. In *Political Parties and Linkage: A Comparative Perspective*, ed. Kay Lawson, pp. 3–24. New Haven, CT: Yale University Press.
Le Bon, Gustave. 1960 [1895]. *The Crowd: A Study of the Popular Mind.* New York: Viking Press.
Leff, Nathaniel H. 1972. Economic retardation in nineteenth-century Brazil. *Economic History Review* 25 (3): 489–507.
Levine, Daniel H. 1973. *Conflict and Political Change in Venezuela.* Princeton, NJ: Princeton University Press.
  1989. Venezuela: The nature, sources, and future prospects of democracy. In *Democracy in Developing Countries. Vol. 4: Latin America*, eds. Larry Diamond, Juan J. Linz, and Seymour Martin Lipset, pp. 247–90. Boulder, CO: Lynne Rienner Publishers.
Levine, Daniel H., and Brian F. Crisp. 1999. Venezuela: The character, crisis, and possible future of democracy. In *Democracy in Developing Countries: Latin America*, 2nd ed., eds. Larry Diamond, Jonathan Hartlyn, Juan J. Linz, and Seymour Martin Lipset, pp. 367–427. Boulder, CO: Lynne Rienner Publishers.
Levitsky, Steven. 2003. *Transforming Labor-Based Parties in Latin America: Argentine Peronism in Comparative Perspective.* Cambridge: Cambridge University Press.
Levitsky, Steven, and Maxwell A. Cameron. 2003. Democracy without parties? Political parties and regime change in Fujimori's Peru. *Latin American Politics and Society* 45 (3): 1–33.
Levitsky, Steven, and María Victoria Murillo. 2007. Argentina: From Kirchner to Kirchner. *Journal of Democracy* 19 (2): 16–30.
Levitsky, Steven, and Lucan Way. 2002. The rise of competitive authoritarianism. *Journal of Democracy* 13 (2): 51–65.
Lichbach, Mark Irving, and Alan S. Zuckerman, eds. 1997. *Comparative Politics: Rationality, Culture, and Structure.* Cambridge: Cambridge University Press.
Lievesley, Geraldine. 2005. The Latin American left: The difficult relationship between electoral ambition and popular empowerment. *Contemporary Politics* 11 (1): 3–18.
Linz, Juan. 1988. Legitimacy of democracy and the socioeconomic system. In *Comparing Pluralist Democracies: Strains on Legitimacy*, ed. Mattei Dogan, pp. 65–113. Boulder, CO: Westview Press.
Linz, Juan J., and Alfred Stepan. 1996. *Problems of Democratic Transition and Consolidation: Southern Europe, South America, and Post-Communist Europe.* Baltimore: Johns Hopkins University Press.
Lipset, Seymour Martin. 1981. *Political Man: The Social Bases of Politics.* Extended ed. Baltimore: Johns Hopkins University Press.
  1994. The social requisites of democracy revisited: 1993 Presidential address. *American Sociological Review* 59:1–22.
Lipset, Seymour M., and Stein Rokkan. 1967. Cleavage structures, party systems, and voter alignments. In *Party Systems and Voter Alignments: Cross-National Perspectives*, eds. Seymour Martin Lipset and Stein Rokkan, pp. 1–64. Glencoe, IL: Free Press.

Little, Daniel. 1991. *Varieties of Social Explanation: An Introduction to the Philosophy of Social Science*. Boulder, CO: Westview Press.

López-Maya, Margarita. 1997. The rise of *Causa R* in Venezuela. In *The New Politics of Inequality in Latin America: Rethinking Participation and Representation*, ed. Douglas A. Chalmers, pp. 117–43. New York: Oxford University Press.

López Maya, Margarita. 2003. Hugo Chávez Frías: His movement and his presidency. In *Venezuelan Politics in the Chávez Era: Class, Polarization and Conflict*, eds. Steve Ellner and Daniel Hellinger, pp. 73–92. Boulder, CO: Lynne Rienner Publishers.

2008a. Caracas: The state, popular participation and how to make things work. Paper presented at the Yale Conference on the Popular Sectors and the State in Chavez's Venezuela, 6–8 March, New Haven, CT.

2008b. Gobierno y sociedad a cuatro años del referendo revocatorio. *Ultimas Noticias*. 6 July.

Madsen, Douglas, and Peter G. Snow. 1991. *The Charismatic Bond: Political Behavior in Time of Crisis*. Cambridge, MA: Harvard University Press.

Magaloni, Beatriz, Alberto Díaz-Cayeros, and Federico Estévez 2007. Clientelism and portfolio diversification: A model of electoral investment with applications to Mexico. In *Patrons, Clients, and Policies: Patterns of Democratic Accountability and Political Competition*, eds. Herbert Kitschelt and Steven Wilkinson, pp. 182–205. Cambridge: Cambridge University Press.

Mainwaring, Scott P. 1999. *Rethinking Party Systems in the Third Wave of Democratization: The Case of Brazil*. Stanford, CA: Stanford University Press.

Mainwaring, Scott, and Timothy R. Scully, eds. 1995. *Building Democratic Institutions: Party Systems in Latin America*. Stanford, CA: Stanford University Press.

Mainwaring, Scott, and Timothy R. Scully. 2008. Latin America: Eight lessons for governance. *Journal of Democracy* **19** (3): 113–27.

Maldonado, Ana, university student. 2005. Interview with author, 5 May, Caracas/Provo, Utah.

Marcano, Cristina, and Alberto Barrera Tyszka. 2004. *Hugo Chávez sin uniforme: Una historia personal*. Caracas: Grupo Editorial Melvin.

Márquez, Patricia. 2003. The Hugo Chávez phenomenon: What do "the people" think? In *Venezuelan Politics in the Chávez Era: Class, Polarization, and Conflict*, eds. Steve Ellner and Daniel Hellinger, pp. 197–214. Boulder, CO: Lynne Rienner Publishers.

Martín, Guillermo. 2000. La República Bolivariana: ¿Relaciones Intergubernamentales en el Siglo XXI Venezlano? *Perfiles Latinoamericanos* 17:123–51.

Martz, John. 1966. *Acción Democrática: Evolution of a Modern Political Party in Venezuela*. Princeton, NJ: Princeton University Press.

Martz, John D., and David J. Myers. 1977. *Venezuela: The Democratic Experience*. New York: Praeger.

Mascareño, Carlos. 2000. *Balance de la descentralización en Venezuela: logros, limitaciones y perspectivas*. Caracas: Editorial Nueva Sociedad.

Mauro, Paolo. 1995. Corruption and growth. *The Quarterly Journal of Economics* **110** (3): 681–712.

1997. The effects of corruption on growth, investment and government expenditure: A cross-country analysis. In *Corruption and the Global Economy*, ed.

Kimberly Ann Elliot, pp. 83–108. Washington, DC: Institute for International Economics.

Mayobre, José Antonio. 2002. Venezuela and the media: The new paradigm. Chapter In *Latin Politics: Global Media*, eds. Elizabeth Fox and Silvio Waisbord, pp. 176–86. Austin: University of Texas Press.

Mazzoleni, Gianpietro, Julianne Stewart, and Bruce Horsfield, eds. 2003. *The Media and Neo-Populism: A Contemporary Comparative Analysis*. Westport, CT: Praeger.

McAdam, Doug, John D. McCarthy, and Mayer Zald, eds. 1996. *Comparative Perspectives on Social Movements: Political Opportunities, Mobilizing Structures, and Framing*, Cambridge: Cambridge University Press.

McAdam, Doug, Sidney Tarrow, and Charles Tilly. 1997. Toward an integrated perspective on social movements and revolution. In *Comparative Politics: Rationality, Culture, and Structure*, eds. Mark Irving Lichbach and Alan S. Zuckerman, pp. 142–71. Cambridge: Cambridge University Press.

2001. *Dynamics of Contention*. Cambridge: Cambridge University Press.

McCarthy, John D., and Mayer N. Zald. 1977. Resource mobilization and social movements: A partial theory. *American Journal of Sociology* 82 (6): 1212–41.

McCoy, Jennifer L. 2004. From representative to participatory democracy? Regime transformation in Venezuela. In *The Unraveling of Representative Democracy in Venezuela*, eds. Jennifer L. McCoy and David J. Myers, pp. 263–96. Baltimore: Johns Hopkins University Press.

2005. One act in an unfinished drama. *Journal of Democracy* 16 (1): 109–23.

McCoy, Jennifer L., and David J. Myers, eds. 2004. *The Unraveling of Representative Democracy in Venezuela*. Baltimore: Johns Hopkins University Press

McCoy, Jennifer L, Andrés Serbin, William C. Smith, and Andrés Stambouli, eds. 1995. *Venezuelan Democracy Under Stress*. Miami, FL: North-South Center, University of Miami.

McGuire, James W. 1995. Political parties and democracy in Argentina. In *Building Democratic Institutions: Party Systems in Latin America*, eds. Scott Mainwaring and Timothy Scully, pp. 200–46. Stanford, CA: Stanford University Press.

1997. *Peronism without Perón: Unions, Parties, and Democracy in Argentina*. Palo Alto, CA: Stanford University Press.

Medina, Pablo. 1999. *Rebeliones: Una larga conversacion con Maria Cristina Iglesias y Farruco Sesto*. Caracas: Edición del Autor.

Mendoza, Rubén, Coordinador Estatal de Círculos Bolivarianos MBR-200, Estado de Miranda. 2004. Interview with author, 21 July, Sabana Grande.

2005. Interview with author, 3 May, Caracas/Provo, Utah.

Mercal C.A. 2005. *Mercal...acelera el nuevo modelo económico y social de Venezuela*. Pamphlet. Caracas.

Mercal, C.A. Website. 2006. Available at http://www.mercal.gov.ve.

Merkl, Peter H. 1981. Democratic development, breakdowns, and fascism. *World Politics* 34 (1): 114–35.

Merolla, Jennifer L., Jennifer M. Ramos, and Elizabeth J. Zechmeister. 2006. Crisis, charisma, and consequences: Evidence from the 2004 U.S. presidential election. *Journal of Politics* 69 (1): 30–42.

Milliken, Jennifer. 1999. The study of discourse in international relations. *European Journal of International Relations* 5 (2): 225–54.

MINCI (Ministerio de Comunicación y Información). n.d.a Untitled document on Mission Barrio Adentro. Manuscript in possession of author.
  n.d.b Untitled document on Mission Mercal. Manuscript in possession of author.
Ministerio de Alimentación. n.d. *Reseña histórica del Ministerio de Alimentación*. Available at http://www.minal.gob.ve.
Ministerio de Energía y Minas, Dirección de Hidrocarburos, Dirección de Economía de Hidrocarburos. 1997/1992/1987/1983/1979. Petróleo y otros datos estadísticos. Caracas, Venezuela.
Ministerio del Poder Popular para la Economía Comunal. 2008. Misión Che Guevara. Available at http://www.minec.gob.ve/.
Ministerio para la Economía Popular. n.d.a *Cómo se constituye un Núcleo de Desarrollo Endógeno: Guía para autoridades y organismos públicos*. Pamplet in possession of author. Caracas.
Ministerio de Energía y Minas, n.d.b *Nuevo Modelo Socio-Productivo y Desarrollo Endógeno: El Proyecto Nacional-Popular Bolivariano*. Slide presentation in possession of author.
Minogue, Kenneth. 1969. Populism as a political movement. In *Populism: Its Meaning and Characteristics*, eds. Ghita Ionescu and Ernest Gellner, pp. 197–211. London: Macmillan Company.
Misión Barrio Adentro. n.d. *La misión avanza: Historia y avances*. Available at http://www.barrioadentro.gov.ve.
Misión Ribas. n.d.a. *Formación de la ciudadanía en el marco de la refundación de la República*. Pamphlet in possession of author. Caracas: Mission Ribas.
  n.d.b. *Orientaciones generales para la facilitación*. Pamphlet in possession of author. Caracas: Mission José Félix Ribas.
  n.d.c. *Política Educativa de la Misión José Félix Ribas: Nueva etapa*. Pamphlet in possession of author. Caracas: Mission Ribas.
Misión Robinson, Comisión Presidencial. n.d. *Una Sola Mission: Tercer Taller Nacional Mision Robinson*. Caracas: Misión Robinson, Comisión Presidencial.
Molinar Horcasitas, Juan, and Jeffrey A. Weldon. 1993. Electoral determinants and effects of Pronasol. In *Transforming State–Society Relations in Mexico: The National Solidarity Strategy*, eds. Wayne Cornelius, Ann. L. Craig, and Jonathan Fox, pp. 123–42. San Diego, CA: Center for U.S.-Mexican Studies, University of California–San Diego.
Morgan, Jana. 2007. Partisanship during the collapse of Venezuela's party system. *Latin American Research Review* 42 (1): 78–98.
Morsbach, Greg. 2006. What comes next for Venezuela? *BBC News*. Available at http://news/bbc.co.uk.
Mudde, Cas. 2004. The populist Zeitgeist. *Government and Opposition* 39 (Fall): 541–63.
  2007. *Populist Radical Right Parties in Europe*. Cambridge: Cambridge University Press.
Mullins, Willard A. 1972. On the concept of ideology in political science. *American Political Science Review* 66 (2): 498–510.
Naím, Moisés. 1993. *Paper Tigers and Minotaurs: The Politics of Venezuela's Economic Reforms*. New York: Carnegie Endowment for International Peace.
  2004. Foreword. In *The Unraveling of Representative Democracy in Venezuela*, eds. Jennifer L. McCoy and David J. Myers, pp. ix–xiv. Baltimore: Johns Hopkins University Press.

Neuendorf, K. A. 2002. *The Content Analysis Guidebook*. Thousand Oaks, CA: Sage Publications.
Newcombe, Nora S. 2005. Language as destiny? Or not. Essay review of *Space in Language and Cognition: Explorations of Cognitive Diversity* by Stephen C. Levinson. *Human Development* 48:309–14.
Nolia, Alberto. 1993. Requiem por un gran partido. *Zeta* 945 (20): 20–3.
Noriega, Roger. 2007. The end of democratic solidarity in the Americas? *Latin American Outlook* 5: 1–5. Available at http://www.aei.org.
North, Douglass C. 1990. *Institutions, Institutional Change and Economic Performance*. Cambridge: Cambridge University Press.
North, Douglass C., and Robert Paul Thomas. 1973. *The Rise of the Western World: A New Economic History*. Cambridge: Cambridge University Press.
Novaro, Marcos. 1998. Populismo y gobierno. Las transformaciones en el peronismo y la consolidación democrática argentina. In *El fantasma del populismo: Aproximación a un tema (siempre) actual*, ed. Felipe Burbano de Lara, pp. 25–48. Caracas: Editorial Nueva Sociedad.
O'Donnell, Guillermo. 1973. *Modernization and bureaucratic-authoritarianism: Studies in South American politics*. Berkeley: Institute of International Studies, University of California.
  1992. Transition, continuities, and paradoxes. In *Issues in Democratic Consolidation: The New South American Democracies in Comparative Perspective*, eds. Scott Mainwaring, Guillermo O'Donnell, and J. Samuel Valenzuela, pp. 17–56. Notre Dame, IN: University of Notre Dame Press.
  1999. Polyarchies and the (un)rule of law in Latin America: A partial conclusion. In *The (Un)Rule of Law and the Underprivileged in Latin America*, eds. Juan E. Méndez, Guillermo O'Donnell, and Paulo Sérgio Pinheiro, pp. 303–37. Notre Dame, IN: University of Notre Dame Press.
  2001. Democracy, law and comparative politics. *Studies in Comparative International Development* 36 (1): 7–36.
  2004. Human development, human rights, and democracy. In *The Quality of Democracy: Theory and Applications*, eds. Guillermo O'Donnell, Jorge Vargas Vargas Cullell, and Osvaldo M. Iazzetta, pp. 9–92. Notre Dame, IN: University of Notre Dame Press.
O'Donnell, Guillermo, Philippe C. Schmitter, and Laurence Whitehead, eds. 1986. *Transitions from Authoritarian Rule: Prospects for Democracy*. Baltimore: Johns Hopkins University Press.
O'Donnell, Guillermo, Jorge Vargas Cullell, and Osvaldo M. Iazzetta, eds. 2004. *The Quality of Democracy: Theory and Applications*. Notre Dame, IN: University of Notre Dame Press.
OCEI (Oficina Central de Estadísticas e Información). 2002. Muestro de Hogares. Available at http://www.ocei.gov.ve.
Offe, Claus. 1985. New social movements: Challenging the boundaries of institutional politics. *Social Research* 52 (4): 817–68.
Ojeda, William. 1995. *Cuánto vale un juez*. Valencia, Venezuela: Vadell.
Olson, Mancur. 1982. *The Rise and Decline of Nations: Economic Growth, Stagflation, and Social Rigidities*. New Haven, CT: Yale University Press.
Ortega, Daniel, and Michael Penfold. 2007. Does clientelism work? Electoral returns of excludable and non-excludable goods in Chavez's Misiones programs in Venezuela. Paper presented at the XXVII International Congress of the Latin American Studies Association, Montreal, Canada, 5–8 September.

Ortega, Daniel, and Francisco Rodríguez. 2008. Freed from illiteracy? A closer look at Venezuela's *Misión Robinson* literacy campaign. *Economic Development and Cultural Change* 57 (1): 1–30.

Oxhorn, Philip. 1998. The social foundations of Latin America's recurrent populism: Problems of popular sector class formation and collective action. *Journal of Historical Sociology* 11 (2): 212–46.

Panebianco, Angelo. 1988. *Political Parties: Organization and Power*, trans. Marc Silver. Cambridge: Cambridge University Press.

Panizza, Francisco. 2005a. Introduction: Populism and the mirror of democracy. In *Populism and the Mirror of Democracy*, ed. Francisco Panizza, pp. 1–31. London: Verso.

Panizza, Francisco, ed. 2005b. *Populism and the Mirror of Democracy*. London: Verso.

Pantín, Guillermo. 1997. *LatinoMafia: crónica de la corrupción del sistema*. Caracas: Pomaire.

Pappas, Takis S. 2008. Political leadership and the emergence of radical mass movements in democracy. *Comparative Political Studies* 41 (8): 1117–40.

Parker, Dick. 2005. Chávez and the search for an alternative to neoliberalism. *Latin American Perspectives* 32 (2): 39–50

Parma, Alessandro. 2005. Corruption report claims business as usual in Venezuela. *Venezuelanalysis.com*. 20 October. Available at http://www.venezuelanalysis.com/news/1422.

Peñaloza, Pedro Pablo. 2004. Sanifa saca cuenta y arrebata. *Tal Cual*. 4 August.

Penfold-Becerra, Michael. 2008. Clientelism and social funds: Evidence from Chávez's *Misiones*. *Latin American Politics and Society* 49 (4): 63–84.

Pérez Perdomo, Rogelio. 1995. Corruption and political crisis. In *Lessons of the Venezuelan Experience*, eds. Jouis W. Goodman, Johanna Mendelson Forman, Moisés Naím, Joseph S. Tulchin, and Gary Bland. Washington, DC: Woodrow Wilson Center Press.

Perón, Juan. n.d. *Mensaje leído ante la Asamblea Nacional por el General de Brigada D. Juan Perón con motivo de su juramento como Presidente de la Nación 4 de Junio de 1946 y discurso pronunciado ante el pueblo el 12 de Febrero de 1946 al proclamarse su candidatura*. Pamphlet.

Petkoff, Teodoro. 2004. Prólogo. In *Hugo Chávez sin uniforme: Una historia personal* by Cristina Marcano and Alberto Barrera Tyszka, pp. 7–23. Caracas: Grupo Editorial Melvin

Pion-Berlin, David, and Harold Trinkunas. 2005. Democratization, social crisis and the impact of military domestic roles in Latin America. *Journal of Political and Military Sociology* 33 (1): 5–24.

Piven, Frances Fox, and Richard A. Cloward. 1977. *Poor People's Movements: Why They Succeed, How They Fail*. New York: Pantheon Books.

Poleo, Rafael. 1993. Los candidatos vistos uno por uno. *Zeta* **949**. 17 June, pp. 6–8.

Primicias. 1998. *Primicias*. 10 February, p. 10.

Putnam, Robert D. 2000. *Bowling Alone: The Collapse and Revival of American Community*. New York: Simon & Schuster.

Quinn, K. M., B. L. Monroe, M. Colaresi, M. H. Crespin, and D. R. Radev. 2006. An automated method of topic-coding legislative speech over time with application to the 105th–108th U.S. Senate. Manuscript in possession of author.

Randall, Vicky, and Lars Svasand. 2002. Party institutionalization in new democracies. *Party Politics* 8 (1): 3–29.

Red Universitaria de Estudios Políticos. 1999. Elecciones y democracia en la hora constituyente. *Boletín RedPol*. 1.

República Bolivariana de Venezuela. 2001. *Líneas Generales del Plan de Desarrollo Económico y Social de la Nación 2001–2007*. Caracas. Available at http://www.mpd.gob.ve/pdeysn/pdesn.pdf.

República Bolivariana de Venezuela: Presidencia. 2007. *Proyecto Nacional Simón Bolívar Primer Plan Socialista (PPS): Desarrollo Económico y Social de la Nación 2007–2013*. Caracas. Available at http://www.mpd.gob.ve/Nuevo-plan/plan.html.

Reuters. 2008. Oil powerhouse Venezuela struggles to keep lights on. 22 October. Available at http://www.nytimes.com.

Rey, Juan Carlos. 1998. *El futuro de la democracia en Venezuela*. Caracas: Facultad de Ciencias Juridicas y Politicas, Universidad Central de Venezuela.

Riker, William H. (1982). *Liberalism Against Populism: A Confrontation between the Theory of Democracy and the Theory of Social Choice*. Prospect Heights, IL: Waveland Press.

Roberts, Kenneth M. 1995. Neoliberalism and the transformation of populism in Latin America: The Peruvian case. *World Politics* 48 (1): 82–116.

2000. Populism and democracy in Latin America. Paper presented at the conference Challenges to Democracy in the Americas, Carter Center for Democracy, Atlanta, 16–18 October.

2001. Party–society linkages and democratic representation in Latin America. Paper presented at the XXIII International Congress of the Latin American Studies Association, Washington, DC, 6–8 September.

2003. Social correlates of party system demise and populist resurgence in Venezuela. *Latin American Politics and Society* 45 (3): 35–57.

2006. Populism, political conflict, and grass-roots organization in Latin America. *Comparative Politics* 38 (2): 127–48.

2007. Latin America's populist revival. *SAIS Review* 27 (1): 3–15.

Roberts, Kenneth M., and Moisés Arce. 1998. Neoliberalism and lower-class voting behavior in Peru. *Comparative Political Studies* 31 (2): 217–47.

Roberts, Kenneth M., and Erik Wibbels. 1999. Party systems and electoral volatility in Latin America: A test of economic, institutional, and structural explanations. *American Political Science Review* 93 (3): 575–90.

Robinson, W. S. 1950. Ecological correlations and the behavior of individuals. *American Sociological Review* 15 (3): 351–57.

Rocha Menocal, Alina. 2001. Do old habits die hard? A statistical exploration of the politicisation of Progresa, Mexico's latest federal poverty-alleviation programme, under the Zedillo administration. *Journal of Latin American Studies* 33:513–38.

Rodríguez, Francisco. 2007. Sharing the oil wealth? Appraising the effects of Venezuela's social programs. *LASA Forum* 38 (1): 22–25.

2008. An empty revolution: The unfulfilled promises of Hugo Chavez. *Foreign Affairs* 87 (2): 49–62.

Romero, Simon. 2007a. In Venezuela, Chavismo is dissected by fans and foes. *New York Times*. 24 January, p. 4.

2007b. Chavez plans one big Venezuela leftist party, led by him. *New York Times*. 4 January, p. 3.

2007c. Chavez moves to nationalize 2 industries. *New York Times*. 9 January, p. 3.
2007d. Chavez threatens to jail violators of price controls. *New York Times*. 17 February, p. A3. Available at http://www.lexisnexis.com.
2009. As oil wealth slips, so fade Venezuela's hopes of extending sway in the region. *New York Times*. 20 May, p. A6.
Ross, Michael L. 2001. Does oil hinder democracy? *World Politics* 53:325–61.
Rousseau, Jean-Jacques. 1993. *The Social Contract and Discourses*. Trans. and intro. by G. D. H. Cole. Rev. and augmented by J. H. Brumfitt and John C. Hall. Updated by P. D. Jimack. Rutland, VT: Everyman.
Roxborough, Ian. 1984. Unity and diversity in Latin American history. *Journal of Latin American Studies* 16 (1): 1–26.
Rucht, Dieter. 1996. The impact of national contexts on social movement structures: A cross-movement and cross-national comparison. In *Comparative Perspectives on Social Movements: Political Opportunities, Mobilizing Structures, and Framing*, eds. Doug McAdam, John D. McCarthy, and Mayer Zald, pp. 185–204. Cambridge: Cambridge University Press.
Salamanca, Luis. 2004. Civil society: Late bloomers. In *The Unraveling of Representative Democracy in Venezuela*, eds. Jennifer L. McCoy and David J. Myers, pp. 93–114. Baltimore: Johns Hopkins University Press
Santander, Sol, Coordinadora de Planificación Académica, Misión Sucre. 2005. Interview with author. Caracas, 30 June.
Sartori, Giovanni. 1976. *Parties and Party Systems: A Framework for Analysis*. Vol. 1. Cambridge: Cambridge University Press.
Schady, Norbert R. 2000. The political economy of expenditures by the Peruvian Social Fund (FONCODES), 1991–95. *American Political Science Review* 94 (2): 289–304.
Schamis, Hector. 2006. Populism, socialism, and democratic institutions. *Journal of Democracy* 17 (4): 20–34.
Schedler, Andreas. 2002. The menu of manipulation. *Journal of Democracy* 13 (2): 36–50.
Schedler, Andreas, ed. 2006. *Electoral Authoritarianism: The Dynamics of Unfree Competition*. Boulder, CO: Lynne Rienner Publishers.
Schiller, Naomi. 2006. Catia sees you: Community television, clientelism, and everyday statemaking in the Chávez era. Paper presented at the XXVI Congress of the Latin American Studies Association, San Juan, Puerto Rico, 15–18 March.
Schumacher, Paul, Dwight C. Kiel, and Thomas Heilke. 1996. *Great Ideas/Grand Schemes: Political Ideologies in the 19th and 20th Centuries*. New York: McGraw-Hill.
Scott, James C. 1969. Corruption, machine politics, and political change. *American Political Science Review* 63 (4): 1142–58.
Seligson, Mitchell A. 2002. The impact of corruption on regime legitimacy: A comparative study of four Latin American countries. *Journal of Politics* 64 (2): 408–33.
2006. The measurement and impact of corruption victimization: Survey evidence from Latin America. *World Development* 34 (2): 381–404.
2007. The democracy barometers: The rise of populism and the left in Latin America. *Journal of Democracy* 18 (3): 81–95.

Selznick, Philip. 1957. *Leadership in Administration: A Sociological Interpretation.* Evanston, IL: Row Peterson.
Shifter, Michael. 2006. In search of Hugo Chávez. *Foreign Affairs* 85 (3): 45–59.
  2007. *Hugo Chávez: A Test for U.S. Policy.* Washington, DC: Inter-American Dialogue.
Shils, Edward. 1956. *The Torment of Secrecy: The Background and Consequences of American Security Policies.* Glencoe, IL: Free Press.
Silva, Irina, Promotora Estatal de Círculos Bolivarianos MBR-200, Estado de Carabobo. 2004. Interview with author. Valencia, 19 July.
Sjöö, Jenny. 2006. "For my president and for my country": The Círculos Bolivarianos – a minor field study from Venezuela. Unpublished master's thesis. Uppsala, Sweden: Uppsala University.
Skidmore, Thomas E., ed. 1992. *Television, Politics, and the Transition to Democracy in Latin America.* Washington, DC: Woodrow Wilson Center Press.
Smilde, David, and Daniel Hellinger, eds. forthcoming. *Participation and Public Sphere in Venezuela's Bolivarian Democracy.* Durham, NC: Duke University Press.
Smilde, David. forthcoming. Seeing and not seeing Venezuela's Bolivarian democracy. In *Participation and Public Sphere in Venezuela's Bolivarian Democracy,* eds. David Smilde and Daniel Hellinger. Durham, NC: Duke University Press.
Smith, Peter H. 2008. *Talons of the Eagle: Latin America, the United States, and the World.* 3rd ed. New York: Oxford University Press.
StataCorp. 2003. *Stata Base Reference Manual, Vol. 2, Release 8.* College Station, TX: Stata Corporation.
Stein, Stanley J., and Barbara H. Stein. 1970. *The Colonial Heritage of Latin America: Essays on Economic Dependency in Perspective.* New York: Oxford University Press.
Stokes, Susan. 1995. *Cultures in Conflict: Social Movements and the State in Peru.* Berkeley: University of California Press.
  2005. Perverse accountability: A formal model of machine politics with evidence from Argentina. *American Political Science Review* 99 (3): 315–25.
Sudweeks, R. R., S. Reeve, and W. S. Bradshaw. 2005. A comparison of generalizability theory and many-facet Rasch measurement in an analysis of college sophomore writing. *Assessing Writing* 9:239–61.
SUNACOOP (Superintendencia Nacional de Cooperativas). 2008. Sunacoop ha registrado a 241 mil cooperativas a nivel nacional. Available at http://www.sunacoop.gob.ve/index.php?option=com_content&view=article&id=163:sunacoop-ha-registrado-a-241-mil-cooperativas-a-nivel-nacional&catid=34:nnoticias.
Taggart, Paul. 1996. *The New Populism and the New Politics: New Protest Parties in Sweden and in a Comparative Perspective.* New York: St. Martin's Press.
  2000. *Populism.* Philadelphia: Open University Press.
Tanaka, Martín. 2005. Peru 1980–2000: Chronicle of a death foretold? Determinism, political decisions, and open outcomes. In *The Third Wave of Democratization in Latin America: Advances and Setbacks,* eds. Frances Hagopian and Scott P. Mainwaring, pp. 261–88. Cambridge: Cambridge University Press.
Tarre Briceño, Gustavo. 1994. *4 de febrero: El espejo roto.* Caracas: Editorial Panapo.
Tarrow, Sidney. 1994. *Power in Movement: Social Movements, Collective Action, and Politics.* Cambridge: Cambridge University Press.

Templeton, Andrew. 1995. The evolution of popular opinion. In *Lessons of the Venezuelan Experience*, eds. Jouis W. Goodman, Johanna Mendelson Forman, Moisés Naím, Joseph S. Tulchin, and Gary Bland, pp. 79–114. Washington, DC: Woodrow Wilson Center Press.

The Carter Center. 2005a. *The Carter Center and the Peacebuilding Process in Venezuela June 2002–February 2005: Summary*. Atlanta: The Carter Center.

2005b. *Observing the Venezuela Presidential Recall Referendum: Comprehensive Report*. Atlanta: The Carter Center.

n.d. Report on an Analysis of the Representativeness of the Second Audit Sample, and the Correlation between Petition Signers and the Yes Vote in the Aug. 15, 2004 Presidential Recall Referendum in Venezuela. Unpublished electronic manuscript. Available at http://www.cartercenter.org/documents/1834.pdf.

Tinsley, H. E. A., and D. J. Weiss. 1975. Interrater reliability and agreement of subjective judgments. *Journal of Counseling Psychology* 22 (4): 358–76.

Toro, María Milagros. 2005. *Mercal C.A.* PowerPoint presentation. Manuscript in possession of author.

Transparency International. 2007. *Report on the Transparency International Global Corruption Barometer 2007*. Available at http://www.transparency.org/policy_research/surveys_indices/gcb.

Transparency International. 2008. *TI Corruption Perceptions Index*. Online dataset. Available at http://www.transparency.org/.

Trinkunas, Harold. 2002. The crisis in Venezuelan civil–military relations: From Punto Fijo to the Fifth Republic. *Latin American Research Review* 37 (1): 41–76.

van Dijk, Teun. 2008. *Discourse and Power*. New York: Palgrave Macmillan.

Velasco, Alejandro. forthcoming. "We are all still rebels": Popular protest and political consciousness in Venezuela's Fourth Republic. In *Participation and Public Sphere in Venezuela's Bolivarian Democracy*, eds. David Smilde and Daniel Hellinger. Durham, NC: Duke University Press.

Venturi, Franco. 1960. *Roots of Revolution: A History of the Populist and Socialist Movements in Nineteenth-Century Russia*. Trans. by Francis Haskell. New York: Alfred A. Knopf.

VHeadline. 2001. VHeadline News Briefs. 18 December. Available at http://www.vheadline.com/readnews.asp?id=9309.

Vilas, Carlos. 1992/1993. Latin American populism: A structural approach. *Science and Society* 56 (Winter): 389–420.

Vivas, Jesús, Coordinador Estatal de Círculos Bolivarianos MBR-200, Estado de Aragua. 2004. Interview with author. Maracay, 16 July. Transcript in possession of author.

2005. Interview with author. Maracay/Provo, Utah, 3 May. Transcript in possession of author.

Wagner, Sarah. 2005a. Mercal: Reducing poverty and creating national food sovereignty in Venezuela. *Venezuelanalysis*. 24 June. Available at http://www.venezuelanalysis.com.

2005b. Venezuela: Illiteracy free territory. *Venezuelanalysis*. 21 April. Available at http://www.venezuelanalysis.com.

Waisman, Carlos H. 1987. *Reversal of Development in Argentina: Postwar Counterrevolutionary Policies and Their Structural Consequences*. Princeton, NJ: Princeton University Press.

Walicki, Andrzej. 1969. Russia. In *Populism: Its Meaning and National Characteristics*, eds. Ghita Ionescu and Ernest Gellner, pp. 62–96. New York: Macmillan Company.

Way, Lucan A. 2005. Ukraine's Orange Revolution: Kuchma's failed authoritarianism. *Journal of Democracy* 16 (2): 131–45.

Weber, Max. 1958 [1946]. *From Max Weber: Essays in Sociology; Translated, Edited, and with an Introduction by H. H. Gerth and C. Wright Mills*. New York: Oxford University Press.

Weffort, Francisco C. 1973. Clases populares y desarrollo social. In *Populismo, marginalización y dependencia: Ensayos e interpretación sociológica*, eds. F. C. Weffort and A. Quijano, pp. 17–169. Costa Rica: Editorial Universitaria Centroamericana.

    1978. *O Populismo na política brasileira*. Rio de Janeiro: Paz e Terra.

Wendt, Alexander. 1999. *Social Theory of International Politics*. Cambridge: Cambridge University Press.

Weyland, Kurt. 1996. Neopopulism and neoliberalism in Latin America: Unexpected affinities. *Studies in Comparative International Development* 31 (3): 3–31.

    1999. Neoliberal populism in Latin America and Eastern Europe. *Comparative Politics* 31 (4): 379–401.

    2001. Clarifying a contested concept: Populism in the study of Latin American politics. *Comparative Politics* 34 (1): 1–22.

    2003. Economic voting reconsidered: Crisis and charisma in the election of Hugo Chávez. *Comparative Political Studies* 36 (7): 822–48.

White, Edward M. 1985. *Teaching and Assessing Writing*. San Francisco: Jossey-Bass Publishers.

Wibbels, Eric, and Kenneth Roberts. 1999. Dataset on union density. In possession of author.

Wiles, P. 1969. A syndrome, not a doctrine. In *Populism: Its Meaning and National Characteristics*, eds. Ghita Ionescu and Ernest Gellner, pp. 166–79. New York: Macmillan Company.

Willner, Ann Ruth. 1984. *The Spellbinders: Charismatic Political Leadership*. New Haven, CT: Yale University Press.

Wilpert, Gregory. 2007. Corruption in Venezuela. *Venezuelanalysis*. Available at http://www.venezuelanalysis.com/analysis/2654.

Witt, Emily. 2007. The fugitive. *Miami New Times*. 1 February. Available at http://www.lexisnexis.com/us/lnacademic/search/newssubmitForm.do.

World Bank. 1997. *Helping Countries Combat Corruption: The Role of the World Bank*. Washington, DC: World Bank.

    2007. *World Development Indicators*. Washington, DC: World Bank.

World Bank Group. 2008. *Governance Matters 2008: Worldwide Governance Indicators, 1996–2007*. Online dataset. Available at http://info.worldbank.org/governance/wgi/index.asp.

World Values Survey. 2006. European and World Values Surveys Four-Wave Integrated Data File, 1981–2004, v.20060423. The European Values Study Foundation and World Values Survey Association. Aggregate File Producers: ASEP/JDS, Madrid, Spain/Tilburg University, Tilburg, the Netherlands. Aggregate File Distributors: ASEP/JDS and ZA, Cologne, Germany.

Wüst, A. M., and A. Volkens. 2003. Euromanifesto coding instructions. Working Paper Nr. 64. Mannheim: Mannheimer Zentrum für Europäische Sozialforschung.

Zago, Angela. 1992. *La Rebelion de los Angeles*. 4th ed. Caracas: Warp Ediciones.
Zakaria, Fareed. 2003. *The Future of Freedom: Illiberal Democracy at Home and Abroad*. New York: W.W. Norton & Company.
Zapata, Roberto. 1996. *Valores del Venezolano*. Caracas: Conciencia 21.
Zeta. 1993. La guerra verde. *Zeta* **949**, 17 June, pp. 15–16.
Zúquete, José Pedro. 2008. The missionary politics of Hugo Chávez. *Latin American Politics and Society* 50 (1): 91–121.

Index

AD (Acción Democrática/Democratic Action), 44, 89, 92, 100, 113, 188
Agreement for Cooperation, 200
Ahmadinejad, Mahmood, 76, 78, 133, 136, 140
Alessandri, Arturo, 4
Alfaro Ucero, Luis, 92
Alfonsín, Raúl, 198
Alvarado, Velasco, 246
Álvarez Paz, Oswaldo, 91
Argentina, 102, 135, 144
Arias Cárdenas, Francisco, 20, 93
Armony, Ariel C., 70
Armony, Victor, 70

Bachelet, Michelle, 51, 197
Barrio Adentro. *See* Missions
behavioralism, 10, 238
Belarus, 135
Berger, Oscar, 28, 45
Berlusconi, Silvio, 138, 235
Betancourt, Rómulo, 89, 103
Blair, Tony, 82, 133
Bolaños, Enrique, 28, 45
Bolívar, Simón, 57, 83
Bolivarian Circles, 20, 167
  decline of, 180–1
  disruptive tactics, 184–90
  history of, 176–7
  institutionalization, 178–81
  insularity, 190–3
  movement structure, 181–4
  as populist movement, 178–93
Bolivia, 25, 101, 102, 144
Bossi, Umberto, 235
Bryan, William Jennings, 42

Bucaram, Abdalá, 248
Bush, George W., 76, 78, 81–2, 133

Caldera, Rafael, 17, 61, 87, 89, 90–1, 103, 162
Campaña de Santa Inéz, 2
Canovan, Margaret, 35, 37
Cárdenas, Lázaro, 75, 80
Castro, Fidel, 25, 57, 84
Causa R (Causa Radical/Radical Cause), 17, 91, 100, 113
CD (Coordinadora Democrática/Democratic Coordination), 3
charisma. *See* charismatic linkages
charismatic linkages
  definition of, 41
  relation to populism, 41–3, 163–5
Chávez, Hugo
  charismatic leader, 41–3, 162–4
  coup of 2002, 1, 20–1
  discourse: "anything goes" attitude, 65–9; Christian imagery in, 20, 56–7; conspiring elite in, 61–3; historical references in, 57–8; Manichaean outlook in, 55–8; systemic change in, 63–5; will of people in, 58–61
  as leftist, 52–3, 83–5, 245–7
  personal history of, 16–25, 92–3
  as populist, 43–8, 50–3
Chavismo
  future of, 243–9
  history of, 16–25, 92–3, 162
  international relations, 4, 25, 46–7
  and leftism, 50–3, 83–4, 246–7
  and news media, 67–8, 191–3
  and scholarship, 26–7, 47–8

287

Che Guevara Socialist Mission. *See* Missions
Chile, 102, 165, 235
China, 19, 23
Christ Mission (Misión Cristo). *See* Missions
CNE (Consejo Nacional Electoral/National Electoral Commission), 1, 22
Communal Councils (Consejos Comunales), 24
Communist Party of Venezuela, 25
competitive authoritarian regimes. *See* democracy
constructivism, 10–11, 238
Convergencia, 90, 100, 113
COPEI (Comité de Organizacion Política Electoral Independiente), 89, 90, 109, 113
Coppedge, Michael, 109
Correa, Rafael, 78, 197
corruption
  under Chavismo, 245
  definition of, 95–6
  measurement of, 96, 150–2
  during Punto Fijo system, 46, 103–10
  relation to populism, 96–8, 148–53
Costa Rica, 99, 165
coup of 1992, 17
coup of 2002. *See* Chávez, Hugo
CTV (Confederación de Trabajadores de Venezula/Worker's Confederation of Venezuela), 101
Cuba, 19

Dahl, Robert, 36
de la Torre, Carlos, 148
de Miranda, Francisco, 57
de San Martín, José, 79
democracy
  competitive authoritarian regimes, 27
  hybrid democracy, 45
  normative definition, 15
  procedural definition, 15
  semidemocracy, 27
Diamond, Larry, 29
Dieterich, Heinze, 59, 64, 83
discourse, 237–42
  definition of, 30
  and ideas, 31–2, 237–9
  measurement of, 70–2, 239
  and worldview, 30–1
discourse theorists. *See* constructivism
disruptive tactics. *See* organizational theory of populism
Drake, Paul, 164
Duarte, Nicanor, 28
Durkheim, Emile, 9

economic voting theory, 134–7, 154
Ecuador, 25
El Salvador, 165
elitist discourse, 33, 97
Ellner, Steve, 109

fascism, 37
Fermín, Claudio, 91, 93
Fernández de Kirchner, Cristina, 51
Florentino y el Diablo, 2
Forza Italia, 235
Fox, Vicente, 47
FPÖ (Austrian Freedom Party), 235
Fujimori, Alberto, 198, 199, 248

Glistrup, Mogens, 235
Gutiérrez, Lucio, 248
Guzmán, Abimael, 42

Haider, Jörg, 235
Harnecker, Marta, 59, 67, 83
Haya de la Torre, Victor Raúl, 246
Hellinger, Daniel, 109
Hofstadter, Richard, 35
holistic grading, 71–2, 239
Honduras, 108
Huntington, Samuel, 169
hybrid democracy. *See* democracy

ideology, 30
India, 23
institutionalization. *See* organizational theory of populism
insularity. *See* organizational theory of populism
Insulza, Jose Miguel, 47
interaction effect, 154–60
Iran. *See* Ahmadinejad, Mahmood
Iraq, 19
Italy, 235

Jagers, Jan, 70
Juan Carlos, King, 47

Kahnemann, Daniel, 103
Kennedy, John F., 57
Kirchner, Néstor, 51, 79

Laclau, Ernesto, 35, 43
Lagos, Ricardo, 51
Ledezma, Antonio, 93
legitimacy, 94–5
Leoni, Raúl, 103
Libya, 19

Index

Lukashenko, Aleksandr, 42, 76, 78, 133, 140
Lula da Silva, Luiz Ignácio, 51, 75, 79–80
Lusinchi, Jaime, 104

macroeconomic policy. *See* populism
Mainwaring, Scott, 169
Maisanta Command, 2, 179
MAS (Movimiento al Socialismo/Movement for Socialism), 91, 113
mass society theory, 137–41, 158
MBR 200 (Movimiento Bolivariano Revolucionaro 200/Bolivarian Revolutionary Movement 200), 16, 176, 200
McCoy, Jennifer L., 109
MCGN (Movimiento de Concentración Gente Nueva/Movement of New People Gathering), 184
McGuire, James, 36, 171, 174
media, news. *See* Chavismo
Menem, Carlos, 80–1
Mercal Mission. *See* Missions
Mexico, 25
military in Venezuela, 16–17, 44
Milošević, Slobodan, 138
Miquilena, Luis, 20
Missions, 22, 199–210
　Barrio Adentro, 200, 207–209, 226
　Christ Mission (Misión Cristo), 199
　as result of clientelism, 211, 227–9
　and leftism, 202–10
　Mercal Mission, 201, 207–209, 220, 225
　patronage machine: district level targeting, 217–20; open conditionality, 220–3; partisan profile of participants, 225–7
　as result of populist worldview, 211–15, 227–9
　Ribas Mission, 200–1, 202–5, 204, 218
　Robinson Mission, 200–1, 202–5, 204
　Sucre Mission, 200–1, 202–5, 204, 218, 225
　Vuelvan Caras, 201, 205–6
Montt, Efraín Ríos, 42
Morales, Evo, 42, 76, 78, 133, 135, 197
Moreno, Mariano, 79
movement structure. *See* organizational theory of populism
Mudde, Cas, 42
MVR (Movimiento Quinta República/Fifth República Movement), 100, 113, 177, 181

Nicaragua, 161
normative theory of populism, 148–53, 154, 234

O'Donnell, Guillermo, 98
Organization of American States (OAS), 1
Organization of the Petroleum Exporting Countries (OPEC), 23
organizational theory of populism
　disruptive tactics, 172–4
　institutionalization, 169–70
　insularity, 174–5
　movement structure, 171–2
Ortega, Daniel, 78

Páez, José Antonio, 57
Panebianco, Angelo, 172
Paraguay, 108, 161
Paris Commune of 1871, 83
party system breakdown
　cognitive theory, 103
　deepening of democracy theory, 93, 99–100, 113, 125–6
　economic voting theory, 94, 102–3, 110–11, 114–29
　normative theory, 94–5, 103–10, 111–12, 114–29
　structuralist theory, 93–4, 100–2, 111, 125–6
　in Venezuela, 88–92
Pérez, Carlos Andrés, 17, 28, 61, 101, 104
Pérez Delgado, Pedro "Maisanta," 57
Pérez Perdomo, Rogelio, 109
Perón, Juan, 4, 42, 77, 78, 246
Peronism, 38
Peru, 25, 101, 144
Petroleos de Venezuela, S.A. (PDVSA), 20
PJ (Primero Justicia/First Justice), 188
Plan Bolívar 2000, 19, 22, 199–200
Plan for Economic and Social Development (*Plan de Desarrollo Económico y Social*), 19
pluralist discourse
　and corruption, 98
　definition of, 29
　and democracy, 36–8
　and majority rule, 34
　pragmatic outlook, 34
　and respect for democratic procedures, 36
　and systematic change, 35
　and tolerance for dissent, 35
populism
　and "anything goes" attitude, 34, 36
　definition of, 5–6
　and democracy, 36–8
　discursive definition, 38, 39–41, 48–9, 233
　economic definition, 38, 40
　and "Evil," 35

populism (*cont.*)
  and "Good," 34–5
  macroeconomic policy, 196–9
  Manichaean outlook, 33–4
  measurement of, 8, 53–5, 69–75, 233
  and pluralism, 5
  political-institutional definition, 39, 40
  and rational choice, 11–12
  structural definition, 38, 39–40
  systemic change, 35–6
populism, organizational theory of, 167–9, 236–7
Populist Party in the United States, 42, 197
postmodernists. *See* constructivism
PPT (Patria Para Todos/Fatherland for All), 25, 113
presidential recall referendum, 23, 201
presidential recall referendum of 2004, 1–3
Préval, René, 28
Primera, Alí, 57
Progress Party (Denmark), 235
Project Venezuela (Proyecto Venezuela), 92, 113
Proyecto Nacional Simón Bolívar, 25
PSUV (Partido Socialist Unido de Venezuela/ United Socialist Party of Venezuela), 24
Punto Fijo system, 3, 44, 89–92
Putin, Vladimir, 42
Putnam, Robert, 175

radical-right populism, 234–5
rationalists. *See* behavioralism
Red Nacional de Círculos Bolivarianos, 182
Rey, Juan Carlos, 109
Ribas, José Felix, 57
Ribas Mission. *See* Missions
Robinson Mission. *See* Missions
Rodríguez, Simón, 57, 83
Rosales, Manuel, 24, 93
Rousseau, Jean-Jacques, 34, 60
rule of law, 95
Russia, 161

Sáez, Irene, 92
Salas Römer, Henrique, 92, 114, 118, 119, 124, 125, 128
Salinas de Gortari, Carlos, 199
Sarney, José, 198
Sartori, Giovanni, 175

Scully, Timothy, 169
semidemocracy. *See* democracy
socialism
  and Chavismo, 83–5, 245–7
  and ideology, 30
  and Missions, 208–10
  and populism, 84
South Korea, 165
Spain, 165
Stokes, Susan, 246
strike of 2002, 21, 201
structuralism theory
  dependency theory, 145–8, 159
  modernization theory, 141–5, 158–9
Sucre Mission. *See* Missions

Taggart, Paul, 35
Templeton, Andrew, 109
Trienio, 44
Tversky, Amos, 103
Twenty-First Century Socialism, 6, 24

Ukraine, 135
United States. *See* Bush, George W.
UNT (Un Nuevo Tiempo/A New Time), 93
UPC (Unidad Patriótica de Carabobo/ Patriotic Unity of Carabobo), 184
URD (Unión Republicana Democrática/ Union for Rebublic and Democracy), 89
Uribe, Álvaro, 42
Uruguay, 99, 102, 165, 235

Vargas, Getúlio, 4, 77
Vásquez, Tabaré, 51, 197
Velasco Ibarra, José María, 42, 77
Velásquez, Andrés, 91
Villalba, Jóvito, 89
Vuelvan Caras. *See* Missions

Walgrave, Stefaan, 70
Weber, Max, 9, 41, 240
Wendt, Alexander, 239
Weyland, Kurt, 103, 110
work stoppage of 2002. *See* strike of 2002
worldview, 29–32, 237–42

Yushchenko, Viktor, 75, 76, 78, 133, 140

Zamora, Ezequiel, 57, 83

For EU product safety concerns, contact us at Calle de José Abascal, 56–1°,
28003 Madrid, Spain or eugpsr@cambridge.org.

www.ingramcontent.com/pod-product-compliance
Ingram Content Group UK Ltd.
Pitfield, Milton Keynes, MK11 3LW, UK
UKHW040414060825
461487UK00006B/507